HUMAN SURVIVAL?

Absolute Requirements

PROFESSOR MICHAEL R W BROWN

CONTENTS

Detailed contents precede each section

DEDICATION AND THANKS

I have a strong feeling of closeness to the numerous people who, over six decades, have educated me and thus helped form this book. I express gratitude. To the brave truth-tellers about exploitation and evildoing that I've read, some of whom I've met, and a few became friends. To those recent authors emphasising the need for social unity, for kindness and altruism: especially Karen Armstrong, the late John Berger and Dan Berrigan, recently died, William Blum, Joanna Blythman, Noam Chomsky, Robert Fisk, Owen Jones, Yuval Harari, the Dalai Lama, Michael Lewis, Senkenesh Gebre-Mariam, George Monbiot, Michael Moore, John Pilger, Jeremy Scahill, Nicholas Shaxson, James Wickstead and Mark Zepezauer.

To those organising and contributing to Amnesty International (https://www.amnesty.org.uk), the networks Avaaz (avaaz. org), SumOfUs.org (us@sumofus.org), the 'Occupy' Movement (occupywallstreet.org), 38 Degrees (38degrees.org.uk), WeMove. EU, Change.org, Global Citizen (http://www.globalcitizen.org), Truthout (messenger@truthout.org) and to the other numerous and increasing, altruistic groups and individuals working to help the needy, the oppressed and to reduce violence in human society. To all the beautiful, inspiring humans who attempted to make the peaceful 'Arab Springs' and the current 'Occupy Wall Street' in New York City and back to the 'Hungarian Spring', Fidel Castro's liberation of Cuba and Mahatma Ghandi's pacifist, inclusive and successful approach to moving control of India from Britain to the Indians and further back to Kyros The Great (500 BC) who abolished slavery in Persia, and then beyond through early human history.

And gratitude to all the numerous women who have suffered ridicule and worse and worked for their rights in the past and today. While still missing out numerous heroines, in the UK we have Mary Wollstonecraft (1759-1797) and Emmeline Pankhurst (1858-1928) a leader of the British Suffragette Movement. There were countless courageous women worldwide who fought for civil rights in numerous countries and still do so. An important fighter who has been ignored and forgotten is Olympe de Gouges. She was a radical female activist of the French Revolution. In the 18th century, French (and likely worldwide) men 'believed' that women did not have the intellectual capacity to participate in public debate! In 1791, a new constitution was ratified by the French National Assembly with a preamble, the *Declaration of the Rights of Man and Citizen*. De Gouges wrote a pamphlet response to the preamble, the De Gouges *Declaration of the Rights of Woman and Citizen* and called for women to gain rights equal to men and protection of their rights as mothers. A striking statement in her document is 'a woman has the right to mount the scaffold'. Wikipedia gives timelines for feminist success in different countries and lists the names of the numerous women in each country. And gratitude also to the living women that I've heard and read about: UK Professor Mary Beard and Queen Noor of Jordan, a country that amazed me during a scientific visit by its humanity, especially to refugees.

And gratitude to the brilliant students of evolutionary biology, sociology, psychology and economics who, although almost entirely unknown to me personally, have educated me by their writings and who offer explanations of human existence uncontaminated by the need to conform to *a priori* and often contradictory truths from the sacred texts of numerous religions. They are Daron Acemoglu, Richard Dawkins (The Richard Dawkins Foundation for Reason and Science https://richarddawkins.net/), Jared Diamond, Yuval Harari, Steve Jones, Iain McGilchrist, Paul Krugman, Kate Pickett, Matt Ridley, James Robinson, Joseph Stiglitz, Chris Stringer, Spencer Wells, Richard Wilkinson, Frans de Waal and back to Charles Darwin himself. To Dawn Wood, poet, painter and microbiologist who introduced me to

Lucretius. Thanks to Terry Gibson (www.inventing-futures.org) for his positive criticisms, helpful advice and insights.

Thanks to my friends John and Clare Prangley, Cyril Cooper and the late Paul Murphy for numerous creative conversations. And to Bill Watkins, John Farwell and Roz Baird for helpful discussions. To Christine Atkinson for many philosophical discussions, to Jocelyn Bell Burnell for humanising our former work environment and to Jackie Heath for advice on the content and layout.

And thanks to Melvyn Bragg for his BBC radio series presenting conversations by different, relatively unknown, truly scholarly, non-celebrity humans expertly discussing any and every humanising subject. And thanks also to Neil MacGregor whose exhibitions at the British Museum and 2017 BBC radio talks have illuminated the faith of ancient peoples from objects that have survived for as long as 40 Millenia. And to the BBC morning programmes by human, feminine presenters, humanely covering every possible human issue of importance.

I also express gratitude to my lovely, extended family for many discussions over the years: my wife Margaret, our children Michael (whose recent death devastated our extended family), his wife Trudi, Sarah and her husband Andrew, Paul and his wife Rosslyn, Elizabeth and her husband Steven, Jessica and her husband David, and our grandchildren: Joseph, Eleanor, Jerome, Sophie, Gregory, Duncan, Gabriel, Olivia, Timothy, George, Georgia and to the memory of Jessica, the twin of Jerome, who died shortly after birth and while alive in her incubator instinctively held my finger with a grip of steel, *squeezing it white*. Thanks to Johanna Köckeis-Grüner and all her colleagues at the Hotel Turmhof in Gumpoldskirchen (Austria), where I've spent many peaceful hours working on this book. I've stayed at hotels all over the world and Turmhof is the best quality, most *human*, most hospitable hotel that I've ever stayed at. It's at the head of the wine village, overlooking and adjacent to a hillside of vines and with beautiful walks – an appropriate place to write about humanising society.

.

LETTER TO THE READER

Dear Reader,

I'd like to introduce myself and explain how this book came about: to describe the origins of and explain the world's mega problems and especially how to mitigate them. The book has the perspective of addressing the role of evolutionary forces in contributing to the mega problems of the 21st century. These problems are unprecedented in magnitude in biological history and may prove catastrophic. But before doing so, I need briefly to explain the depth and complexity of the subject matter and my inevitable lack of expertise in so many aspects. Biological evolution affects every aspect of life from cells to higher animals – social and personal. It has given rise to the mechanisms underpinning the workings of our metabolism, our anatomy, our minds and the arrangements of our social life; all are interrelated. Currently, findings in molecular biology are explaining the molecular control mechanisms, potentially of every aspect of cells and organisms, including humans. It's now possible to 'edit' genes (see later) and their expression and thus we are within sight of eliminating many dreadful diseases.

Humans inherit innate tendencies and impulses – *instincts* – that assisted the survival of prehuman apes living in small groups in trees. We share the same instincts, as well as additional, human ones, that can lead to behaviour such as altruism, language, art, sculpture, poetry, music and dance. And importantly, we no longer live and find safety in trees in small groups, but in the main we have huge populations living mostly in cities. Partly for these reasons and partly because my job was focussed elsewhere, writing this book about the effects of evolution on human survival has taken several decades. Despite much clear evidence, we humans ignore aspects of instinctive alpha-male behaviour and our instinctive obedience to these leaders. We are also impelled by instincts about territory, fear of the foreign and the male subjugation of women.

An important question is why is it that humans typically act as if our behaviour is largely or solely the consequence of rational thought? Why do such socially bad things *continually* happen? The role of instincts, innate impulses, in our life, especially in the behaviour of large groups, e.g. nations, is typically overlooked. Why? One explanation of the bad events is the presence of the above instincts regarding territory, fear of the foreign, male suppression of women, alpha males *and obedience to them*. Alpha males have instincts that enable them to provide rapid, coordinated responses to change, including dangerous ones and importantly, non-alphas have instincts to obey, including by 'would-be alphas'. And it's obvious that alphas typically take their powers for granted, as if by right. This all helps the group by having a healthy, well-fed leader. In the ape world, Mother Nature curtails these powers; would-be alphas can remove the greedy, overweight, unfit leader. Although we humans also have basic instincts including obedience to alpha males, we are different in that our alphas are uncurtailed and may not, and usually do not, share our lifestyle. They may even live elsewhere.

This probably explains why the same bad things continue to happen again and again throughout history and across cultures. It is the same instinctive behaviour of alphas and their subjects that is responsible. For this reason, even risking the smooth flow and narrative of the book, I have repeatedly emphasised this blindness to the otherwise obvious failings of our alphas. The purpose of the book is, for me, to publicise as strongly as I can the importance and reality of evolutionary impulses in contributing to our society's mega problems. We are handicapped by instincts that prevent us from taking needed action and even make us blind. Simply look at any photograph of hundreds of thousands of people *in unison* with Nazi salutes, smiling and cheering the delusional leader Adolf Hitler in the1930s (see later). It's now clear that we are all capable of such behaviour, given appropriate circumstances and history.

On a personal note, my normal work has been, and to a large extent still is, that of a university scientist studying the survival of microbes, both in the natural environment and in infections. My English childhood was spent in Wallasey, Merseyside and was occupied mostly with sport. Perhaps I should mention that I was 'born' a Roman Catholic, but am now an agnostic, although for the numerous conventional Gods of the various cultures I'm an atheist. After qualifying as a Pharmacist and gaining research degrees in microbiology, in my long career I've had appointments at the universities of Manchester, London, Bath and Aston, and on sabbatical at the universities of Calgary, Florida, Lille, Oxford and Stanford. I was a Visiting Professor at Warwick and Dundee Universities. I've been a consultant for several pharmaceutical companies worldwide and had sabbaticals at Industrial Research Institutes: Sandoz (later Novartis) Vienna, Ciba Geigy (later Novartis) Basel.

In recent years, I've published ideas about the origins of life – mainly the possible role of the polymer polyphosphate – but human evolution and attendant social problems have not been central to my regular academic research. Until recently, the nearest I've been to this subject was early in my career at the start of Bath University, decades ago. I was Director of the Science and Religion Group at the University which was part of a wider study of Science and Society. But my main job by far was as a microbiologist studying microbial survival, and in recent years being struck by the parallels that exist between the survival mechanisms of *all* living organisms. Nevertheless, for much of my life, I have been thinking, reading, attending seminars by and speaking to philosophers, theologians and psychologists and writing notes for my personal interest about the nature of reality and about religion. These activities have led on to considering the influence of evolution on perception, and later to its influence on every aspect of life. I had no idea whatsoever that these notes would coalesce into this book.

My life was greatly influenced when, as a late adolescent undergraduate (aged about 21 and at Manchester University), I read 'The Last Days of Socrates' by Plato (Socrates wrote almost nothing). It was in a bookshop in Manchester and I did not leave the shop until I had read the entire chapter. I was overwhelmed. It turned out to be the start of this book, which in a way is a kind of autobiography, an intellectual journey. There was the (possibly spontaneous) cheek of Socrates' opening, as he defended himself in a trial that led to his death. He was well aware of the spurious authority that power so often brings (see later regarding the alpha male and the power 'phenotype'). I especially recall his often-quoted teaching that 'Wealth does not bring goodness, but goodness brings wealth and every other blessing, both to the individual and to the State'. And there were other things in his 'defence' that affected me greatly. He prized the purity of his 'soul', his integrity above all else, including above his life, and he proved it by drinking the hemlock. For me, it was a new world. Today, I am still smitten by Socrates and I recommend any reader who has not done so to read 'The Last Days'. I also recommend a lovely book by Bettany Hughes entitled 'The Hemlock Cup' about Socrates' life and world and also her several BBC documentaries about him.

Another major stage in my life was when I recently discovered (through the writings of Karen Armstrong – see section later on Religion) that the Axial Age leaders of different cultures and times (notably, the Buddha, Confucius and the Daoists) and also Jesus at the end of his life (Matthew's Gospel – entry to Heaven is the result of helping others) and at the beginning of his public life (quoting Isaiah – 'I have come to give hope to the poor') all taught that the essence of religion was altruism – responding to human need. For them, religion is *not* sacred texts, doctrines and pious practices: these have an important role to play in helping society adhere and survive biologically. This important *social* role is carried out by the alpha (usually male, often exclusively so) clergy. On the other hand, religion, according to the above prophets, is primarily kind behaviour – how one behaves. Your religion is *actually how you behave.* So, we have two separate, innate impulses for human behaviour: one, the ancient primate instincts for short -term, small-group survival, and the other, later human impulses notably for altruism, language, rationality, art, sculpture, poetry, music and dance. Empathy in humans facilitates altruism.

Now, towards the end of my life (as I revise this book yet again, I am 86) my interests in survival have merged. The last decade or two, while still working on microbial survival (and the role of polyphosphate), has also seen my further education in studying broader evolutionary biology with increasing intensity. This book is the result, with its message, based on empirical evidence, that humanity's major problems are <u>not</u> the result of outbreaks of sin. They are mainly the result of the inappropriate expression of powerful, basic instincts evolved for the short-term, small-group survival of apes living in trees, typically overwhelming any powers of reasoning. That is, these *impulses* evolved for short -term survival in an arboreal, pre-human world greatly different to ours and *where the alphas lived closely with the rest.* Our current, partly human world is where our alphas do not return with us to our habitat, which is no longer arboreal and we are millions.

Also contributing to our problems is the lack of expression of specifically human instincts and our unmet primate <u>and</u> human needs – of being *connected*, of *belonging* (a need shared with other animals) and of having *inclusive* social structures. Contributing to problems can sometimes be mentally ill leaders. Our world remains to some extent a pre-human one. Definitions are given later, essentially restricting the word 'human' to primates who have evolved into humans with consciousness and vastly greater brain power. Our alpha males possess massively more nuclear, world-destroying and polluting powers, and world-disruptive powers through digital information technology (IT) and its job-destroying use in artificial intelligence (AI) than ever previously imagined. This book is a personal attempt to contribute towards a human world by shining needed light on its current, mainly primate (i.e. pre-human) nature, especially regarding the major social structures and large groupings such as nations.

Why have I persisted in the writing of this book when others have more gifts in this area than me? I am under no illusion whatsoever about my place among these writers. Remarkably knowledgeable, brilliant writers have written about evolution, and are acknowledged in my dedication. Also, remarkably knowledgeable, brilliant writers and documentary makers have written about many of humanity's social problems. Notably, Noam Chomsky, Robert Fisk, George Monbiot, Michael Moore, Owen Jones and John Pilger have superbly and *bravely* analysed many of the world's problems and their immediate causes – often national governments or large corporations. Surprising to me is that these true giants have analysed the how and where of the wrongdoing and stopped at that point. The world's problems exist because nasty, bad people do nasty, bad things *and have always done so*. Despite my own shortcomings, my broad ignorance, I believe that I have something important to say not mentioned elsewhere.

Please excuse the following repetitions. Our behaviour is massively affected by instincts that evolved eventually to enhance the survival of pre-human animals living in small groups in trees – instincts that are now often inappropriately expressed. Notably, these instincts include ones about territory, fear of the foreign, male fear of and suppression of women, alpha males and related obedience to them, _helpfully_ enabling concerted responses to change and danger. One such instinct, connected with the alpha male, is for the group not to see (and never mention) that 'the Emperor has no clothes on'. This facilitates obedience to orders from alphas – coordinated responses to change, especially danger. I have not found a single account suggesting that a major factor in our current human problems is our mindless (avoiding reason and evidence) enacting of *instincts,* broadly fear-evoked, about territory, the foreign, male suppression of women, especially not expressing public authority, 'would-be alphas', alpha males and associated obedience to them. If such a book had existed, I would not have pursued this one. The style of the book, sometimes repetitive, is also affected by these facts. Its purpose is to point out that human behaviour, especially strife and war, is often propelled *not* by our reason but by instincts about territory, the foreign and alpha males, often evoked by fear and sometimes by the prospect of more power (frequently expressed as money). Our alphas typically evoke fear of the foreign as they push us to war. Michael Moore has produced a documentary (2016) entitled 'Where to invade next?' and offers a humorous attack on the mega powerful USA's propensity for war. And, towards the end of my writing, USA's President Donald Trump came on the scene unexpectedly and went way beyond my worst fears. In June 2017, he announced his plans to change Cuba to be more like the USA. He started with threats. We must bear in mind that the USA has the worst social statistics of any nation for which there is data (see 'The Spirit Level' by Wilkinson and Pickett). Now in March 2018 his record shows unrelenting attacks on the budgets for social services and the USA has *never* had an effective universal health service for all of its citizens.

An unexpected consequence of this book has been my own education.

I have been advised to aim at a non-specialist readership and with a specific, non-specialist friend in mind. This I have tried to do to help the book read in an accessible, *personal* way. *I'm attempting to write to this friend, trying to explain my findings and my feelings.* For similar reasons, in some cases, I've illustrated biological points with examples from my own research and from people that I know personally. Naturally, I've also given most references to works by others. It's possible that I've given too many references, in which case please skip them. But if a reader wishes to dig into an aspect, then a starting reference is provided.

An attempt at clarification. I have used the word 'humanise' to mean increasing the expression of the altruistic, artistic and rational qualities of human culture. That is: kindness, treating others as we would wish for ourselves or even before our own needs (altruism), as well as expressing art forms and human powers of *reason*. I also imply a reduction of violent behaviour, including inter-human group violence. Other species do not have aspects of human culture such as art, sculpture, music, dance, literature, poetry and especially our advanced capacity for language and rationality (of course, other species do communicate with sounds and gestures and have forms of reasoning). This usage of 'humanise' could imply that other species do not have altruism and are always violent. This is not so. There are numerous acts of altruistic behaviour observed and recorded in our current evolutionary relatives. In terms of violence, our genetically closest relatives vary in the use of violence. For example, bonobos are exceptionally peaceful (and exceptionally sexually active; maybe both are connected), while chimpanzees are frequently violent. Authoritative comparisons of primates and humans are given extensively in superb books by Frans de Waal: for example, 'Our inner ape' and 'Are we smart enough to know how smart animals are'. He also edited the excellent 'Tree of origin'.

For decades, I have been aware that my ambitions for this book could be pretentious: nothing less than explaining the origins of the world's mega problems (and without recourse to the Devil or to God) and how to reduce them. Without doubt, I could go on correcting and adding new material for another 64 years. I summarise numerous quotations of Picasso in – 'No painting is ever finished'. But I must stop. Today, 30th March 2018, as I re-read these words, I am 86 and amazingly 64 years since the start when I read Socrates defence. Ezra Pound describes my situation

And the days are not full enough
And the nights are not full enough
And life slips by like a field mouse
Not shaking the grass

I've done my best and it cannot wait any longer. It will be out there, and the way ahead is simple even though perhaps impossible. I hope to convince readers of the following.

Human survival *absolutely* requires each of us to:
Increase the expression of human instincts and control basic ones.

Even as a religious agnostic, I'm at one with the Axial Age leaders/sages in believing that one's religion is not portrayed in pious practices, sacred books and not in what one *says* is one's belief, but rather how we *behave*. They recommended kindness and altruism. Later, Jesus in Matthew's gospel and immediately before he was executed put it succinctly. He stated his *absolute* criteria for entry to Heaven as follows:

Help the ill, naked, thirsty, hungry, imprisoned and strangers (acronym – 'in this').

I agree with these sages that this is the highest form of human behaviour for us all.

Sincerely,
Mike Brown

A SHORT PRE-ABSTRACT

A child cries out, 'But he isn't wearing anything at all!'

In 'The Emperor's New Clothes' by Hans Christian Andersen ('Fairy Tales Told for Children'), two weavers promise the Emperor a new suit of clothes. They say it's invisible to those who are unfit for their positions, are stupid or incompetent. When the Emperor appears before his subjects in his 'new clothes', no one dares to say that they don't see any suit of clothes on him for fear that they will be seen as 'unfit for their positions, stupid or incompetent'. Only a child speaks out.

A SHORTER PRE-ABSTRACT

*The world's mega problems are
the results of biology.*

We need to free our expression of human instincts for altruism, empathy, art and reason and to control our basic ones regarding territory, fear of the foreign, the male suppression of women, alpha-male leaders and our obedience to them.

ABSTRACT

A Greek tragedy

History illuminates our present by showing where we came from and casting light on our consistent behaviour – our innate tendencies, our character. Evolutionary history casts light more deeply on where humans came from and the innate instinctive, impulsive behaviour inherited from our pre-human ancestors who lived in a very different, arboreal world. In Greek tragedies, at the start of the drama, the outcome is visible in the characters of the participants: what follows appears an inevitable consequence of character. So it is with human life.

Life is characterised by a competitive, commonly cooperative, struggle for survival, aided by programmed stress responses in cells, evolving into instinctive behaviour in higher animals. Such behaviours facilitated the essentials for survival. In addition to 'housekeeping' instincts regarding such as nutrition and metabolism (much in common with all life forms) and those regarding shelter and procreation, there are instincts for *effective, rapid and concerted responses to change, notably dangerous ones*. One might describe these particular survival instincts as the 'Golden Rules' for biological survival. These ancient instincts (Oxford dictionary definition: innate propensity, innate *impulse*) are imbedded in the pre-human parts of the brain more or less unaffected by the consciously thinking parts of the newer, human regions of the brain. They helped and enabled the short-term survival of small groups of animals living and curtailed within 'nature'. This is not to say that these pre-human animals could not think to a considerable extent – they could, and to an underappreciated extent as emphasised in the writings of Frans de Waal. But they also had instincts that impelled them regarding danger. Broadly, they are about hierarchies with *alpha males* that lived closely with their group, and sensing and making 'decisions' about perceived danger. Alphas take the best of limited resources (this behaviour maintains healthy leaders and hence helps those that are led) and there is associated *obedience to elites* as well as *structural inequalities* such as gender role divisions, often including male anti-feminism (see later); *defence of territory* (fight or flight); latent and actual hostility to and fear of 'otherness' (self/non-self, us/them); inflicting collective punishment, i.e. on all who appear like 'them' (i.e. 'others'); and *competitiveness* (especially the male expression of competition).

These same instincts, evolved to bring about the short-term survival of small (20-30 ish) groups of animals within and curtailed by *arboreal* nature, are now also characteristic of humans operating in huge groups (millions) and with elites having God-like powers. Today, virtually unbounded by nature, we are causing catastrophic damage to humanity and to the world that sustains life. Our consciousness and our *potential* human instincts towards altruism, creativity, rationality and human culture have not prevented this. Humans, for the first time, have the capacities to influence and damage 'Mother Nature', have *already twice used nuclear weaponry* and also misuse information technology for personal gain, creating worldwide financial and other havoc. The same IT enables our alpha males to follow our personal use of the internet on a massive scale – the surveillance society. Human alphas have never had such power and have never been so separated from other fellow humans. Commonly, the alphas 'belong' not with the society they lead but with other alphas. Offering this as an argument supporting Trident nuclear weapons, a recent UK Prime Minister (David Cameron) stated that Trident bought us (him) a seat at the 'top table', i.e. with the other alphas.

Those watching a Greek tragedy can see the characters of the participants and can link these with the outcomes. Whereas we humans ignore or even deny our evolutionary character, propelled by our instincts – including the instinctive, mindless (literally) following of and obedience to our alpha-male leaders, unrestrained by 'nature' and paranoid about territory and 'the foreign' – and the inevitable outcomes of this. The modern world and its subunits are still led largely, but not entirely, by alpha males with little in common with those who are 'led'. These 'leaders' have their relatively mindless, primate instincts fully functioning, including the taking of whatever resources are available and constructing a competitive, 'winner takes all', fearful, anti-feminine, disconnected world where reason is hardly valued. This book is essentially about inappropriate evolutionary influences on the modern world, ideas about how to mollify them and how to provide unmet basic human needs. These human needs include belonging, being connected, being employed/*working* in a communal/group endeavour, expressing the *human* instincts / attributes of altruism, creativity and rationality and having inclusive economic and political structures. Despite our new intelligence, we are still primates with the same old instincts, but with extra, underused, new human ones and living in a very different, man-made world. In the process of survival, primate instincts typically trump human ones.

The founders of the major religions overcame their own basic instincts to achieve the short-term survival of themselves and their group, and typically offered a common, *humane and altruistic* path forward for the long-term benefit of humankind as a whole. Indeed, most of the 'Axial Age' sages (around 900 to 200 years BCE) were hostile to and had no interest whatever in doctrine, creeds or metaphysics (see Karen Armstrong's 'The Great Transformation'). A person's theological beliefs were a matter of indifference to somebody like the Buddha. *What mattered supremely was not what you believed (or <u>said</u> that you believed) but how you behaved*: <u>how you behaved</u>. It's no coincidence that these cultural leaders separately emphasised altruism, possibly intuitively, as being at the heart of their teaching. This same core, altruistic, humane teaching has been expressed in different languages, cultures and times.

In Matthew's gospel, Jesus's account of the criteria for entry to Heaven on the Day of Judgement consisted *solely* of responding to the needs of others, closely similar/identical to the Axial Age sages. Thus, to achieve a place in Heaven it was not *group* obedience to leaders (which was good for primate survival in an earlier, different world of small groups living in trees), but altruistic *individual* behaviour – helping others – that counted. Part of the tragedy is that these sages were rapidly replaced by hierarchical, competitive institutions ('corporations') largely exhibiting the basic, small group-serving, short-term survival instincts from earlier primates. In biological terms, the primacy of the founders' teachings was replaced by the absolute primacy of <u>institutional survival</u>. The survival and safety of the religious institution *per se* trumps all: that is, its competitive increase in numbers, wealth, prestigious buildings, social influence and ability to respond rapidly to change, especially to dangerous (to the institution) change trumps all. To that extent, the institutions have become corporations; humanist leaders offer advice similar to the sages about altruism and with no reference to any God.

Nevertheless, however much religions ignore the altruistic teachings of their founders, they typically play an important biological role in enabling members to feel and experience community and belonging. Religious 'corporations' can help adherents to feel safe such as when their own religion is their state religion with its attendant State security. Naturally and inevitably, problems arise when multiple religions exist in the same place and teach contradictory dogma, all claimed to come from one God. This book describes the main problems facing humanity which are commonly ignored. It outlines the basics of evolutionary biology – especially instincts often inappropriate for modern society, notably those associated with alpha males and their rich, unbounded, alienated lifestyle, and those regarding territory, obedience and the 'foreign'. The widespread and historical prevention of women from having public power and 'voice' seems likely to be a male instinct. Exceptions exist where the woman has male characteristics, including the willingness to obey or even to blow the war bugle. These same instincts apply also to powerful social institutions and nations: there is much conclusive evidence to show that nations work best when the economic and political structures are inclusive. There is also conclusive evidence that individual, basic, *human* social needs include the reality of belonging and of being connected. Similarly, social structures help towards healthy societies if they are inclusive.

The causes of our problems are dealt with: inappropriate instincts and unmet human needs often in proportion to social inequality. By definition, Capitalism is about capital inequality managed by alpha males and this needs controlling. We have alpha males no longer belonging with those they 'lead', misusing unprecedented powers over money, weaponry and digital communication. The world is largely 'managed' as if only money matters. It seems highly _unlikely_ that social change towards reduced influence of primate instincts and more towards human instincts and thoughtful, rational behaviour will develop from the existing structures led by our alpha males. Widespread, *peaceful* and *individual* participation in social affairs is needed and happily has started to happen on an accelerating scale. Examples include Amnesty International, the network Avaaz (avaaz.org), SumOfUs. org (us@sumofus.org), the 'Occupy' Movement (occupywallstreet. org), 38 Degrees (38degrees.org.uk), WeMove.EU, Change.org and the brilliant 'truthout', mostly analysing the immediate origins of the world's problems (messenger@truthout.org). We need a change that takes us away from mindless (literally) primate obedience to our primate alpha males and towards thoughtful participation as individual humans: altruistic, creative and rational. The feminine side of males needs more expression as does the natural, feminine voice of women. It's less to do with men and women than masculine/ macho and feminine qualities.

Early education and upbringing is hugely important for the individual and for society. Child development should acknowledge and be based on established biological needs, including emotional, physical and brain development. There is now massive empirical evidence for these statements. Improvement led by alpha male individuals or alpha states seems highly unlikely. Suggestions point at incremental ways to meet the essential human needs for healthy early development: *to belong* (be less unequal – see later 'The Spirit Level', Wilkinson and Pickett), to *be connected* to one another and to express widely our human instincts of altruism, and also our creativity in art, poetry, literature, sculpture, music and dance. Human males need more expression of feminine behaviours: less macho, softer and intuitive and *not limited solely to fight or flight*. These aims apply within the social structures as well as to the society they serve. The hugely malevolent and antisocial role of mega-rich industries such as energy and tobacco in undermining the idea of global warming or the dangers of cigarette smoking are an old as well as a current threat. Under the false cloak of impartiality, they and other powerful corporations relentlessly attack trade unions and pay for fake 'think tanks' using 'dark money' to oppose any regulations for corporations and to oppose taxes.

Even disregarding corruption and misuse of power, the *increasing speed* of change of numerous aspects of society is too fast for politicians and current political structures to manage. We are increasingly ill-equipped to solve our problems: nuclear weapons, environmental destruction, misuse of information technology (IT) with widespread and colossal looting of national resources, artificial intelligence (AI) with consequential massive loss of jobs and predicted social disorder. Humans have unmet needs regarding belonging and having inclusive social structures. Also, especially in large groups such as nations, we see the inappropriate expression of primate instincts, notably regarding territory, fear of the foreign and alpha males. And we witness the widespread suppression of women (especially a public voice) and femininity. Allow me to emphasise that, unlike today, these basic instincts evolved to assist the survival of small groups of apes in small communities in trees and with their leaders living in intimacy with them and sharing their lifestyle.

This book has a final focus on the extent to which specific major social structures <u>in</u>appropriately express instincts (dictionary definition: *innate* propensity or impulse) still shared with pre-humans and how we can ameliorate them. What is crucial is how our social structures could facilitate greater expression of the human impulses of altruism, culture and rationality and how they require change to do so. Ways are suggested gradually and incrementally to humanise society, increase inclusiveness, minimise inappropriate personal and institutional 'instincts' and answer essential human needs. Thus, from this perspective, there is a final focus on:

1. The State/Politics, Justice, Law, Education and the Military;
2. Religions; and
3. Commerce, The Media, Habitats and overall Culture.

The inclusion of the section on Religion may surprise readers because *despite the typically altruistic teachings of the <u>original</u> prophets,* religious structures tend strongly to express primate instincts related to alpha males and obedience to them, fear of the foreign, including of women by men, and territory which all facilitated an arboreal existence. Religions typically suppress women from having official power.

Broadly, modern humans are sick. The sickness is not from Satanic evil or from a punishing God. The adverse social statistics are *symptoms*. The *disease* is a disease of the mind brought about by individual and social disconnectedness and not belonging, linked to changes in our brains. Repetition of the following seems appropriate. Human society is impelled by ancient instincts evolved for short-term survival of small groups of apes living <u>together</u> in trees. It needs greater expression of human instincts of altruism, rationality and creativity.

Animals imprisoned in unnatural, municipal zoos have elevated levels of stress hormones and exhibit stressed behaviour. Modern humans are commonly (though nations vary) in a 'zoo' of our own making and alpha 'primates' are in charge with all their instincts intact. We are diseased. Generally speaking, the symptoms include mental illness, obesity, violence, petty crime, murder, rape, drug addiction, lack of community life, large prison populations and feral, *disconnected*, predatory leaders. The intensity of these symptoms are proportional to national inequality (see later). Societies tend to treat these symptoms, but not the disease. The core of the disease is people not belonging, being disconnected, living in non-inclusive states and sometimes even being victims of their predatory alpha-male leaders. The pathological consequences that occur for the human brain and hence the mind are inevitable. We need to change society from being largely <u>non</u>-human primate in character to largely human.

Q. Can it be done?

A. As the world is substantially driven by primate instincts with roots going back billions of years to the origins of life and to a different world, with alpha males in charge and with ever-increasing powers, it is likely that change is *almost* impossible.

In the short term, we can at least try incrementally to move the most primate societies towards the existing most human. The embryonic social movements by *individuals* are promising and may be the only way forward. George Monbiot's advice is for *everyone* to start now and do something constructive today. Thus, change from being a largely obedient and mindless, mass primate to being a more thinking, altruistic individual and socially aware human is essential. All the great sages of different cultures and epochs recommended this.

INTRODUCTION

Contents

EVOLUTION AFFECTS PERCEPTION: INFLUENCE OF ELITES ON INDIVIDUAL PERCEPTIONS

A personal, subjective start

My early, intense adolescent thoughts about reality led me on to considering the influence of evolution on *how* we think about reality or indeed about anything – our perceptions. What is reality? How do we even start to think about it? I was aware that numerous people had puzzled over reality, very probably since the first humans and including the world's greatest intellects. Nevertheless, for me, almost the only satisfying ideas that I read were not overtly philosophical works, but poetry or literature: T S Eliot's 'The Four Quartets', Robert Pirsig's 'Zen and the Art of Motor Cycle Maintenance', John Berger in 'Ways of Seeing' and much more recently 'The Master and his Emissary' by Iain McGilchrist. The subjectivity of perceived reality was strikingly illustrated to me (possibly because I read it on my honeymoon) in a passage in 'Anna Karenina' when Levin, deeply in love with Kitty and waiting to see her and aware that she loves him, is walking around the town. Tolstoy writes: 'What he (Levin) saw that day he never saw again'. Levin was of the view that everyone he met that day, all strangers, loved him and shared his joy. Another interesting view on the perception of reality is from Socrates who is thought to have taught that reality is 'what you see as you seek goodness'. And later, personally, was my own change to agnostic from being a Roman Catholic mindlessly 'believing' all that the clergy taught, including an infallible Pope living in a Vatican palace and the 'faith' consisting almost entirely of pious practices absolutely controlled by celibate priests or monks, often shorn of personality by titles and rank and uniforms and sometimes shaven heads.

Surprisingly, the kindest, most intelligent people who influenced me included numerous RC priests and nuns. And now, about 60 years from my first musings, I marvel at the workings of the brain as it unravels sensory perceptions of taste, smell, touch, sight, sound and speech and *creates a reality*. And how it creates pathways in specific parts of the brain for the electrochemical movements that hold and *create* meaning and a sense of reality. And I marvel at how it's now possible to visualise such movements *as they occur* and their brain locations using non-invasive physical techniques. And I marvel at how the optimum functioning of such pathways requires *healthy child development from before the day of birth.*

Obedience to authority

It's clear that of the numerous religions, differing in many ways including theology and philosophy, they typically do not differ in terms of the intelligence of their leaders. It's not possible to distinguish Islam from Christianity or Sikhism or Buddhism or Hinduism or Judaism on the basis of the IQ or theoretical knowledge base of their theologians and leaders. What is often common is theological indoctrination and attempts to isolate the adherents to the 'faith'. For example, in my youth, 'mixed' (Catholic and Protestant) marriages and also socialisation were actively discouraged in numerous ways. I have seen Protestant election literature in Northern Ireland describing the Pope as actually being Satan in human guise and gaining sufficient support to win the election. It thus seems that humans are able to 'believe' almost anything and possibly *actually* anything – including not seeing that 'the Emperor has no clothes'. Not seeing that the Emperor is naked (unlike Socrates who clearly recognised naked Emperors) is one of the themes of this book. One biological explanation is that humans have an instinctive propensity to obey our alpha-male leaders and not 'see' fault, as this usefully helps, for example, the survival of their religious *institutions* to which they belong and the culture of which they are a part. The needs of survival, driven by instincts (notably, fear of foreign, territorial, obedience to alpha-male leaders, competitive and anti-feminine), typically trump everything. Social unity and obedience is a major requirement for biological survival.

It also seems that, as a society, the overall, common view of reality (the culture, 'the way things are') is strongly influenced by power relationships. What a society sees as good (or bad) art, dress, table manners, music and general behaviour is strongly influenced by how the powerful see things. The important biological role of elites is discussed shortly, in terms of leadership, sensing danger and also *helping to glue society together and hence facilitate speedy and concerted responses to danger and thus survival*. The artist and social commentator Grayson Perry has produced a book of ideas and paintings to illustrate them, 'The vanity of small differences'. In it, he comments on the longevity of social class. I quote:

> '*Class is something bred into us like a religious faith. We drink in our aesthetic heritage with our mother's milk, with our mates at the pub, or on the playing fields of Eton. We learn the texture of our place in the world from the curlicue of a neck tattoo, the clank of a Le Creuset casserole dish, or the scent of a mouldering hunting print. A childhood spent marinating in the material culture of one's class is soaked right through you.*'

The need to identify leaders is related to the need for rapid response to change, especially dangerous changes.

'Reality'

Before dealing with brain development and its consequences, it seems useful to consider some poetic accounts of reality. The following are assorted ideas about reality that affected me along my journey. Very often it's the *primate* version that is described as the 'real world'. But poetry is a *human* activity. John Lennon is quoted as saying, 'The more real you get the more unreal the world gets'. If I may make a comment on someone as sensitive and human as John Lennon, then it's that the 'real world' of primates and right-wingers is largely what we have today. Humans still have much to do to construct a human world.

'A good poem is a contribution to reality. The world is never the same once a good poem has been added to it. A good poem helps to change the shape of the universe, helps to extend everyone's knowledge of himself and the world around him.'

Dylan Thomas

'There's real poetry in the real world. Science is the poetry of reality'

Richard Dawkins

'Love is the source of reality'

Susan Polis Schutz

'How many legs does a dog have if you call the tail a leg? Four.
Calling a tail a leg doesn't make it a leg'

Abraham Lincoln

'The eye sees only what the mind is prepared to comprehend'

Robertson Davies, Tempest-Tost

'Religion is a system of wishful illusions together with a disavowal of reality, such as we find nowhere else but in a state of blissful hallucinatory confusion. Religion's eleventh commandment is "Thou shalt not question".'

Sigmund Freud, 'The Future of an Illusion' (The Standard Edition)

'Memory has its own special kind. It selects, eliminates, alters, exaggerates, minimizes, glorifies, and vilifies also; but in the end it creates its own reality, its heterogeneous but usually coherent version of events; and no sane human being ever trusts someone else's version more than his own'

Salman Rushdie, 'Midnight's Children'

'Reality exists in the human mind, and nowhere else'

George Orwell, '1984'

'Art is not a mirror held up to reality but a hammer with which to shape it'

Bertolt Brecht

'We become slaves the moment we hand the keys to the definition of reality entirely over to someone else, whether it is a business, an economic theory, a political party, the White House, Newsworld or CNN'

B.W. Powe, 'Towards A Canada Of Light'

Context and predisposition leads us to varying views of reality. In social situations of dispute or of actual violence, perceptions of what is happening and of the causes, typically vary greatly. Even at an ordinary social gathering, there will often be large differences in what each person 'sees'. A frequently quoted extreme example is when a panel was asked to take part in an experiment to monitor a specific aspect of group behaviour. Most, intently focussed on the details of their task, failed to notice someone dressed as a gorilla ostentatiously moving through the control group. And obviously, falling in love is an especially intense modifier of one's perception of reality: *so is fear*.

Information about brain function and structure has long come from correlating behaviour changes with brain damage, sometimes observed during surgery, sometimes observed *post-mortem* (see later 'Brain development'). Today, non-invasive techniques continue to yield important information about functions associated with behaviour or thoughts (calculations, recognition of words or not) or feelings of various kinds (fear, sexual arousal). Briefly, the names of techniques are listed so that any reader can look into them further: magnetic resonance imaging (fMRI) can monitor aspects of brain function; positron emission topography (PET) involves injecting radioactive glucose into a subject and monitoring where it accumulates while the subject has exercises about words or feelings or whilst relaxing with eyes closed; electroencephalography records brain waves through the use of electrodes on the scalp. Brain scans have shown the effects on nerve cell growth in different sections of the brain after prolonged activity of different kinds, such as a particular kind of physical activity. Also shown are the nullifying effects on rational thought of 'falling in love', with the obvious consequences for procreation. Similarly, brain scans show that rationality is reduced or eliminated when *danger is perceived*, thus leaving instincts to propel us rapidly down well-trodden primate paths that increased the chances of primate survival. Well before MRI or other scans existed, Edmund Burke wrote, 'No power so effectually robs the mind of all its powers of acting and reasoning as fear.' It's now clear that fear is a major trigger for instinctive behaviour.

A striking idea that will also be referred to again is that *humans should not be seen as separate beings.* William Condon (in 'Beyond Culture', pages 72-77, Ed. E.T. Hall) thought that it made no sense to view humans as 'isolated entities', but rather as bonded together in 'shared organizational forms'. Howard Bloom (in 'You are still being lied to', pages 10-18, Ed. Russ Kick) furthers the idea of humans being intrinsically *not* isolated beings. He gives numerous references about how social influences shape the brain. Bloom says that in an effective learning machine, the connections deep inside far outnumber windows to the outside world. He quotes evidence that in the cerebral cortex about 80% of the nerves connect with *each other*, and not with input from eyes or ears. He calls human society a 'learning device'. Such ideas are supported by the evidence that 'belonging' within a community is an *absolutely essential need: without it, there is social pathology.*

We are not only or simply individuals. Thousands of years ago the Greek philosopher Aristotle said something that is often quoted; 'Man is a social animal'. And in recent times there are the frequently quoted ideas in the poem by Thomas Merton, 'No man is an island'. This is enlarged upon later. Also dwelt on later is the work on social inequality (see 'Basic human needs'), showing a strong correlation between income inequality and adverse social statistics. How can it be that, at the extremes, there are several-fold differences in the incidence of *various* crimes and illnesses between equal and unequal societies, and in a linear manner? The answer may lie in the work mentioned above regarding humans not being simply separate, isolated entities. Being unequal could mean a lack of something essential and basic, namely not belonging and a lack of broad community. Thus, the adverse social ailments are *symptoms* of this lack. Money is broadly a measure of power; hence income inequality can also be seen as power inequality.

Genes and environment: nature and nurture

It's a truism that, in general, the behaviour of all organisms is determined by their genetic make-up (see later section on evolutionary biology) and by their environmental influences, *notably those experienced during early development.* Environmental influences include social ones – the society we live in can be healthy or pathological. Later, I deal with conclusive empirical evidence regarding the bad effects of social inequality and of having non-inclusive social structures. Not 'belonging' makes us physically as well as mentally ill. When the environment changes, a living organism characteristically changes itself in an advantageous way; that is to say, it can adapt without genetic change (loss or gain of genes). Of course, there can be new genetic activity. Occasionally the genetic material itself alters due to loss or to acquiring new ('foreign') genetic material or to a change resulting from a relatively random genetic alteration within itself. This can be a handicap or have no significant effect, but can sometimes result in increased positive options for the organism.

Do these ideas apply to changes in the intellectual environment? Are perceptions affected by our genetic make-up and by environmental changes? It clearly seems so. When prevailing ideas propagated by the elite change, then commonly, perhaps slowly, human followers adapt their ideas to conform to those of the elite. Indeed, there seems to be hardly any limit to the ideas that are acceptable (or apparently so) to many when propagated by a sufficiently powerful elite. Consider the situation in North Korea with numerous severe social ills including widespread starvation. Currently, as I write this section, there are scenes of people openly weeping and wailing at the death of their leader – commonly referred to as 'dear leader'. For millennia and today there are numerous religions with related holy scriptures that adherents 'believe' are the literal words of their one (or multiple), true God. Sigmund Freud, mentioned above under 'Reality', suggests that religion's eleventh commandment is 'Thou shalt not question' ('*The Future of an Illusion*'). Some degree of non-questioning and having a common perception of reality are powerful social adhesives: they help group survival.

Shortly after the time of the initial prophets, who commonly taught altruism, official religions greatly reduced the significance of the prophets' teaching. They mainly served a truly important *biological* function as powerful, man-made, mostly male corporations, often contributing to social adhesion. Behaviour conducive to biological survival is selected: behaviour inappropriate to survival is eliminated. Official religions largely consist of male hierarchies requiring obedience and acting as an intermediary / interpreter between God and people.

The 'Golden Rule' of survival

Given an anatomy and metabolism appropriate for the environmental niche, then the Golden Rule of survival is to have *'an effective, rapid, coordinated response to change, especially dangerous ones'*. Mother Nature eliminates ineffective responses. For primates, leadership and unity (with obedience) facilitate such responses. Leadership without obedience is obviously ineffective. Thus, for numerous prehuman species, the chances of survival were optimised by alpha-male decision-makers and associated obedience. Instincts that facilitated such behaviour are still alive and well.

Another related predisposition is that of obedience to leadership: as mentioned earlier, without it leadership would be impotent. Facilitating obedience is the common practice (possibly instinct) of not seeing that 'the Emperor has no clothes on', which is especially evident whilst the Emperor is a successful alpha male. The strong tendency to suppress the public expression of women's views is likely because they may be unreliable when the war bugle sounds (see later, sexism). Women broadly may even be psychologically 'allergic' to military bugles! Then, going backwards, it occurred to me that the background to <u>what</u> one 'sees' and even <u>how</u> one sees, especially when feeling threatened, is provided by our evolutionary background. In addition, we have the varying consequences of foetal, infant and adolescent development. How we see and what we see was shaped over aeons of time by the requirements of survival. It now seems clear that common social perceptions of reality and acceptance of 'our place in society' are powerful parts of the glue binding society together. My original interest in the concept of reality thus became more than merely autobiographical and hence of more general scope.

INSTINCTS FROM PRIMATE ANCESTORS AND BEYOND

The Oxford English dictionary defines an instinct as an 'innate propensity' or 'innate impulse'. As I considered the very consistent behaviour of human groups, especially under stress or even under perceived stress, it began to occur to me that evolution plays a vastly more prominent role than merely as a background influence: humans do not face life and its problems solely with their high intelligence and consciousness and make free, rational choices. Although few people would think that they choose in a totally pure, 'free' form, I have come to see (evolutionary biologists might well say, 'about time') that evolution plays a much greater role in our behaviour than is generally assumed. This is so in absolutely everything, but especially so in situations that threaten oneself or one's own group. Innate, non-conscious impulses from our primate ancestors (and beyond) play a major role in behaviour, and the widespread *downplaying or ignoring* of this is an important focus of this book. Notably these impulses are about territory, the foreign, competition, alpha-male leaders facilitating rapid, concerted responses to danger and associated obedience/compliance and group compliance. Male suppression of the female occurs in many primate species and occurs in humans, notably over women having public power (see later). These non-conscious, innate impulses are part of the 'Golden Rule of Biology' regarding survival of all organisms: 'an effective, rapid, concerted response to change, especially dangerous ones'. In the modern, human world, where alpha males typically do not share a common environment with their followers and where the taking of the best for themselves is no longer restrained by nature, pathology often results. Innate impulses associated specifically with humans will be discussed later; namely, altruism, creativity, language, rationality and the various forms of art – music, poetry, sculpture and literature. In the case of language, human right-wing behaviour appears to overcome human rational thinking and behaviour. When under stress/threatened, right wing speech and behaviour tends to avoid reason and express assertions, ridicule and sneering. Is such behaviour an instinct (see later)?

In addition to the variation in perceptions of reality as determined by such as nutrition and our social environment, especially influenced by behaviour of the powerful, different stages of brain development in the young and past adolescence will predispose us as to what and how we 'see' the world. Interference with normal brain development leads to lasting harm, i.e. a reduced ability to play a useful social role. Recently, there is evidence to show that the most ancient part of the brain (similar to reptiles) that deals with fear and perceived danger, overrides other, more recent parts. Thus, instinctive response to perceived danger trumps consciousness. Similarly, as mentioned earlier, 'falling in love' interferes with the reasoning areas of the brain, with the obvious consequences for procreation. Such facts have led to a reassessment of the idea of 'free will' (see later).

Mismatch of old instincts and new world

Today, humankind is faced with global problems requiring global cooperation. It seems clear that our ancient instincts for *small group, short-term* survival, which have successfully got us through evolution so far, are now hindering behaviour needed for the long-term survival of large-scale *humankind* as a whole. Potential for inter-state, inter-race and inter-religion conflict is always present. Indeed, somewhere on Earth numerous such conflicts always exist including as I write now or at any time since I started this enterprise. The more powerful a religion is, with its greater cohesive properties, then the more intense is the clash with a different religion or ideology. It's not the religion *per se*, but its role as a differentiating feature of a culture or nation. This is the case despite the fact that the founding religious prophets virtually all advocated altruism as a central tenet! We have human instincts, commonly swamped by primate ones, especially for actions by large groups or nations. Also, it is now clear from

DNA studies that there are not now several human races, just the one: skin colour is insufficient to define a species. Dark human skin colour is mainly about reducing harm, including cancer, from sunlight. Light skin does not confer 'racial' superiority: it facilitates vitamin D synthesis initiated by sunlight. Instincts are considered more fully elsewhere in this book, including definitions under 'Background ideas on evolutionary biology' and also under 'Causes of humanity's problems'.

Brain development, consciousness, intuition, empathy and altruism
My initial task of how to think cleanly and objectively about reality has now been largely abandoned. My thinking apparatus and how it operates is so obviously linked to survival that a clean view of reality, uncontaminated by the overriding need for survival, could well be impossible. Consciousness, too, is beyond me in terms of my saying anything useful. It seems clear, certainly to me, that what is usually described as conscious thought is at least inaccurate. Complex thought (and language) comes from non-conscious sources – the unconscious mind. Does anyone construct sentences, speak coherently or produce original ideas by conscious thought? It seems that the 'conscious' mind, in the sense of being aware of one's surroundings, especially of dangers and of opportunities, can trigger the thoughts that come from somewhere else. Sometimes, it seems that thoughts come from nowhere, especially the most original. Intuition is often used to describe the origin of such 'thoughts'. For years, I have been intrigued about the fact that it's possible to recall verifiable facts about events years ago, including people, movement, colours, smells and impressions. Under hypnosis, forgotten events can be recalled. It's as though everything that we have ever seen or heard or thought or sensed is recorded in our brain. If we had a digital camera and recorder to simulate this, how much memory would we need? It must be unimaginably large.

As happens to me so often in writing this book, I had stumbled into one of the numerous (probably all) areas of life affected by evolution and find that many others have been there many years before me. Timothy Wilson in 'Strangers to ourselves: discovering the adaptive unconscious' points out that the human mind can accept colossal amounts of information per moment! Yet, as David Brooks points out (see immediately below), we can be conscious of only about 40 at any one time. Consequently, on a *momentary* basis and very approximately, we are *unaware* of vastly more bits of information taken in than we are *aware* of. Wilson suggests that the role of the unconscious is to help us in our normal, daily lives. The unconscious mind provides our decisions. He argues that it is an adaptive unconscious, defined as '*mental processes that are inaccessible to consciousness but that influence judgments, feelings or behaviour*'. He argues that whilst the unconscious mind plays a role in day-to-day decisions, it also does so in key life decisions such as those regarding marriage and career. His book also argues that, despite what we think, it's unlikely that we are consciously in charge of what we perceive to be our *intentional* actions.

David Brooks has written a popular, readable book, 'The social animal', about the impact of the unconscious mind on individual and group behaviour. He points out that both the conscious and what he calls the 'adaptive unconscious' minds (as per Timothy Wilson) receive information and construct stories. But the consciously constructed self can bear little correspondence to the non-conscious self. *Wilson gives numerous examples throughout the book and considers how we came to have two personalities: conscious and non-conscious.*

More on the book's structure
Intended to be accessible to the non-biologist, this book emphasises the major problems facing humanity, then considers broad, background ideas about evolution, the decisive role of primate, short-term instincts in survival and essential *human* needs. These human needs include the expression of the human instincts of altruism and art. Based on this approach, it goes on to outline the

causes of our problems in terms of instincts that are inappropriate for humans in the modern world, unmet essential human needs and the existence of unprecedented powers available to our alpha males. Then it examines possible ways to reduce our problems, partly by answering our basic needs. Finally, the major human social structures are considered from the *perspective of addressing inappropriate instincts and essential but unmet human needs.* It is proposed that progress will come only partly, *if at all*, from existing primate, hierarchical structures (and associated obedience), and partly from mass demands from *individuals* for structural changes, which are often relatively small.

Advocated is supporting the peaceful, mass exposure of injustice via social media including the already existing mass movements Occupy, Avaaz, SumOfUs, 38 degrees, Amnesty, 'truthout' and others including those suggested by George Monbiot (see later www.monbiot.com). Needed are parliaments or senates whose actual constitution represents the *community mix,* and parliamentarians and public servants who serve the people and *live lifestyles at least similar to those served.* Somehow, the connection needs to be cut between politicians, political parties and corporations / 'big business' with its 'big money' buying laws favourable to them. Such connections have been recognised since the earliest presidents of the USA, but without success. A major improvement would be religions that focus on the key and simple altruistic teachings of their founders and commercial enterprises that involve their employees as participating fellow humans and not as disposable objects, and a 'media' that informs, educates and entertains in the absence of individual media 'moguls' determining a commonly '*over-primate*' agenda.

Broadly, we need to move society from being mostly primate to more human.

It seems appropriate to start with an account of humanity's problems, for biological reasons, often understated by leaders or even ignored. Later, I will go on to consider how to reduce these problems along the lines mentioned above.

**Note: A quick way to learn more about a
scientific reference or 'paper'**

I've given references to the key books, people and sources of information that I have found most useful. Where I'm referring to human features in common with all organisms, I've sometimes used my own work to make the book more personal. To find a scientific paper in a journal, simply use Google and type in Home-PubMed-NCBI (an excellent USA database). Then, in the empty space in PubMed, type in the details of the paper or the journal or the author(s) of interest. Then, immediately the paper will come up or at least the abstract or perhaps other papers of the specified author. To find out more about a publication that is quoted or a person with a public profile, it can sometimes be easiest to use Google directly. Simply type the name of the person into the space on the Google page. For example, in my own case, simply type in MRW Brown (there are hundreds of thousands of scientists named 'Brown', often causing confusion for me, so I use the initials of all my forenames: Michael, Robert, Withington) and instantly masses of information about me appears. I've just checked right now and to my surprise, as well as my published work and other information, there is included a reference to **MRW Brown – Google Scholar Citations**. And clicking on this reference directly shows detailed, statistical information about my published work (with titles and fellow co-authors) and how often each has been quoted and over how many years! I have previously seen such data, but not found it simply by 'Googling' my name. So, as a start, to find out more about any reference or author (with a public profile) that I quote or any other topic of interest, I recommend that you simply type it into Google. It's amazing.

BACKGROUND IDEAS ON EVOLUTIONARY BIOLOGY

Contents

Preamble

Broad timetable of human evolution
(simplified and approximate timescales)

'Big Bang'
13.7 billion years ago the 'Big Bang' happened and matter appeared. If we extrapolate back from the trajectory of components of our expanding universe, then we arrive at the same place and at the same time – the 'Big Bang'. Many, possibly most, cosmologists believe it likely that other universes exist, obviously of unknown dates of origin.

Earth

Molten earth	4.6 billion years ago (i.e. it took 9.1 billion years to coalesce) Molten for 800 million years
Solidified earth	3.8 billion years ago (acquired water and an atmosphere capable of supporting life as it circled the sun)

Life

'Simple' cells	3.6 billion years ago i.e. life appeared after <u>200 million years of solid earth with water</u>
Cyanobacteria and photosynthesis (*importantly <u>utilising the energy of the sun</u>*)	3.4 billion years ago
'Complex' cells (eukaryotes)	2 billion years ago i.e. 1.6 billion years after the first simple cells
Multicellular life	1 billion years ago i.e. 1 billion years after first eukaryotes

Simple Animals	600 million years ago
Fish	450 million years ago
Mammals	200 million years ago
Birds	150 million years ago
Flowers	130 million years ago
Primates	60 million years ago
Family *Hominidae* (great apes)	20 million years ago
Genus *Homo* (human predecessors)	2.5 million years ago
Anatomically modern humans in Africa	200,000 years ago
Anatomically modern humans left Africa to populate the rest of the world	60,000 years ago

Abbreviated summary of timescale for human evolution

13.7   million millennia ago matter appeared from the 'Big Bang'

3.8   million millennia ago earth solidified with water and a life-supporting atmosphere

3.6   million millennia ago life started, i.e. <u>life took 200 million years to appear on solid earth</u>

2.5   million years ago *Homo*. Then, 2.3 million years later – i.e. <u>200 millennia</u> ago, anatomically modern humans appeared in Africa, i.e. it took 3.4 million millennia from the first cell.

60   millennia ago <u>anatomically modern humans</u> left Africa to populate the rest of the world

Comment: If we humans are defined by where we come from, then we are all Africans.

Additional notes on (a) primates,
(b) early humans and (c) nomenclature
(a) Primates
Defined by the Collins English dictionary as 'Any <u>placental mammal</u> of the *Primates*, typically having flexible hands and feet with opposable first digits, good eyesight and, in the higher apes, a highly developed brain: includes lemurs, lorises, monkeys, apes, and man'. *Primates arose from ancestors that lived in the trees of tropical forests; many primate characteristics represent adaptations to life in this challenging three-dimensional environment.* Most primate species remain at least partly arboreal. With the exception of humans, who inhabit every continent, most primates live in tropical or subtropical regions of the Americas, Africa and Asia. The primate family line goes back at least 55 million years, maybe 55. It's suggested that they may have evolved from insectivores, although this is not universally accepted.

Bonobos, genetically closest to humans, have fluid social groupings similar to the common chimpanzees, although bonobos are less excitable and aggressive. Male-female alliances also are more important for bonobos. Older females at times even become group leaders. Bonobos are unique among non-human primates in primarily engaging in sexual intercourse face to face. Gorillas do so occasionally. Both heterosexual and homosexual intercourse are common among bonobos. Copulation occurs frequently as a means of reducing tension in the community and has become recreational for them. In this and other traits, bonobos are similar to humans. Today, their range is limited to the forests south of the Zaire River in West Central Africa, and there are considerably fewer of them than common chimpanzees.

(b) Early humans and later population increases
Homo habilis is the earliest known species in the human lineage. Named in 1964 by Richard Leakey, the term 'habilis' refers to 'being handy'. This name was suggested because the hand and foot remains of this species were of special interest to the anthropologists studying locomotion. *H. habilis* had the ability to grasp objects and make

stone tools. This evidence allows researchers to conclude that *H. habilis*, a species that existed in Eastern Africa over a million years ago, exhibited a mode of locomotion very similar to that of modern humans. Most *H. habilis* fossils derive from Olduvai Gorge, Africa and several fragmentary specimens indicate that this species possessed an <u>enlarged brain</u>, around 550 to 690 cubic centimetres (cc). Anthropologists date *H. habilis* as originating between 2 and 1.9 <u>m</u>illion <u>y</u>ears <u>a</u>go (MYA), followed by *Homo erectus*, which dates to approximately 1.7 MYA. As a result, *H. habilis* was the first species that possessed the characteristic enlarged brain. This enlarged brain is also closely associated with the ability of <u>using stones for tool-making</u>. (**Note**: The brain of *Homo sapiens* (1130 cc for women and 1260 cc for men) is about double that of *H. habilis*).

Homo erectus appeared about 2 MYA and spread throughout Eurasia. It was likely the first hominine (any of a taxonomic tribe (Hominini) of hominids that includes recent humans together with extinct ancestral and related forms) to live in a hunter-gatherer <u>society and make use of fire</u>. The species disappeared about 0.4 million years ago. *H. sapiens* (anatomically modern humans) emerged about 0.2 MYA and is the only surviving species of the genus: all of several others became extinct. Archaic humans did survive alongside *H. sapiens* until around 40,000 MYA (e.g. *H. neanderthalensis*) and possibly until as late as about 12,000 years ago. There is evidence of interbreeding of archaic, notably Neanderthal, and modern humans. Anatomically modern humans migrated from Africa around 60,000 years ago. In recent years, a further species has been discovered with human *and* ape-like features. Notably, the paleoanthropologist Lee Berger discovered *Homo naledi* (and *Australopithecus sediba*) at the Rising Star Cave, South Africa. The significance of this finding and questions raised are discussed by the eminent anthropologist, Chris Springer of the Natural History Museum UK ('Human evolution: the many mysteries of *Homo naledi*'. eLife 2015; 4:e10627). Thus, life started around 3.6 million <u>millennia</u> ago and *H. Sapiens* appeared 3,400 <u>millennia</u> later, i.e. 200 millennia ago. Hence, *H. Sapiens* has had about 200 millennia to adapt to a new world with our:

a. human consciousness and brain power giving us nature-destroying capacity and
b. massive, 'unnatural' populations.

Adaptation

It seems that not enough time has elapsed for healthy adaptation. At the start of widespread agriculture, about 8000 BC, the world population was approximately 5 <u>million</u>. Over the 8,000-year period up to 1 AD it grew to around 200 <u>million</u>, with a growth rate of under 0.05% per year. In around 1800 AD the world population reached about one billion, the second billion was achieved in only 130 years (1930), the third billion in less than 30 years in 1959, the fourth billion in 15 years (1974), and the fifth billion in only 13 years in around 1987. Thus, during the 20th century, the world population had grown from around 1.65 billion to about 6 billion. In 2015, it was just over 7 billion. Population size is, itself, a human stress that we still need to adapt to.

Note: Because of reducing growth rates, it could take over 200 years to double again if current rates are maintained (Historical Estimates of World Population – US Census Bureau; The World at Six Billion, World Population, Year 0 to near stabilization [Pdf file] – United Nations Population Division).

(c) Nomenclature: primate and human

To avoid repetitive definitions and clarifications throughout the book, reminding the reader that humans are also classified biologically as primates, I now emphasise the following. Although humans are primates and *possess their basic instincts*, the word primate will be used to describe late, <u>pre</u>human primates. The word human will be used to describe the conscious, vastly more intelligent, language-using primate *Homo sapiens*, which also has additional innate, *human* tendencies, including altruism, language, creativity in art, poetry, music, singing, sculpture and dance.

Note: There are well-established, rare accounts of altruistic behaviour carried out by apes. Frans de Waal has written about the closeness of apes and humans in many ways and of occasional altruistic behaviour in apes.

How ideas about evolution arose

1. 'Early' thinkers, using mainly intuition with observation, came up with ideas similar to Darwin's but millennia before him. Many other ideas of numerous kinds arose, including rational ideas that were wrong, and those from sacred books, many of which were also factually wrong.

2. Empirical evidence, relying on experiment, not on speculation or theory, supported the Big Bang creating elements and atoms, the same as those we have today. Extrapolating the movement of matter in the universe backwards shows that all material originates at the same time and place. Polyphosphate (present from before biological evolution) is a possible template for assembly from units with *pre-existing affinities* and on a self-assembled surface such as a membrane, or on clay. Membrane vesicles can be self-assembling. Even DNA is assembled from units with pre-existing affinities: the base units of DNA have preferences; thus, there is order from apparent chaos. And was everything present in essence and potentially at the very beginning, about 14 billion years ago? Self-replicating, microbial life took about 200 million years from when the earth became a suitable habitat. Microbes changed, evolved, remain in astronomical numbers and are essential for soil and its quality. They are also essential for animal health, notably the gut population (microbiome), in numerous ways. At the same time, life evolved to be increasingly complex, leading to intelligent animals. Is it inherent and potential in matter to increase in complexity in this way? Given the inevitable 'errors' in DNA replication, then diversity of progeny is also inevitable. Thus, increasing complexity could occasionally lead to enhanced survival ability.

3. Putting aside the direct influence of a God, then it must follow that the possibility of life and of human life and thus altruism and love were potential in matter from the beginning.

Introduction

> *Evolution is just a theory?*
> *Well, so is gravity and I don't see you*
> *Jumping out of buildings.*

Richard Dawkins

This book is mainly about addressing the broad influence of our evolutionary background on human survival, social structures *and on happiness.* Specifically, the influence of:

a. unmet but essential human needs, including healthy early development and

b. the sometimes overwhelming negative influence of mindless primate instincts, including those related to leaders and hierarchies, on human institutions and human survival.

A theme is the discrepancy between instincts suitable for the short-term survival of individuals and small groups, together living an arboreal life within nature, and the same instincts operating in 'unnaturally' large human groups relatively unbound by nature. My purpose is not to present personal theories but rather to point out important, empirically determined facts that are obvious, yet are typically unrecognised or ignored despite contributing to human misery. What follows is about the basics of evolutionary biology and human evolution. Evolution has given us our character, including our basic as well as our human instincts: we are human primates.

Apart from natural disasters such as tsunamis, earthquakes and plagues, primate instincts inappropriate to the modern world are the cause of much human suffering. In addition, inappropriately exclusive social structures are correlated with the failure of nation states. According to Oxfam, we have about 1% of the world's population owning more than the rest of us put together! In the UK, this is rarely reported. Much attention by the UK press (mostly right wing, with right-wing *overseas* owners) is focussed on reducing the welfare bill (health, education and unemployment assistance).

Throughout human history, conflicts and wars have existed and caused misery. About a third of all countries are currently at war and virtually all states spend much of their resources on the military (see details later). In my own country (the UK), among many massively expensive weapons, we have submarines patrolling the seas with nuclear weaponry of unprecedented power and *no clear enemy to fire at!* And this is at a time when the UK government is attacking welfare 'scroungers' and expressing concern about how the elderly have 'unfairly' escaped significant financial cuts. UK leaders frequently state that these weapons give 'us' (i.e. our top alpha males) 'a seat at the top table': an attitude unadapted since the UK had a massive empire and matching power and owned the top table. And these specific weapons alone cost many tens of <u>billions</u> of pounds. In addition, if they were used, the deaths and injury of millions of humans and the associated environmental damage would make their use immoral by any standards of morality, including that of the official UK state religion of Christianity.

God as an explanation of the origin of life

Under 'Religion as a social structure' I will refer to God and also the Devil at greater length. A large proportion of the world believes that much, if not all, of what happens is not the consequence of biology, but the will of God and/or the evil activities of the Devil. For example, about 40% of the citizens of the USA do not believe in biological evolution but rather in special creation. For more detail, see Richard Dawkins' 'The Greatest Show on Earth'.

Cultural norms and myths

Norms

Not only are physical attributes selected for in evolution, but numerous authors have pointed out that ideas are also selected in human cultures and become norms. As mentioned earlier, a basic consensus on the perception of reality obviously can act as powerful social glue. Social conformity, obedience to social norms, helps concerted action at times of social danger. And also obvious is that such a consensus can act as a break on necessary social change. Individual value systems are affected by the overall values of the culture. Cultural values can be considered as being on a spectrum between extrinsic and intrinsic. People towards the intrinsic end have high levels of self-acceptance, strong bonds of intimacy and a desire to help other people. People at the extrinsic end are drawn to external signifiers, such as fame, financial success, image and attractiveness: they seek praise and rewards from others (T. Kasser, November 2011. Values and Human Wellbeing. The Bellagio Initiative. http://www. bellagioinitiative.org/wp-content/uploads/2011/10/Bellagio-Kasser. pdf). The social commentator, George Monbiot, has drawn attention to much worldwide social research indicating that intrinsic values are strongly associated with an understanding of others, tolerance, appreciation, cooperation and empathy (S. H. Schwartz, 2006. Basic Human Values: Theory, Measurement, and Applications. Revue Française de Sociologie, 47/4. http://bit.ly/1hL1JFJ; F. Grouzet *et al*, 2005. The structure of goal contents across fifteen cultures. Journal of Personality and Social Psychology, 89, 800-816. http://psycnet. apa.org/journals/psp/89/5/800/).

Those with strong extrinsic values tend to have lower empathy, a stronger attraction towards power, hierarchy and inequality, greater prejudice towards outsiders and less concern for global justice and the natural world (see T. Kasser, November 2011 above). These differing social norms can exist in opposition to each other: as one set of values strengthens, the other weakens. There thus exists a tendency for individuals to conform to the overall social value system. Clearly, this tendency contributes to the likelihood of coordinated social responses as per a primate instinct.

Religious ideas are another good example. They contribute to social glue and work as a social enforcer. With exceptions, they maintain cultural norms and adjust to maintain their own power, teaching and imposing ideas about reality that support the existing power structures. This probably explains why there are so many religions and sub-religions: they have changed as different societies have changed. As the local culture changes, religions adapt and change (see section below on adaptation and phenotypes) so as to increase the chances of their own institutional survival and that of their culture. Thus, in my own country, the UK, bishops sit in Parliament (the House of Lords) and the Queen is the Head of State and of the Church of England. In Christianity, for example, Heaven awaits the obedient and the disobedient literally (it is taught) spend eternity in hellfire. This role of religion continues across the world today, despite possible philosophical errors being implied. Wittgenstein pointed out that eternity is not time (and change) going on forever, but is a state of timelessness. Also, eternal fire is a dubious concept. Nevertheless, biologically speaking, the fear (erroneous or not) can act as a deterrent to disobedience.

On the other hand, the strongly adhesive qualities of religion become antisocial when different religions or belief systems clash and are the cause of violence and even wars. The extreme rewards (Heaven) and punishments (eternal hellfire) that help to bring about obedience and glue people together, then justify the strife and war to carry out the will of their God – as if their God is unable to do such things himself. Another drawback to conservative cultural ideas that have positively helped glue society together is that they can become a barrier to change when change is needed. When the teaching is objectively wrong, such as in the story of the creation of the world and its timing or of the relative movement of the sun and the Earth or of the origin of plagues and tsunamis (God's wrath) or whether the Earth is flat, then either the teaching should change or be discarded or extinction of the religion looms. History records hundreds of extinct religions.

Myths

Individual and collective memory often (maybe always) selects memories as representative of the past that are especially flattering or that support a defined identity and contributes to the social adhesion.   Sometimes events never happened, or perceptions are mistaken. Concepts such as ethnicity, 'people' and nation are powerful adhesives to bind people together. Given that there is convincing evidence that modern humans left Africa around 60,000 years ago and settled the rest of the world with much breeding between groups, then today there is relatively little likelihood for highly distinct and 'pure' genetic groups to remain highly distinct and pure, unless geographically isolated over long periods.

Although this is my own subjective impression, my country, the UK, with its recent large, powerful empire partly retains a current aspect of our national identity that is related to a God-given right to power. We are a 'land of hope and glory'. 'We take freedom and democracy across the world'. During a week when long-term cuts in 'welfare' were predicted by our Chancellor because of huge debts, we invested in an overseas military base and we continue our ultra-expensive 'Trident' nuclear weapons programme that adds to the prestige of our elite, alpha males. Compared to other colonial powers, it seems that the British Empire was far from the worst empire: nevertheless, we accepted slavery for centuries and we did commit atrocities. I have seen the Church of England prayer book displaying a picture of God sending down rays of grace towards our monarch and supporting the myth of 'Royal' blood and the 'Divine right of Kings'.

Similarly, the current world power, the USA, has a myth of also being designated by God to lead the world towards freedom and democracy. The former President Obama has spoken (which was surprising to me) of the US historic mission to lead the world. A former US Vice President, Al Gore, in his book on the world's problems ('The Future') has stated surprisingly (at the start and at the end of the book) that only the US nation can lead us out of these problems. Given that the USA is the most unequal country (for which there's data) with attendant severe social ailments (see later), these assertions make no sense. Even so, Al Gore is successfully leading a campaign that points out the imminence of catastrophes caused by global warming and highlights the dishonest propaganda coming from the USA far right, including the President, Donald Trump, and funded indirectly by the energy billionaires.

One prominent myth relates to the origins of the State of Israel and ideas about the 'Holy Land', the 'People of Israel' and the 'Exile', referred to later under 'Key problems'. The Israeli historian Shlomo Sand in 'The invention of the Jewish people' destroyed the myth of the Roman-enforced exile. There is *no evidence* that the Romans deported the population of Judea – 'The Exile'. I'm not an historian, but clearly if Shand can be refuted, then all that his opponents need to do is to reveal the evidence. This has not happened. And this myth can join many of the other myths of other nations that help sustain them.

The well-known, long-lasting and appalling 'racism' against Jews has *biological* explanations. Historically, Jews aroused instincts about foreignness and territory. They aspired, not to the land where they actually lived, but to their Holy Land. They also had a foreign, alien religion, a foreign language (often Hebrew) and adhered to their 'foreign' dress customs. Almost everywhere, they were seen as foreign in every sense, with the virtually inevitable arousing of suspicions of the indigenous people against foreigners. Today, this myth of God's people and their Holy Land is at the centre of the problems of Palestine. Adding to these problems is the knowledge that one cannot distinguish the inhabitants of Israel genetically (see earlier under 'Violent aggression'), at least partly because the early Jews often proselytised and had converts (again, see Shlomo Sand's 'The invention of the Jewish people'). It's hard not to agree with Sand's view that Israel must become a democratic state for all of its citizens or else perpetuate the current disaster. As for many countries, the State of Israel's origins in violence, land theft and involvement in global politics (West versus East, and Middle East oil) does not bode well.

As a kind of appendix to myths about the Jews, we have Hitler, fanning the flames of anti-Semitism and adding to the myth of Jews intrinsically being deeply different and evil. In his short book 'Hitler', A. N. Wilson details how Hitler gathered around himself a 'grotesque gang of misfits and semi-criminals who would, for a nightmarish decade, be the most powerful political clique in Europe' which helped in his own myth of being the 'Great Leader'. In 'Mein Kampf' there is a remarkable passage: 'With Satanic joy in his face, the black-haired Jewish youth lurks in wait for the unsuspecting girl whom he defiles with his blood, thus stealing her from her own people'. In such ways, Hitler propagated the myth of a German purity and of a Jewish impurity. It would all be unbelievable, absurd and even mad if Hitler had not actually existed and the Holocaust had not actually happened. But it did happen. Later (under 'Education'), I describe the intense, prolonged and successful indoctrination of German youth by Hitler's policies.

In parenthesis, it's interesting to note today's outbreaks of 'terrorism', mostly by people claiming adherence to Islam and with real grievances from past misuse of power by Western nations. It seems that historically 'the wandering Jews' rarely (if ever) used terror prior to the establishment of the State of Israel. Yet they did so at its creation.

Animal group size

Another factor that seems underrated is group size (see publications from the anthropologist, Robin Dunbar). Our ape predecessors, up to human hunter-gatherers, lived in small groups relative to today's human societies. Whether a consistent small group size (up to approximately 50 for chimpanzees) qualifies for being an instinct is less important than that group size, physiology, brain anatomy, psychology, behaviour (including that of alpha-male leaders) and diet all developed together over millions of years, compatible with and within the natural (i.e. little influenced by human activity) environment. Modern behavioural studies indicate that a task-driven human group, e.g. a committee, is commonly most successful if numbered around seven, with members of varying personalities and backgrounds. It is likely that in an ape or early human group each individual would feel that they belonged. The deep need for humans to belong is stressed later.

Basic needs for survival
Recognition of environmental change, especially danger and an effective, rapid and coordinated response. 'The Golden Rule of Survival' (again).

All organisms have basic requirements of anatomy, physiology and metabolism, and for higher organisms, psychology appropriate to their habitat. To put it another way, a habitat is required that is appropriate to an organism's anatomy, physiology, metabolism and psychology. The habitat provides nutrition, shelter and facilitates procreation. It's obvious that survival is most likely if an organism has an effective and rapid response to change, especially dangerous changes. In the case of groups of organisms, chances of survival are increased if the rapid response is also coordinated. The elimination of ineffective responses to threats by biological extinction takes care of the effectiveness criterion and for primate groups, hierarchies facilitate the rapid and concerted requirement as well as playing a major role in the sensing of the danger. Coordination and control are obviously needed to achieve the rapid and concerted response, including conditioning between threats. Thus, animal survival (and the evolution of life) is based on the requirement to respond to stress: *recognition of danger and an effective, rapid and coordinated response.* This will involve effective control during and between threats.

Origins and evolution of life

Life's origins

The origins of life remain obscure. It has been suggested that life arrived on Earth from another planet, leaving the origin still obscure. A widely held theory is that biochemicals came together on the surface of self-assembled lipid vesicles or perhaps on clay or rock. Another widely held theory is that RNA was important for life's start (The dawn of the RNA world. RNA, vol. **15**, pgs 743-749 (2009). C. Briones, M. Stich and S. C. Manrubia). One theory proposed by myself and my former colleague, the late Arthur Kornberg, was that a polymer of phosphate groups facilitated the assembly of important macromolecules. Polyphosphate was available on prebiotic Earth and has several properties that make it a good candidate for assisting such assembly, e.g. creating polymers from amino acids. Any reader interested in finding out more about this is referred to the following paper: Inorganic polyphosphate in the origin and survival of species. Proceedings of the National Academy of Sciences of the USA, volume **101**, pgs 16085-16087 (2004). M. R.W. Brown and A. Kornberg.

Evolution

Evolution is a 'universal solvent'

Much of this book is not original, though emphasising the negative effects of the power phenotype is possibly new. Almost always, when I thought that I'd had an original idea, it proved later that someone (often many) had got there before me, even centuries before. In several instances, unexpectedly, I had ideas that were shared with great thinkers of thousands of years ago and I felt an extraordinary and personal affinity with them. Because the scope of this book is so wide and covers all fields of life, it's likely that many other ideas are also already proposed by others. Daniel C. Dennet in Darwin's Dangerous Idea' put it clearly (despite and possibly because of the mixed metaphor): 'There is no denying ... that Darwin's idea is a universal solvent, capable of cutting right to the heart of everything in sight'. It's clear that evolution is the basis of every aspect of the life of every organism. Whilst I am a microbiologist with my career focussed on microbial survival and adaptation, I do not and cannot claim to be an expert in all areas of evolution and its application to major social structures: politics, the military, religion, professions, commerce, media, culture. Involved are all the major disciplines of science, notably molecular genetics, neurobiology and anthropology as well as history, sociology and psychology. Together with my 'day job', this is why the book has taken me so long to write; personal notes for about 45 years and then turning into something more structured about two decades or so ago and then a book about ten years or so ago.

My slight consolation is that the same dilemma applies to everyone else. There is a continuing explosion in knowledge and understanding about the basics of biology: genetics, structure and function. Ever more sensitive, non-intrusive physical techniques are being devised to examine brain development and function. Molecular genetics is expanding with extraordinary speed and casts light in every biological direction. Everywhere in biology, 'expertise' is becoming diluted as new knowledge increases rapidly. Where I have failed, including inadvertent failure to give credit to others, I apologise. My purpose is to point out hugely important drivers of destructive human behaviour that are generally ignored, despite being visible: the 'elephant in the room'. In fact, it would be more accurate to say the 'rampaging elephant in the room'. Likely, this ignoring or rather *not seeing the elephant* is also instinctive and applies to numerous aspects of human perception. We see with decreasing clarity those things that reduce our chances of survival, often as determined by our elites, with behaviour also impelled by instincts.

Proof of evolution

*By considering the embryological structure of man
the homologies which he presents with the lower
animals we thus learnt that man is descended from
a hairy quadruped,......probably arboreal in its habit,
and an inhabitant of the Old World.*

Charles Darwin

A basic and still contentious idea is that humans share ancestors with the great apes (and beyond): chimpanzees, gorillas, orangutans and bonobos. In fact, we share *almost* 100% of our genes with the apes: the bonobos being closest to us genetically (about 98.5% identity).

When an undergraduate at Manchester University, I attended lectures by an eminent zoologist on embryology – the development of the embryo. He pointed out how different stages of the human embryo corresponded to different stages in evolution.

Fresh insights into humanity's most recent relatives have come from recent findings near Johannesburg, SA. A system of caves known as 'Rising Star' yielded initially 1,500 human bones and later, many more. This and other work has cast new light on our origins, including interbreeding with Neanderthals and others (Human evolution: fifty years after *Homo habilis*. Nature, volume **508**, pages 31-33. 2014. Bernard Wood; Evolution: the human saga. Scientific American, volume **311**, Number 3 September 2014 – special edition of Scientific American edited by Kate Wong). Indeed, DNA analysis has revealed the previously hidden 'promiscuity' of humans and other close species (see later).

It is not my intention to argue the case for evolution at length. Others have done so far better than I could. I am not normally given to being in awe of other scientists, but the entire field of evolution benefits from numerous, truly brilliant authors who have also written for the non-specialist public. My selection is idiosyncratic. My personal preference for the interested reader would be definitely to read Charles Darwin himself: 'On the origin of Species' (1859). Jerry Coyne has written the excellent, well-received and comprehensive

'Why evolution is true'. It's a broad sweep of all the evidence for evolution written in a readable style. I strongly recommend books by Richard Dawkins. For interested newcomers, I suggest that the propaganda of religious 'fundamentalists' against him is to be ignored. He is entirely rational, and his books are beautifully written. His 'The Greatest Show on Earth' is a detailed, meticulous, humorous and totally convincing account of the overwhelming evidence for evolution. It is also an annihilation of the assertions and faith statements of the opponents of evolution. He takes their statements seriously and does so with extraordinary good humour. I would love him to write a book proving that the Earth is not flat.

'The origin of our species' by Chris Stringer is a meticulous, authoritative and detailed account that addresses all the major questions about our evolutionary origins. 'The Journey of Man' is a clear, detailed description of human origins in Africa and subsequent dispersals, written by a former experimental molecular geneticist, Spencer Wells. Jared Diamond has written exceptional books on humanity's origins and social development: 'Collapse', 'The third chimpanzee' and 'Guns, germs and steel'. A relatively recent book of his is 'The world until yesterday' and is a comprehensive account of our human past and offers valuable lessons from our ancestors. Another suggestion with an easily readable style that I especially like and obviously with a genetic emphasis is 'The Language of Genes' by Steve Jones, based on his series of BBC Reith Lectures and also his book 'Y: the descent of man'. His 'The Serpent's Promise: The Bible Retold as Science' is a scrutiny of the Bible from the perspective of science. Jones believes that science is the Bible's direct descendant and he, with the light of science, explores the factual, if not the spiritual, questions raised millennia ago. 'Genome: The autobiography of a species in 23 chapters' by Matt Ridley is a brilliant, erudite account of the human genome, indeed our 'autobiography'. His novel approach is to consider the 23 pairs of chromosomes and to explain the function of a specific gene in each that plays an important and different role in human life. I found it superb.

'Only' a theory

Creationists often make the devious assertion that evolution is 'only' a theory. This was beautifully and seriously dealt with by Richard Dawkins in his book mentioned above, 'The Greatest Show on Earth', especially his first chapter (headed 'Only a Theory?') which, for me, is a gem. My collaborator of several years was the Nobel Laureate, the late Arthur Kornberg, mentioned above. He discovered and purified enzymes that make DNA. He was acknowledged as a giant in the field and his work was at the base of the biotechnology revolution in terms of adding/removing genes. His preference was to refer to the *laws* of evolution. It is now clear that predictions can be and are made as a result of genetic knowledge. 'Only a theory' implies something half-baked, analogous to a transient fashion. Whereas a scientific law enables *predictions about the future*. The science of genetics, aided by developments in computing, has progressed with astonishing speed and is casting light on the detailed genetic composition (genomes) of numerous species including our own and of our relatives, and *linking specific genes with specific functions and processes*. Interventions in gene make-up, 'gene editing', are occurring daily to improve agriculture, medicine and our general understanding of organisms. An example, as I write now (August 2017), is the removal of several harmful viruses from the pig genome so that pigs can be used to provide organs for transplantations for humans.

Religions that deny evolution are digging within their own graves. In their denial, they are also diverting attention from the needed insights and accurate intuition of their founders, e.g. regarding the primacy of altruism. It's noteworthy that the Roman Catholic Church changed and now accepts biological evolution: similarly, and reluctantly, some time ago it accepted the relative movements of the planets.

Readers sceptical of evolution are asked to note the following established facts.

a.   All the atoms composing our bodies come from the same set of elements as those in the rest of the universe arising from the 'Big Bang' about 13.7 billion years ago.

b.   Individual human cells share much cell machinery and structure with all other organisms in the whole of nature.

c.   Humans are one species of animal closely related to apes metabolically and genetically, as well as being a species with unique powers of rational thought, empathy, intuition and altruism.

Given that life and consciousness exist, then matter from the 'Big Bang' must have had and has the potential for mind. Or to put it another way, matter has always had the potential for rationality, empathy, intuition and altruism. Essentially, all humans now belong to the same species. Consequently, where I later refer to specific cultures, nations or religions, it's helpful to think of the people within such social structures as ourselves but with their environment (geography, history and culture) to shape them (us). In that sense we are all Egyptians, we are all Americans. If anything, we are all Africans (see section earlier on our evolutionary past). To repeat: the first humans to leave Africa did so only about 60,000 years ago.

Those who are sceptical of the influence of genetics should also consider the following very basic facts. Humans cannot fly unaided, but birds can with their DNA coding for bird anatomy, physiology, brains and at least some bird behaviour; nor can unaided humans remain underwater for hours, although fish can with their fish DNA coding for characteristics necessary for underwater existence. Humans have the wrong DNA for these activities. There are definite differences between men and women as specified by our DNA. Twenty-two chromosomes (DNA arranged in separate strands: see below) are common for humans, but women also have two large X-chromosomes, while men have a single X-chromosome paired with a smaller male,

Y-chromosome. The latter has the codes for the testes. Genes and combinations of them specify everything about a human, including gender with its associated anatomical, physiological and psychological differences. And importantly, gene activity is influenced by the environment, including and especially our early development. Today, in numerous organisms of various types, specific genetic changes are being made for commercial and medical reasons with results that prove the link between the gene and the characteristic. It can be predicted as a result of specific genetic changes, that a crop will survive desiccation better than the plant without the change. Susceptibility to various cancers is affected by the presence or absence of specific genes. Other examples are given later.

The heredity chemical – deoxyribose nucleic acid (DNA)

Why, when animals mate, are the offspring of the same species? Why, when plants are pollinated, do the seeds give rise to plants of the same species? How scientists showed that it was indeed the DNA and not another chemical such as a protein that conveyed inherited characters is, itself, a fascinating and remarkable story that I must deal with, only very briefly. Over the last 150 years the following broad developments have occurred in understanding inheritance. Charles Darwin published 'On the Origin of Species' about evolution by natural selection in 1859; Gregor Mendel, working with pea plants and crossing different strains, studied the inheritance of specific, clear-cut characteristics (height, flower colour and position, seed shape) and published rigorous, quantitative results in 1866; Frederick Griffiths found that a 'transforming principle' from a virulent strain of the bacterium *Streptococcus pneumoniae* could change a non-virulent strain into a virulent one, and in 1944 Oswald Avery and colleagues showed that the 'transforming principle' was DNA. This was the point at which studies in genetics and DNA blended. Subsequently in 1952, Hershey and Chase used bacterial viruses again to confirm DNA as the carrier of hereditary information. Another milestone in the 1950s was the discovery and isolation by Arthur

Kornberg of DNA polymerase, the enzyme synthesising DNA. I had the extraordinary education of working with Arthur Kornberg for several years before his untimely death. And, of course, then came the spectacular elucidation of DNA structure by Watson and Crick, aided by several others in the field.

Since then, it has been verified beyond reasonable doubt that DNA is the heredity material of a cell (collectively called the genome) and determines a cell's or an organism's spectrum of capabilities. It's a long 'poly-mer', i.e. a chain of repeating chemical units. In higher organisms, the bulk of the DNA is arranged in separate strands called chromosomes, located within the cell's membrane-bound nucleus. Before briefly describing a little more about DNA, it's important to point out that this *determination of any organism's properties is the result of the sequence in the chain links of chemical compounds and their physical-chemical properties.* Even such as a human brain, mental tendencies and human personality originate in the chemical configurations of DNA. With all organisms, expression of these characteristics is influenced by their environment, including for humans, the mother's womb and state of mind and later the 'environment' through infancy and adolescence. How such complexity stems from relative simplicity is still partly a mystery but is slowly unfolding. That it occurs is quite certain. Repetition could be helpful: any organism's properties, including its adaptive range, are the result of the sequence in a specific chain of chemical compounds and of their physical-chemical properties and of their intra and external environmental interactions. It's not surprising that many people find this difficult to believe. As a former Roman Catholic, I did not believe it for much of my life. But it is true.

A further note about DNA: The finding and functions of DNA illustrate the multiple origins of much scientific discovery. DNA was first identified in 1869 by the Swiss chemist Friedrich Miescher. Then other scientists, notably Phoebus Levene and Erwin Chargaff discovered its primary chemical components and how they joined with one another, e.g. bases on opposite strands paired off. Also, important X-ray crystallography by English researchers Rosalind Franklin and Maurice Wilkins contributed to James Watson and Francis Crick's derivation of the three-dimensional, double-helical model for the structure of DNA. In the 1950s Arthur Kornberg isolated and purified the enzymes involved in synthesising DNA. Watson and Crick's model was also made possible by advances in model-building, or the assembly of possible three-dimensional structures based upon known molecular distances and bond angles, a technique used and advanced by biochemist Linus Pauling. In fact, Watson and Crick were worried that they would be 'scooped' by the scientific genius Pauling, who proposed a different model for the three-dimensional structure of DNA just months before they did. In the end, however, Pauling's prediction was incorrect. An account of this history is given in: Pray, L. (2008) Discovery of DNA structure and function: Watson and Crick. Nature Education 1(1):100. Also, Watson published the best seller 'The double helix'. A revision was later published, *'The Annotated and Illustrated Double Helix' by James Watson, edited by Alexander Gann and Jan Witkowski (Simon & Schuster).*

Code for any organism

The chemical polymer DNA has a four 'letter' genetic 'alphabet' consisting of four specific chemical compounds, 'nucleotides', with about three billion of these 'letters' comprising the code for developing and maintaining a human. Genes are composed of a limited, specific sequence of these 'letters'. When the cell divides into two, the DNA replicates itself by a complex, highly organised machinery with numerous components. Like all machines, the products are not always identical in an absolute sense and sometimes (see the section below on diversity) there are 'copying errors' (mutations), usually minor. Furthermore, it's now clear that different organisms are able to, and do, exchange DNA thus expanding the organism's genetic 'code' and the options and range of characteristics. Some DNA exists outside the nucleus and some is associated with 'organelles' called mitochondria.

The latter are important in energy metabolism and are thought to be derived from bacteria originally living within the cell in a mutually beneficial way.

Thus, diversity is inevitable.

Much work has been carried out on the sequence of the chemical components of DNA, initially gradually and recently more swiftly as techniques improved. Given the billions of units (or 'letters') in the genetic code, manual analysis and comparison of the sequences characteristic of species is unrealistic. Genomics is the application of computer analysis to such data about DNA structure and component sequences. This greatly facilitates the discovery of evolutionary pathways and connections. This field casts a bright light on the specifics of evolutionary progress including its 'timelines'. And the field is expanding rapidly.

Human genome
Discovering the chemical sequences in the strands in the entire human genome, broadly in the year 2000, more fully in 2003 and accelerating, is possibly the greatest scientific advance ever. This initial work cost about $3 billon. Affordable genomes are available in 2017 for about $1,000, with 'next-day delivery' and prices dropping. Computer study of the sequences in the human genome is leading to numerous advances in medicine. For example, several hundred genes contributing to cancer have been identified, leading to increased understanding and options for treatment. Herceptin, an anti-breast cancer drug is active against the one in five sufferers with HER2-positive disease, but not in those lacking this protein. The anti-cancer drug Gefitinib is active in about 15% of lung cancer patients. The cost of current genetic screening to discover which patients have which mutations can add to and subtract from the medical and drug costs. France, a world leader in its national public health service, introduced genetic testing facilities in university hospitals

and of about 15,000 lung cancer patients tested, only 1,700 were appropriate for subsequent treatment. The cost was £30 million, i.e. about £2,000 per patient per genetic screen. Naturally, financial and human savings are made by not using drugs that are ineffective for some patients. Another recent advance is in the mis-functioning of platelets where workers at Birmingham University (UK) discovered a gene designated G6b that regulates platelet production: platelets play a role in blood clotting. A mutant version of G6b causes platelets to behave in a hyperactive manner, resulting in an immune response destroying most of the body's blood platelets with pathological consequences. This discovery opens up pathways of understanding of the rare disease 'platelet function disorder' and will hopefully lead to therapies to prevent heart attacks and strokes from blood clots.

Current studies comparing the genomes of humans with near relatives such as Neanderthals or primates such as chimpanzees offer the possibility of better understanding of the key qualities that make us human. Neanderthals, the closest evolutionary relatives of present-day humans, lived in large parts of Europe and western Asia before disappearing as late as about 12 to 30,000 years ago. In 2010 a draft sequence of the Neanderthal genome was published, allowing comparison with the human genome. It's remarkable that bonobo chimpanzees (the closest primates to humans) share 98.5 % of their DNA 'letters' with humans. Obviously, the unshared bit is of huge interest. Several other extinct species close to humans have been discovered recently, one solely via analysis of genomes. In evolutionary terms, the 150 years from the publication of Darwin's broad insight into our biological antecedents up to the specific sequencing of the human genome and its editing is the blink of an eye.

Gene editing – I recommend any reader not to skip this section, it's amazing
For some decades, scientists have used techniques to remove nucleotides (the 'letters' of the DNA 'script') from the genes of one organism and paste them into another organism – recombinant

DNA – and also recognised the dangers. One danger is the possibility of transferring unwanted viruses integrated in the chromosome. In recent years an exceptionally important technique has been devised that enables the real editing of a genome. It's now possible to <u>alter or delete or rearrange</u> the DNA of almost any organism, including humans.

This ability to change the code of life gives us power over nature previously unimaginable. The technology goes by the name CRISPR-Cas9 (<u>c</u>lustered, <u>r</u>egularly <u>i</u>nterspaced, <u>s</u>hort <u>p</u>alindromic <u>r</u>epeats, with Cas9 being an enzyme that can precisely cut out an unwanted DNA sequence). For any interested non-specialist reader, the August 2016 edition of National Geographic has a popular account by Michael Specter of this amazing technique. Another more detailed popular review is given by Heidi Ledford in Nature (News and Comment), 7th March 2016: 'CRISPR: gene editing is just the beginning: the real power of the biological tool lies in exploring how genomes work'. An early account in the journal Science is 'Multiplex genome engineering using CRISPR/Cas systems'. Science, 2013 Feb 15;339(6121):819-23. doi: 10.1126/science.1231143. Epub 2013 Jan 3. Cong et al.

For anyone wanting more detailed information about its uses in medicine, Anthony James of the University of California, Irvine has been working on mosquitoes for decades with the intention of adjusting their genes so that they can no longer spread the diseases they can carry. These include yellow fever, dengue fever, chikungunya, West Nile virus and Zika: diseases that infect and kill millions of humans. In 2015, he and colleagues published successful results showing Anopheles mosquitoes incapacitated for the spread of the malaria parasite ('Highly efficient Cas9-mediated gene drive for population modification of the malaria vector mosquito Anopheles stephensi'. Gantz et al. PNAS (2015). vol 112 no. 49 E6736–E6743, doi 10.1073/pnas.1521077112). It would be difficult to exaggerate the importance of this approach in every area of biology including human medicine: similarly, for the ethical questions raised. Unsurprisingly, CRISPR-Cas9 genome editing kits are now on the market, prices starting at around $150. Simply 'Google' CRISPR/Cas9.

Molecular clock

Broadly speaking and influenced by the importance and consistency of the 'copying error' (mutation) to the organism's survival, genomics provides a form of molecular clock that measures the rate at which mutations are made and accumulated. It can show how long ago it was that organisms shared a common ancestor. In such studies, the fact that mitochondrial DNA with 37 genes is transmitted through generations *only* via the mother is also helpful in establishing ancestral lines. Even more helpful to ascertaining timelines are studies of the Y-chromosome, transmitted only via the male. This is because it is about 3,000 times longer than the mitochondrial DNA and offers far more sites for previous mutations, but with only 21 genes. Consequently, mutations of non-gene sections are not selected for and the timelines are more reliable. Human chromosomes other than the Y have vastly more genes – about 1,500. Several other techniques in population genetics such as radioactive decay are also used to identify the occurrence of changes in the DNA and corroborate their timing. Among many findings is one that is startling. It's possible that all modern humans alive today are descended from a man who lived in Africa about 60,000 years ago. We are all 'Africans'. Life was not created in its entirety over six days a few thousand years ago, any more than the flat Earth is the centre of the universe with the sun encircling it.

Elsewhere, I refer to widespread *gene mixing* as the result of births where, unknowingly (to some), the marital husband is not the father. The mixing can be greatest when the father is from afar such as a visiting sailor or foreign soldier or traveller. This can commonly be approximately 15 % of births. On a broader sweep, genomics gives us a molecular clock about the mixing of entire human populations over millennia: which populations and when. Two examples follow.

Firstly, is a study about genetic mixing of a specific people in the Middle East – the Jews. The study was based on samples of 526 Y chromosomes representing six Middle Eastern populations (Ashkenazi, Sephardic, and Kurdish Jews from Israel; Muslim Kurds; Muslim Arabs and Bedouin from the Negev). Among several findings, they showed that Kurdish and Sephardic Jews were indistinguishable from one another, whereas both differed slightly, yet significantly, from Ashkenazi Jews. This study helped elucidate the complex demographic history that shaped the present-day genetic landscape in this troubled region. Without such genetic studies of timelines, it would be much more difficult to trace the origins and mixing of populations. ('The Y chromosome pool of Jews as part of the genetic landscape of the Middle East' was published in the American Journal of Human Genetics in 2001, volume 69, November, pages 1095-112, authors A. Nebel and several others).

Secondly, a more expansive study reveals information about timelines and world-wide mixing over millennia. The study produced an atlas of worldwide human admixture history, constructed by using genetic data alone and encompassing over 100 events occurring over the past 4,000 years. They identified events whose dates and participants indicated genetic impacts of the Mongol empire, Arab slave trade, Bantu expansion, first millennium CE (Common Era or AD) migrations in Eastern Europe, European colonialism, as well as unrecorded events. *They showed admixture to be an almost universal force shaping human populations* ('A genetic atlas of human admixture history'. Published in the journal Science. 2014 volume **14**, February, pages 747-51, author G. Hellenthal and several others).

'Simple' life forms

Single-cell microbes such as bacteria have the same survival requirements as higher life forms (microbial survival has been the subject of my research for my entire career). To survive, they also require *effective, rapid and concerted responses to stress*. I currently work on an aspect of microbial survival and try, in various ways, to test the idea that a particular polymer (polyphosphate) plays an important and general role in survival. The idea arose a couple of decades or so ago from the work of the late Arthur Kornberg with whom I was privileged to collaborate. In our last paper, we wanted to review the existing evidence and show polyphosphate's importance. We did this by listing the basic requirements for microbial survival and showed with numerous references that polyphosphate was necessary for optimising each requirement.

We listed the following broad requirements for microbial survival, either within a host or in the natural environment as:

a. an efficient, competitive basic metabolism;
b. the ability to detect and the capacity for rapid adaptation to minor environmental changes;
c. existence mainly in the surface-adherent mode of growth (i.e. having its own territory); and
d. response to changes at the limits of the adaptive capacity of the organism – stress responses.

These requirements are broadly necessary for all life, from microbes to humans and also human institutions. They broadly apply to professions, universities and all social institutions. To summarise, these are survival criteria for human organisations: organisations efficiently focussed on purpose, their ability to sense and respond to environmental change, including danger, and the need for 'territory', i.e. familiar 'landscape' where nourishment, dangers and havens are known.

In microbes, specific stress responses evolved to cope with danger from such as toxic chemicals, UV light, freezing, heat and desiccation. For example, a consistent response evolved to repair DNA damage caused by UV light or desiccation. Another response is for toxic chemicals to be pumped out of the cell. Yet another is to protect cell structures *en route* to dormancy by analogy with seeds of higher plants. Microbes have several such responses to major stresses: they are rapid and aid survival. So far, every stress response studied for the role of polyphosphate found that it was involved in the response.

During evolution, developments in the metabolism and structure of some microbes took place without handicapping these responses. They are like well-oiled, familiar tracks that facilitate survival. In addition to the selection of intra-cellular biochemical and structural changes, there also occurred a selection of gross 'behavioural' changes. Thus, chemotaxis is a process that directs a motile microbe towards food or else away from toxic material. It seems likely that these programmed, predetermined responses are continuous through evolution up to instincts in higher animals.

It's important to note that the vast majority of microbes do not exist as cells growing independently in aqueous suspension, either in the natural environment or within animals. Individual cells in suspension have no control over their environment and are vulnerable to any physical or chemical change in the external environment or to predation. Instead, microbes exist almost entirely as surface-adherent 'biofilms' and have properties substantially different to those of cells growing in suspension. In this way, microbes can make and control their immediate environment. For microbes, it's typical to survive as dense, surface-attached aggregates, often of mixed species. This field was virtually invented by a good friend, the late J. W. (Bill) Costerton.

> *The benefits of surface-attachment for microbes are analogous to the importance of familiar territory to higher animals.*

Such consortia, typically coated with exopolymer, are protected against predation by other organisms and often from UV light and offer yet more protection to the microbial world. The exopolymer can itself attract water and reduce dehydration under dry conditions. Microbial survival is assisted by communication between them. As a cell population increases, chemical signals are produced that modify behaviour. Proximity to a surface induces metabolic changes that enhance the sticking to the surface. The survival advantages of possessing territory apply widely across the whole of biology. Anyone interested in further information about signalling of microbes can obtain it from 'Googling' the name of a Professor eminent in this field, Paul Williams and add the word 'signals'.

The heading to this section could be misleading. In reality, there are no simple organisms. They are all highly complex. The highly complex social behaviour of bacteria extends even more so to lower animals such as ants and insects, in seeking food and in response to threats and is relatively constant over time and across climates. *How* highly complex social behaviour occurs consistently in such animals remains an unsolved mystery, but *that* it occurs is quite certain. Thus, such populations have predispositions to specific behaviour patterns, analogous to 'instincts' in higher organisms. These include task specialisations related to reproduction, food supply and its location and also response to stress.

Diversity

Another important and basic idea to consider is biological diversity – vital to evolution. It's the 'food' of selection. Without it evolution does not and cannot occur. Even if we consider growing bacterial populations from a genetically pure, single culture, the cells show massive heterogeneity. At any moment, cells will be at different stages of replication and of varying dimensions. As the cell numbers increase, the cells adapt in numerous ways from the original growth environment to the new growth circumstances. Then, with increasing population, the environment may become hostile such as one or more nutrients starting to become scarce and the cells adapt to this in various ways. In fact, the cells adapt *before* the nutrient runs out. As starvation approaches, these heterogeneous cells start a stress response in which, commonly, each cell protects its key structures before stopping growth and becoming dormant. Not all cells in the population complete this process. None of this is done in a synchronous way; each cell in the population copes according to its state when it sensed that the food was disappearing.

Thus, even in a 'pure' culture of single-cell organisms, much non-genetic diversity exists. Even during one subculture, it is possible that mutations can occur, but typically of genes with no significant consequence. *Repeated* subculture in media consistently causing, say, starvation of one essential nutrient could lead to selection of mutants more suited to coping with that particular starvation. It is well established that mistakes ('copying errors') in DNA replication are relatively common and often of little consequence to the initial population. But sometimes the consequences are important, e.g. antibiotic-resistant mutants appear as a result of antibiotics eliminating sensitive bacteria and leaving the resistant mutants (perhaps about 1 in 100 million of the original population) supreme and causing human infection.

In the case of higher animals, we have numerous possibilities for diversity: the sperm and the eggs; the fertilisation process; the influences of the mother's body and state of mind on development, followed by post-birth development within the social environment. A few years ago, I heard a seminar about an aspect of DNA replication during a period at the Stanford University Department of Biochemistry. The content of the talk implied that DNA likely never replicated 'perfectly' in an absolute sense. Afterwards, on the way back to the lab, I asked my collaborator, pre-eminent in DNA research, what he thought. He thought it likely that this was so. *In other words, diversity is built into biology. It is inescapable.* This is probably the basic cause of why there are so many religions and sub-religions and sub-sub-religions, and political ideologies and sub-ideologies and sexual preferences (straight, gay, 'cross-dresser' etc., etc., etc.) and dietary styles and views on literature and indeed diversity about every human (or other organism) activity.

Diversity is *natural* in every sense.

Absolute conformity is not possible even with human, controlling intervention of extreme kinds such as in Stalin's Russia or the numerous church-dominated societies claiming direct intervention by God. *Diversity is natural and inevitable.*

Adaptation

> *'Life is like riding a bicycle.*
> *To keep your balance,*
> *you must keep moving.'*

> **Albert Einstein**

An essential characteristic of living organisms is their power to adapt appropriately to environmental change. This contributes to diversity (as mentioned in the previous section) and can happen without any genetic changes, but of course with gene *activity*. Einstein's quotation has it right. The environment varies, sometimes unpredictably, and survival requires adaptation to the new circumstances – 'You must keep moving': adapt or die.

Within limits set by its genetic material (pigs cannot fly), the organism changes itself so as to be better able to cope with the new situation. Thus, existing genes are 'switched' on or off according to the new circumstances. Changes that are difficult to cope with can result in the organism following a metabolic 'stress' pathway. In some cases, such as higher plants, seed formation is a way of surviving the winter until spring allows germination of the seeds. Yet another example is the bending of a plant towards the sunniest direction. The characteristics of an organism in its environment, or the adapted and changed characteristics for a new environment, are called its *phenotype*. Another example is human skin temporarily and slowly turning brown in the sun, i.e. a 'tanned' phenotype. Also, see the section below on the *'power phenotype'* – that is, the characteristics of (typically) male animals as they acquire power and adopt the behaviour pattern (power phenotype) of the alpha male, i.e. broadly demanding obedience to the alpha's choice of response to danger and taking the best of everything for themselves.

Much of my scientific career has been spent on the study of the microbial response to stress, much of it adaptation. A good example of adaptation comes from my own research as follows. Several cultures of a bacterium were separately grown in the same basic nutrient medium, but each with an <u>in</u>adequate concentration of a specific and different essential nutrient. Thus, growth occurred and then ceased due to a lack of an essential nutrient: carbon or nitrogen or phosphate or magnesium, or potassium, or sulphate or oxygen or iron. In essence, each culture grew and then stopped due to a specific starvation. The chemical composition of the cells from these separate cultures differed greatly, as did their cell structures. Also, their physiological properties varied such as susceptibility to antibiotics, biocides or to being phagocytosed, i.e. being 'eaten' by human white cells or by environmental amoebae. They had adapted to the lack of each essential nutrient in different ways:

> *each adaptation was highly appropriate in terms of survival under the specific conditions.*

When the starved bacteria were sub-cultured in rich medium, the 'original' properties reappeared, i.e. there had not been a significant mutation. When similar experiments were carried out with bacteria that form resistant spores, the spores formed under each condition also varied in composition, structure and physiological properties. Not only had the cells adapted to the stress of starvation by sporulating, but the spores were adaptations to the specific starvations. What happens is that genes are switched on or off according to the needs caused by impending starvation, such as the need to be more efficient in getting the scarce nutrient and also more economical in using it. Then, when starvation seems inevitable, the cell switches on specific stress genes, e.g. protects structures, and becomes dormant. Continuous growth under the above conditions would lead to genetic selection of mutants better fitted to survive in an environment deficient in the particular nutrient.

An extreme example is the development of a complex, higher animal. After the female egg is fertilised by the male sperm, the growing cells that differentiate into differing tissues and organs broadly have identical genes. But the genes that are switched on or off determine the nature of the tissue or organ. The other side of the coin of adaptation is when a single organism or even something as complex as a human society has adapted so well and for so long (numerous generations) to an environmental situation, then when the environment does change, especially when this is a rapid and large change, then adapting to the new situation can be slow. The response may be too slow to ensure survival. For highly complex human cultures, long accustomed to power and wealth, adapting painlessly to their loss typically proves impossible. Bonner and Wiggin trace the eventual catastrophic 'natural history' of human empires in their book 'Empire of Debt', and Niall Ferguson has written a topical book about empire. Its title is apt: 'The Colossus: the rise and fall of the American empire'. Surprisingly to me, he believes and provides detailed argument to show that the world broadly benefits from this empire. It is tempting to wonder whether my own country's (UK) extensive and costly weaponry (at the cost of basic living standards for the poor) is a futile attempt by the alpha élite to deny loss of empire and wealth.

Species
Earlier, reference was made to differences in DNA causing different species. Species evolve and change over time, often aeons of time. Nevertheless, they have been classified according to their consistent properties that define them. Thus, oak trees although never identical in an absolute sense (diversity is always present), have characteristic shape, leaves and root systems and clearly differ from other trees such as elms even when cultivated across a wide variety of environments and at different times. This indicates genetic determination of the characteristics of the oak

tree. Microbes have long been classified and identified by their morphological and biochemical properties. Today, solely the DNA profile of an organism is characteristic of a species and plays a major role in classification. As I write this section, the origins of a specific hospital bacterial contamination have been confirmed by DNA profiling, as has the path of a worldwide spread of *Clostridium difficile* infection. Indeed, increasing knowledge of the specific details of the DNA of a species also provides clear, direct evidence of evolutionary origins, pathways and timelines as indicated earlier. Such timelines are corroborated by other, independent measurements such as radiation decay.

It could be helpful for the sceptical non-biologist to consider the following. If an acorn is planted, it *never* produces an elm tree (or never a rose or a cat or dog). Why not? Answer: it has DNA specifying an oak tree. Also, biological evolution selected organisms such as trees and other plants with adaptive capacities predisposing them to survival, e.g. leaves turning towards the light or roots growing towards water. Selection means, in practice, the *removal* by competition of those less fitted to survive as in the example of plants that are less able to optimise acquisition of light energy. The broad story of evolution is about competition *within diversity* and subsequent survival, typically involving *astronomical time periods and numbers of organisms*.

Similarly, our primate ancestors had characteristics that distinguished them from other animals, regardless of environment. Primate mothers give birth to babies of their own species. Obviously, this is genetically determined: they had primate DNA. Likewise, primates have critical behaviour patterns that also seem remarkably constant for the species across a variety of environments and over time. These patterns would thus appear to be genetically determined, pre-disposing instincts such as male-dominated hierarchies, sexual behaviour, the defence of territory, the rearing of offspring, and potential and actual hostility to and fear of 'otherness'. These constant behaviour patterns of higher animals, overlapping with those of humans, may be described as programmed behaviours related to important survival needs. Broadly speaking, a species is defined as a group of related organisms whose common characteristics distinguish them from other groups. Genetic composition plays a major role in classification. Pragmatically and traditionally, capacity for interbreeding has conferred membership of a species.

Brain development
Introduction

The brain, our source of rationality, develops as part of a foetus and during life, and is influenced by its environment, with development mostly in the first few years. Even so, it can continue until after late adolescence. See S-J Blakemore in The Lancet (www.thelancet.com Vol 382 October 26, 2013. Blakemore's 2013 Royal Society Rosalind Franklin Award). I quote, '...the old idea that if something goes wrong in the first 5 years of your life, it's too late to do anything about it, is contradicted by new research, which suggests that developmental neuroplasticity can continue. The human brain undergoes very protracted development right throughout adolescence and into the 20s. Adolescence might even represent a second sensitive period of development. what the brain research suggests is that adolescence is not too late in terms of learning, training, and intervention.'

Thus, it's an empirical fact that our nature does not develop independently of our environment. In any event, genetic influences cannot be used to justify policies such as eugenics. In recent years, it has become clear that there are not different human races, there is only one. Genetic differences within broad human groups are greater than those between groups: Africa, Middle East, Asia, Europe. As mentioned earlier, it has also been shown widely that there is much genetic 'mixing'. In most groups, commonly a proportion of the fathers of children are not the biological father but is someone else. In some groups this can be of the order of 10-15%. Some years ago, before this was known generally, my wife and I were entertaining a Russian geneticist who was studying DNA profiles of people in an area of Europe of very mixed ethnicity. He told me of his surprise at the proportion (about 15%) of legal 'fathers' who were not the biological father and were unaware of this fact (he did not enlighten them).

Although it is now clear that there is a genetic component in all aspects of individual behaviour, this is a far cry from biological determinism of specific acts of individual behaviour. Furthermore, given the interaction between genes and also the large influence of environment on gene expression, including during the early development of humans from the foetus onwards and through adolescence, then talk of determinism is entirely theoretical. Predisposition, related to personality type, seems more rational and with little link to free will in any absolute sense. It is well established (see later) that an interruption of the natural development of the embryo has long-term and sometimes permanent effects. Early nutrition and learning environment also have lasting effects. The 'wiring' of the brain, mostly established in the early years, but also into and after the teens, is vital and depends partly on the social environment of the developing child. It is now established that chronic abuse leads to lasting damage to such brain development, including the absence of important connections between neural centres. In 2013, it was shown that abuse at home results in harm to the brain development of children and that abuse to the mother had a worse effect on the child's development than abuse directly of the child! This baffled me until my wife pointed out that the mother is the main source and symbol of security to the child. There is also the almost universal evidence from schools that disruptive, antisocial child behaviour is closely associated with disturbed homes and parenting. This is a form of 'determinism' that contradicts the later, almost inevitable, punitive, right-wing response to 'crime', which ignores the most likely cause i.e. disturbed homes and parenting.

Especially important is that animals learn advantageous behaviour from other animals. Provided that the group structure is unbroken, then this learning is passed on *as if* it were genetic. Humans, with their high intelligence, pass on learning and do so with the great advantage of language, itself a huge asset and associated with the brain development that underpins language. Even with the intrinsic genetic equipment, lack of a suitable early environment can be devastating, including the development of language. There are numerous examples worldwide of children from deprived homes being handicapped in many ways regarding social development and language skills. There are even a few extreme examples of young children surviving with animals, totally away from humans: they were devoid of language and other human social attributes. So, behaviour is affected by genes, influenced by internal and external environments during development and later by learning. With language, learning cannot be solely from one's specific group, but also from other sources. It thus seems difficult to justify the concept of 'free will' in any absolute sense with such powerful forces influencing behaviour.

Brain structure and behaviour

The correlations between brain structure and behaviour have long been studied via accidental brain damage and from autopsies. Today, non-invasive, sophisticated equipment is used to study correlations between brain responses and environmental changes of various kinds. Thus, a human subject can experience various emotions and the equipment can measure the specific parts of the brain's neural networks 'lighting up' under the various circumstances. *In this way it has been shown that fear closes down the thinking parts of the brain and pushes us down the well-trodden paths to instinctive behaviour, e.g. fight or flight.* It may be useful to remember that instincts played and still play a major role in human survival. If a wide-eyed, mad-looking man with a blood-stained axe runs towards you, it's not the time to suggest that he sits down to discuss his issues. We still have primate instincts and they can still help short-term survival even though they also can and do cause harm as discussed later. Without basic, prehuman instincts, we humans are unlikely to have evolved as such. We remain primates, but of a special kind and we also have an absolute need to express our <u>human</u>, innate impulses. Lack of expression leads to illness – personal and social.

A key idea in biology and for this book is that when an organism, individually or as a group, has a characteristic appearance and behaves in a consistent and characteristic pattern at different times and in different geographical climates and environments, then that characteristic range of appearances and behaviours is likely to have complex genetic components. In other words, the organism is programmed to exhibit the appearance and behaviour. Or, to put it in yet another way, behaviour that was less likely to lead to survival led either to extinction or to its replacement by other, successful patterns of behaviour. For higher animals and especially humans (with language), short-term, social learning can be passed on <u>as if</u> it were genetic.

As mentioned earlier, for centuries, animals and plants have been classified into species in this way. It is unlikely that a pattern of, say, animal appearance and behaviour that is characteristic could be the chance consequence of a specific 'local' environment when it occurs across geographical environments, cultures and historical times. It would seem likely that instincts in animals – an innate tendency to behaviour more or less likely to help survival – are continuous back through evolution to the point of being stress responses in microbes. Evolution has eliminated microbes with less helpful responses to stress and also eliminated animals that have behaviour patterns that are less helpful to survival. This process continues.

As with many other areas of biology, the speed of scientific progress regarding the brain, its genetics and its interactions within itself and with the outside world and subsequent behaviour is accelerating. It is now well established that interference to brain development by social abuse or by direct injury or chemical influence affects subsequent behaviour, even dramatically. Apart from such ill effects, the normal, relatively healthy brain influences many, perhaps *all*, aspects of behaviour and even disease and is itself influenced by its social environment. 'The Master and his Emissary' by Iain McGilchrist is a comprehensive, at times poetic, account of brain development and function and will be referred to later, notably in an account of empathy and social behaviour. Another notable and readable account of human brain development can be found in 'We are our brains' by Dick Swaab. The title is an apt description of the contents, although I wonder why the English title was not 'We are our minds'. 'Why love matters – how affection shapes a baby's brain' by Sue Gerhardt is also considered elsewhere, but essentially gives much recent empirical evidence that loving relationships are vital to early brain development, including during pregnancy and later to health in general. Two other superb books by the psychiatrist Norman Doidge give amazing evidence of the 'neuroplasticity' of the brain, also referred to in 'The Master and his Emissary' – one I had somehow missed, 'The brain changes itself' (2007) and recently (2015) 'The brain's way of healing'. Perhaps I should not have been amazed because, apart from the reproductive cells of male sperm and female eggs (with half the full number of chromosomes), all cells of the body contain the same, full complement of chromosomes and are *potentially* capable of performing the tasks of every cell.

Recent stem cell research has shown this in numerous tissues and organs. In other words, undifferentiated, embryonic stem cells can become differentiated into those needed for any kind of tissue or organ. Put another way for those unfamiliar, when the sperm fertilises the egg, the first new, undifferentiated cells with the full number of chromosomes, broadly speaking can become any other kind of human cell. In June 2016, it was reported that pigs are being used to grow much-needed human organs, initiated by undifferentiated, human stem cells.

Life-changing benefits of language. Language itself and also, perhaps separately, the complex ideas characteristic of humans conveyed by language, surely come from the extra brain developments resulting from mutations of the prehuman, primate brain. Humans characteristically use reason in solving problems – perhaps instinctively. Fear may interfere. The word consciousness is widely used and accepted to imply the relatively huge capacity for thought (even if mostly, *perhaps entirely* <u>sub-</u>conscious) unique to humans and, reluctantly, I will use it in that ill-defined sense. The brain is the place of reason, even when sub-conscious. Naturally, our old instincts (alpha males and associated group obedience, territory, competitiveness, hostility to 'strangers', possibly male subjugation of women) are unlikely to be isolated from influencing our 'new' human consciousness (mainly sub-) and our behaviour.

In addition to instincts in common with other primates, constant and characteristic behaviour of human groups includes the complex culture, religion, legal framework, art and artefacts that distinguish them from other primates and are a consequence of the conscious (see earlier comments on definitions of consciousness) human mind. Qualifying as a human instinct is altruism, advocated by the major religious prophets, but later almost ignored by the subsequent religious / corporate institutions in favour of obedience and so-called pious practices. I consider later the possible interactions between conscious thought and the earlier, programmed instincts predisposing to short-term, small group survival behaviour, selected over aeons of time. It seems clear that when a clash occurs, the primate instincts win and are expressed: religion is a good example. The altruism advocated by the original religious prophets loses in a clash with *institutional survival i.e.* the gaining of territory, fear of the foreign, the demands of alpha-male leaders and the suppression of women from public discourse.

Determinism

The possibility of determinism has been a subject for philosophical debate ever since philosophy began e.g. everything pre-determined by God or by 'nature'. Particularly with the continuing results of the Human Genome Project and with accelerating developments in neuroscience, there is more acceptance of genetic influence on behaviour. Given that nature obeys laws, some argue that, in an absolute sense, everything is predetermined from the 'Big Bang' onwards, including genes, their changing environment and changing interactions. On the other hand, libertarianism propounds human free will. What is clear is that, like religion, proponents and opponents of these positions cannot be classified simply by their differences in knowledge and intelligence. Numerous, eminent and reputable philosophers differ on this issue as on so many, maybe all, major philosophical issues. As this is the case, I propose mostly to leave the debate to the people possibly best qualified – the philosophers and neuroscientists. I merely comment:

a. that the laws of nature are partly to do with probability and chance rather than absolutes and
b. that 'nature' is not fixed. Variation is the food of natural selection.

In 'We are our brains' by Dick Swaab (mentioned earlier), he is unequivocal regarding free will. In this book, he states 'Our current knowledge of neurobiology makes it clear that there's no such thing as absolute freedom. Many genetic factors and environmental influences in early development, through their effects on our brain development, determine the structure and therefore the function of our brains for the rest of our lives'.

Social life predetermined?

The phrase 'biological determinism' also seems inappropriate to social life. Even if there is an argument of predetermination of social behaviour, based on nature following laws existing from the 'Big Bang', only a God could predict the precise, specific behaviour. And likely so, only if the God eliminated probability from the laws of nature, thus totally altering nature. For humans, such a complex matter as human behaviour is not susceptible to precise prediction.

On the other hand, if the behaviour is defined loosely, e.g. exhibiting broadly antisocial behaviour such as episodes of violence, then one could indeed broadly predict a high probability that children from disturbed and violent homes are more likely to continue to behave in a similar way than those not so disadvantaged. This is already well established and supports the idea of remedying poor, early development as opposed to automatic and solely punitive approaches. Thus, behaviour could be seen as broadly predetermined but unknowable *a priori.*

For practical purposes, the least bad approach may be to act as if humans have free will, are broadly predisposed to specific behaviour by personality and environmental upbringing and should accept responsibility for their actions. Nevertheless, in response to antisocial behaviour, attempts at rehabilitation are a necessary and logical component, given the clearly established major influences of the social environment, especially early on. Clearly, society should pay especially great attention to the early development of all babies and infants and treat this as a major priority. Surely, this approach must be an important part of how we reduce humanity's problems.

Also, aberrant behaviour by people with violent or otherwise grossly inappropriate childhood upbringing should not be considered simply as evil and punished as such. Can one label the consequences of aberrant development as evil? The close correlations between inequality and numerous social evils referred to earlier strongly indicate the limits of 'free' will. Why do evils, many of them termed 'sins' (e.g. theft, murder, rape) occur more in unequal societies and less in equal societies? Just as infections and tsunamis are no longer seen as the punitive work of a God (or a Devil), but rather as the result of microbes and massive earth movements, so animal and human behaviour is seen partly as the consequence of development, especially that of early and adolescent life.

Social cohesion – belonging

Early human and prehuman ape societies were relatively small and intimate. All individuals would have had a sense of 'belonging'. Studies of current 'stone age' communities of hunter-gatherers also indicate this. At the end of the day, the human hunter-gatherer group would likely discuss the day and future needs around the fire. To some extent, it is reminiscent of my own early childhood. I was born in 1931 and, as referred to earlier, the life of myself and my parents has seen possibly the biggest social changes since the introduction of large-scale agriculture and large human populations. My working-class family would all eat breakfast and dinner together around the dining table every morning and evening. As a child, radio had recently arrived. After dinner, my family and friends gathered at home around the fire or occasionally adults gathered at the pub (commonly with a fire) to socialise, Wednesday and Saturday evenings and Sunday lunch times. Entertainment was by talking or by individuals having a 'party piece' such as playing a musical instrument, singing, telling jokes and anecdotes. A variation occurred during good weather, when almost all children in my ('working class') area 'played out', either in the street or in the park and often well after it was dark. During the second world war, when my town (Wallasey, Merseyside) was bombed regularly, after the warning air-raid sirens sounded, we would sit in a local air-raid shelter and everyone would have a party piece – mine (aged from about 9) was to recite a poem. Now, the widespread custom in the West is for families to sit around a television watching celebrity strangers entertain them. Commonly, it is an individual pursuit or for a couple. Also, common in the West is for children to play solitary games on computers or electronic devices and to do so for several *hours a day*.

It would also seem likely that evolution, with primate instincts suited for small groups surviving within nature, did not prepare humans for huge, disconnected, modern societies controlling nature, with massive degrees of income inequality and the negative consequences in proportion to the inequality: murder, imprisonment, mental illness and even obesity!   The consequences of social inequality are dealt with at greater length later, but it's important to emphasise that the social ills are *in proportion* to the degree of inequality and similarly related to social disconnectedness! The ill effects are surprisingly (to me) not restricted to the financially poor: it's the *difference* in inequality and the gradient includes the relatively rich societies (see 'The spirit level', Wilkinson and Pickett and also later). Also, information about successful human teams comes from the empirical work of the management consultant Meredith Belbin (http://www.belbin.com). He found that the success or failure of teams related to the presence of individuals with <u>different</u> behaviour characteristics. Thus, a successful team needed several people of varying personality. Of likely evolutionary significance is that each of the various characteristics useful to a team is relatively common and of the order of 5% or more frequent. Given the likely small size of early human groups (great apes: around 20-50) then such groups were likely to contain all or most of the personality types needed to optimise 'success'.

Today's huge societies, of a complexity vastly greater than that of primitive groups, requires less of the primate, single alpha-male as leader and *more leadership teams of varying characteristics along the Belbin lines*. Nevertheless, a leadership group balanced in personalities does not help socially if the purpose is predation on the community. Today (as for many decades), numerous multi-national organisations owe virtually no allegiance to any country and are predators upon the world at large. They move manufacturing facilities to places with the lowest wages and minimum restrictions regarding health and safety, workers' pensions, paid leave/holidays and where taxes are minimal or zero. It is literally a world away from small communities living and hunting together and supporting one another.

Sociobiology debate

Some decades ago in the West, this debate about 'nature or nurture' / 'free will' became especially inflamed, sparked off by a book authored by Edward O. Wilson called 'Sociobiology: the new synthesis'. The debate was well described 25 years later by Ullica Segerstrale in 'Defenders of the Truth' and after interviewing many of the participants.

Biological explanations of behaviour were generally thought by Wilson's opponents to be intrinsically objectionable. In some cases, it seemed that this was so even if the biological explanation were true. Some participants felt a deep repugnance to genetic determinism with implications of denying 'free will' and the idea that innate behavioural tendencies could justify existing social inequalities. They could also be used to justify attempts at eliminating traits from humankind deemed to be undesirable: eugenics, sterilisation, genocide and developing a 'master race'.

But, *even if* some races could ever be intrinsically inferior, how can that justify such things? The answer is never unless one worships biological 'superiority' i.e. the worship of power. And that would be the strangest God of all! In fact, genetics gives no evidence whatsoever for superior 'races' of humans. We all descend from humans that came out of Africa about 60,000 years ago and survived the best we could. A related interest, existing today, was about the influence of genes on moral behaviour. Some think that altruistic or evil behaviour may both be the inevitable consequence of our genes and not a matter of choice: *in which case*, 'true' good and evil may not exist. There have been huge, costly and misguided efforts at social manipulation, notably the appalling, inhuman Nazi Holocaust of Jews. Given the solid empirical evidence about the role of environment on human development, reason would demand that much attention is given to healthy human development, especially at early stages. Unreasonably, politicians, especially of the right, prefer to ignore evidence about the consequences of harmful human development and socialisation and advocate punitive retribution for the consequential antisocial behaviour.

Postscript

A postscript regarding E. O. Wilson relates to 'Group Selection'. In a paper in Nature by Wilson and colleagues, 'The evolution of eusociality' (Nowak et al., 2010. Nature, 466,1057-1062) described 'Eusociality' (Greek eu: 'good/real' and 'social') as the highest level of organisation of animal sociality. It was defined by the following characteristics: cooperative brood care (including brood care of offspring from other individuals), overlapping generations within a colony of adults, and a division of labour into reproductive and non-reproductive groups. This paper contributes to a continuing and heated debate about the possible role of 'group selection' in which a 'fit' society may also be selected for survival. Any reader interested in this important idea is also directed to an article in 'The Science Creative Quarterly' (Momoprice, 2006. The controversy of group selection theory. 3rd February 2006).

What follows next is an account of basic human needs, our key problems and their causes, then ideas on ways of reducing our problems and improving human life generally.

Instincts – introduction and definitions

(Oxford dictionary: non-conscious, innate survival tendencies. The role of instincts in driving social behaviour is so important that instincts deserve special attention and clarification, especially over *definitions*. Also, helpful to refer to is 'The Chimp Paradox' by Steve Peters.)

'We've never learned anything from the past'
Nicholas Winton (a centenarian who helped over 600 Jewish children escape the Nazis)

*'Life
is what happens to you
while you're busy making
other plans'*

John Lennon

Nicholas Winton has pointed out that the same bad things continue to happen, despite repeated intentions to the contrary. And John Lennon's aphorism could be rewritten, less poetically, as basic primate instincts often continue to be expressed even when conscious thought is planning other activities. So, an important question is why do so many unwanted events *continuously* happen such as war, racism, slavery and general abuse of human rights? Why are the brilliant, detailed, crystal-clear analyses of such social evils by the truly human and insightful thinkers Noam Chomsky, Robert Fisk, George Monbiot and John Pilger ignored, time after time after time?

One answer is the existence of basic instincts that constantly, repeatedly and mindlessly impel us towards behaviour that evolved to assist the short-term survival of individuals and small groups of animals that preceded humans and in a different environment. Immediately prior to the first humans, apes lived in trees in small groups of around 20-50. Given an appropriate anatomy and metabolism suitable for an environmental niche, one might describe

'The Golden Rule of Survival' as having *effective, innate, rapid and concerted responses to change, notably dangerous ones*. Danger is associated with fear, and fear is a major trigger for the expression of basic instincts. The definition of an instinct is necessarily broad. Also, related ideas about the meanings of liberal or left or right-wing or conservative innate human behaviours also require broad definitions and are dealt with later in this section. The use of these words in normal discourse and by newspapers and other media also contributes towards definitions: how widespread and consistently is the word instinct used to describe an innate impulse?

Microbes have innate propensities to behaviour: general metabolic responses to change broadly, such as to fluctuations in the concentration of a nutrient and also to changes at the extremes of capacity to cope i.e. stress. All are innate propensities in responding to *change*. Those changes that endanger the cell imminently, evoke responses called stress responses as mentioned earlier (see 'Simple' life forms, above). They mainly relate to short-term survival. However, the intrinsic, broad metabolic spectrum relates to more long-term survival. For example, is *any* organism's basic metabolism appropriate for the current habitat? If not, then survival is under threat. Of course, without short-term survival, there is no long-term survival. The biochemical and genetic mechanisms behind microbial stress responses, analogous to instincts, are being elucidated in some detail. (For anyone interested, there is a summary in 'The long and short of it – polyphosphate, PPK and bacterial survival'. Trends in Biochemical Sciences, volume 33, pages 284-290 (2008). M. R. W. Brown and A. Kornberg). The precise programmed mechanisms leading to the consistent stress responses of humans are largely unknown, whether they be biochemical, developmental, neurological or other genetically programmed impulses. Fear is known to be important. Socially learned consistent behaviour is dealt with below. Nevertheless, that there *is* consistent response to stress, individual and group, across cultures, climates and time is beyond doubt. This consistency offers a pragmatic 'definition' (see later, below) of an instinctive response to stress.

Habits

(Also see above – 'Brain development')

For humans, we also have numerous innate tendencies, not all called instincts in everyday language. An example is having a habit. The brain treats a habit as a single unit of behaviour (see 'Good habits, bad habits', Graybiel and Smith, Scientific American June 2014; 'Habits, rituals and the evaluative brain', A. M. Graybiel (2008), 'Annual Review of Neuroscience, volume. 31, pages 359 - 387). Much current research is on identifying the brain regions and connections responsible for creating and maintaining a habit. As a habit started to develop in experimental rats (on instruction, they travelled down a maze towards a reward), the neurons in the brain's striatum were highly active; as the habit became formed, brain activity declined. Once established, brain activity was high only at the start and finish, indicating one unit of behaviour. Different brain circuits take the lead as deliberate actions become habitual. Multiple circuits connect one brain region, the striatum, with another, the neocortex and these circuits are more or less engaged as we act deliberately or habitually. This important work *could lead to interventions that control habits and, hopefully, instincts, especially inappropriate ones.*

Habits and instincts have partly similar consequences – non-thinking behaviour. Humans have reflexes, conditioned reflexes and habits with similar characteristics – non-thinking behaviour such as kicking a football or hitting a tennis ball with a racket. 'The Chimp Paradox' by the psychiatrist Steve Peters mentioned earlier, describes a simplified account of how the mind works and how to manage what he describes as the 'chimp' in all of us. The 'chimp' is an emotional machine that 'thinks' independently from the human and data-storage parts of the brain. Using the principles of his book, Peters has had remarkable, objective success with individual elite sports people and also executives of corporations in giving insight into their behaviour and how to control it. It will be referred to later in the sections on reducing humanity's problems.

For the purposes of this book with a focus on survival, the

instincts of main interest are those leading to behaviour most directly linked to perceived imminent danger, regardless of their biological basis. Whilst every aspect of metabolism and organism structure probably helps survival in a specific niche, those impulses that help short-term survival are the ones commonly called instincts. Notably, these include defence of territory, fear of the foreign / 'the other', 'fight or flight', instincts connected with alpha-male power and related obedience and conformity to social norms. *Such instincts are typically triggered by <u>fear</u>.* Sexual instincts, especially but not exclusively in young men, would seem to require little in the way of fear triggers. The suppression of women from public discourse is discussed later as a possible male instinct. It would seem obvious that the survival instinct is also linked to the human impulse for power (and money), expressed so strongly in alpha males.

Anthropologists commonly use creative art as indicative of prehistoric human settlements as opposed to animal sites. Creativity has been suggested as a vital and characteristic feature of humans. As it is an innate propensity, it qualifies as an instinct. Immediate human predecessors, the genus *Homo*, appeared 2.5 million years ago, and only 200,000 years ago did anatomically modern humans appear. Modern humans left Africa around 60,000 years ago. The oldest *surviving*, dated art is from around 40,000 years ago. The Altamira cave paintings are about 19,000 years old and sites with abstract symbols are possibly from 70,000 years earlier (shell beads and engraved ochre). The 'National Geographic' has an issue partly devoted to the first artists (January 2015).

It seems clear that our instincts dealing with imminent danger are closely similar to those of earlier animals. However, we humans have other consistent behaviour patterns – innate tendencies – that are analogous to broad metabolic facilities in animals and ourselves. They are needed for long-term human health and survival. Whilst some animals are known to express altruism, we humans have a well-developed capacity for altruism and the complex culture arising from consciousness listed in the table given later under 'Instincts'.

We have a need to be creative. It also seems that whilst expressing primate instincts, our human intellects can be used to justify this otherwise mindless behaviour.

Instinct and intuition – a clarification

The word instinct is sometimes used in the West to mean intuition. Indeed, the Oxford English dictionary offers intuition as an alternative meaning for the word instinct. Obviously, in normal language, the context will indicate the actual meaning intended. Nevertheless, for the purposes of this book, it's important to distinguish instinct from intuition. The artist Joseph Beuys taught that intuition is the highest form of subconscious thinking where numerous experiences are put together to produce an original idea. I have referred earlier to the evidence that most 'thinking' is subconscious and involves new parts of the brain associated with the transition to being human. It would seem that intuition in this sense is synonymous with subconscious thinking.

Individual and group identity

Instincts evolved when the gap between individual identity and the group identity was small or non-existent. The identity of the individual was inextricably bound up with that of the group. The separation of individual and group identities is a modern development and where apparently real, can be associated with pathology: we *need* to belong. Thus, it's difficult to separate instincts characteristic of the primate group from those of the individual. I have referred earlier to William Condon (in 'Beyond Culture'. pages 72-77, Ed. E. T. Hall) who thought that it made no sense to view humans as 'isolated entities', but rather as bonded together in 'shared organizational forms'. This was supported by others such as Howard Bloom ('You are still being lied to'. pages 10-18. Ed. Russ Kick): the idea of humans being intrinsically *not* isolated beings). A table of instincts follows under 'Instinct Classification', page 67).

Consistent, widespread human behaviour

Much of what follows is obvious and is based on historical fact. Yet people act as if the reality were different. Human group behaviour, although in numerous and obvious ways is vastly rich and varied, is also remarkably constant when the group is under threat. Threat evokes fear and *fear evokes basic instincts*, notably regarding territory, the foreign, alpha-male leadership and obedience. This constancy occurs across cultures and historical periods and therefore again would appear to be genetically predisposed, together with learned behaviour. It could be imagined, for example, that a human group with much territory could be generous towards human neighbours with little. In fact, an almost universal response to a serious territorial threat is for young men to go out and kill other young men and sometimes, to a lesser degree, young women. Indeed, refusal by the young men (across cultures it is almost always men) to fight is typically met with a brutal response from their own group. Similarly, groups with great power (alphas) commonly take whatever they want. For millennia, towns have had fortified walls and standing armies exist everywhere.

Also, during relatively stress-free periods, the group may:

a. learn obedience to elites, usually male;
b. bond with their group in numerous ways; and
c. acquire hostility to potential aggressors and thus be predisposed to a rapid response when for example, their territory is (perceived to be) threatened.

There is a recent example of consistent, widespread and thoughtless behaviour regarding the UK's 'Brexit'. Is it instinctive? In 2018 there was a UK civil service economic analysis of several scenarios regarding UK Brexit. The gloomy analysis was derided/ sneered at by right wing spokesmen. The analysis was not examined for flaws of approach or omissions or illegitimate conclusions. Simply, it was condemned, without evidence, as biased. Unlike the politicians who made the derisory remarks and sneers, the professional reputations of the civil servants were vulnerable to any analysis that revealed poor approaches, false assumptions and illegitimate conclusions. Their economic forecasts were open to rational criticism. A leading right-wing 'Brexiteer', Jacob Rees-Mogg simply made instant, unsubstantiated *assertions* about bias by the civil servants. The viewer/listener was asked to accept Mr Rees-Mogg's evidence-free *assertions* rather than the reasoned conclusions of a study by a group of government civil servants, expert professionals in economics. It's hard not to conclude that the absence of reasoned adverse criticism of the report was that it was not possible. If the report *was* flawed, surely the flaws would have been exposed? Should we disregard the professional's evidence-based advice because an alpha-male, Jacob Rees-Mogg says so, even if he was educated at Eton and Trinity College, Oxford?

Q. Is the tendency, when in a dispute or when fearful, to avoid evidence and simply sneer and ridicule, a sign of an instinctive (primate) approach?

A. Yes.

Survival is helped by social control

Much of human culture involves conditioning for obedience to social elites and conformity to social norms – forming the social adhesive. Reinforcing obedience to leaders/rulers increases the chances of survival via the essential, basic response to threat by all organisms: effective, rapid and concerted. Without social obedience, leadership cannot function. Thus, basic fear and hostility to 'the different', especially the foreign, is associated with assisting a rapid, concerted response to danger. <u>Conformity</u> helps this response: no foreigners, no gays or other sexual 'deviants' and no women in power. Alpha males have a key role in concerted responses to danger and contributed to the survival of our predecessors living in trees in small groups. Now, human society is very different. Nevertheless, concerted responses to danger are often still necessary, bearing in mind that the dangers are more complex than when occurring in an arboreal population of about 30- 40.

The instincts behind this typical behaviour have served our ancestors well in the sense that they survived evolution and we humans were able to evolve with our consciousness. The addition of human consciousness to the primate mind does not appear to involve loss of the basic instincts, although the possibility of choice of behaviour appeared in a unique way. Thus, consciousness potentially reduces the predetermined tendency of behaviour and allows the *possibility* of a more flexible pre*disposition* to modes of behaviour. But the instincts are still there, constantly predisposing and unobtrusively influencing actions that we think are conscious. Clearly for humans, many personal and group problems are the result of the tension between instincts and choices available through consciousness.

'Primate' instincts evolved in the absence of consciousness
It's clear that much individual human behaviour is caused less by conscious decisions than by these instincts inherited from evolution, typically related directly to the survival of primates. The influence of these instincts is commonly ignored when analysing the causes of conflict. Commonly, the evil character of the opponents is given as the root cause and is often preceded by our alpha males propagating a sense of fear. A modern example is the correlation between nations described as evil and in need of 'democracy and freedom' and their possession of oil, much needed by the powerful aggressor. The precise biological mechanisms of group instincts, as such, are mysterious, but consistent group behaviour, predisposed by individual instincts clearly does exist. As indicated above, there is conformity of human group behaviour, especially when the group perceives a threat. This constancy, especially in response to imminent, life-threatening danger, must surely come from inherited instincts together with learned behaviour. Religious institutions are no different and quickly become 'primate-ised' (see under 'Religion').

When human consciousness evolved, with its huge qualitative and quantitative change in capacity to store and manipulate data, the existing instincts did not thereby disappear. It's important to emphasise that instincts evolved in the absence of the human consciousness which came later. Just as our digestive system works independently of our conscious mind, so our behaviour regarding key survival attributes is predisposed to specific patterns – instinctive patterns. It needs to be pointed out that prehuman animals have intelligence in that observations about changes in their environment can be analysed and influence behaviour. A bonobo may 'weigh up' what to do. This is thinking. Humans can obviously 'weigh up' what to do in a more complex way, assisted by their extra brain equipment, even when the thinking is subconscious. It's likely that this subconscious thinking is the highest, most creative form of thinking. For an authorative and detailed account of how primate behaviour can inform us about human social evolution, see the multi-authored book edited by Frans de Waal, 'Tree of Origin' and also 'Our Inner Ape' by the same author.

As mentioned earlier, even organisms low down in the evolutionary tree such as microbes have pre-existing stress responses: they sense danger and have *appropriate, speedy and concerted responses.* As the metabolism of single-cell microbes evolved, e.g. the making and degradation of proteins, carbohydrates, lipids and cell structures, so did metabolic pathways respond to potentially lethal stresses. That is, stresses of various kinds can be responded to appropriately with specific, pre-existing metabolic pathways – stress responses. Furthermore, microbes typically live in complex communities adhering to surfaces: such communities offer numerous mutual advantages for survival with much inter-cell communication. Microbes that responded inappropriately to their environment are no longer with us: they are extinct. Like microbes, animals not having an innate propensity to optimum behaviour (conducive to survival) patterns, have also become extinct.

Instinctive behaviour, innate impulses to behaviour not needing the conscious brain, arose in the far distant, evolutionary past, likely continuous with and going back to microbial stress

responses.   In this book, they will be referred to as 'primate'–
our immediate ancestors. It could be useful to bear in mind that
microbial stress responses of some kind have existed for about 3.6
billion years, animals have had instinctive responses for about 600
million years, in mammals for about 200 million years, in primates
for 60 *million* years, in the great apes for about 20 million years, in
our human predecessors (genus *Homo*) for about 2.5 million years
and anatomically modern humans for about *200,000* years. If this
longevity for responses to change and stress seems unlikely to any
reader, then one should remember something mentioned in the
earlier section on 'Proof of evolution'. All organisms have much in
common, namely that all the atoms composing our bodies come
from the same set of elements as those in the rest of the universe,
arising from the 'Big Bang' about 13.7 billion years ago. Individual
human cells share much cell machinery and structure with all other
organisms in the whole of nature. For example, there's a uniformity
in response of individual cells whether single-cell microbes or
cells that form part of the animal anatomy when dealing with
desiccation or UV damage to DNA. Gross animal(s) response to
danger regarding territory or fear of the foreign is another matter
of extreme complexity. That such instinctive behaviour exists is
without doubt, even though the mechanisms behind the responses
are still obscure. Often, an instinctive, fearful response to danger
is intellectually justified in humans.

One may wonder if specifically human instincts exist *based on
our genes*. But behaviour learned and passed on from one generation
to another would have the advantage of language. It's probable that
there is an interaction between 'hard-wired', genetically predisposing,
primate tendencies to survival behaviour and social learning.
Following the dictionary definition of instincts as an innate tendency,
i.e. consistent, characteristic behaviour across time, place and
cultures, then humans do have 'instincts' not shared with primates
as shown in the Table of Instincts below (section on Instincts, page
67). Whether these are 'true' or not, programmed instincts are less

important for this book except that they do represent consistent behaviour characteristic of humans. However, these consistent, human behaviour patterns serve the *long*-term 'health' and survival of humanity: altruism and human culture in which *creativity* is expressed in such as literature, poetry, art, music, dance, sculpture, cooking and home-making. Given that these basic instincts have existed for so long, it's not surprising that they trump the recent, human ones when they clash e.g. a fearsome stranger evokes 'fight or flight'.

Social learning – language

In addition to instincts (as innate predispositions analogous to 'reflexes' as part of the make-up of animals and arising from natural selection over millions of years), there is learning by personal experience and also from one's social group. Clearly, human consciousness and high intelligence further assists learning from experience. Language and rationality are obviously major assets in acquiring life skills and learning from the experience of others. Thus, survival behaviour results from genetic predisposition *together with* learning from the social environment. The predisposition is analogous to a conditioned reflex that is performed without thought. In general, it is not proposed to distinguish between the two when using the word instinct to describe consistent behaviour across cultures, climates and time.

Culture will be referred to later, but briefly as <u>overall</u> lifestyle, including altruism, art, music, dance and poetry. Individual instinctive behaviour aiding survival includes that which occurs in the absence of imminent external threats, such as seeking food, shelter, sex and procreation and the rearing of offspring. Similarly, in peaceful times, social behaviour includes much conditioning so that in times of stress the correct, coordinated behaviour occurs conducive to survival, e.g. the expression of instincts that assist social bonding and community adhesion. Social *conformity* increases the chance that in times of danger leaders will be obeyed and the likelihood of survival will be increased. As mentioned previously, group survival is obviously enhanced when the group can mount a coordinated and rapid response to danger.

It is becoming ever more evident that individual social learning is strongly influenced, even determined, by brain development in its social environment, especially during the early stages. Correlations between brain activity, function and behaviour are being elucidated and clarified almost daily. At the risk of oversimplifying, whilst both hemispheres of the brain can deal with any kind of information, they do so in different ways. And while there is flexibility of function, different components have broadly different specialities: feelings and emotion, including empathy (or not); language and/or its emotional content (see Iain McGilchrist's 'The Master and his Emissary' and also 'We are Our Brains' by Dick Swaab).

An important question relates to the extent to which the human mind influences, if at all, the expression of primate instincts. As a basic instinct is being expressed, does the thinking part of the human mind *ever* have any role? I've attempted to find an answer, but failed. The nearest I've got to an answer is that the thinking part of the brain shuts down when frightened. For example, instinctively fight or flight when faced with a potential aggressor or when sexually aroused (just do it – leads to more babies). It's a common tactic of alpha males, consciously or not, to evoke fear in order to enhance obedience: for example, the 'war' on terror, the 'war' on drugs. Our alpha males retain the sole right to determine which person or group is a terrorist, which country to fight in a war and which chemical is a drug. In the latter case, the drugs causing the most deaths and illness in the West (directly or indirectly) are *legal*: cigarettes causing numerous expensive diseases and alcohol with its related diseases and associated and hugely expensive road deaths and injuries. Apart from drugs *per se*, the punitive, so-called 'war on drugs' mentioned earlier is enormously expensive and of the order of $100 billion per annum. Similarly, leaders commonly manipulate basic instincts to elicit widespread fear regarding *foreigners* trying to *control* us (instead of our own alpha males) or wanting our *territory*. What appears evident is that the human aspects of the mind are used to justify instinctive behaviour regarding territory or the foreign. Thus, the basic instincts trump the human. Instincts regarding sex or art would seem to require few or no triggers, certainly not fear. Expressions of sex or art activities are on a 'hair trigger', likely to appear unpredictably and at any time.

Effective, speedy and coordinated responses to danger again
As mentioned previously, during the evolution of our predecessors, instincts for key behaviour patterns assisted survival. Crucially important instincts are those predisposing to appropriate, speedy and concerted responses to perceived danger. They are about leadership, hierarchies and group obedience. Typically, this is grossly underestimated or ignored in considering human behaviour. It would seem that when threatened (or perceived to be), human group behaviour is largely instinctive, and that consciousness plays a much smaller role than generally accepted. Individual behaviour under threat is similarly predisposed to make an instinctive response, but with many more examples of conscious responses. Typically, almost universally, the path advocated (but rarely taken) to resolve group conflict ignores these instincts and exaggerates the role of reason. When a powerful group wishes to acquire territory or material from a less powerful group, commonly they take it and use their human minds to justify the primate behaviour. In my lifetime, a major example of this came about when a US Republican politician, Barry Goldwater, saw the Soviet Union as part of the second coming of Christ and said that the 'evil Soviets' justified the use of nuclear weapons and the bringing on of the end of the world – the apocalypse. If Mr Goldwater had read the New Testament's Matthew's gospel he would have noted that it would be God who decided the time and place and that the sole entry criterion for Heaven was responding positively to need and did not include starting a nuclear holocaust with catastrophic consequences for much of humankind.

Instincts occur without the need for conscious thought. Specific primate groups also have characteristic behaviour patterns shaped by inherited instincts and reinforced by learned behaviour, e.g. hunting as a pack. These instincts have special significance in short-term, immediate, life-threatening situations where they predispose to life-saving behaviours. Thus, during the evolution of our primate ancestors, group behaviour favouring survival was selected: that is, *effective, rapid and coordinated responses.* This may well explain why the thinking parts of our brain are shut down when in fearful situations, thus leaving instincts in control – help from ancestral 'experience'. Similarly, inappropriate behaviour leads not only to individual elimination but also, eventually, to group extinction. Whilst there will have been and are a vast variety of behaviour patterns, the literally vital aspect is related to the threat of death/extinction. At that point, the role of an instinct is to push behaviour along an evolutionary 'tried and trusted' path to survival. Individuals and groups with inappropriate (for prehuman dangers) responses are no longer with us. Commonly, in each generation there is a competitive loss of the weaker members and an increase of the stronger. So, for the particular environmental conditions, the stock is strengthened *in primate terms*.

Alphas and hierarchies
It's not difficult to understand why evolution has come up with human and prehuman hierarchies. A group of animals, including humans, acting in concert is likely to cope with a threat better than a group where each member acts in a disparate, individualistic way, e.g. getting food and/or surviving an attack. Thus, selection will favour groups with effective and concerted responses to serious threats (see earlier, E. O. Wilson, 'Group Selection'). As stated previously, it would also seem likely that a speedy, effective and concerted response to threat would be selected. These instincts do not absolutely determine the precise details of how the group behaves, but strongly predispose to broad patterns of survival

behaviour. For example, kill the potential aggressor or take flight. Groups may hunt for food in packs and attack the weakest member of the quarry group, and also defend themselves as a group. Also, in between threats, there is selection for behaviour that increases the probability of appropriate group behaviour when the next threat occurs. Generally speaking, human society ignores the role of instincts, impulsive non-rational behaviour, and pretends that behaviour is the result solely of reason.

One obvious method that has been selected during evolution for achieving such a response by a threatened group is via a leader and obedience by the rest: for this obedience, control is important. Hierarchies help rapid and concerted group responses. Across human cultures and history, obviously the 'choice' of leader or a leading group is typically confined to males, but with rare exceptions. Historically, having such a visible leader has been regarded as vital. At the moment of death of a monarch, the next in line *simultaneously* becomes the monarch. Hierarchies are *alpha groups*. A recent UK government led by David Cameron is an interesting example of group leadership selection. It starts very early. The UK educational system has *widely recognised* 'top', most expensive, private schools (Eton, Harrow, Winchester), other less recognised private schools, then state schools stratified into 'grammar' (pupils are selected) and then the 'rest'. There is also the use of top 'finishing' schools (e.g. in Switzerland) for girls who then provide suitable top spouses for top alpha males. Cameron and four of his most trusted aides went to Eton, while more than half of his cabinet were privately educated. Out of his last cabinet of 28 members, 10 went to Oxford and 4 to Cambridge. An earlier Cameron cabinet had a similar composition with much of his inner cabinet of the most senior appointments being old Etonians.

Such a narrow focus of backgrounds has been widely criticised. That is, it's elitism for no reason. But surely, Cameron's underlying impulse must be *instinct* to do with safety and national and personal survival. 'Formally', Eton and Oxbridge (mostly from his own University, Oxford in his cabinet) are the 'best' backgrounds to have, but there is also a *shared* background with shared assumptions, including that they are indeed the best. By sharing their backgrounds, they 'know' one another. It isn't simply 'top people, alphas together', it's the safety and comfort of belonging to a shared alpha cultural background. And they are 'formally' the best. It's a form of *a priory* identification of alphas before they express actual personal talents. The system's function is to provide alphas, so *designating* institutions as 'the best' mechanically and inevitably leads to perceptions of 'the best'. This may *not always be true*, of course. Decades ago, President Kennedy was concerned about science in the USA because of Russia's apparent lead in science/the space race. His enquiries revealed that the most *creative* workers did <u>not</u> come disproportionately from the so-called 'top' universities such as Harvard, Yale, Stanford and Princeton.

In the section on Education, I comment on the potential negative consequences for creativity of spending much of the child's early years learning what others have decided for them. In the same vein, going to boarding school, away from family and home may well affect development and result in a child becoming more detached and with reduced empathy. For readers wanting more evidence in this area, the journal 'the Psychologist' has discussions and references on this ('Effects of boarding school' https://thepsychologist.bps.org.uk/volume-29/june-2016).

Educational priorities

It's clear that in many human cultures, early education is not led by the well-established developmental needs of children, but is led by the biological need to identify our alphas. Perhaps identify is the wrong word. Maybe it's to label *a priori* the alphas (e.g. in the UK, Eton is followed by Oxford, Harrow is followed by Cambridge). In the early primate, arboreal world, *any leader is better than none* in the absolute need to survive. In the modern, human world, surely early education must be led by established *developmental* needs. It could be beneficial to recall that bonobo mothers carry their child on their body for the first two years.

> *This widespread behaviour of selecting alphas could be associated with the widespread, almost universal, neglect of the poor and impoverished: they will very rarely ever be alphas.*

Currently (August, 2017), we have a USA President assuming that he has virtually unlimited (alpha) powers and proposing to reverse policy regarding US military in Afghanistan and demanding that other nations join in and provide extra military. He feels as a global alpha (leader of the USA) the world must follow his alpha lead. It's hard not to recall the film by Michael Moore, 'Where to invade next?' Surely, when it comes to national leadership, the world, perhaps through the UN, should consider advocating a multiple leadership group of perhaps five and abandon the one alpha mode. Likely, such a group would seriously consider having health services for everyone, including the poor.

> *Having one alpha male leader is indeed natural: natural for around 30-40 apes living in trees.*

Instincts: classifications and tables
Introduction

> 'The condition of man ..... is a condition of war of everyone against everyone.'
>
> **Thomas Hobbes**

As indicated earlier, some human societies can exhibit extreme selfless, altruistic behaviour, especially from individuals. But *under threat*, when brain function is disturbed, obedience to leaders has increased emphasis and behaviour to non-members of the society is characteristically very different. If one accepts the definition of instinct as non-conscious, innate survival tendencies, then it seems clear that there are indeed group behaviours characteristic of human society that are consistent across time and geography and culture. They bear repetition: male-dominated hierarchies with personal conditions and rewards related to position in the hierarchy (the 'power phenotype'), group obedience to elites and social conformity (glue), hostility to and fear of 'otherness' (us and them), defence of territory (fight or flight, building fortified habitations), inflicting collective punishment on other groups, competitiveness (especially, but not exclusively, male), and structural inequalities such as gender role divisions. In addition to basic behaviour more or less shared with primates, religion can and does serve as a cause of cohesion as well as of conflict.

Moral codes are typically abandoned or weakened in times of conflict and empathy is rarely expressed. The needs of survival swamp everything. After all, instincts evolved to increase the chances of survival. It's well described in the aphorism: '*There are no rules in love and war*' (derived from John Lyly's novel 'Euphues: The Anatomy of Wit', published in 1579. '...the rules of fair play do not apply in love and war'). This behaviour of human groups under threat is consistent across cultures, climates and historical periods and is reinforced between times of threat and danger by social conditioning. In the extreme case of territorial threats and war, young men characteristically fight opponent men with extreme violence. In specialist niches, different behaviours may occur, but the broad thrust of human group behaviour, particularly under threat, is relatively constant. Despite numerous discussions and books and articles I have read, I have no explanation of why humans torture and humiliate other humans, especially captive ones, sometimes for no apparent reason. It seems to be a pathology of humans.

The poor – an almost universal characteristic of human societies
Why has every culture over many millennia had a majority at the 'bottom', often large, of the poor? The proportion of poor has varied. Western society now has a 'middle' class. But relative to the alphas (see below), the poor are characteristically numerous. It's a characteristic typical of human communities. In the past and especially in so-called religious societies, the influence of the Devil or of their God is invoked as an explanation. Also, the genetic superiority of the alphas is given as an explanation, e.g. the 'blue blood' of the Royal alphas or 'breeding', or the poor are the ones inherently lazy and/or stupid. The ancient Greek playwright Aristophanes reflected on the universality of the poor in his play 'Plutos' (wealth): the poor always come off badly versus the rich.

Biology and evolution are importantly about survival. Another explanation of poverty, from those most influenced by primate instincts, could be that the poor are unlikely to provide alphas, so money spent on the poor is 'wasted'. This majority has been under regimes of the left as well as of the right. The poor, i.e. the 'lower' classes, have been needed for work (less so in the future) and for armed conflict, so society provides the minimum for maintenance. Social inequality (see later) is directly related to numerous social ailments. In more equal societies (e.g. Scandinavian societies) there are many less social problems: several-fold compared to the least equal (USA). It seems likely that in the modern world, some of the instincts associated with an arboreal life of a small group (30-40) of monkeys are inappropriate for humans, even harmful.

Classification of instincts
Primate instincts
As mentioned earlier, instincts have origins that appeared long before primates, but it's convenient to call them primate. These broadly include hierarchies and obedience to elites, typically male (alpha male) and the instinctive taking of 'the best' by alpha males thereby optimising their own survival (*and* that of the led). Others are defence of territory, potential and actual aggression to and fear

of 'otherness', competitiveness (especially male) and sex. We have structural inequalities such as gender role divisions. They are listed in more detail below. *Humans share these instincts*, typically for short-term survival.

Human instincts

In addition to possessing the above primate instincts, there are innate behaviour patterns that are specifically human, connected with brain developments associated with the capacity for conscious thought and also giving us intuition. All assist survival by answering human needs and by binding society together. *Whether these behaviour patterns are 'true' instincts in the sense of being genetically programmed seems unclear.* But the interaction on the one hand of the enhanced brain power and also specific brain developments, e.g. the capacity for empathy and altruism associated with consciousness, have given rise to the reproducible, innate cultural behaviour of humans. And, as discussed earlier, brain developments enabled language and the complex ideas / rationality communicated by it. Language facilitates learning and thus affects social behaviour *as if* it were genetic.

There is one area where the expression of primate instincts seems clearly influenced by human consciousness. It seems likely that primate drives are often facilitated and justified by rational, human advocacy. For example, when the USA was contemplating a nuclear attack on Russia (referred to earlier), the basic instinct was supported by an explicit 'argument' that Russia was evil and resembled the 'Apocalyptic Beast' of the Day of Judgement. It's hard not to assume that Christ's judgement was to have been accelerated by US foreign policy. Frequently, individual and national acts of violent aggression are 'justified' by rational discourse. The Paris attacks by so-called IS would seem to be an expression mainly of primate instincts to kill the opponents, but modified indiscriminately to include anyone in the West, even co-religionists. It's hard to untangle the primate from the human leading to this pathological behaviour claimed to be religious.

Human societies characteristically give rise to complex human culture: religion; language, the need for creativity, poetry and literature; art, sculpture, architecture, music and gastronomy. Altruism is a special instinct in that it involves putting the interests of others before one's own. The basic primate instincts can pervade in terms of competition and hierarchies, e.g. as part of the religious and art structures, especially <u>official</u> ones. *In times of danger, the primate instincts typically override the human ones.* If one considers nations and cultures worldwide and attempts to list characteristics that remain common and hence similar to instincts, they include the familiar characteristics listed in the table of primate instincts given at the end of this section. Nations have instincts for artistic aspects of human culture. From time to time, nations can exhibit altruism, e.g. the taking in of migrants and refugees in need. Currently as I first write this section (November 2014), the UK and other EU countries are planning to *abandon* schemes to save the lives of migrants who attempt the crossing from Africa to Europe in unsafe boats that capsize. The reason given is that rescue boats only 'encourage' the migrants to attempt the crossing. Allowing them to drown will discourage them: similar to the approach for eradicating vermin. I suggest that altruistic instincts are not linked to short-term survival but are analogous to *metabolic* innate tendencies. They assist long-term health and the survival of humans. We have a definite need for human culture with its altruism, creativity, art, poetry, music and dance. Without it, society becomes sick, with pathological social symptoms.

Instincts for left and right-wing human behaviour
Also considered broadly as instinctive and tabulated below, are individual and group tendencies to 'left' (liberal) or 'right' (conservative) wing opinions and behaviours. Again, *whether these 'left-wing' behaviour patterns are true instincts in the sense of being genetically programmed seems unclear.* Nevertheless, individual humans as well as groups (across time, geography and cultures) characteristically show left as well as right-wing behaviour. The definitions and *broad* descriptions of left wing,

right wing, liberal, neoliberal, conservative and neoconservative vary in precision.

Two notes:

1. I attempt to clarify definitions by referring to the words' origins, to dictionary definitions and also to common usage in everyday speech (Western), newspapers, radio and TV. I actively seek not to invent new or private definitions.

2. A cause of confusion is the use of the word liberal by USA political and religious 'conservatives' (but not with a focus on conserving the teaching of Jesus as in Matthew's gospel: an absolute requirement to help the needy). Apart from this single group, there is uniformity of meaning applied to these words and such use is shown in the lists that follow.

Tables of instincts

Instincts are defined as propensities or innate impulses to individual and group behaviour patterns that are constant over time, climates and cultures and are thus innate. These patterns are more or less related to important survival needs.

Primate 'Housekeeping' instincts

Shared with humans and evolved in the absence of consciousness: broadly supporting the short-term survival of one's group. Instincts broadly involved in short-term individual and group survival: seeking nourishment, shelter, sex and procreation, the rearing of offspring.

- Alpha males who gain personal rewards by maintaining the health of the group – the 'power phenotype' (see earlier): sensing need and facilitating rapid and coordinated responses to perceived danger, 'authoritarian'. In humans, one alpha could be replaced by a small group of 3 to 5 and this would probably reduce the overwhelming role of instinctive behaviour and increase the likelihood that considered thought would contribute more.

- Linked instinctive obedience to the leaders by those led, and whilst the leaders remain successful, not seeing that the leader is 'naked': conformity of social behaviour including dress codes in humans.
- Other structural inequalities such as gender role divisions.
- Defence of territory (includes nationalism in humans).
- Aggression, potential and actual hostility to and fear of 'otherness' (self and non-self; 'us and them'). Fear of inter-group ('other') contact.
- Competitiveness.
- Communication between individuals, including sound and touch.
- Altruism exists, typically between mothers and their offspring.

Human instincts

Broadly related to the long-term. They exist in humans *in addition to* the short-term survival, primate instincts listed above. For humans and apes, individual survival and group survival are closely related.

- Rationality and reason
- Altruism, facilitated by empathy.
- **Note**. Whilst language is weak regarding absolutes, it might help to clarify such a key concept as altruism. The meaning is related to that of a selfless act, of love or a state of loving. One reason for situations where altruistic acts are rare, is that under some circumstances they can be difficult, hard to do: people in need can be out-of-work foreigners. The philosopher Thomas Aquinas described love as an act of the will – choosing the other's good. Across cultures, willing the good of another and acting upon it is thought of as the highest form of human behaviour.
- Home-making, gastronomy.
- Complex culture arising from human 'consciousness' (I've used inverted commas here because creative ideas and culture arise sub-consciously).
- The need to be creative.
- Language – spoken and written and linked to the instinct for

rationality/reason.
- Literature – poetry, drama and story-telling.
- Art and artefacts.
- Music, dance, singing, choirs.
- Painting.
- Sculpture.
- Architecture.
- Religion.
- Legal social frameworks.
- A special, innate (i.e. reproducibly occurs across cultures, times and places) behaviour pattern of humans is to subjugate women, sometimes with vicious cruelty. It might be considered as an instinct of men and <u>maybe</u> of women to obey.

Note: In clashes of human versus primate instincts, the basic, primate instincts tend to prevail, especially in times of social danger and in <u>*official*</u> social structures, e.g. 'high' ART and 'official' RELIGION.

Characteristics of right-wing (conservative) individuals and groups
(Broadly they accord with primate instincts. These characteristics are <u>generalisations</u>, based on every day and media usage.)
- Less discussion using rationality, the 'right' tend to 'argue' by making *assertions*. Support for and obedience to the authoritarian power (alpha-male) phenotype: tendency to govern/manage by command and control.
- The 'winner takes all' approach is used: 'might is right'. This tends towards non-inclusive social structures. The 'right' is typically united in times of stress because of the predominance of basic instincts common to all and they commonly see things more in terms of 'black or white'.
- Especially in 'arguments' with the left, tend to make non-rational assertions; use sneers and derision.
- Attracted to <u>short-term</u> 'solutions'.

- Socially conservative. Religious 'fundamentalists'. The word 'fundamentalist' is typically used to imply a rigid application of religious rules and regulations from a previous time, but not from the original religious prophet who typically taught altruism as fundamental. Commonly involved is a rigid, clerical interpretation of a sacred text. Conformity of social behaviour including 'conservative' dress codes in humans.
- Individualistic except in times of danger. Anti 'big government', anti 'the state', i.e. typically anti-government spending on health, education, welfare and tax: the exception is national defence, this being strong.
- Tendency to advocate privatisation of main public services: health, education, roads and railways, energy and also aspects of the military. One result is to pay less taxes.
- Anti trades unions. Anti workers' rights. The role of the 'worker' is to obey.
- Attracted to power. Showing symbols of power, e.g. national flags.
- Punitive approach to crime ('hanging and flogging'), emphasis on 'law and order' and 'rules'.
- Suspicious of the poor; they see them as 'other' and not 'us' and are often labelled as lazy, inferior and definitely not alphas.
- Suspicious of 'welfare' from taxes.
- Suspicious of 'non-normal' diversity: anti-gay, anti foreigners, anti 'other' religions.
- Macho male supremacy: low regard for the feminine quality of compassion. At the extreme end, commonly unimaginative, uncaring and/or unaware of what others are thinking. Little empathy.
- Emotionally shallow.
- Emphasise and encourage competition: strongly conscious of 'winning and not losing'.
- **Note**. Competition can be considered as on one side of a coin where the other side is explicitly emphasised/designated as 'them' or the 'foreign'.

- In elections, they are exceptionally nationalistic and emphasise 'defence', territory and anti-foreigners. Commonly promote their own top alpha leader and denigrate their opponents' leader/s.
- Tend to soften right-wing behaviour in times of safety and plenty.
- They hold a strong belief in the correctness of their cause, possibly because they correctly sense that their instincts are real and authentic and wrongly assume that they totally define the 'real' (primate) world and downplay the 'human' world.
- They demonstrate behaviour that requires the suppression of or an absence of empathy: collective punishment for adversaries ('them'); indifference to the weak, related to a large, relatively poor underclass; aggression, group and individual; tendency towards bullying, sexism, racism, systematic torture (especially during wars). This last point is <u>not</u> characteristically primate.

Characteristics of left-wing ('liberal') individuals and groups
(Broadly they accord with human instincts, which is possible because of the 'new' human brain. These characteristics are also generalisations, based on every day and media usage)
- In times of stress the 'left' is typically more disunited than the 'right' because they are less influenced by basic instincts and more by intellect. Thus, they see things in shades of grey and there are numerous options to proceed. The left characteristically use reason to analyse problems.
- Generally altruistic: they favour increased expenditure on health, education and welfare. The 'left' is commonly attacked by the 'right' for their 'tax and spend' (for health, education and welfare) policies.
- The 'left' tend towards having empathy with the poor, sick and powerless.
- Tendency towards <u>in</u>clusive social arrangements. They advocate *communal* control of the main public services: health, roads and railways, education, energy. Policies for the *'common good'*.
- Socially less conservative than the 'right', including a liberal approach to dress codes.

- Attacked for being 'soft' (rehabilitation) on crime and 'soft' on national defence.
- Strong belief in the correctness of their cause, possibly because they believe in the moral superiority of selfless altruism (as taught by the major religions) over selfish individualism.
- Tend to move their views towards the 'right' in times of social danger and hardship.
- One could broadly characterise the 'left' as driven more by altruism and community need, and the 'right' more by individualism and the expression of basic primate instincts.
- **Note**: In terms of the meaning of 'left' and 'right' from the 'everyday' use of language in Britain, former UK Deputy Prime Minister (Nick Clegg, 2013) cited examples of the Prime Minister's move to the 'right' as being anti welfare, Europe and climate change. The Prime Minister's sympathy for funds from the aid budget possibly going to the military were described widely by the press as reaching out to the 'right'. Similarly, the UK coalition government's internal strife (May 2013) was described by the press as being due to the right-wing desires to leave the European Union, stop immigration and reduce 'welfare' for the poor. The BBC typically refers to racist views as being right wing.

Meanings of the word 'liberal'

Associated with definitions of left wing is the meaning of 'liberal'. The original meaning(s) of liberal has been used in a confusing way by 'neoliberals' who oppose central government and are broadly anti-democratic. Confusingly, they are also described as 'neoconservatives' and have close links with evangelical Christians who are widely spoken of as right wing and as 'fundamentalists'. The fundamentalism is not linked to the fundamental teaching of Jesus regarding the primacy of helping the needy. Instead, they refer to belief in the literal meaning of *selected* words in the Bible as if God had dictated the contents to be interpreted by the official clergy. In the USA, there has been an alliance between the political right and the religious right.

Random quotations and definitions of 'liberal' from newspapers, wireless and TV

'Willing to respect or accept behaviour or opinions different from one's own; open to new ideas'

'Western countries pride themselves on their supposedly liberal acceptance of different cultures'

'Favourable to or respectful of individual rights and freedoms: liberal citizenship laws'.

Some widely used synonyms are: tolerant, unprejudiced, unbigoted, broad-minded, open-minded, enlightened, forbearing, permissive, free, free and easy, easy-going, laissez-faire, libertarian, latitudinarian, unbiased, impartial, non-partisan, indulgent, lenient.

Note: Later, I comment on the incomplete development of or inactivation of those parts of the brain that enable empathy with other humans and their predicaments and correlations with right-wing views. Also, I consider the significance of the power phenotype existing on the socially right _and_ on the left.

That is, *left-wing behaviour <u>on achieving power</u> can change into the powerful leaders/alphas exhibiting the power phenotype with little or no difference from the right-wing power phenotype.*

There is also the fact that in clashes of human versus primate instincts, the basic <u>primate instincts tend to prevail especially in times of social danger</u> and in <u>official</u> social structures in, for example, official ART and institutional RELIGION. Under 'Instincts of special interest', I consider further ideas about 'left' and 'right'.

Instincts of special interest for human behaviour

It should be noted that at *times of crisis, primate instincts tend to override human ones.* The following specific instincts will now be highlighted: power phenotype, indifference to the weak, altruism, culture, tendencies for left and right-wing behaviour and aggression. Aggression, perhaps linked to indifference to the weak and associated with much human suffering, is dealt with at some length later under 'Humanity's Key Problems.

Instincts of special interest: power phenotype
> *'Power is not a means, it is an end... The object of*
> *power is power.'*
> **George Orwell in 'Nineteen Eighty-Four'**

> *'The fundamental concept in social science is Power,*
> *in the same sense in which Energy is the fundamental*
> *concept in physics.'*
> **Bertrand Russell in 'Power: A New Social Analysis'**
> **(Routledge Classics)**

George Orwell was well aware of the instinct leading to the phenotype associated with power. It is common for people with power to confuse the possession of power with the simultaneous possession of knowledge, sensitivity and intelligence. It's as if power changes people into believing that they have become Leonardo da Vinci, the Italian polymath (painter, sculptor, architect, scientist, musician, mathematician, engineer, inventor, anatomist...). And Bertrand Russell was also well aware of this transformative phenomenon. So was Socrates. And people with power, expressing this characteristic, typically take the transformation for granted.

To remind the non-biologist, a phenotype is behaviour not involving a genetic mutation, but an adaptive response to environmental circumstances – in this case the assumption of power. In non-human primates, the alpha male is typically identified by his strength, size and possession of leadership and power. The alpha-male primate has a special role in perceiving and responding to threats and hence plays a key role in what could be described as the 'Golden Rule of Biology' referred to earlier, namely identifying and facilitating *effective, rapid and concerted responses to change, notably dangerous ones*. He also commands the best resources of food, shelter, sleeping place and the healthiest mate. Once established, the alpha-male phenotype is to take these superior circumstances as normal – that is, they are 'taken for granted'.

It aids the survival of the primate group (around 20-50, living in trees) to keep their leader relatively fit and healthy and ready for decisive responses to danger. It's vital for group survival that danger is recognised, and a rapid response made and, if necessary, coordinated.

In fact, the main task of the alpha-male ape is to recognise and coordinate group responses to such danger. It is the biological reason he has the best of resources such as food and shelter. Also, there is an increased chance of strong, healthy offspring. The resources used by him are unavoidably restricted and limited by the natural circumstances. Simultaneous with having an alpha male, is constant competition and rivalry, thereby keeping the alpha male 'on his toes' and having a replacement available. And he lives, hunts and sleeps *with* his group.

Note: Identification of alphas *a priori*

To emphasise, we can identify alphas *a priori* – the <u>rich</u> and their children, who also have power in other forms. Also, we can identify alphas <u>*a priori*</u> via their exclusive schools. In the UK, and elsewhere, it's possible to identify potential alphas by their going to 'posh' schools such as Eton, Harrow and Marlborough, which are also characterised by having highly qualified staff, a high staff/student ratio, excellent facilities of every kind and very expensive fees. These 'top' schools being private facilitates rich alpha-hood. In the UK, for example, the cabinet has often contained half or more of its members educated at Eton/Harrow (and Oxford or Cambridge). Such cabinets, especially the 'inner cabinet', therefore have a largely common culture, despite it being alien to the national wider culture.

For humans, the need for a coordinated, rapid response to danger is no less necessary than for other animals and we still use the 'previous' primate method of following alpha-male leaders. Unlike our arboreal predecessors, human alphas rarely cohabit with the people they lead. In an original way, the UK artist, Grayson Perry, has used tapestry, paintings, drawing and writing to illustrate the precision of the distinctions between social classes with their different visible 'tastes'. He created six remarkable tapestries that were reprinted in his beautiful book, 'The vanity of small differences'. The following is a quotation that I repeat: 'Class is something bred into us like a religious faith. We drink in our aesthetic heritage with our mother's milk, with our mates at the pub, or on the playing fields of Eton.... A childhood spent marinating in the material culture of one's class means taste is soaked right through you.' The reason for such a deeply imprinted predisposition comes from evolution.

Class makes the alpha and the alpha class clearly visible.

Although today, we need a change from the single alpha male leading a group or a huge nation with great dangers of a complexity far beyond that of an ape, tree-living society. The distinction between the leaders and the led has also been supported by ideas of 'blue blood' and 'breeding' i.e. the leaders and leading class are genetically different and superior. And every opportunity is taken in many cultures to use every possible method to support the authority of alphas. Even God is recruited to support the top alpha. For example, during the coronation ceremony of the current UK Head of State, Queen Elizabeth, the Archbishop alpha cleric refers to the Queen as the 'Anointed of the Lord'. She rules with the approval of the Lord and is the formal Head of the Protestant Church of England.

In modern human society, often with a huge population (millions, compared to apes of around 20-50), the resources taken by alpha males and associated elites are relatively unlimited. And they characteristically do not live and work with their 'group'. They are often, probably typically, leading lifestyles alien to much of the population. The power phenotype is no longer as healthy and useful for the human group as when we lived within 'Mother Nature'. Furthermore, the modern human alpha male can be a predator on the society to which he 'belongs' – a pathology leading to a disconnected society that makes it difficult to 'belong'. An interesting example is a widespread human practice, carried out up to the 16th century, of discovering the truth of a problem: one should ask the highest ranking (alpha) male. The scientific revolution later offered a new, open, testing, evidence-based approach.

Power phenotype exhibited by individuals, groups, corporations and nations.

The idea of the human power phenotype will be further developed later. It seems self-evident that the power phenotype applies not only to individuals but also to organisations and to nations. An interesting example comes from my own experience as a consultant. The behaviour of executives in pharmaceutical companies can often be influenced by what the 'top' (alpha male) company does. It would be rare to be dismissed for doing what a top company does. Before IBM's decline, it was common for individuals to say, 'Nobody gets sacked for buying IBM.' Alpha males attending 'top level' meetings with other alphas thereby <u>receive endorsement of their alpha status, as do other attendees</u>. One can well imagine that it was not evil, but alpha behaviour when UK Prime Minister Tony Blair was taken into the top USA group of President Bush's circle and was then impelled to do everything he could to get the UK to join in the Iraq war and was blind to the absence of any plan for post-victory. Also, this could easily have blinded him regarding the absence of any evidence whatsoever for weapons of mass destruction. Instinctively, he likely wanted 'in' with the world's top alphas and the UK too, to join the alpha USA.

The UK Prime Minister David Cameron claimed publicly that the unaffordable Trident missile system gained us (him) a seat at the 'top table', i.e. he could be pals with other top alphas. Like Blair, he was clearly not stupid, nor necessarily personally evil. At least to some extent, they were both mindlessly, instinctively acting as alphas. Similarly explained has been expenditure on numerous alpha projects *worldwide* whilst extreme national needs are unmet. Even where there is homelessness, hunger, unemployment and no available health service, we continue to have massive expenditure *worldwide* on international prestigious Olympic 'games', prestige palaces for leaders, prestige and ultra-expensive 'space' projects and unaffordable wars of aggression involving top alphas. *The instinctive and mindless behaviour of the world's alphas, together with our instinctive and mindless <u>obedience,</u> is endangering us all in today's world.*

How about having nations led, as well as by a cabinet, also by a top leadership of 3-5 people, men and women, rather than one alpha male? Having such a group, including women, could have the consequences of making less vulnerable: a health service for all, public parks, galleries, libraries, nurseries and it might increase the likelihood of housing the homeless. It might also result in less wars.

If any reader is unsure, then consider the irrational behaviour of the current USA President. And also, note that the USA spends as much on armaments as the next ten nations put together, despite having an over-expensive *private* health service that <u>ex</u>cludes large numbers of the poor. And in 2018 is a proposal for a *massive reduction* in funds for social services.

President Trump has proposed deep cuts to programs used by millions of low-income American families including food stamps, Temporary Assistance for Needy Families and the Children's Health Insurance Program (CHIP). The following is a report abstracted from 'Newsweek' (March 2018). "The Senate passed stopgap spending with only temporary funding fixes for CHIP, the health insurance program that covers about 9 million children in the U.S. If Congress does not re-authorize CHIP funding, an estimated 1.9 million children in 25 states will lose their health insurance by the end of this month, and an additional 1 million will lose out in February, according to a Georgetown University report. In addition to health care, Trump plans to target food assistance for the poor. More than 42 million people in need, including children and elderly individuals, across the United States last year used food stamps, part of the Supplemental

Nutrition Assistance Program (SNAP). In his 2016 budget, Trump proposed cutting SNAP funding by $192 billion over 10 years, kicking millions of people off food stamps. Only 75 percent of people who qualify for food stamps actually use them".

One explanation for the 25% could be the shame of being poor. President Trump justifies this programme as helping to get people back to work. In other words, these lazy people need forcing into work.

Instincts of special interest: indifference to the weak

> *'I will support the financing of public art when the last homeless person is housed.'*
> **Abbé Pierre (French priest dedicated to the homeless)**

Another human characteristic and the source of much human suffering, maintained over cultures, climates and time is widespread indifference to the weak, related to a large, poor underclass. The mysterious origins and purpose of this latter characteristic are discussed above, partly as the consequence of the 'power phenotype' and the primate need to have healthy leaders (making those led, safer) and also the huge increase in group size, facilitated by the move from 'hunting and gathering' and social 'belonging' to large-scale agriculture and animal husbandry.

The poor are unlikely to become national alphas, hence may not be considered worth the cost of housing and other needs.

Other negative features, also occurring across cultures, climates and time which can thus be classified as at least similar to human instincts, are unbounded aggression (group and individual – see below); bullying, especially of women by men, systematic torture, racism, homophobia and sexism. In so-called 'developing' countries, i.e. including mainly the victims of colonialism and the very poor, there has developed a culture of often *discarding* the severely disabled. For example, those who are immobile may be forced to sit ignored in a corner. Happily, as always there are some people who respond positively. One such organisation is 'Motivation', fighting for such people and providing wheelchairs to enable motility. I quote, 'Without mobility, millions of disabled people in the developing world are unable to leave their homes, go to school or to work. Many are left to lie on the floor. Many more die from preventable complications.' 'Motivation' helps people to acquire the right wheelchair in the right way – to stay healthy, get mobile and play an active part in their communities. See more at: http://www. motivation.org.uk/#sthash.IA2bzgVm.dpuf

Instincts of special interest: altruism and culture
Altruism does not fit precisely into a definition of an instinct. Instances of altruism appear to have occurred in all human societies in different places, times and cultures and in that sense, it is indeed a kind of innate tendency. As well as individuals, society obviously benefits from such acts.

Human consciousness and associated intuition have influenced the expression of at least some spontaneous, individual, selfless behaviour. There are numerous examples in all societies and at all times of individuals behaving in an altruistic way when faced with human need. The Oxford dictionary defines altruism as 'Regard for others as a principle of action'. Such individuals, some later seen as prophets, see beyond the immediate survival of their own group and look towards the well-being of humankind as a whole, advocating altruism as a core belief. It appears that altruism is at least latent in all humans, but not always expressed, perhaps similar to the power phenotype. Also, there are many examples of societies acting in a selfless, altruistic way and helping other communities suffering from some catastrophe such as tsunamis, fires, volcanoes or famine. There are some examples of animals acting in a selfless way and are an early, uncommon, 'embryonic' appearance prehuman. Mothers' instincts towards their young are usually selfless. It's possible that the evolution of altruism came via the feminine instincts regarding their children. If any reader is further interested, the following references may help. 'Altruism and Helping': Jane Allyn Piliavin (2008). The Evolution of a Field: The 2008 Cooley-Mead Presentation Social Psychology Quarterly September 2009 vol. 72 no. 3 209-225; Toth, *et al.* Wasp gene expression supports an evolutionary link between maternal behaviour and eusociality. *Science* **318**, 441–444 (2007); 'Our inner ape' by Frans de Waal.

But when a human group is itself under threat, then the collective behaviour tends strongly to be not altruistic, with many examples of ruthless aggression, willingness to fight and even systematic torture, especially during wars. At which time there is increased obedience to elites, nationalism, hostility to and fear of 'otherness' and the inflicting of collective punishment. Fear is obviously a major trigger for releasing basic, primate instincts.

It has been suggested that empathy is a prerequisite for altruism. It would seem at the least that empathy facilitates altruism. Studies of brain function and development (described in 'The Master and his Emissary' by Iain McGilchrist) have identified specific areas (right frontal hemisphere) and even specific cells (mirror neurones) that are associated with understanding another person's intentions and our capacity to empathise with them. These areas are 'silent' when autistic children attempt to achieve this understanding. It has been suggested, and it seems plausible, that right-wing tendencies are associated with a lack of human empathy. I have written earlier about social values existing on a spectrum between extrinsic and intrinsic: *these individual values vary with the general social culture.* People towards the intrinsic end have high levels of self-acceptance, strong bonds of intimacy and a powerful desire to help other people. People at the other end are drawn to external signifiers, such as fame, financial success, image and attractiveness (T. Kasser, November 2011. Values and Human Wellbeing. The Bellagio Initiative. http:// www.bellagioinitiative.org/wp-content/uploads/2011/10/Bellagio-Kasser.pdf). They seek praise and rewards from others.

Research across 70 countries suggests that intrinsic values are strongly associated with an understanding of others, tolerance, appreciation, cooperation *and empathy* (S. H. Schwartz, 2006. Basic Human Values: Theory, Measurement, and Applications. Revue Française de Sociologie, 47/4. http://bit.ly/1hL1JFJ; F. Grouzet *et al*, 2005. The structure of goal contents across fifteen cultures. Journal of Personality and Social Psychology, 89, 800-816. http://psycnet.apa.org/journals/psp/89/5/800/). Those with strong extrinsic values *tend to have lower empathy*, a stronger attraction towards power, hierarchy and inequality, greater prejudice towards outsiders and less concern for global justice and the natural world. Clearly, manifestation of an intrinsic culture with the widespread expression of art, music and literature would help to humanise society – in particular, local, small-scale art of every kind presented in homes, schools, libraries and galleries.

Instincts of special interest: left and right-wing tendencies
A consistent feature of human societies is the presence of a substantial segment of society or of an entire *society*, commonly described today either as 'right' (conservative) or 'left' (liberal) wing and demonstrating <u>broad</u> social opinions and behaviour attributes – generalisations are listed in the table above with broad definitions also described above. Similarly, entire groups (or nations) can be classified broadly as left or right-wing. It is thought that these terms first arose in the French Revolution of 1789 and referred to the seating arrangements in the 'Estates General'. Those sitting on the left broadly opposed the monarchy and wanted a republic and supported secularisation. Those seated on the right wanted to retain traditional social institutions of the 'Ancien Régime': that is, the religious, political and aristocratic system in which all were subjects of the King of France blessed by God. Use of the term 'left' became more prominent after the restoration of the French monarchy in 1815 when it was applied to the 'Independents'. More recently, the phrase left-wing has been used to describe an increasing group of movements including the civil rights movement, anti-war

movements, and environmental movements. Opposition to these is commonly described as right-wing.

Difficulty of precise definitions

As for instincts generally, precision in defining 'left' and 'right' is not possible. Commentators have frequently had difficulty over the concept of a continuous spectrum from left to right, as I have; some have suggested multiple dimensions. Altruism is defined as 'regard for others as a principle of action'. Other human instincts are related to the complex culture arising from consciousness; language especially (spoken and written), literature (poetry, drama and story-telling), religion, legal social frameworks, home-making, art and artefacts, music, dance, painting, sculpture, architecture, gastronomy. How can there be a continuous spectrum of such human impulses with such primate instincts as those concerning territory, the foreign, competition, suppression of women and alpha males? I have avoided using multiple dimensions as the key distinction for this book is between basic (primate) and human instincts.

As well as the historical roots of the words, the dictionary definitions and also the actual use of 'left' and 'right' wing in the media casts some light on broad definitions. The Oxford English dictionary refers to the left as 'holding relatively liberal or democratic opinions'. It refers to the right as 'a group or section favouring conservatism: similar to the monarchical right in the revolutionary French 'Estates General'. As for the media usage, the previous UK Prime Minister Cameron was widely accused of moving to the 'right' to appease his right-wing and hardened policies regarding 'welfare', immigration and the European Union (May 2013). He was attacked by his own right wing for softening regulations regarding homosexuality and marriage. Belief in the literal truth of the Bible coming directly from God is associated with the right. Similar associations occur with other religions having sacred books believed to be derived from their God. It's clear that the UK press considers negative attitudes to homosexuality, foreigners, non-Christian religions and 'welfare' payments as separating left from right.

Generally speaking, innate right-wing tendencies correspond to primate instincts and innate left-wing tendencies correspond to human instincts, notably altruism (**but**, importantly, see later, below). The human instincts for left or right-wing tendencies are listed above as separate tables. As explained, one could broadly characterise tendencies of the left as driven more by altruism and social justice. The 'left' wants to alter inequalities regarded as unjustified whilst the right regards them as 'natural' or 'traditional'. The right is characterised more by basic primate instincts: hierarchies and authoritarianism and the consequential social inequalities, including those that enhance the lifestyles of the alpha males; defence of territory; fear of/hostility to foreigners; conserving existing social norms, suppression of women (see more later). As discussed earlier, perhaps the biological mechanisms of the human, innate tendency towards left-wing opinions and behaviour are not identical to instincts as listed, but the tendencies are at least similar to instincts in that these tendencies clearly do exist within human societies and individuals across culture, climate, geography and time.

It is clearly of interest to separate, if possible, the genetic from the environmental influences leading to left and right-wing behaviour i.e. 'nature-nurture'. There have been studies that have cast some light on this. In 'Bright minds and dark attitudes: lower cognitive ability predicts greater prejudice through right-wing ideology and low intergroup contact' by Hodson and Busseri (Psychol Sci. 2012 Feb;23(2):187-95), the IQ scores of several thousand British children were compared with their later, stated views as adults on things such as the treatment of criminals and openness to working with or living near people of other races. Also considered was US data which compared IQ scores with homophobic attitudes. It was found that lower general intelligence in childhood predicts greater racism in adulthood, and this effect was largely mediated via conservative ideology.

A secondary analysis of a US data set confirmed a predictive effect of poor abstract-reasoning skills on anti-homosexual prejudice, a relation partially mediated by both authoritarianism and low levels of intergroup contact. All analyses were controlled for education and socioeconomic status. Because the correlation was between IQ at a young age and attitudes in adult life, it consequently minimised environmental influences. These results suggest that cognitive abilities play a critical and underappreciated role in prejudice.

Speaking personally and with hesitation, I find this hard (but not impossible) to accept despite their evidence and wonder if agreeing with right or left-wing statements on a paper form correlates with actual behaviour towards needy people. Even so, general right-wing tendencies could also be the consequence of a lack of development of those parts of the brain associated with the capacity for empathy, especially a lack of understanding of the poor and powerless. It would seem that empathy is a prerequisite for altruism (or at least facilitates it) and it is a late brain development. Decades ago, the psychologist Jean Piaget and his followers published much evidence about the development of 'higher order' brain function moving up from such as personal identity to understanding complex concepts such as justice and truth. Empathy comes late in development and may be relatively poorly established in some adults who may develop later into 'right-wingers'.

This lack could be inherited or be the result of interrupted brain development or could be suppressed because of the *nature of the society lived in*. For example, stress and/or fear affect brain function. Almost all human societies and many subunits are governed by leaders exhibiting primate, alpha-male behaviour in a society and in a permanent state of stress. In this sense, we are largely governed by primates in an unsuitable world. Possibly, this is connected to the extent of violent social aggression that has long existed and which may suppress feelings of empathy and associated acts of altruism.

Extrinsic values are strongly associated with conservative politics.

Experiments reported in the journal Motivation and Emotion suggest that when people feel threatened or insecure they gravitate towards extrinsic goals (K. M. Sheldon and T. Kasser, 2008. Psychological threat and extrinsic goal striving. Motivation and Emotion, **32**:37-45. Doi: 10.1007/s11031-008-9081-5 http://www.selfdeterminationtheory.org/SDT/documents/2008_SheldonKasser_MOEM.pdf). Threats of crime, war on terror, war on drugs and so on, result in primate, fear-driven, instinctive responses. These arise directly to protect oneself and one's small group's short-term survival. People at the extrinsic end tend to report higher levels of stress, anxiety, anger, envy, dissatisfaction and depression than those at the intrinsic end of the spectrum (T. Kasser, 2014. Changes in materialism, changes in psychological well-being: Evidence is from three longitudinal studies and an intervention experiment. Motivation and Emotion, **38**:1–22. doi: 10.1007/s11031-013-9371-4; K. M. Sheldon and T. Kasser, 2008. Psychological threat and extrinsic goal striving. Motivation and Emotion, **32**:37–45. Doi: 10.1007/s11031-008-9081-5 http://www.selfdeterminationtheory.org/SDT/documents/2008_SheldonKasser_MOEM.pdf). Significantly, societies in which extrinsic goals are widely adopted are more unequal and uncooperative than those with deep intrinsic values.

Left-wing politics good: right-wing politics bad?
The consequences for improving society of having left and right wings are considered later in terms of reducing humanity's problems. In particular, I consider the fact that

> *historically, idealistic left-wing (altruistic) movements and revolutions on achieving power can rapidly change with leaders exhibiting the <u>same</u> primate power phenotype as before, often with similar, disastrous consequences.*

The possession of power tends to change the left-wing altruistic group into one exhibiting the power phenotype: if not, then it is rapidly replaced by people who do. It would seem that this is an example of primate (right-wing) instincts trumping the human. A major issue blocking the way of facilitating altruistic behaviour, as advocated by virtually all the major religious and humanistic leaders (but not so prominently later by their institutions), is that primate, right-wing instincts have such deep and widespread roots. For example, mammals with their instincts have existed for around 200 million years and primates for 60 million years. The 'left' have often recognised this difficulty and wrongly felt instinctively (primate) that only a swift, radical change can work: the slaughter of all the existing leaders of a conservative regime and the uprooting of such deep social structures. Another influence is that the basic instinct related to power (the power phenotype) is shared by all and on gaining power, the 'left' tends to become united by the ancient, mindless and inappropriate instinct to eliminate all opposition – 'them'.

In other words, with the assumption of power, the human tendencies of the left are commonly trumped by the primate instinct associated with power.

BASIC HUMAN NEEDS

Contents

INTRODUCTION

'Man is a social animal'

Aristotle

Before dealing with aspects of the inhuman behaviour of modern institutions, it may help to comment further on basic human needs and the consequences if they are not met. These needs occur as a consequence of our evolutionary history. I will then consider the extent to which social institutions serve these needs. A frequently quoted, and sometimes disputed, hierarchy of human needs was originally proposed by Abraham Maslow several decades ago (Maslow, A. H., 1943. A theory of human motivation. *Psychological Review, 50*(4), 370-96). He lists needs for basic physiology in order: safety, belonging, esteem, self-actualisation and self-transcendence. I prefer to consider needs in the following condensed way that also embraces Maslow's hierarchy:

1. 'Housekeeping' needs: *early healthy, personal development.* For survival and safety: nutrition, shelter and 'territory'/ habitat, sex and procreation.
2. To be part of and connected to a human community and its culture – to 'belong'. This includes socially useful work that confers dignity and is recognised as such.
3. Expression of the human instincts of altruism and human, creative culture: art, poetry, music, dance, sculpture. An associated need is to be and feel part of the natural world: animals, plants, land/soil, the universe.
4. The human need to make sense of the universe.

Early healthy, personal development

Numerous forms of life do not emerge fully capable of healthy survival. Plants in inadequate soil are unhealthy. Microbes have requirements for healthy survival and these requirements vary depending on the immediate environment. How can humans be thought of as so different, with much behaviour explained as morally good or evil?

Some housekeeping needs are well understood despite not being met in many parts of the world. In particular, despite much empirical work by eminent workers and government reports referred to elsewhere and including Maslow above, *healthy child development should receive much greater emphasis*. To some extent, healthy child development is related to loving parents, especially the mother, and a generally healthy habitat. Such requirements are affected by a healthy overall society in human terms.

Later, under 'Reducing Humanity's Problems' (Broad and Specific), issues regarding territory and habitat are dealt with: city and urban planning, including housing. While the importance of the healthy, early development of humans is recognised by science and commonly by parents, its importance has not adequately been recognised by the educational and criminal justice systems of the world. But this is slowly being remedied (see earlier – 'Reducing the long-term harm of child neglect'). In this section, it's intended to focus on needs 2 and 3, as listed above. The crucial importance of healthy early development has been elaborated on earlier and will be later. It seems likely that meeting needs 2 and 3 will also contribute to answering developmental needs.

Basic needs: community, to belong, to be connected, to be part of an 'us'

'No man is an island,
Entire of itself,
Every man is a piece of the continent
A part of the main
If a clod be washed away by the sea,
Europe is the less.
As well as if a promontory were.
As well as if a manor of thy friend's
Or of thine own were:
Any man's death diminishes me,
Because I am involved in mankind,
And therefore, never send to know for whom the bell
tolls;
It tolls for thee.'

John Donne

The need for community, to belong, is at the base of human needs. John Donne's poem was written well before much empirical evidence (discussed elsewhere) stated that it's a mistake to consider a human as a separate entity. Belonging to a group is necessary for one's health. Earlier, I've referred to evidence about brain development and social life being connected. Even organisms as low down the evolutionary tree as microbes act in a coordinated way. As mentioned earlier (in 'Simple life forms'), they mainly exist as surface-attached, multi-species, cooperative consortia. This biofilm mode of existence enables them to construct and control their environment. Likely, this mode of existence is continuous through evolution and demonstrates itself in higher animals as an instinct regarding territory: know where there is food, safety, danger and where to hide. Typically, cooperative behaviour helps survival. For humans without the feeling and reality of community, little makes sense and chaos often reigns. In the UK in summer 2011, there were riots and mindless destruction in several cities, commonly attributed to an alienated, feral, dispossessed underclass. No comment was made about the feral, alienated, alpha-male overclass.

The alienated, feral, alpha-male overclass
As mentioned elsewhere (see the section entitled 'Causes of humanity's problems'), in recent years there has been much sociological research into the negative consequences of social inequality and also the consequences of a lack of connectedness. Non-inclusive social structures add to the negative consequences. It will be seen later that these strands of human needs merge. Clearly, the power phenotype flourishes under such conditions and is likely to accelerate a sense of exclusivity.

The 2008 UK Commission on Social Determinants of Health concluded that 'Social injustice is killing people on a grand scale'. Reducing health inequities is, for the Commission on Social Determinants of Health, an ethical imperative. It also concluded that 'Together, the structural determinants and conditions of daily life constitute the social determinants of health and are responsible for a major part of health inequities between and within countries'. The Chairman of this commission, Michael Marmot, authored a book with a similar message, '*The Status Syndrome: How your social standing directly affects your health and life expectancy*'. In this he again argues that socio-economic position is an important determinant for health outcomes. This holds even if we control for the effects of income, education and risk factors (such as smoking) on health. The causal pathway Marmot identifies, concerns the psychological benefits of 'being in control' of one's life. Autonomy in this sense is related to our socio-economic position.

Several other eminent authors have written popular books explaining the findings of inequality to a wider audience, in particular, two Nobel Laureates, Krugman and Stiflitz. In 'End this depression now!' Paul Krugman points out the growing isolation of America's economic and political elite from the lives of ordinary Americans. For middle-income families, even before the recent financial crisis, there was only a modest rise in income under deregulation, achieved mainly through longer working hours and mostly *not* higher wages. For an influential tiny minority – the decision-makers – the era of financial deregulation and increasing debt saw massive growth in personal income. Joseph E. Stiglitz in 'The Price of Inequality' writes indignantly about inequality and its consequences. He is sympathetic to the 'Occupy Wall Street' protesters. Stiglitz insists that the huge and growing divide between the richest 1 per cent and 'the 99 per cent' (a slogan of the protesters) is *not* just one concern among many, but the precise, defining characteristic of a pathological economy. A brilliant, lucid analysis and sifting of these two books is given in a review by two eminent political scientists in 'The New York Review of Books' (September 27th 2012): Jacob Hacker (Yale) and Paul Pierson (Berkeley). In a later (2015) book, 'The Great Divide', Stiglitz expands on his earlier book with a series of essays and continues to offer solutions. He emphasises that inequality is a choice made by the elite, manifested through mistaken, unjust policies and priorities.

Another remarkable book, mentioned earlier, and one that struck me greatly because of the clarity of the presentation of empirical findings, is 'The Spirit Level' by Richard Wilkinson and Kate Pickett. Here, overwhelming, detailed and quantitative evidence is given about the close correlation between negative social behaviour and the income gap between the 'top' and 'bottom' of society. It's a straight line. The book presents evidence of close correlations between income inequality, as measured by the difference in income between the top 20% and the bottom 20% of society, and the frequency of numerous specific social ills. It is not to do with the *amount* of income, but with the *difference*. When the gap widens, negative social indices increase. One interpretation (but see below) that springs to my own mind is that in extreme cases there is not one society; the bottom and the top of the line belong to different 'communities', with different 'foreign' lifestyles. In a 'them and us' world, the top and the bottom are both 'them'. At the top of the list, largely not referred to and with the world's worst social statistics (apart from dysfunctional states without such statistics) are the USA closely followed by the UK.

However, surprising to me, the correlation is <u>not</u> simply between the extremes. As inequality increases incrementally, so do *numerous* negative social indices about such as crime and health. There is a straight-line relationship. In 'The Spirit Level', the authors suggest that inequality may be measuring how hierarchical societies are. The bigger the inequality, the bigger the social differences and social stratification becomes increasingly important. It seems likely that we 'belong' most strongly within our social strata. The word belonging (or not) seems a good one to describe something very basic that influences health or disease – individual and social. Once again, in writing about a subject so broad, I've an idea (or rather my wife Margaret had the idea), possibly not original, but I've not found it anywhere else. Money quantifies power. Thus, the straight-line graphs in 'The Spirit Level' (Wilkinson and Pickett), with income inequality plotted against incidence of negative social indices (e.g. rape, theft, murder) for the different countries, could replace 'income inequality' with the word 'power'. It may help to clarify *why* it's a continuous line as opposed to simply a difference between top and bottom nations: no power, no belonging.

Shockingly, even as I write this, my last revision in April 2018, the work above is ignored or misunderstood. The UK BBC and reputable newspapers such as the UK 'Observer' still refer to gross inequality as somewhat distasteful or inappropriate. In the Observer article (8th April 2018) as part of an article headed 'Richest 1% on target to own two-thirds of all wealth by 2030' reference is made to polls asking what people *thought* about power distribution by 2030. Most respondents thought that the super-rich would have the most. They (41%) feared that the consequences of wealth inequality would be rising levels of corruption or having unfair influence on government policy (43%). It seems that the wealth of hard evidence listed above was ignored. Why? My suspicions of widespread ignorance by our leaders are hardening. Do politicians read? The evidence referred to immediately above shows the effects of social inequality upon numerous evils such as rape, murder and numerous other *crimes*. 'The Spirit Level' by Wilkinson and Pickett was published in 2009 and 'The Great Divide in 2015 and including evidence going back *decades*. It's not inequality *per se*, it's the social pathology that follows.

Finding out that citizens fear that by 2030 the super-rich may have unfair influence on government policy is absurd. They have this influence *now* and have had for decades via fake, massively funded, think-tanks and magazines helping to delay actions against the harm from such as alcohol or global warming. There are documented numerous meetings between UK Prime Ministers and media moguls negotiating favourable media coverage in exchange for political favours etc, etc.

As for primates, the idea of not belonging or of being disconnected could not exist. It is probable that early human hunter-gatherers would have had difficulty understanding a question about belonging. And as for the leaders living separately from and acting *against* the interest of the rest of the group and instead acting in their own interests or even as predators – this is a modern social pathology. Earlier, I mentioned ideas about humans essentially not being individuals but intrinsically part of a social group. In exteme individual isolation there is mental disease, less extreme and belonging to a group simply increases the sense of 'us and the other groups - them'.

Group size

One factor affecting the sense of belonging that seems generally underrated is group size. Some animals such as birds or fish can achieve relatively huge group sizes. But the group size of our ape predecessors up to human hunter-gatherers was tiny, relative to today's human societies. Chimpanzees have an average group size of about 50 (according to Robin Dunbar in his readable 'The Human Story'). It's not obvious whether consistent small group size qualifies for being an instinct: perhaps it does in a literal, dictionary sense. What is clear is that group size, physiology, psychology, diet, exercise, instincts and behaviour (including that of alpha-male leaders) all developed together over millions of years and within the natural (i.e. little affected by human activity) arboreal environment. It seems likely that group size would indeed be selected for.

Behavioural studies indicate that a modern task-driven group, e.g. a decision-making committee, is commonly most successful if consisting of several people with varying personalities (see Meredith Belbin). It is highly likely in an ape or early human group that each individual would feel that they belonged. 'Belonging' would have been taken for granted in early human societies. As mentioned earlier, personal identity would be bound up in the group identity, perhaps even indistinguishable from it. It seems clear that the need for a widespread actual sense of belonging is a requirement for a healthy society. Its absence is associated with a socially diseased state. And it seems that this has been grossly under-recognised. Even in the mundane activity of building homes on working-class 'housing estates', the need in the design for facilitating a sense of community has not always been recognised. It could well be that living together in numerous <u>tents or caves</u>, with crude but common eating, cooking, recreational and toilet facilities could generate a better sense of belonging than could merely bricks and mortar with nothing else in common.

A contribution to the age old and widespread success of religion in its various forms and adapted to the differing cultures is that it provides belonging. In my own experience as an English Roman Catholic (now ex-RC, agnostic) there are typically the following in all parishes: Sunday (compulsory) and weekday (voluntary) masses, and various other services. These typically involve singing and in some Christian denominations, dancing. There are numerous clubs such as youth clubs (often with singing and dancing), scouts, guides, cubs and charitable organisations of different sorts. Also, in terms of belonging, a change of job and location is facilitated by joining in at the new parish and immediately being welcomed by the local people.

BASIC NEEDS: TO BE PART OF THE NATURAL WORLD (ANIMALS, PLANTS, LAND, THE UNIVERSE)

The timescale of biological evolution is hard to imagine. The 'Big Bang' occurred about 13.7 billion years ago and the coalesced Earth had circled the sun for 4.6 billion years. So-called simple cells have existed for the last 3.6 billion years and anatomically modern humans have existed for only 200,000 years and probably left their African home a mere 60,000 years ago to colonise the world. Thus, humans have a physiology and a set of instincts suitable for primates living in a world vastly different to ours. The phrase 'a fish out of water' comes to mind. It's not just a question of 'bad' instincts: after all, without them primates would not have evolved. It is rather that they are often inappropriate today, having been developed for a different environment and for organisms without human consciousness and a vastly smaller population size living in trees.

So, it's becoming clear that departing greatly from early human diets, physical activity and social arrangements can cause serious issues of personal health and social disorder. Prehuman primates and early humans lived in small communities where each member belonged, and all were in close contact with each other and with nature (i.e. the natural environment was little affected by human activity) in the raw. Lack of contact with 'nature' for some city dwellers, ignorance of the origin of food, whether vegetation or animal, lack of 'kinship' with animals and even other humans, living in isolation in densely populated cities and cut off (disconnected) from one's rulers/leaders or even so-called 'representatives' by very different lifestyles all have negative effects. Societies cannot truly be represented by people with a lifestyle that is vastly different to that of the people they 'represent'. Clearly, discussions about salaries for our leaders/politicians/alphas should bear this in mind.

BASIC NEEDS: TO BE CREATIVE, TO MAKE SENSE OF THE WORLD VIA INTUITION, ART, SCIENCE AND RELIGION

> *'The eternal mystery of the world is its comprehensibility.... The fact that it is comprehensible is a miracle.'*
>
> **Albert Einstein**

Also, near the base of human needs is the need to be creative and to make sense of the world around us. In this search for understanding we have always used our creativity and also intuition. It seems that art too, has long played a role in offering insights, often unwelcome, about the 'human condition': art and intuition are inextricably linked. Science plays an increasing role in explaining the physical world. As a global explanation of everything, numerous religions have offered versions of God as the creator, sustainer and controller of the universe. These words: intuition, art, science and religion have often been used with different meanings, potentially causing confusion. It might be helpful, if not to define them, at least to clarify the differences in these approaches to understanding the world.

Intuition making sense of the world

By intuition is meant the putting together of numerous, even all, of one's experiences by the subconscious mind to produce an insight. The link with art is shown by the definition of poetry given by T. S. Eliot (quoted in 'Staying Alive' Ed. Neil Astley Page 18) which is simultaneously a definition of intuition: '... it is neither emotion, nor recollection, nor, without distortion of meaning, tranquillity. It is a concentration, and a new thing resulting from the concentration of a very great number of experiences... a concentration which does not happen consciously or with deliberation...' Intuition has been described by several authors (notably the artist Joseph Beuys) as the highest form of mental activity. In the same context, Einstein described intuition as our highest activity.

As mentioned earlier, the word instinct is sometimes confusingly used to mean intuition. Instinct is programmed survival tendencies, whereas intuition is defined by several eminent thinkers and artists as the highest form of subconscious thinking, giving rise to insights, often original.

Art making sense of the world

Art of any kind – broadly poetry, literature, theatre, painting, sculpture, architecture, music, dance and gastronomy – can offer insight into the human condition. Such insights, typically (maybe always) intuitive, are there to be considered, accepted or rejected for what they are: take them or leave them. Although arising within a culture, art is typically individual. Official, bureaucratic 'ART' can offer something, but its main function is to maintain the cultural norms and current views of the artistic elites: it contributes to social control and to the social glue. Art has more similarities to science than may seem to be the case at first consideration. Attempts are made in art to express a truth about reality. Intuitive guesses are made as to what may 'work' regarding the words written or colours and shapes painted or sculptured or the flow of the music. Then publish or exhibit or perform. A difference from science is that the 'usefulness' is more profound than technology: it lifts the spirit and reminds us that we are human. Art can inform us about the human condition. In both art and science, there is the need for openness; both benefit from it. Also, the reproducibility desired in scientific measurement is not applicable to art: generally speaking, the insight is accepted or not.

Science making sense of the world

Science, although involving insight, is different to insight. In popular culture, science is thought of as cold, impersonal and involving incomprehensible equipment and techniques used by cold, unfeeling, inhuman, clever people, mostly men. Science is seen as driven solely by this cold, impersonal, mechanical logic and hence can and does cause devastation to humans. In contrast to this popular belief and in reality, science may be considered as a *technique*, a method for approaching truths about the natural world: attempting to understand an unknown in the natural world and a gradual revealing of the truth, but never entirely getting there – provisional truth. Intuition plays an important role in this. The connection with religion is tenuous and indirect. The explanation of phenomena such as plagues or tsunamis as God's actions has been replaced by science offering microbes and earthquakes or eruptions as the causes.

Science is a method of approaching some kinds of truth, mainly about the physical, material world. People have carried out science for thousands of years, with examples of great success. But broadly speaking, until the 16th century, the main source for learning about the natural world was to ask the opinion of a high-status man. This reinforced the power of the elite, the alphas. In practice, the method of science is simple and effective. An informed guess is made as to the cause of a phenomenon in the natural world or even an intuitive 'leap'; then think what else would likely happen if the guess or 'leap' were true and test these predictions by experiments to see if it 'works out' or not. Such provisional 'guesses' are commonly called hypotheses. Then, if interesting, the results are published, together with the methods used to obtain them, so that they can be *verified or disproved* by others. The 'guesses' or insights often come from nowhere, especially if exceptionally original, and are intuitive. Sometimes the scientific finding can be applied in a useful way – e.g. technology.

Essentially, the work of science is communal and *open*. An individual, having a novel idea, will probably have worked for years with other scientists, had numerous laboratory discussions/ presentations, been to conferences, published scientific papers and had responses from referees and editors and then had the idea. When the idea is tested and results and methods published after criticism by colleagues, referees and editors, then the scientific community has the opportunity to respond. The *process* is essentially an *open and a communal one*. That is not to say that those in science meetings/ discussions, editors, reviewers and scientific committee members are different as people to the rest of humanity. In my own personal experience, they are, broadly speaking, little different, if at all, to the non-scientific community as people, and the world of science also has alpha-male hierarchies and alpha elite institutions, competitiveness, hostility to novel ideas, misuse of power and the power phenotype.

But the *scientific method*, with its openness and publication of the ideas/guesses, methods and results, has led to the massive advances visible to all. At this very moment, the field of molecular genetics is reaping rich crops regarding human brain development and personality, on disposition to diseases and in every area of biology. As mentioned earlier, science's connection with religion is indirect. Science has eliminated the need for God as a cause of natural phenomena. Science has increased understanding of the physical mechanisms of phenomena such as earthquakes; movements of the planets and disappearances of, for example, the moon or the sun, showing that the Earth is not the centre of the universe; and, of course, biological evolution with genetics and physical dating techniques establishing timelines for the origins of life and the appearance of humans. Even so, some religions simply deny the evidence without discussion or state that God, through the Bible, draws out, for example, the timescale of life's creation.

The bad consequences of science are the result of human activity and not science *per se*. The nuclear bombs that destroyed Hiroshima and Nagasaki were human designed and manufactured, put on planes by humans, flown by air crew, and a human pressed the switch that dropped them. In the case of the fire-bombing of Dresden (Germany) and of the destruction of Coventry (UK) in World War 2, with many thousands burned alive, similar numerous human activities were needed and many more planes and air crews. The destruction was carried out as a result of the collective activity of living humans, not by the concepts of science. For millennia, moral and philosophical leaders have pointed out that each human has a personal responsibility for his or her actions. Logically and morally it is not enough for evil to be justified on the grounds of 'obeying orders'. But leaders exhibiting the power phenotype rarely accept such morality. They are in the grip of 'Mother Nature' with her emphasis on short-term survival: they are the alpha males and we must instinctively follow. Typically, local and world religious leaders keep quiet when faced with the wrongdoings within their own culture – likely for reasons of their own biological survival. Yet an important role for religion is to point out such evils.

On one occasion I had a bright, likeable PhD student who seemed to have lost some enthusiasm. I sent another, personal account of science and the scientific method. It was a kind of poem. It's below. The student's name is changed.

Dear Sam,

It seemed a good idea
maybe
to write you
a kind of poem
an odd kind
about what I know
of Mother Nature

I have some responsibility
not as much as yours
for your learning
as I also am trying to learn
her secret ways

I write because
I'm a bit worried
it seems to me
that perhaps
you do not take her
seriously enough
maybe if you knew more about her

You may wonder
as I do
why things are so secret
despite being so connected
to everything else
but I can't help you there
way too deep for me

So, here are a few scraps
I have discovered
from my own relationship
over many, many years
but mostly by accident
despite my intense
deepening commitment

First of all,
don't be fooled by her name
it's misleading
of course, it's true
she's the source of life
some say she is life
but she can be utterly,
un-motherly ruthless
and relentlessly destroys life
without mercy

To reveal anything important
she yields only after commitment
a choice
to be faithful to her

This may seem surprising
but remember
many philosophers
define love essentially
as an act of the will
the will
a decision, a choice
to commit

She reveals nothing important
unless addressed with honesty and good will
scientific rigour
means not compromising
with half truths

Any signs of disrespect
poorly designed experiments (an insult)
questions without insight
no commitment
not enough thought
you are shunned

It's as though
she has a perverse side
(she does not)
lays lots of false trails
leading nowhere
but especially
for the short-sighted

Careful, gentle
and patient pulling
at a loose thread
left from a former suitor
eventually
may expose something
of her
and can sometimes be a way
to reveal much more

And yet
she is known to yield
quite suddenly
inspiration from nowhere
though usually
after a lengthy courtship

She yields
not always
to the most intelligent
but
more often
to the most ardent

She is
never, never, never, never, never, never, never, never
fooled
ever
and Sam
do I need to repeat this?

I may be quite wrong
but it seems
you
might be after
casual sex
with Mother Nature
she really doesn't like it
doesn't even like flirting
and Sam
it's not the age difference

Try to woo her
start slowly, gently
lots of little presents
of what she likes
beautiful experiments
much more attention -
she can't get enough
lots more thought
read lots
speak to other suitors
go to meetings/seminars
she responds to all this

And, of course
if you are able
wholehearted commitment
and
where does that come from
(if at all)?
there's another mystery for you.

Sincerely,

Mike

PS
And her other name, Sam?
Her real name is Reality

Religion making sense of the world

Religions are quite different to the above and they make sense of the world in various ways. One common way is to attribute everything to the will of a supreme creator – God. It must be pointed out that many religions describe their God in anthropomorphic terms: a powerful, male ruler wanting to be constantly praised and reminded of his power and often, defying moral philosophy, delivering collective punishment to the enemies of his religion, commonly associated with a different, specific, competing culture. In such ways, together with extreme rewards and punishments, religions help bind specific societies together.

Unlike the provisional laws of science, religions commonly teach explicit, absolute truth: absolute because it is revealed by God. And in some cases, even written, 'sacred' texts can be seen as conveying absolute truths even though no language can ever carry absolute truth. Language is too frail to carry such a burden and is dependent on the influences of cultures we're not sure about. We are never *absolutely* sure about any culture and language, modern or old. In practice, the interpretation of God's wishes, or of sacred texts, is given solely by the clergy. This clerical power is jealously guarded: *at one time, the Christian laity was forbidden to read the Bible under pain of <u>hellfire for all eternity</u>.* This added more power to the social control and social adhesion exerted by the alpha clergy and thus usefully (in *biological*, survival terms) added to the likelihood of rapid and concerted responses to danger. William Tyndale was the first man ever to print the New Testament in the English language. Tyndale also went on to be the first to translate much of the Old Testament from the original Hebrew into English, but was executed in 1536 for the 'crime' of printing the scriptures in English. I repeat – Tyndale was executed for printing the Bible in English. Is this not pathological control by the clergy? His friends published entire Bibles in the English language for the first time, and within one year of Tyndale's death. These Bibles were primarily his work. For many people, the teaching of a God-given account of the universe and our place in it, gives a feeling of absolute certainty to our understanding.

It is striking that numerous religious prophets advocated altruism as the actual, practical core of their teaching.

From another perspective, it's interesting that the French theologian and <u>non</u>-believer Simone Wiel described the essence of prayer as a state of openness. It is not the obedience to practices demanded by alpha clergy. She taught students in the order of St. Dominican that being open is being open to everything and according to Wiel is more truly prayer than is merely petitioning God for something. The same concept of openness has been applied to art of all kinds and also to the idea of love. The reasons for the variety of religions and their often-contradictory truths are discussed in more detail later, as is their role as social glue and social 'enforcers'. It's also interesting that the *process* of science is intrinsically open, despite any inadequacies of its participants: testing ideas, discussions, seminars, editors, referees, open publication and availability to anyone.

HUMANITY'S KEY PROBLEMS

Contents

BROAD INTRODUCTION

The knowledge on waking
That in this legal wilderness
No rights exist

The humiliation of being able
To change almost nothing,
And seizing upon the nothing
Which then leads to another impasse

The example of those who resist
Being bombarded to dust.

Verses from 'Seven levels of despair by John Berger ('Collected Poems' 2014).

A largely unmentioned and sometimes unmentionable aspect of cultures is that of past evil behaviour. We tend to hide it. We tend to become oblivious of past evil behaviour or perhaps believe that gross evil behaviour is likely only from others. This is why this book is initially emphasising the many instances of extreme evil behaviour that we are *all* capable of. I'd like to make it clear that in mentioning the problems caused by people in any particular country or nation, I mean humans with the history, intellectual and other environmental influences and overall culture of the particular society. It's obvious that the humans of one country are *potentially* no more violent or territorial or intelligent than those of another. There are bigger genetic differences within so-called 'racial' human groups than there are between them: similarly, for the members of any religious faith.

Incompatibility of rationality and instincts

> *The evolution of the brain not only overshot the needs*
> *of pre-historic man, it is the only example of evolution*
> *providing a species with an organ which it does not*
> *know how to use.*

Arthur Koestler

Human reason finds it difficult / impossible to cope with the swamping effects of instincts. The Buddha and others used meditation as a means of dealing with instinctive behaviour. But, the purpose of an instinct is to propel us down biological survival paths such as leading to procreation or away from danger to safety, the acquisition or protection of territory, or obedience to leaders (alphas) and the instincts associated with alpha behaviour.

Unmet needs

Any unmet *human* need, as given in the earlier section, is associated with social problems. These will arise in individuals and in all aspects of human society. For example, not belonging/lack of community, not being part of the natural world or suppression of creativity, all result in problems of numerous and various sorts. Inadequate habitation or even *homelessness* is an immediate problem that requires resolution in numerous countries, even rich ones such as the UK (in 2018, there is a disgraceful, predictable shortage of housing) and the USA. Surely homelessness needs to be addressed *before* any expenditure on public art or on a space race? Unmet needs contribute to the problems dealt with below.

Problems caused by humans of all nationalities and in different historical periods

For example, swept up in a particular medieval, religious tide, we can broadly have clerical participation in the vicious, intensely cruel, *official* Roman Catholic Church's Spanish Inquisition.

There were unspeakable horrors of human torture and humans burnt alive in the name of God. And in the same place but at a later time, have peaceful, kind descendants of largely the same faith. We now have the same church denouncing such things and also expressing guilt at these past sins via a papal commission. The USA, currently the world's only superpower, is widely criticised for the violent and widespread use of this power and its earlier racist slavery. In fact, until relatively recently, the USA was almost entirely populated by people from Europe, originally with their different languages and cultures, together with, more recently, Spanish-speaking people. The indigenous inhabitants are a tiny minority, having been 'ethnically cleansed' by the colonising *Europeans*/new Americans. The racist, ethnic cleansing of indigenous Australian Aborigines was started by the *British*. The appalling, racist, white Afrikaners' treatment of indigenous black South Africans was by former Dutch people.

Like everywhere else, these countries are populated by humans, notably influenced by their history, including the power of their alpha males. In recent years 'we' British have also reviled Germans because of the inhuman, disgusting Holocaust, Japanese because of their cruelty in World War 2 and Israelis because of their ruthless and continuing vicious treatment of the dispossessed Palestinians. And we British, without our powerful, former empire, have much to regret and others to remember. It's probably wrong to see the *people* (so-called 'races') doing these evil acts as evil 'them' (not us); it's also unhelpful. Much of this evil, human *behaviour* is a result of instincts and circumstances – humans *driven* by innate, mindless, primate forces. Hopefully we can alter the circumstances: instincts are quite another matter. It is not the Germans or Americans or Australians or Dutch or English *per se* – it's we humans. It's also clear that not seeing the nakedness of the alpha-male Emperor helps towards our social glue as well as giving him relatively unopposed powers to seek more powers. We should constantly bear in mind that potentially humans can all, individually or collectively, do appalling acts of extreme evil. It's not always 'them' who do such things.

Genetically, we are closely similar. To repeat myself, our human predecessors (*Homo*) have been in Africa for about 2.5 million years. Anatomically modern humans appeared in Africa only about 200,000 years ago and started to leave Africa as recently as about 60,000 years ago. Lately, several reputable authors (notably Steven Pinker in his 'The Better Angels of our Nature' – see later) have shown that in numerous ways the world has become less violent. For example, if violent deaths are normalised to deaths per unit of population, then such deaths are declining. Violent deaths in Europe and elsewhere have thus been shown to decline. The RC Church no longer burns people alive or drowns so-called witches or has arbitrary power to do as it wishes. Nevertheless, do these selected statistics show that the world is improving and is less dangerous? Nation states carry out torture in secrecy, although sometimes it is later exposed. As I type, the situation in Syria is beyond bad, with hospitals and schools bombed by Russians! Dr Lina Khatib of Chatham House, UK has pointed out that torture has been unchanged and important in Syrian prison life for *decades* since the rule of Bashar al-Assad's father (see later under 'A grim reminder'). And we humans have nuclear weapons, mini versions already used twice and near accidents several times.

The grossly adverse/cruel situation for women has improved in some places but many nations tolerate widespread extreme cruelty. An important, unresolved issue is the deeply rooted antagonism towards women having public power or voice (this is specifically dealt with later). But crucially, our basic, primate instincts have not disappeared, and extremely bad things still happen frequently and on a huge scale. These instincts are alive and well: they do not change quickly. Their massive role is largely unrecognised and needs to be addressed explicitly – that is, innate impulses (dictionary definition) that miss the human, thinking parts of the brain.

Growing inequality and its correlates

Significantly, power in the shape of money is now and increasingly concentrated as never before in the hands of very few people, often called 'the 1 per cent'. Oxfam is publicising the fact (2015) that this 1 per cent will shortly own more than the rest of us put together!

The world population was around 7 billion in 2012. Given that about a quarter to a half of the world's GDP (about $78 trillion) is owned by merely some thousands of people (much in tax havens), then very approximately we should perhaps talk about 'the 0.000001 per cent'. This statistic was unknown to me until recently and is not publicised. It is surely shocking. It's interesting to calculate, given that the amount stashed away in tax havens is about $20 trillion (figures vary somewhat), for a world population of about 7 billion, and assuming a cost-free recovery, then each human could receive about $2,800 from this money. This would leave the 'owners' with their homes and very likely much more than adequate personal finance, relatively unharmed. They could also be de-criminalised. In other words, without damaging these people, everyone else could receive about $2,800. If the money was distributed unevenly, say to the bottom 1 billion, then they would each receive about $20,000. This would leave the world's disclosed total expenditure on armaments ('defence') still at about $1.4 trillion. In a sane (human) world, the cost of providing homes, food and clean water for everyone would be relatively easy. Likely it's impossible, alas, alas. It is not simply that income inequality is rather distasteful – it's linked to serious social pathology.

My own country, the UK, is demonstrably and rapidly descending into an extraordinarily unequal society with the proven, attendant social evils closely associated with inequality. We are moving up the straight lines that show the correlation between inequality and numerous social ills ('The Spirit Level' by Wilkinson and Pickett) and getting ever closer to the most *unequal* of those countries with reliable statistics, the USA. More slowly, the EC is moving in the same direction. A UK right-wing coalition government dealt with an extreme financial crisis – in common with many other nations – and did so by a rapid reduction in 'welfare' (designated as 'The Nanny State') and eliminating numerous social supports, including those for the poor, the elderly and the 'working poor'. The UK Joseph Rowntree Foundation (2014) has monitored the rise in poverty for young adults and those in work as a result of insecure employment such as zero-hours 'contracts'. Lack of affordable housing plays a role.

Political commentators are pointing out that the UK Tories, recently (2015) and continuing (2017), elected with a barely workable majority under the cloak of a financial crisis, are implementing long-standing right-wing ideologies regarding reducing 'the state' (welfare, education and health, but not armaments). The International Red Cross is now opening food kitchens in the rich UK. There are also current reports of large increases in child abuse published by the UK National Society for the Prevention of Cruelty to Children (NSPCC). UK prisons are overcrowded: riots and suicides in prison are at a high. A dismantling of the UK NHS by privatisation is taking place as I write. All this, our leaders repeatedly say, is partly in order to afford our standing army and nuclear submarines that will gain 'us' (i.e. 'them') a 'seat at the top table' (the former Prime Minister David Cameron's phrase) for our elite. In February 2016, a senior US diplomat strongly advised the UK to renew trident when the time comes on the grounds that it will maintain us as a leading nation and maintain the UK 'special relationship' with the USA. Is this not entirely alpha 'power talk' by the world's most powerful (but socially deprived) alph-nation?

The UK did extremely well at the 2016 Olympic Games, astonishingly coming in second place, before China, with its gold medals. But this has been linked to the precision targeting of pre-games funding of about £4-5 million *per medal.* This helps towards our alpha status. The homeless, the hungry and the ill-educated could have used this finance. The crucial education of our infants and young could have benefitted by a few hundred million £UK. But this would not have contributed *soon* to our alpha status, if at all. The UK has a diseased society and the above are the *symptoms* of the pathology. Little attention is given to the feral, ultra-rich who caused the financial catastrophe – their taxes have been *reduced* on the stated grounds that it will assist our economy and attract rich people to live with us! It is *not* well-being and happiness that was the object of the recent UK right-wing coalition government: it was the 'economy' and

> in the last decade or so it barely benefits 'the 99 per cent' (similarly in the USA).

But, as shown by numerous studies (see above and later), the economy greatly benefits the '1 per cent'. The main UK parties are *not* proposing a tax on financial transactions and *not* a land value tax and *not* a progressively-banded council tax and *not* a windfall tax on the wealth of the numerous *multi-billionaires*. And how about the widespread tax avoidance and evasion? No, that's the 'us'. It's the already poor, 'the them' that will carry the burden through reduced welfare and other public spending cuts. Recently (November, 2014), 'legal' tax avoidance on an 'industrial scale' involving the EU state of Luxembourg, the UK and some of the world's largest multinational corporations, has been exposed. Later, I mention evidence that the UK itself already is a tax haven. And there is massive UK state propaganda labelling tax virtually as evil and those on welfare as being 'scroungers'. And the former UK Prime Minister announced that he was putting together tough anti-strike laws to reduce the only human powers that some workers possess.

'Humans' with fully expressed alpha-male instincts cannot tolerate dissent from those led. And we have relentless propaganda about 'over-regulated', 'rule-mad', foreign Europe. Much of which, in fact, are rules to protect workers' rights and workers' safety at work:

such protections cost money that could go to the 1 per cent. And in 2016 the UK voted to leave the EU (Brexit) by a small majority which has resulted in a split nation. In 2017, it has become clear that few, if any, had any <u>idea of the consequences</u>. It seems possible that a big influence on the vote was the *instinct* to escape the foreign influence on UK affairs – foreigners, territory and obedience to our right-wing political alphas. In many institutions and nations, such an important, potentially divisive change requires a decisive majority such as two thirds or more. Otherwise, there could be a divisive split within the nation or organisation.

As well as the bad social consequences mentioned above, the increasing inequality in my home country is also linked to insecure jobs not generating a living wage or not even a so-called minimum wage. Attracting rich entrepreneurs is adding to our non-living-wage economy and with the entrepreneurs and their companies paying little or no taxes in our country, money is disastrously being *siphoned <u>away from</u> the local economy*. Such behaviour propels us towards our low wage, 'working poor' society, as in the USA with its extreme inequality and associated bad social statistics. In the UK of centuries ago, wealthy landowners would build 'stately' homes and huge 'stately' gardens but using mostly local labour for both the building and the maintenance. Today, much of the generated wealth is instantly siphoned off and locked in secret, off-shore tax havens, depriving the local economy.

The 'economy' does not reflect well-being or happiness, merely turnover. It seems likely that for *biological* (<u>not</u> evil) reasons, we (and much more slowly, the EC) are following the individualistic, antisocial trajectory of the USA. The USA, with the world's richest economy, has the worst social statistics for which reliable data exists (see later). Also, there are shocking USA statistics about how rich people and rich companies are heavily subsidised, avoid taxes and hide profits, documented in 'Take the Rich Off Welfare' by Mark Zepezauer and in numerous, detailed publications (simply Google his name) by Noam Chomsky.

Labelling the Americans or 'the rich' as evil is unhelpful. I wonder if the USA has *ever* been an integrated, relatively equal 'community'. At the risk of over-generalising, Europeans (mostly), with their *different* languages, *different* religions and *different* cultures, colonised *different* regions of (the now) USA. They (still mainly European) slaughtered the indigenous people and fought amongst each other in wars of different kinds and developed a large, Southern, slave economy. The USA culture is varied, but so-called 'rugged individualism' (or more accurately, 'winner takes all') is prominent in much of the art forms and in popular culture. Later, I comment on my personal, family experience of life in the USA and the extraordinary, consistent generosity and kindness of 'ordinary' Americans. With my family, legally domiciled in the UK, I have also lived for extended periods in the USA, Canada, Austria, Switzerland and France. For our family, without question, the Americans were the most hospitable. How this is compatible with such aggressive, violent and dangerous (for the world) US foreign policy is dealt with later (USA as a special case).

Obviously, there is some truth in such labels and numerous *acts* are evil, but such labels alone are unhelpful in solving these problems. The underlying causes of these evils are biological:

a.   primate instincts that evolved for the short-term survival of small groups of animals living in trees (without human consciousness) are often inappropriate for today's heavily populated, different world; and

b.   unhealthy, early human development, unmet human needs, including connectedness, belonging and expression of human instincts including those for creativity; and

c.   the need to live in a society with inclusive economic and political structures.

After now, after briefly listing the obvious individual and large-scale problems facing the world, I will then focus on the exceptionally serious examples of violent aggression. What I write is not new, but it is instinctively ignored or even unrecognised. This ignoring and not recognising is part of the problem. For this reason, I feel obliged to add myself to those attempting to make the true situation as explicit and clear as possible and with specific examples.

Individual and global problems

Apart from the above, currently <u>much of the world</u> faces on an individual, daily basis: crime, poverty, disease, unemployment, housing shortage, hunger, sexism and violence against women, racism, pornography, ageism and homophobia. On a daily, *global* scale: war, ethnic 'cleansing', organised atrocities, slavery and human trafficking, sexism, unsustainable population increases, environmental destruction, insufficient food and energy, poverty, organised crime, web pornography and loss of community. We now have the <u>increasing primacy of money</u> over almost all the world's structures and the associated behaviour of the '1 per cent', successfully devising ways to siphon off large chunks of the world's GDP. This process is enabled/facilitated by massive and ongoing developments in IT and Artificial Intelligence (AI). And we have widespread, numerous, nuclear weapons *already catastrophically used twice* and of a world-damaging power barely imaginable as well as real risks with near accidents, rarely mentioned, from nuclear technology, which will be dealt with later.

On an evolutionary basis, one might ask the question, how long will it be before they are used again in anger, or by accident? Is it in the immediate future, or in the next decade, or the next century, or in the next millennium? What are the actuarial odds on them never being used again? *These odds are surely affected by them having already been used twice and by the several near accidents.* But our alphas are impelled towards short-term fixes. A nuclear explosion by accident or design has catastrophically long, long-term consequences. But being an alpha with access to nuclear weapons is a badge of honour and a sign of 'alpha-hood'.

Imminent problems
Water shortages
Imminently, the world will have shortages of water and fuel, and global warming (UN Reports), leading to mass migrations. Indeed, China is reported to have problems of water availability currently (2017).

Global warming
I will not attempt a comprehensive account of global warming but give a brief account. Numerous independent sources accept the imminent dangers of global warming – simply 'Google' global warming. For example, the World-Wide Fund for Nature (WWF) is an international non-governmental organisation founded in 1961, working in the field of wilderness preservation, and the reduction of humanity's footprint on the environment. It was started by eminent, reputable naturalists and ecologists. It reports that a mere 2°C rise in temperature will put 30 per cent of species at high risk of extinction, marine food chains will collapse and ecosystems could completely disappear, while shortages of food and water are predicted to trigger massive movements of people, leading to migration, conflict and famine. In 2013, the planet passed a dangerous milestone when atmospheric levels of carbon dioxide exceeded 400 parts per million, prompting the scientific community to advocate renewed vigour in efforts to combat climate change. However, current commitments by the world's governments fall *far short* of the greenhouse gas reductions needed to limit the global temperature rise to 2°C by 2020. We need to take urgent measures to slow down and reduce the extent of the climate crisis. Global temperatures have been rising for over a century, speeding up in the last few years, and are now the highest on record. This causes massive negative impacts such as the melting of Arctic sea ice, prolonged heatwaves and rising sea

levels. Bangladesh is in danger of being totally submerged. The situation is further harmed by the activities of 'climate deniers', with bogus 'think tanks' funded by energy companies and *now in President Donald Trump's cabinet*, discussed below.

Recent and current wars

The vicious war in Syria has escalated from attacks on 'ordinary' civilian, domestic targets to napalm and poison gas attacks on *schools*. The snipers on President Assad's side have targeted unborn babies in wombs as part of a sick 'game' in which the body area targeted changes on a daily basis (The London Times, October 19th, 2013). And their opponents have responded also with vicious reprisals. In April 2017, after the earlier catastrophic destruction of Aleppo and elsewhere, Syria, with the backing of others, has illegally used poison gas against its own citizens. And the USA has responded by destroying the airfield used in the illegal gassing.

The disasters/wars in Africa and the Middle East have led to people trying to escape via sea and in inadequate boats which sink and require rescue. In November 2014, humanitarian attempts were made to alter a proposed *policy* of *not* helping. It is unkindly said (including by people of a religious faith) that such help stimulates yet more migrants to travel, as if they were unwanted animals. Similarly immoral, so-called Eurosceptics have warned (December 2015) that providing the 'living wage' as opposed to the 'minimum wage' will lead to a new boom in migrants. So, not paying fellow citizens a living wage is a way to deal with a more important problem – the migration of unwanted refugees!

Unmanageable speed of change

There is little evidence that political leaders are aware of the social dangers of rapid change. We are accelerating towards problems of mass unemployment and the downgrading of quality employment by the use of smart machines. These have massive and increasing digital power, capable of replacing humans and altering entire professions. It's noteworthy that in writing this book, over the last few years, I have asked questions directly to 'Google' and usually and increasingly, get an instant, helpful answer. It has learned to 'understand' questions. An account of the various causes of the inevitable and massive social problems are given later ('Causes', page 153).

Early USA presidents' warnings fulfilled: Triumph of corporate money

Warnings from early presidents about misuse of corporate power
It might be judged strange to list the election of Donald J. Trump as posing a major global danger. But his election is important more for what and who is behind him than for who he is, although the two are related. Later, ('Political Structures – USA as special case'), reference is made to the repeated warnings of early presidents about corporate power destroying democracy. For example, a quotation from *over two centuries ago* from Thomas Jefferson, President of the USA, <u>1801</u>-09, states: 'I hope we shall… crush in its birth the aristocracy of our moneyed corporations which dare already to challenge our government in a trial of strength and bid defiance to the laws of our country'. From the very beginnings of the *dis*united USA there have been relentless attempts by corporations to reduce workers' rights on such as pay, holidays, pensions, security and hours of work. Some corporations have increasingly seen their workers as not fellow citizens but as 'them, not us' – that is, a means to wealth that needs to be exploited. Concerted, repeated and successful efforts have prevented a humane national health service *for all*, including the poor, from being established. Similarly, corrupt attempts were successfully made to reduce/eliminate tax worldwide by corporations. These 'successes' are linked to the gross inequality of USA society with its attendant, extreme and world-leading statistics on social illnesses.

'Misinformation Machines', fake 'Think Tanks' and the election of President Donald J. Trump
There are now numerous publications detailing the 'how' of the corporations' shady successes that led to the election of President Trump. His election and his irrational behaviour are shocking examples of an alpha male (and of those behind him) assuming a right to almost absolute power. For this reason, I now spend some time on the people surrounding the President of the USA.

For example, the investigative journalist George Monbiot has exposed details of fake 'think tanks' and the origins of the 'dark (hidden) money' sources that support them. Put all together as a system, Monbiot calls it a 'Misinformation Machine'. He writes regularly in the UK's 'The Guardian', is rational and provides key references to people and organisations. For example, 'Dark Arts', issue 3rd February 2017: 'How a dark (hidden) money network is taking power on both sides of the Atlantic'. Also, 'The Misinformation Machine 2017', issue 30th November 2017: 'Donald Trump's staff are drawn from an opaque network of fake, corporate-funded 'think tanks' and fake 'grassroots campaigns'. These fake 'think tanks' are funded by mega-rich corporations or mega industrial conglomerates such as military, tobacco, energy or alcohol. The media (ultra-rich owners) offer their biased views as a 'balance' to conventional science. They clearly do not understand what science is. Science is *not* unsubstantiated *assertions*. President Trump's instant outpourings of presidential edicts surely did not come from President Trump directly, but from corporation-funded fake experts. George Monbiot (The (UK) Guardian, Tuesday 4th April 2017) has pointed out that '…. billionaires and the organisations they run, demand freedom from something they call 'red tape'. What they mean by red tape is public protection'. This can include a 'living wage', pensions, vacations, reasonable job protection and working conditions.

And now (March 2018), we have the evidence from investigative reporters (UK Observer, The Guardian and UK Channel 4 documentary) of their malign influence on social matters, notably hundreds of elections worldwide and involving a network including billionaire Robert Mercer and his company Cambridge Analytica. It is dealt with in more detail below and later.

Appointment of zealots

In recent times President Trump has appointed extremist zealots – i.e. non-rational, non-evidence-based, 'Chimp'-behaving extremists to his cabinet (see classification in 'The Chimp

Paradox' by Steve Peters). In December 2016, he put Myron Ebell, a *climate-change denier* who's been paid by Exxon Mobil and the Koch brothers, *in charge* of the Environmental Protection Agency (EPA) transition! Ebell is not a scientist and has no degrees or qualifications in climate science. He serves as director of global warming and environmental policy at the Competitive Enterprise Institute (CEI), a libertarian advocacy group in Washington DC. In practice, that means he spends his time rejecting and trying to discredit scientists who work to understand the global climate. Ebell says that he 'believes' climate scientists are part of a coordinated 'global warming movement'. In an interview with 'Business Insider' in August 2016, Ebell repeatedly referred to climate scientists as 'global warming alarmists' and *asserted* that climate research is in fact an arm of a coordinated political movement.

Fake disagreement about global warming
Scott Pruitt, Donald Trump's later head of the US EPA, has dismissed a basic scientific understanding of climate change by denying that carbon dioxide emissions are a primary cause of global warming. Pruitt has said that he did not believe the release of CO_2, a heat-trapping gas, was pushing global temperatures upwards. 'I think that measuring with precision human activity on the climate is something very challenging to do and there's *tremendous disagreement* about the degree of impact, so no, I would not agree that it's a primary contributor to the global warming that we see,' he told the US CNBC. No, that assertion is not true. There is not tremendous disagreement among scientists. It's fake, paid-for disagreement by fake 'think tanks' whose purpose it is to disagree. This stance puts Pruitt at odds with his own agency, which states on its website that carbon dioxide is the 'primary greenhouse gas that is contributing to recent climate change'. This finding is backed by NASA, which calls CO_2 'the most important long-lived 'forcing' of climate change'. It is also backed by the equivalents of the UK Royal

Society worldwide. As I write, Scott Pruitt is seeking to annul the rules protecting rivers from pollution, workers from exposure to pesticides and everyone from climate change!

Q. How can this happen?
A. By having Donald Trump as President of the USA.

Scientists have understood for more than a century that CO_2 traps heat. Atmospheric concentrations have increased by more than a third since the Industrial Revolution, driven by the burning of fossil fuels and deforestation. The Intergovernmental Panel on Climate Change Report from 2014, which summarised the findings of *2,000 international scientists,* states it is 'extremely likely' that the steep rise in CO_2, along with other greenhouse gases such as methane, has caused most of the global warming experienced since the 1950s. Yet, the Trump administration has announced (2017) that 'EPA studies data must undergo *political* review before release'.

**Appointment and resignation of White House
National Security Advisor**
Another dubious, high-level appointment was ex-General Michael Flynn as the White House national security advisor. The US House Oversight Committee was examining the General's activities before he joined Trump's White House. It was likely to focus on Flynn's contacts with foreign nationals and look at fees he may have received from foreign governments, including Russia and Turkey. US intelligence officials had serious concerns about him because of his history of contacts with Moscow and his encounter with a woman who had trusted access to Russian spy agency records. Numerous sources claimed that US and British intelligence officers discussed Flynn's 'worrisome' behaviour well *before* his appointment last year by Donald Trump. Flynn was forced to quit in February, after 24 days in the job. He resigned

when it emerged *he had lied* to Vice President Mike Pence. Flynn said he had not discussed lifting US sanctions on Russia with Sergei Kislyak, Moscow's US Ambassador, but later admitted this was untrue. Flynn indicated he was willing to testify before the FBI and congressional committees about potential links between the Trump campaign and Russia *in exchange for immunity*. Recently (2017), the FBI Director, James Comey, confirmed that his agency was investigating possible collusion between Trump and Russia to influence the outcome of the US election! And in January 2018, we have Donald Trump praising himself as a 'stable genius'! All this would be a laughable farce if Donald J. Trump was not President of the USA.

Non-evidence-based assertions by President Donald J. Trump
Mr Trump is definitely not Leonardo or Aristotle. He has boasted that he never reads anything. Examples of Donald Trump's *non-evidence-based assertions are as follows*. He *asserted* that the 'concept of global warming was created by and for the Chinese in order to make US manufacturing non-competitive'. He *asserted* that it as 'junk science'. In March 2017, Mr Trump was openly planning the following: to pull out of the Paris Agreement for Climate Change *asserting* that it was 'living in cloud cuckoo land'. He plans to cancel payments for UN climate programmes, shut down President Obama's Clean Power Plan, thereby allowing coal plants to emit unlimited amounts of climate pollution, revive the Keystone XL Pipeline and open protected *public lands to coal mining and fracking*. And as Christmas 2016 approached, he 'tweeted' that the USA needed a *massive increase in expenditure on its nuclear weapons programme*. This despite the USA spending as much as the next 10 or 11 countries combined on defence! He is cancelling 'Obama Care', the only significant healthcare available to the poor of the USA. Trump is proposing to remove funds from the US Chemical Safety Board that investigates lethal industrial incidents.

All of this is entwined with the overall corrupt practices

of the ultra-rich and the siphoning off of around 20-30% of the world's GDP out of local economies and into foreign locations including tax havens. There has been an effective and coordinated campaign to make tax an ugly word. Happily, this has not (yet) corrupted the more equal societies at the good end of the equality/inequality graph. But without taxes, who will pay for road repairs and cleaning, public transport, public libraries, parks and art galleries, schools, hospitals and other public health facilities? These facilities humanise our living environment. The mega-rich alphas typically use privately funded institutions. Inappropriate alpha instincts propel them. And now they have acquired Donald J. Trump as a spearhead.

On a daily basis, in the first few months since his election, President Trump is making extreme, controversial decisions and dealing with scandals related to his senior appointments. President Donald J. Trump and his corporate backers are increasingly appearing to be a serious threat to the world's natural ecology, are dehumanising society, reducing community, increasing feelings of 'us and them', looting vast sums of money and are a threat to preventing nuclear disasters and to world peace. A modestly hopeful sign is the widespread opposition by individuals, notably by American women, with house meetings taking place across the country.

Even so, the hopes of USA President Thomas Jefferson over two centuries ago (**1801**-09) and numerous presidents since then, are further away from being realised. May I again quote him 'I hope we shall... crush in its birth the aristocracy of our moneyed corporations which dare already to challenge our government in a trial of strength and bid defiance to the laws of our country'. Alas, they are now running the USA.

How to hijack democracy: a major threat

Light was cast on an otherwise shadowy global operation involving big data in the UK weekend newspaper, 'The Observer', Sunday May 7th, 2017. The writer was Carole Cadwalladr. She showed how a secret network of computer scientists 'hijacked our democracy'. It involved Cambridge Analytica, 90% owned by billionaire Robert Mercer, a closely linked company 'AggregateIQ' and a network of influential people, mostly on the far, far right. Techniques had been devised for the military to influence propaganda and elections in nations that were of interest to the UK and USA military. These techniques, involving detailed knowledge of individuals' preferences, were used to influence electioneering. They were called 'digital targeting campaigns'. They were used for Donald Trump's presidential campaign and multiple other Republican campaigns, mostly funded by Mercer, who also 'helped' the UK's Nigel Farage 'Leave.EU' campaign.

The network was laid out in a centrefold in the newspaper, giving details of the various people and organisations involved. Briefly, notable linked individuals were Robert Mercer, President Trump and his chief strategist Steve Bannon, and Nigel Farage. In 2014, Bannon opened the London arm of his vicious news website Breitbart to support UKIP (the UK Independence Party). Bannon told the New York Times that this was the latest front 'in our current cultural and political war'. Carole Cadwalladr has indirect evidence that:

a. Bannon considers Britain as key to his plans for changing the *entire world order*; and
b. he believes that to change politics, you first have to change the culture.

And on a daily basis, President Trump and his inner team are attacking journalists, attacking the FBI (investigating his links with Russia) and appointing far right extremists to important judicial posts. This is a truly dangerous development for democracy, especially when considered with the evidence unravelled by George Monbiot (see above) and others about the influence of billionaires financing fake think tanks, defending their interests over many decades by telling untruths about, for example, military danger, tobacco, alcoholic drinks and energy, and denying global warming. The world now faces unprecedented danger. As emphasised under 'Politics', allowing corporations' money to buy power and to influence elections is proven to be bad in many ways. Telling untruths about the harm caused by major industries is despicable. But using the latest IT and AT, via mega personal data, to influence the results of elections must also be stopped. Cadwalladr's article deserves to be read widely.

In a further development, an undercover investigation by the UK Channel 4 News (19th March 2018), in association with the Observer, Cambridge Analytica executives claimed to offer a range of dark services. The UK Guardian (20th March 2018) reported (Graham-Harrison, Cadwalladr and Osborne) boasts of the dirty tricks used to swing elections. Undercover reporters of Channel 4 were told by bosses of how honey traps, former spies from Britain and Israel looking for political dirt and fake news can be used to help clients. The UK Information Commissioner, Elizabeth Denham, criticised Cambridge Analytica for being un co-operative with an investigation as she confirmed that her watchdog would apply for a warrant to help her examine the firm's activities. It was also reported that 'Number 10' was 'very concerned' over Facebook data breach by Cambridge Analytica.

> *Did a non-UK billionaire, aided by non-UK, far-right-wing zealots, spending huge sums of money, bring about Brexit by tipping the election?*

Note: Was it not a mistake for an issue so deeply important for the UK as leaving the EU (regardless of the consequences or terms) to be based on a yes or no 51% vote? It's common elsewhere, in such exceptionally important and potentially divisive circumstances, to require a two-thirds majority.

A brief note on Donald J. Trump, the person

Sidney Blumenthal, a former advisor to President Clinton and a biographer of USA presidents, has written an article in the London Review of Books – 'A Short History of the Trump Family', volume 39, No 4. 16th February 2017. While reading this article, I felt and still feel strong sympathy for Donald Trump. As a child, he had little chance of developing his humanity. I quote Blumenthal: *'Reckoning with Trump means descending into the place that made him. What he represents, above all, is the triumph of an underworld of predators, hustlers, mobsters, clubhouse politicians and tabloid sleaze that festered in a corner of New York City, a vindication of his mentor, the Mafia lawyer Roy Cohn, a figure unknown to the vast majority of enthusiasts who jammed Trump's rallies and hailed him as the authentic voice of the people'.* A young boy, loving and mimicking his father, had to accept the above. What a start in life! It explains Trump's behaviour. It does not explain why he was elected.

What now follows is a focus on serious examples of violent aggression. That is, anti-women behaviour, war, 'the war on drugs', slavery and racism, religion and any lessons learned.

VIOLENT AGGRESSION: ABUSE AND DISCRIMINATION AGAINST WOMEN

He tells her

> *He tells her that the earth is flat –*
> *He knows the facts, and that is that.*
> *In altercations fierce and long*
> *She tries her best to prove him wrong.*
> *But he has learned to argue well.*
> *He calls her arguments unsound*
> *And often asks her not to yell.*
> *She cannot win. He stands his ground.*
> *The planet goes on being round.*

Wendy Cope

The above poem depicts a relatively normal example of Man's patronising attitude to Woman. But there is much worse. If there was ever a case of society closing its eyes to a gross violation of humanity it involves the treatment of women. It has been a relatively hidden scandal, somehow acceptable and natural. Men and even women are blind to it. Women are a special case of discrimination and are often a target of male violence in different cultures and religions, going back to the earliest recorded history. To me, it has been baffling. I have read numerous books and papers on this 'subject' and spoken with numerous feminists. I'm still baffled by the extreme examples, but now offer some broad explanations below. It may seem surprising to the reader, but *I believe that improving the social situation of women is a key route to improving humanity's problems.* Of special interest and concern is the deeply rooted male objection to women having public power (see below). We need a feminine approach to many issues. The macho male approach, evolved for the short-term survival of small groups of tree dwellers within 'Mother Nature', is a handicap in numerous situations in the modern world. An increase in *femininity* would help save the world from its inappropriate, macho, primate culture.

> *Our problems are less to do with men versus women,*
> *than with macho versus feminine.*

Dimensions of the problem of man's abuse of women

> *The emotional, sexual and psychological*
> *stereotyping of females begins when the*
> *doctor says: It's a girl.*
>
> **Shirley Chisholm**

The huge extent of the abuse of women is only just starting to be recognised widely. It has been under the social radar screen for most of us, possibly since the origin of humans. That the idea of human female inferiority exists across cultures and historical epochs suggests a *biological* source. I had no idea of the extent of the abuse and I believe that I am typical. I recently saw a documentary on the role of women in the life of Jesus. I was shocked that I had missed something so obviously true. The TV programme (Channel 4, 8th April 2018, 8 pm) was presented by Professors Joan Taylor (King's College, London) and Helen Bond (School of Divinity, Edinburgh). I suggest that the reader Google their names and follows their work. In hindsight, what they are revealing is blindingly obvious once one opens one's eyes. First of all, in the middle of the varied circumstances of the writing of the gospels, is the fact that they were all written by men, with the assumptions of men about women at that time (and now). Partly re-interpreting Mark's gospel, Taylor and Bond provide convincing evidence that Jesus had women disciples and that they went about in pairs, so that each could interact with their own gender. They also cast light on the role of Mary Magdalene and the removal of Martha and Mary from the record. Later, there was even a woman bishop. This lack of discrimination lasted until the time of the emperor Constantine who suppressed women, and all returned to 'normal'. If only the sexist church of Constantine and of today could learn from Jesus.

Extreme examples of man's abuse of women
India
In modern India, rape is relatively common. The culture clearly supports it. In India (May 2014), two women were gang raped and then killed by hanging by the neck from trees! The culprits remain free as I write. An Indian woman who disobeyed her family's wishes (also May, 2014) and married a man from another religion was stoned to death by her family outside a courthouse while the police did nothing. Individuals (not all) interviewed on live TV supported such a killing on the grounds of 'honour'. Apparently, for a *woman* to marry someone of a different religion it is to 'dishonour' her family and is deserving of such a vicious death. No, it is not! This is vicious, evil behaviour.

As I write this section, there is much publicity worldwide about an extraordinarily vicious gang rape, torture and murder of an Indian woman <u>carried out on a public bus as it travelled along its route</u> early in the morning. The 'respectable', professional defence lawyer publicly blamed the victim's *male* relatives for allowing her out at *such a time, even to attend her student classes.* I heard him shamelessly say this directly on UK TV. In India, religious and other commentators commonly and also shamelessly blame the <u>victims</u> for wearing clothing or cosmetic make-up that they consider inappropriate. It is as if the wearing of 'inappropriate' clothing is worse than violent rape or even justifies it! On the BBC news (2013), the Indian lawyer defending the accused 'bus' rapists, said that if his daughter wore such unsuitable clothing *'he would burn her alive'*! This lawyer not only thinks that his daughter is his property, and that she can be killed by him, but also that he can torture her and can brazenly say so publicly! I wonder if the India Bar Association disbarred him and dissociated itself from such a view. If not, then women using the 'law' in India need help.

China, Jordan, Bosnia

And, at the same time, there are stories of widespread abuse of women in China, including the frequent use of cigarette burns to humiliate, bully and maim. And it is widely tolerated amid deafening silence. Again as I write, there are camps in multi-religious, exceptionally humane and well-governed Jordan for the victims of the brutal Syrian conflict, with over a million humans in desperate need. Local men take advantage of this terrible situation and buy the marriage of young women and then force them into prostitution. And earlier, the 'rape camps' in the aftermath of the Bosnian war had thousands of women imprisoned and raped. In so many wars women are raped by men, but rarely as systematically as in Bosnia: and worldwide, forced marriages and the absence of human rights are rife. It is a crystal-clear human sickness that is widely tolerated. While women remain a minority among the combatants and perpetrators of war, they increasingly suffer the greatest harm. In contemporary conflicts, as many as 90 per cent of casualties are among civilians, most of whom are women and children. Women in war-torn societies can face specific and devastating forms of sexual violence, which are sometimes deployed systematically to achieve military or political objectives (United Nations Report).

Female genital mutilation.

In the UK and elsewhere today we have the vicious crime of female genital mutilation (FGM), defended as a 'cultural practice'! The Aztecs had the cultural practice of keeping an entire people subjugated mainly for regular, lethal blood sacrifices for their God. 'Cultural practice' cannot of itself be an unarguable justification for any act of violence. In the UK, FGM has been illegal since 1985 with known mutilations occurring since then, and only 3 decades later in 2014 is a prosecution being brought. The UK Department for International Development has recently launched a £35 million programme to address female genital mutilation (FGM) abroad but little has been done to help the <u>20,000 girls at risk from FGM in the UK and the 66,000 women living</u> <u>with the lifetime effects of such mutilation.</u>

Schoolgirl abduction.

A sect claiming to be Islamic, Boko-Haram, abducted 284 schoolgirls from their school in northern Nigeria, destroyed the school and in May 2014 threatened to sell the girls into slavery! In 2016 there was some, but little, hope regarding these lost young women. Some were found later. This so-called 'Islamic' group is against any education of women. Preventing any education and selling girls into slavery is surely not Islamic. But *what* is it?

Nazi camp for women, Ravensbruck.

Sarah Helm has written a book about a Nazi camp, Ravensbruck, used specifically for women. The book is called 'If this is a woman: inside Ravensbruck – Hitler's concentration camp for women'. It is an appalling story of torture and humiliation of about 130,000 women of which 10% were Jewish. About 50,000 women were murdered by shooting, starvation, worked to death or gassed. Syphilis was injected into the spinal cord of victims, women stripped naked and made to stand in the snow until they died. A young woman guard (Dorothea Binz) liked to lash the 'lunatics' locked in a small room in Block Ten. Towards the end of World War 2, the last Nazi mass extermination of 6,000 women was at Ravensbruck and *newly erected* gas chambers were used. The book is illustrated with shocking pictures, including one of a group of Ravensbruck SS members looking happy, healthy and entirely normal.

Major religions accept the inferiority of women
The Bible.

Numerous religions portray women as subservient to men. I focus on Judaism and Christianity partly because of my Christian background. Also, as I write this, the campaigning organisation Avaaz has responded to assertions about the Bible supporting the idea of marriage as being the loving union of one man and one woman. In the figure below are eight examples from the Bible (selected and published by Avaaz) showing the biblical acceptance of the inferiority of women. It adds to Professor Mary Beard's (see opposite) example of early Greek literature

Marriage in the Bible
Abstracted from a note by the Avaaz organisation

Man + woman
Genesis 2:24

- Wives subordinate to their husbands.
- Interfaith marriages forbidden.
- Marriages generally arranged not based on romantic love.
- Bride who cannot prove her virginity stoned to death

Man + wives + concubines

Abraham (2 concubines) Gideon (1), Nahor (1), Jacob (1), Eliphaz (1), Gideon (1 or more), Caleb (2), Manassah (1), Solomon (300), Balshazzar (more than 1)

Man + woman + woman's property
Genesis 16

- Man could acquire his wife's property including her slaves.

Man + woman + woman + woman (Polygamy)

Lamech (2 wives), Jacob (2 wives), Ashur (2), Gideon (many), Elkanah (2), David (many), Solomon (700), Rehaboam (3), Abijah (14), Jehoram, Joash, Ahab, Jeholachin, Belshazzar

Man + brother's widow
Levirate marriage Genesis 38-6-10

- Widow who had not borne a son required to marry her brother in law.
- Must submit sexually to her new husband.

Rapist + his victim
Deuteronomy 22-28-29

- Virgin who is raped must marry her rapist.
- Rapist must pay victim's father 50 shekels for loss of property.

Male soldier + prisoner of war
Numbers 31:1-18
Deuteronomy 21:11-14

- Under Moses' command, Israelites kill every Midlanite man, woman and child, save for the virgin girls who are taken as spoils of war.
- Wives must submit sexually to their new owners.

Male slave + female slave
Exodus 21:4

- Slave owner could assign female slaves to his male slaves.
- Female slaves must submit sexually to their new husbands.

'shutting up' women, even high-ranking ones such as Penelope, wife of Odysseus. The Bible portrays women as the property of men, has arranged marriages, the stoning of women to death who could not prove their virginity, and the acceptance of slavery.

The idea of biblical support for the idea of marriage as a loving twosome is not only not true, but absurd. A striking example, among many, is King Solomon, the epitome of wisdom, with hundreds of wives <u>and</u> concubines. I suggest that anyone who has not looked at the Old Testament should do so, even briefly, for self-education. Attitudes in the Old Testament to women, slaves and enemies are anti-Christian and probably anti any religion or movement advocating altruism as a core value. I suggest a start could be Leviticus; then compare this with Matthew 25 in the New Testament. <u>It is not possible</u> to make the two compatible; any reader can quickly see this for themselves without any clerical lies and manipulations. This incompatibility may partly explain why it was forbidden for laity (non-clergy) to read the Bible under punishment of hellfire for eternity.

Christianity, Saint Paul

The New Testament, through the post-Jesus apostle Paul, supports the inferiority of women. In the Letter of Paul to the Ephesians, he asserts: 'Wives, be subject to your husbands, as to the Lord. For the husband is the head of the wife as Christ is the head of the church ... As the church is subject to Christ, so let wives also be subject in everything to their husbands'. In the First Letter of Paul to Timothy he asserts: 'Let a woman learn in silence with all submissiveness. I (I?) permit no woman to teach or to have authority over men; she is to keep silent'. In the King James version translation of this letter we have: 'But I suffer not a woman to teach, nor to usurp authority over the man, but to be in silence'. These extracts, as well as generally helping to keep women as inferior to men, have served as a barrier to women becoming priests or bishops in the Anglican Church, recently overturned (2014). As for the relatively primate RC Church, such a change is currently unthinkable. I have never heard of any church authority denounce this aspect of Paul's teaching (or rather edict) as wrong and bad.

Christianity, the Virgin Mary
In the Bible's New testament, Mary receives little attention. There is the giving birth to Jesus in a stable and just before his public ministry Mary asks him to attend to the lack of wine at a reception and Jesus performs a miracle. And finally, she is mentioned at the end of Jesus' life. I have long wondered at this through my school years and later. In written work and in art, Joseph is later virtually ignored. And Mary is presented in popular, church art – paintings and statues - as docile, hands together in prayer with her head slightly bowed indicating submission and waiting to be told what to do next. Can it be that someone as developed as Jesus is the result of such a docile mother? Church teaching is that Jesus is fully human as well as being fully God. A human as fully developed as Jesus likely has parents of unusually good qualities as parents. It's unlikely that Mary was a docile, always at prayer and unquestioningly 'religious'. More likely, she and Joseph were strong, sensitive and intelligent parents. Could it be that Jesus' parents taught him the key importance of helping the needy?

Could it be that Mary appears so little in the new Testament simply because she is a woman? See later the ideas of Professor Mary Beard and earlier of Professors Joan Taylor and Helen Bond.

The link between social and personal health
The medical world has taken up anti-women violence as an urgent priority. The British journal, *The Lancet,* is a leader in this respect. It regularly focuses on the strong link between social and personal health. It published online a systematic review of the global prevalence of intimate partner homicide. It shows that, overall, 13·5% of homicides are committed by an intimate partner, and in female homicides the proportion of such murders is six times higher than in male homicides – 38·6% versus 6·3%. A recent issue of

The Lancet (Volume 383, Issue 9934, Pages e19-e20, 14 June 2014) focussed on 'Rape as a weapon of war'. In June 2013, the WHO released the first global, systematic review on the prevalence of violence against women. *Shockingly, it shows that 35% of women worldwide have experienced physical or sexual intimate partner violence or non-partner sexual violence, making such abuse a 'global public health problem of epidemic proportions'* (Published online June 20, 2013 http://dx.doi.org/10.1016/ S0140-6736(13)61222-2. See online/articles http://dx.doi.org/10.1016/ S0140-6736(13)61030-2.) It's about time that this is being investigated. The epidemic has been continuing for millennia and maybe longer.

In the UK Parliament, the Commons International Development Committee published a report (2013) on violence against women and girls. The committee pointed out the failure to address violence *within* UK borders. As mentioned earlier, The Department for International Development launched a £35 million programme to address female genital mutilation (FGM) abroad but little was done to help the <u>20,000 girls at risk from FGM in the UK and the 66,000 women living with the lifetime effects of such mutilation.</u> These official statements of intent and hope are one thing, but no prosecution for FGM has taken place in the UK since it became illegal in 1985: it was considered in 2014 for the first time. For the WHO report on the prevalence of violence against women and clinical guidelines see:

http://www.who.int/reproductivehealth/publications/violence/en/index.html For the International Development Committee report on violence against women and girls see: http://www.publications. parliament. uk/pa/cm201314/cmselect/cmintdev/107/10702.htm

The global momentum for change is building
It's a shocking fact that nowhere in the world is a woman safe from violence. But the above shows that a global momentum for change is at least building. In March 2013, 103-member States at the 57th session of the Commission on the Status of Women at

the UN headquarters in New York agreed to end violence against women and girls and to promote and protect their human rights and fundamental freedoms. Again, sadly, this commission can add only to the consensus for change: they cannot actually do it. We are slowly learning lessons about women's place in society. As described above, official bodies, health authorities, governments and the UN are condemning vicious violence, and women themselves are learning to look after women in 'shelters'. If we humans learn to stop this abuse and widespread suppression of women, we will have moved a long way towards a better, less violent and humane world. And there are some signs of recognition that feminine attributes are greatly needed in our current world. We have the recent (2017) exposure of widespread female suppression and sexual exploitation in the film industry and the brave response of female actors led by Oprah Winfrey who accepted her Cecil B. DeMille Award at the 2018 Golden Globes with a message to the young women watching: "A new day is on the horizon." Another brave advocate for womens' rights is ex USA President Jimmy Carter. In a new book he advocates specific actions: 'A call for action: women, religion, violence and power'. It seems possible that suppression of women is the key problem that might affect and help humanity, including reducing the likelihood of war.

Why does abuse and discrimination against women happen?
Introduction

Abuse and discrimination against women is clearly established. But *why* are women abused and specifically regarded as second-class citizens in so many cultures or even are *without any* citizens' rights and over such long historical periods? Any explanations will cast light on what is needed to eliminate such behaviour. On a BBC radio 'Woman's' programme in the UK, there was an interview with a woman who had campaigned successfully for pictures of women to appear on UK bank notes. Apart from the Queen, Elizabeth Fry and Florence Nightingale, only notable men have tended to appear.

Because of her campaign, *she has had <u>large-scale</u> attacks on social media, received graphic, detailed threats of rape and had her home address placed on 'Twitter' with the suggestion that others harm her!* This, simply for advocating pictures of notable women on UK bank notes! In 2016, it was revealed that in the UK, women Members of Parliament receive rape threats on a daily basis!

A member of the European Parliament Janusz Korwin-Mikke recently (<u>2017</u>) said that women should earn less because they 'are weaker, smaller and less intelligent'. This same Polish MEP has used the parliament to spread hate: comparing migrants to 'excrements' and making a Nazi salute in the chamber! How can one explain such inhuman, irrational behaviour? These waters are deep and murky indeed.

Ideas of Professor Mary Beard

At the opposite end of the 'primate'/human spectrum, and at the extreme human end, is Mary Beard, Professor of Classics at the University of Cambridge. I admire her intellect, her humour and her feminine approach. She gave a London Review of Books lecture on an aspect of this dilemma entitled *'Oh do shut up dear!'* It was broadcast as a BBC Four Lecture on 16th March 2014 (available on BBC websites) and it underlines how ancient is woman's lowly position in society. She has put her finger accurately on an important aspect of the situation. At the beginning of her lecture,

> *'I want to start very near the beginning of the tradition of Western literature, and its first recorded example of a man telling a woman to 'shut up'; telling her that her voice was not to be heard in public. I'm thinking of a moment immortalised at the start of the Odyssey. We tend now to think of the Odyssey as the story of Odysseus and the adventures and scrapes he had returning home after the Trojan War – while for*

decades Penelope loyally waited for him, fending off the suitors who were pressing for her hand. But the Odyssey is just as much the story of Telemachus, the son of Odysseus and Penelope; the story of his growing up; how over the course of the poem he matures from boy to man. The process starts in the first book with Penelope coming down from her private quarters into the great hall, to find a bard performing to throngs of her suitors; he's singing about the difficulties the Greek heroes are having in reaching home. She isn't amused, and in front of everyone she asks him to choose another, happier number. At which point young Telemachus intervenes:

'Mother,' he says, 'go back up into your quarters, and take up your own work, the loom and the distaff ... speech will be the business of men, all men, and of me most of all; for mine is the power in this household.' And off she goes, back upstairs.

There is something faintly ridiculous about this wet-behind-the-ears lad shutting up the savvy, middle-aged Penelope. But it's a nice demonstration that right where written evidence for Western culture starts, women's voices are not being heard in the public sphere; more than that, as Homer has it, an integral part of growing up, as a man, is learning to take control of public utterance and to silence the female of the species. The actual words Telemachus uses are significant too. When he says 'speech' is 'men's business', the word is muthos – not in the sense that it has come down to us of 'myth'. In Homeric Greek it signals authoritative public speech (not the kind of chatting, prattling or gossip that anyone – women included, or especially women – could do).'

Mary Beard was also invited to give another London Review of Books Lecture, 'Women in Power' (Vol. 39, No. 6 pages 9-14. 16th March 2017). She continued her previous theme, exploring how deeply rooted in the language are assumptions about women and power. Notably, she continues to refer to the classical world and to how we are still using Greek idioms to represent the idea of women in and out of power. Medusa was one of the mythical sisters known as Gorgons. As a punishment for a crime Athena transformed her into a monster causing anyone who looked at her face to turn into stone. The later beheading of Medusa by Perseus remains a cultural symbol of opposition to women's power. The symbolic use of the bleeding head of Medusa, with writhing snakes for hair, continued over the centuries. In the recent presidential election, Trump's supporters used images of Cellini's bronze sculpture of Perseus and the head of Medusa. An image of Trump's face covered that of Perseus and Hillary Clinton's face replaced the bleeding, snake covered, severed head. The images were on T-shirts, mugs, laptop sleeves. I quote Mary Beard:

> *'It may take a moment or two to take in that normalisation of gendered violence, but if you were ever doubtful about the extent to which the exclusion of women from power is culturally embedded or unsure of the continued strength of classical ways of formulating and justifying it – well, I give you Trump and Clinton, Perseus and Medusa, and rest my case.'*

The lecturer, Professor Beard, has herself been threatened with vicious, violent behaviour for no special reason other than, presumably, being a woman and prominent on television and radio. I hesitate to write the following in case I offend, but someone threatened to behead totally innocent Mary Beard and rape the head! One wonders if the reason is, like Odysseus's

Penelope, she should not have a public voice? Yet Mary Beard is Professor of Classics at the University of Cambridge. Of course, she should have a public voice, and even if she weren't a Professor she should still be heard and happily, she is. We need to remember that in relatively recent times, women were *excluded* from higher education and in 'socially advanced' UK, *excluded* from having a vote in national elections. Men, especially the elite males, <u>routinely ridiculed</u> the idea of higher education or votes for women in line with Mary Beard's analysis. Several religions have sub-groups remaining opposed to women's education or to women having a public voice. Even rational Aristotle was against women being prominent socially. He thought that, because women's 'souls' were dominated by the irrational, it's natural for them not to be rulers but to be ruled by men. Professor Beard has definitely identified something very deep about *public* utterances by women. Even so, the disgusting violent threats for the above innocent activities is... what? What can we call it? Surely, yet again, we are entering a dark, murky space.

Possible biological explanations of abuse and discrimination against women

The inferior situation of women, despite some improvements, is still widespread across nations and cultures. I believe that solving this issue of femininity is a key to other male, macho problems. I remain shocked by this blot on humanity's record and personally horrified at the position of women <u>*advocated*</u> in the Old and New Testaments of the Bible, as shown earlier. Whilst laws and sanctions may have a place, it will surely be helpful if we can gain some understanding of *why* this has happened for so long and still is happening.

One lesson is that the inferiority of women is based deeply in the human psyche, as referred to earlier in Mary Beard's ideas. An important approach might be to address this problem as biological and not the inevitable will of God or of evil acts by individuals or by the Devil. Numerous suggestions for improvements for all these extreme injustices have been made.

I'm not aware of any proposals for improvement, such as those below with a main focus on instincts. These proposals are now illuminated by scientific, empirical evidence to bring about the massive benefits of social equality, connectedness and social institutions that are inclusive. It has now been established beyond doubt that the most effective way to reduce the above bad characteristics of humans is to focus on these aspects. Numerous problems are closely associated with having a less equal and less inclusive society.

Answering the sound of the war bugle
Whilst writing this book, it has become strikingly clear to me that a subject (human survival) with such broad aspects – all of biology – makes it impossible for me not to be cautious in offering any advice. Nobody can be expert in the whole of such a range of subjects. But if I return to the most basic needs for survival: *effective, rapid and coordinated responses to danger,* then some outlines do appear regarding women's subjugation. Let's consider the influence of instincts about danger regarding alpha males, the speed of response, social obedience, fear of the foreign and competition. It's clear that part of an answer is in Professor Beard's lecture (above). Women are not 'us' (men). We are in charge and in some ways 'they' are foreign and therefore somewhat dangerous. Macho male (alpha) hierarchies are in charge and their instincts are more 'reliable' (in a primate world, this amounts to *automatic* and *instinctive* fight or flight) in times of (primate) danger than the softer, feminine ones. In perceived dangerous (primate) times requiring instinctive rapid, mindless, <u>unified</u> action, women could well be a handicap to this primate behaviour. When the bugle sounds, 'they' may not reliably obey and wish to think first. And as for blowing the bugle...?

Consequently, they must be excluded from official power, official speech. In that narrow sense, 'they' are indeed foreign, when viewed through the the instinctive response of men to the foreign. Characteristically, women are not suited to an instant, instinctive and coordinated response to danger led by (macho) alpha-male primates. It's not about women or men, but about femininity or masculinity. It is he feminine, intuitive approach to life that is unreliable when it comes instantly and mindlessly to obeying the call of the war bugle.

Mysterious bringers of life

The empirical fact is that women *are* excluded and have been for millennia. So, in early (and also present) human societies, women are rarely seen as candidates for being alpha leaders or alpha anything and may be seen as somewhat 'foreign' as well. Also, women propagate life. They are intrinsically mysterious to men. And maybe deep down, men fear them. If so, the last thing men want is for women to have public power because they may interfere with the mindless, rapid, coordinated response to danger led by alpha males. Evolution has selected feminine characteristics as optimum for the rearing and nurturing of children. Possibly because of their vital role in child development, women are typically reluctant to abandon their intuition and simply impel themselves down the paths of primate instincts.

It is not simply gender: women who act as macho men are acceptable. Which male politician is more 'macho' than the former UK Prime Minister Margaret Thatcher? Today, femininity is greatly needed: the feminine, intuitive approach has never been more needed to extend beyond child-rearing and home-keeping, vital as they are.

Another risk to a *rapid, coordinated response to social danger* is internal competition. Alphas are the key to this response. In the ape and in human society there is constant competition associated with the role of alpha male and 'would be' alphas. Women can typically be seen as not bonding in the same way as men do and may constitute a kind of alternative competition to the group's decision-making, macho alpha-male approach. All of these possibilities could contribute to the tendency (male instinct) to exclude women from being visible or leader-like in public discourse, as in Mary Beard's reference to

Odysseus' son Telemachus' orders to his mother Penelope in Homer's Odyssey. 'Mother, go back up into your quarters, and take up your own work, the loom and the distaff ... speech will be the business of men, all men, and of me most of all; for mine is the power in this household.'

But we must remember that these basic, primate instincts were shaped by evolution for a *far different, small population, arboreal world*. Our current and recent mechanistic, man-made world, run by our (mostly) alien alpha males, driven by instincts by-passing the human thinking brain, is surely in great need of a softer, feminine approach. After all, we are humans and we are capable of altruism, a quality taught as the *highest* good by the cultural leaders throughout history: Christianity, Islam, Buddhism, Sikhism and Axial Age leaders generally. Iain McGilchrist (author of 'The Master and his Emissary') has highlighted this in terms of the socially harmful overemphasis of those parts of our brains (notably the left hemisphere) managing mechanistic responses. As for the cruel, vicious, unprovoked bullying, violation and torture of women, I have no explanation other than it's a human pathology: it is a sick, diseased behaviour. Maybe some reader might tell me of another explanation.

Reducing anti-women behaviour

Tackling this deeply ancient issue requires *specific* approaches in *each* of the social structures and this is considered later in: the state, military, religion, commerce, professions, media and the overall culture. Men in power are wedded to the idea that the world is intrinsically macho male, like them. It's natural. It's the 'real world'.

Society needs to recognise the problem via education and somehow increase the numbers of women in positions of responsibility and power. We need to recognise that the world is currently a male one and structured as strongly 'macho', and it naturally prefers and selects women with compatible, macho personalities, e.g. Margaret Thatcher. We must find ways to promote women and men with feminine personalities (e.g. the feminine Angela Merkel).

Violent aggression: war

'That man is an aggressive creature will hardly be disputed. With the exception of certain rodents, no other vertebrate habitually destroys members of its own species...... The sombre fact is that we are the cruellest and most ruthless species that has ever walked the earth.'

Anthony Storr in 'Human Aggression'

'Man was born free, and he is everywhere in chains.'

Jean-Jacques Rousseau in 'The Social Contract'

'Let the ruling classes tremble at a communistic revolution. The proletarians have nothing to lose but their chains. They have a world to win. Working men of all countries, unite!'

Karl Marx and Frederick Engels in 'The Communist Manifesto'

'The only thing necessary for the triumph of evil is for good men to do nothing.'

Edmund Burke

'Nobody made a greater mistake than he who did nothing because he could do only a little.'

Edmund Burke

'Misery, mutilation, destruction, terror, starvation and death characterize the process of war and form a principal part of the product.'

Lewis Mumford

'*War is awful.   Nothing good comes out of it.   It destroys the mind as well as the body.*'

Ex-Special Forces Veteran, speaking while building a memorial to his dead and wounded comrades, National Memorial Arboretum, Alrewas, near Lichfield, UK 2017

Dimensions of the scale of war by humans

Herodotus was a Greek historian who lived in the fifth century BC and was a contemporary of Socrates. He is often referred to as "The Father of History". He was the first historian to treat historical subjects by collecting his data systematically and critically, and then arranging them into a narrative. He wrote a history of the Greco-Persian wars ('The Histories') and focussed mainly on their origins, the major battles and the lives of the key leaders. He notably digressions are an important part of 'The Histories'. I also recommend to any reader the modern book by Ryszard Kapuściński, 'Travels with Herodotus'. Herodotus puzzled on the *regularity* of wars and their association with extreme, vicious violence.

Why do humans behave in a consistently violent and aggressive way and how can we mitigate matters? On the very day I write this section, the BBC reports that there are 27 million displaced people in the world. My purpose is not simply to attempt to shock but, following Herodotus, rather first of all simply describe the huge extent of known large and small-scale violent aggression that *we take for granted and often ignore* and then ask why. As part of the consideration later of the major social structures regarding the extent to which they are substantially primate or human, I will consider possible ways to improve the structures, compatible with the inherent biology and with human needs. The behaviour of the world's only superpower, the USA, is of special interest and will be dealt with as a separate section. Essentially, the nation with the most power commonly expresses the typical behaviour of the powerful most strongly (see 'Power phenotype' earlier in 'Background ideas on evolutionary biology').

Of the biblical horrors of pestilence, war, famine and death, mostly we humans contribute directly to war and death: war is brought about by humans. With the appropriate will, humanity could (and does) hugely influence and reduce the problems of famine and pestilence. The age of natural death is constantly being increased. The regular instances of violent aggression do not receive the attention that one might expect. It is part of the background to life and taken for granted – the elephant in the room. Applying another metaphor, it seems that not seeing that 'the Emperor is naked' (unlike Socrates) is also instinctive and supports the alpha-male leader(s). Having healthy *ape* alpha males was and is crucial to the survival of their small groups: as well as crucial to their leadership function. Unlike our human world, they hunted, ate, slept and groomed *with* their group. In the modern world, not seeing and ignoring the scale of violent aggression on a daily basis perpetuates the appalling reality. And primate instincts tend to bypass the thinking parts of the human brain. For these reasons, the intention here is to make the situation crystal clear, unavoidably clear, with known examples. At the end of this section on war is a brief account of the so-called 'War on drugs'.

The massive world expenditure on arms
I quote Oscar Arias Sanchez: 'When a country decides to invest in arms, rather than in education, housing, the environment, and health services for its people, it is depriving a whole generation of its right to prosperity and happiness. We have produced one firearm for every ten inhabitants of this planet, and yet we have not bothered to end <u>hunger</u> when such a feat is well within our reach. Our international regulations allow almost three-quarters of all global arms sales to pour into the developing world with no binding international guidelines whatsoever. Our regulations do not hold countries accountable for what is done with the weapons they sell,

even when the probable use of such weapons is obvious'.

Oscar Arias Sanchez, President of Costa Rica was awarded the Nobel Peace Prize in 1987 for his efforts to end civil wars across Central America.

As I write (Christmas 2016), President elect, Donald J. Trump has 'tweeted' (4:50 PM, 22 Dec 2016) the following *irrational* statement: 'The United States must greatly strengthen and expand its nuclear capability until such time as the world comes to its senses regarding nukes.' Later, the Trump team's spokesman, Jason Miller, issued a statement saying Trump was referring to 'the threat of nuclear proliferation and the critical need to prevent it – particularly to and among terrorist organizations and unstable and rogue regimes'. Jason Miller had an impossible task; even so, his statement makes no sense. Mr Trump's tweet was clearly proposing nuclear expansion. How can the USA *'greatly strengthen and expand its nuclear capability'*, when it already has a stockpile of 7,000 nuclear weapons (similar to that of Russia), possibly help 'the world to come to its senses regarding nukes'? How can the intention to *'greatly strengthen and expand its nuclear capability'* stop proliferation to small groups of religious fanatics or unstable or rogue states seeking nuclear weapons? Another description of his statement is that the military/industrial complex grows and benefits.

Military expenditure by the top-spending countries is shocking. Not only that, there is the scale of weaponry *sold*, mostly to 'developing' nations as described above by Oscar Sanchez. The table below is a list of the 15 countries with the highest defence (defence?) budgets for the year 2015, which is $1.7 trillion or about 74% of the total world defence expenditures. It's noticeable that the USA spends about twice as much as the next two, top-spending countries (China and Saudi Arabia) put together. To put it another way, USA arms expenditure equals that of the next seven states combined. This table is followed by a list of the top arms exporters where the USA and Russia are outstanding.

US-UK Mutual Defence Agreement.

A 56-year-old nuclear agreement between the United Kingdom and the United States of America was again renewed in 2014 with no parliamentary debate or vote. The British public and parliamentarians initially found out about the latest extension and ratification of the Mutual Defence Agreement (MDA) when President Obama informed the United States Congress. It notably includes the *multi, multi-billion-dollar* Trident programme. The Director of the Nuclear Information Service, Peter Burt, has pointed out that it is not an independent deterrent, with virtually every aspect requiring US technology. A University of York lecturer in international security, Dr Nick Ritchie, described this sharing of the technology as a form of *'legalised proliferation'*. Also, it follows that the UK has to buy into and be dependent upon US security strategy. A shocking question is 'whom can it be fired against?' It seems clear that what these billions actually buy is prestige for our alpha males at the cost of diminishing our welfare system, including our precious NHS. As the recent UK Prime Minister David Cameron put it, 'gaining us (him) a seat at the top table'.

The 15 countries with the highest military expenditure in 2015
Stockholm International Peace Research Institute (SIPRI). (www.
sipri.org)

Rank	Spending ($b)	World share %	Share of GDP %
1 USA	596	36	3.3
2 China	[215]	[13]	[1.9]
3 Saudi Arabia	87.2	5.2	13.7
4 Russia	66.4	4.0	5.4
5 UK	55.5	3.3	2.0
6 India	51.3	3.1	2.3
7 France	50.9	3.0	2.1
8 Japan	40.9	2.4	1.0
9 Germany	39.4	2.4	1.2
10 South Korea	36.4	2.2	2.6
11 Brazil	24.6	1.5	1.4
12 Italy	23.8	1.4	1.3
13 Australia	23.6	1.4	1.9
14 UAE*	[22.8]	[1.4]	[5.7]
15 Israel	16.1	1.0	5.4
Total Top 15	**1350**	**81**	
World total	1676	100	2.3

*Note: Figures in brackets are estimate

Comments on trends in world military expenditure 2015
Sam Perlo-Freeman, Aude Fleurant, Pieter Wezeman and Siemon Wezeman.
The SIPRI Military Expenditure Database, available at: <http://www.sipri.org/databases/milex/> was updated on 5 April 2016 to include new data.

Key facts
- World military expenditure was about $1.7 trillion in 2015.
- Total global spending rose by 1.0 per cent in real terms in 2015, the first increase since 2011.
- The 5 biggest spenders in 2015 were the USA (by far), China, Saudi Arabia, Russia and the UK.
- Military expenditure increased in Asia and Oceania, Central and Eastern Europe and in those countries in the Middle East for which data is available.
- Military spending decreased in North America, Western Europe, Latin America and the Caribbean, and Africa.
- Military expenditure in the USA fell by 2.4 per cent to $596 billion, a slower rate of decline than in recent years, mainly due to steps taken by the US Congress to mitigate the impact of the spending reductions imposed by the 2011 Budget Control Act.
- The decline in military spending in Western Europe slowed to 1.3 per cent, while countries in Central Europe increased spending by 13 per cent, largely prompted by fears of Russian aggression following the Ukraine crisis.
- The fall in world oil prices led to cuts in military spending in several oil revenue-dependent countries that had previously made rapid increases. Others, including Russia and Saudi Arabia, continued to boost spending, but Russia is planning cuts in 2016, and reductions are also likely in Saudi Arabia.

Largest exporters of major weapons as percentage of expenditure 2010-14 (Stockholm International Peace Research Institute (SIPRI). www.sipri.org)

The initial values do not represent precise financial flows but are a crude instrument to estimate volumes of arms transfers, regardless of the contracted prices, which can be as low as *zero* in the case of military aid.

	%
USA	31
Russia	27
China	5
Germany	5
France	5
UK	4
Spain	3
Italy	3
Ukraine	3
Israel	2

Suppose we increase the expression of human instincts and control basic ones?

Suppose humans, currently with their divided and conflicting nations and their divided and conflicting sub-groups, learned how to live peacefully? Suppose we all accepted the truth that there is only one race? Suppose we realised that all humans left Africa around 60 million years ago to populate the rest of our planet? Suppose our basic instincts that evolved for small groups of apes living in trees were controlled by human reason? They are largely about territory, fear of the foreign, including women, competition and the instincts of alpha-male leaders and associated obedience to them. Suppose we gave full expression of our human instincts of altruism, art and culture? There would be no or little need for military personnel or military bases and no or little need for costly weaponry. All humans could have clean water, healthy food, good accommodation and medical services.

A grim reminder: wars and atrocities in my lifetime and back to my great-great-grandparents

One recent morning, my wife told me that during the night, being restless, she had quietly (so as not to wake me) listened to the BBC World Service and was depressed by the constant diet of catastrophes during this one, single night. The programme was about war in Northern Sudan, draught and starvation in Somalia and that day's massacres in Syria. Then, early the same morning, on the BBC 'Thought for the Day' programme, a religious commentator mentioned the statistics of the life expectation of people *living on the streets in the affluent UK*. Life expectation is mid-40s, with women dying earlier than men. As mentioned earlier, the International Red Cross *now* provides food for hungry families in the UK. As I write this book, it has shocked me to realise that on a daily basis, there is new evidence of worldwide extreme, vicious violence.

About a third of all UN countries are today at war and much of the world's population lives in poverty, including the working poor of the USA (see David Shipler's superb, balanced 'The working poor: invisible in America') and those trying to escape the close monitoring / surveillence (by the state) of the inhabitants of inner cities who are often driven into a life of drugs and prison ('On the run: fugitive life in an American city' by Alice Goffman). Millions of people drink pathogen-infected water. Why so much war, so much racism, so much religious intolerance and why does the affluent minority not do more to help the poor within and across countries? Why does India indulge in a 'prestigious' space programme while millions in deep poverty live *on the streets*? Why did poverty-stricken Brazil spend billions on arrangements for a 'prestigious' 2014 World Cup, the 2016 Olympic Games and the extremely rich Qatar not address migrant workers' rights, including safety in buildings, for the 2022 World Cup? Numerous workers have waited more than a year for any pay whatsoever and many workers are paid around €0.50 per hour.

Why do individuals secrete away <u>trillions</u> of dollars that they could not possibly spend: about $20 trillion out of the world's GDP of about $80 trillion? Why? These questions are addressed in detail later, but essentially the answer is not rational, but instinctive by those not paying. Notably and characteristically, alpha males buy prestige with others' money, 'knowing' instinctively that their alpha status gives them the right. These human alphas no longer belong to the group that they 'lead'. Pathologically, they are often predators. And, importantly, the money is removed from the local economy and not re-circulated there. It reappears as virtually useless mega prestigious yachts or empty houses in London's exclusive areas or beside the Mediterranean, again empty. It's a human pathology.

As indicated earlier, some human societies can and do exhibit extreme selfless, altruistic behaviour, especially from individuals. But *under threat* (and sometimes when not, e.g. when relatively very powerful) behaviour to foreign nations is characteristically very different. If one accepts the definition (Oxford English dictionary) of instinct as an innate tendency, then it seems clear that there are indeed innate group behaviours characteristic of human society that are consistent across time and geography and culture. They are male-dominated hierarchies with personal conditions and rewards related to position in the hierarchy (see later, the 'Power phenotype' – individual *and group*), parallel group obedience to elites and social conformity, hostility to and fear of 'otherness' ('us' and 'them'), defence of territory (fight or flight and the need to build fortified habitations), inflicting *collective* punishment on other groups, competitiveness (especially, but not exclusively male), structural inequalities such as gender role divisions, including the male suppression of women. In addition to the basic behaviour more or less shared with primates, religion can and does serve as a cause of conflict as described above.

'...the rules of fair play do not apply in love and war.'
John Lyly in his novel 'Euphues: The Anatomy of Wit',
published in 1579

The needs of survival come first and morals second, if at all. Instincts from primates and earlier override all others. This primate behaviour of human groups under threat is consistent across cultures, climates and historical periods and is reinforced between threats and dangers by extreme social conditioning via, for example, military training. In the extreme case of territorial threats and war, young men characteristically fight opponent men with extreme violence. In specialist niches different behaviours may occur, but the broad thrust of human group behaviour, particularly under threat, is relatively constant.

Recent family history: the world's fastest period of
technological change
If I consider only the main instances of especially cruel wars, major atrocities and avoidable famines over the lifetime of myself, my parents and back to my great-great-grandparents, they are truly shocking. If I attempted to list all the documented instances of major injustice, discrimination and misuse of power, then I'd never finish.

This is the 'normal', realistic state of the world.
When I first considered my family 'memory', I had underestimated its length. I spoke directly to my grandparents and they had spoken directly to their grandparents (born in the 1830s). Beyond this period of around 180 years, the direct connection between myself and my great-great-grandparents gets lost. Even within this relatively recent family history and despite reductions in some kinds of conflicts and other improvements, the list of imposed human misery is long, consistent and dreadful. Interestingly, it's likely that this period from around my great-great-grandparents', or even merely since my grandparents' birth has seen more increase in

scientific understanding and technological change than any period in history and has given humans hugely more understanding of and *vastly more power over 'nature'* than ever before. Humanity and the natural world have never been in such danger.

In 1859 Charles Darwin published 'On the Origin of Species by Means of Natural Selection'. This book was never read or mentioned by any member of my family at any time that I was aware of. My Catholic schooling (many decades ago) later ridiculed biological evolution giving the specific example of the eye's complexity as one of the 'proofs' of the impossibility of its evolution: this teaching, I accepted. Notable examples in my parents' lifetime that affected them were radio and telephonic communication. After earlier failures, commercially viable, undersea, transatlantic telegraph communications began from Valentia in West Ireland to Newfoundland in 1866. Later, it extended to other Eastern USA locations such as Long Beach Island NJ. Coincidentally, I have visited both ends of this historic development in communication, where friends or family live.

Solely in my lifetime are nuclear power and weaponry, digital computing and communications technology and the basic mechanisms of biology: the understanding of the origins of diseases and molecular genetics. In the 1950s Arthur Kornberg isolated the enzymes involved in synthesising DNA and Watson and Crick revealed the structure of DNA. In the early 1950s, I often played squash with a friend doing a PhD in computing, using one of the first (physically huge) computers at Manchester University in the UK. I had a friend working at Ohio State University where a major library facility existed to house much of the world's scientific literature and journals (paper). It occupied *several large, multistorey buildings.* Now, such an amount of data can be satisfied with something around the size of household freezer. My current laptop has a million times more capacity than my first portable computer. Apart from the dangers from nuclear technology and from industrial global warming, information technology has enabled criminal disruption of the world's financial systems and the secret, state surveillance of national and international communications, private and public, of large populations – its own 'citizens'. Are we citizens if 'our' government spies on us? Human alpha males with modern technology are like infant children playing with fire, except that we all get burned.

Two current examples from many: Syria and Afghanistan (Holocaust later under 'Lessons')

What follows is not comprehensive. A third extreme example, Palestine, is considered later under 'Racism' and 'the Holocaust'. I will start with the current (2015 as I first write and again in 2017) Syria and Afghanistan situations. I was deeply shocked as I read about and listed the following individual atrocities. I was unaware of their extent and *continuity*. There is the (2011 onwards) vicious slaughter of people in Syria by its own 'leaders' and eventually the responses from the oppressed which also became vicious. Jessica Matthews, President of the Carnegie Endowment for International Peace, has written a notable account of the Syrian conflict in the New York Review of Books (November 6th 2014) under the title 'Is there an answer for Syria'. This is in the context of the new 'Islamic State', so-called ISIS, sometimes abbreviated to IS. My purpose in writing this section is not to offer my own detailed analysis (although primate instincts are hugely there), just the scale of the horror. So far, the cost is 200,000 dead, 3 million refugees, and 6 million forced out of their homes. Nearly half of Syria's population has been made homeless and there is a similar destruction of its physical wealth. Matthews points out that several powers were fuelling the war by proxy and ensuring that a stable military equilibrium was never achieved. On the one hand, these included Russia, Iran and Hezbollah, backing the Syrian leader, Bashar al-Assad, and on the other, Saudi Arabia, some Gulf States and the USA backing the opposition. On top of this immense suffering, Jordan, Lebanon and Turkey have absorbed enormous, destabilising numbers of refugees. And at the end of 2016, Aleppo has fallen to the government forces amidst terrible carnage.

Amnesty International reported in 2017 that as many as 13,000 opponents of Bashar al-Assad were secretly hanged in one of Syria's most infamous prisons in the first 5 years of the country's civil war as part of an extermination policy ordered by the highest levels of the Syrian government. Many thousands more people held in Saydnaya prison died through torture and starvation, Amnesty said, and the bodies were dumped in 2 mass graves on the outskirts of Damascus between midnight and dawn most Tuesday mornings for at least 5 years. Assad's slaughterhouse defies description, but it's horrifyingly real. The Amnesty report, 'Human Slaughterhouse', details allegations of state-sanctioned abuse that are unprecedented in Syria's civil war, a conflict that has consistently broken new ground in depravity, leaving at least 400,000 people dead and nearly half the country's population displaced. It suggests that thousands more people could have been hanged in Saydnaya since the end of 2015, after which former guards and detainees who spoke to Amnesty no longer had access to verifiable information from inside the prison. And as I revise this section in April 2018, the horror continues with Syria using illegal, deadly gas to slaughter numerous innocent civilians. The pro-opposition Ghouta Media Center tweeted that more than 75 people had "suffocated", while a further 1,000 people had suffered the effects. It blamed a barrel bomb allegedly dropped by a helicopter which it said contained Sarin, a toxic nerve agent. The Union of Medical Relief Organizations, a US-based charity that works with Syrian hospitals, told the BBC that the Damascus Rural Specialty Hospital had confirmed 70 deaths. The legacy of Assad's father and of his employment of Adolf Hitler's chief torturer lives on.

The week that I write the following about Afghanistan, sees the West's troops' withdrawal from that centuries-long, war-torn country. The recent US-led coalition spent $1 trillion and deployed 1 million soldiers and civilians over 13 years. A recent, superb book by Anand Gopal ('No good men among the living: America, the Taliban, and the war through Afghan eyes') benefits from an informed and brilliant review (November 6th 2014) in the New York Review of Books by Rory Stewart, Chairman of the Defence

Committee of the UK House of Commons. Stewart had previously been Ryan Professor of Human Rights at the Harvard Kennedy School and in addition has detailed knowledge about Afghanistan. Stewart wrote 'The Places in between' – a travel narrative about his solo walk across north-central Afghanistan in 2002. Along the way he travelled through some of the most rugged, isolated and poor parts of that country. I strongly recommend Gopal's book and also Stewart's review. Gopal, underlined by Stewart's review, details the deeply rooted, vicious and insane politics of Afghanistan and illuminates the truly crazy things that happen in war as well as the vicious. This account deserves a special place in my list because of the detailed, in-depth, investigative journalism by Gopal and others he quotes as well as for Stewart's review. Three examples stand out regarding the absurdities of war, quoted by Stewart.

First is a US counterterrorist operation in 2002 initiated by US Central Command in Tampa, Florida. Two sites were identified as likely 'al-Qaeda compounds'. A Special Forces team was sent in to eradicate this enemy. In fact, *as was common*, an Afghan 'ally' had falsely informed the US that his rivals were Taliban so that they would be eliminated. The result was 'twenty-one pro-US leaders and their employees died, twenty-six taken prisoner and a few who could not be accounted for. Not a single member of the Taliban or of al-Qaeda was among the victims. Instead, in a single thirty-minute stretch the US had managed to eradicate both of Khas Uruzgan's potential governments, the core of any future anti-Taliban leadership'. The leader and 7 members of the Special Forces team **_received medals_**.

The second example consists of Gopal's account (highlighted by Stewart) of the fate of several principal Afghan politicians. 'Dr Hafizullah, Zurmat's first Governor, had ended up in Guantanamo because he'd crossed Police Chief Mujahed. Mujahed wound up in Guantanamo because he crossed the Americans. Security Chief Naim found himself in Guantanamo because of an old rivalry with Mullah Qassim. Qassim eluded capture, but an unfortunate soul with the same name ended up in Guantanamo in his place.

And a subsequent feud left Samoud Khan, another pro-American commander, in Bagram prison, while the boy his men had sexually abused was shipped to Guantanamo.... Abdullah Khan found himself in Guantanamo charged with being Khairullah Khairkhwa, the former Taliban minister of the interior, which might have been more plausible if Khairkhwa had not also been in Guantanamo at the time..... Nine Guantanamo inmates claimed the most striking proof of all that they were not Taliban or al-Qaeda: *they had passed directly from a Taliban jail to American custody after 2001'.* The above 2 examples reminded me of the insanity of 'Catch 22' by Joseph Heller. Except that Heller's book is meant to be a fictional account of war.

The third example consists of the 'bringing to life' of important Afghan warlords. These number Sher Muhammed Akhunzada, Jan Muhammed and Abdul Rashid Dostum. Rory Stewart mentions the temptation of wrongly seeing them as charismatic rogues and inescapable parts of the Afghan establishment. They have links to organised crime, the CIA, Pakistan intelligence officers and the international narcotics trade. They have scams operating in the form of construction companies, private security agencies, property development, importing and exporting oil and opium poppy. Extreme examples of their behaviour include Dostum *cooking Taliban prisoners to death* in shipping containers. Jan Muhammed ordered death squads to shoot unarmed grandfathers in front of their families, to electrocute and to maim. Nevertheless, unlike the title of Gopal's book ('No good men among the living'), Rory Stewart testifies to his own experience of indeed finding good men during his own journeys through Afghanistan.

And more

As an addendum to Syria and Afghanistan I briefly list other atrocities. Amnesty International (April, 2014) is appealing for help regarding an appalling situation in the Central African Republic where there is ethnic cleansing of Muslims, thousands murdered and over 700,000 forced out of their country. The list goes on. In Afghanistan, Iraq,

Darfur, Somalia, massacres of Tamils in Sri Lanka, Balkan massacres and ethnic cleansing with deportation of about 2 *million* people, complete destruction of towns and villages, massacres, concentration/ death and rape camps, decades of suppression of Palestinians, Lebanon massacres, the Khmer Rouge 'Killing Fields' atrocities in Cambodia (about 2 *million* dead), Vietnam, Congo with 6 *million* killed at the end of the 19th century by Belgians and another 5 *million* killed later; Korea, Sudan, Bengali, Biafra, Rwandan, Angola, Uganda, Nigeria, Indonesia genocides, the many tens of thousands of 'disappeared' people in modern South America with powerful USA connivance. *Given the appropriate circumstances, this is how <u>humans</u> behave.*

The South African Boer war (1899-1902) was followed by the vicious apartheid political system and suppression of the majority indigenous black people. Then there was the so-called World War 1 where my grandfather fought and where tens of thousands of soldier-humans were killed or injured by machine guns in just one morning. Some eminent British historians today (2014) justify the slaughter that occurred during World War 1 by 'arguing' that we (the ruling elite) needed to stop German expansionism! Hatred of the Germans by the Allies led to a 'settlement' at the end of World War 1 that left Germany destitute. It's interesting to learn of the inhumane attitude of the victors illustrated by an extract from a speech by Sir Eric Geddes in 1918: 'We will get everything out of her (Germany) that you can squeeze out of a lemon and a bit more... I will squeeze her until you can hear the pips squeak'. It wasn't pips squeaking that came out; it was one of the most vicious evil regimes ever. It's generally agreed that leaving Germany destitute contributed greatly to the rise of Hitler and World War 2. And there were the British colonialist powers in Amritsa, India in 1919 who shot hundreds of men, women and children 'until their ammunition ran out' – to teach them a lesson. What lesson did the Amritsa massacre teach? Or any massacre?

There was the Kaiser's holocaust in South West Africa of indigenous peoples leading to the worst atrocity in recorded history.

That is, the Nazi factory-efficient Holocaust slaughter of millions of Jews as well as Roma, Slavs, intellectuals, gay people, political dissidents and, in World War 2, prisoners of war.

The destruction of Guernica (Spain) and the massacre of its population in, publicised by Picasso's painting, was a truly extreme atrocity. It was a total, deliberate blitzkrieg and involved the Nazis collaborating with Franco. Almost all buidings (98%) were destroyed by bombing and the heavily populated town market was machine gunned. The life of George Steer, the British reporter who brought the horror of the bombing of Guernica to the Britain and America public, has inspired a major English-language film, due out in 2018. Called *Gernika*, (Basque spelling), it will be the first to depict the terrible events of 26 April 1937 on the big screen and it has been welcomed by the people of the region, many of whom have taken part as extras. It was a French version of Steer's reports for the *Times* and for the *New York Times*, carried in *l'Humanité*, that prompted Pablo Picasso to create the huge monochrome painting, *Guernica*, as testament to the extreme suffering of his countrymen.

Nuclear horror
This holocaust continued during World War 2 when millions were slaughtered, and USA atomic bombs were first used with results devastating far, far beyond anything humankind had ever previously achieved. Today (2018), the widespread existence of an estimated 16,000 nuclear weapons of *vastly greater* power constitutes a permanent threat to humankind, maybe the greatest threat, as does the documented evidence of potential accidental nuclear explosions. In 'Command and Control', Eric Schlosser details near misses, especially an accident at a missile silo in Arkansas involving the most powerful warhead ever built by the USA.

It is still well worth reading a book written shortly after Hiroshima when its citizens were vaporised. 'Hiroshima' is a book by the war correspondent and Pulitzer Prize-winning author John Hersey. It was originally published as an article in *The New Yorker* of August 31, 1946. Hersey was one of the first Western journalists to view the destruction after the bombing. He had originally been commissioned by *The New Yorker* to write a series of articles. The editors wanted to drive home the horror of nuclear war. His article was later printed as a book and has sold several million copies. It describes the horror via the accounts of six survivors of the atomic bomb dropped on Hiroshima and covers the time immediately prior to and one year after the atomic bomb was dropped on August 6, 1945. Containing a detailed description of the bomb's effects, the article was a publishing sensation. In deliberately plain prose, Hersey described the horror and awful consequences of the atomic bomb. People had melted eyeballs and people were vaporised. Only their shadows were left, etched onto walls.

It would seem clear that today we need every means possible to keep us all mindful of the potential horrors of such warfare and 'Hiroshima' should be required reading in the final years of school. In contrast, there is almost unanimous ridicule and scorn in the UK media about the 'extremism' shown by the new leader of the Labour Party, Jeremy Corbyn, by being anti-Trident. Also, President Obama (May 2016) visited Japan and Hiroshima and has widely publicised that he will not apologise for the vaporising of Hiroshima on August 6th, 1945. Why not? Answer: probably because the Democratic party would lose votes.

Recently, there were commemorations for the victims of this first dropping of the atom bomb which vaporised a city and its inhabitants (as did the second bombing). There were numerous accounts and references on the BBC, and in every account that I heard or saw, the annihilation/vaporisation of men, women and children was 'justified' by the *assertion* that it saved many lives by bringing World War 2 to a quicker end. Similarly 'justified' is the current bombing of enemies by manless drones involving the destruction of inhabited blocks of apartments and the inevitable death of numerous innocent people. Such 'reasoning' defies moral philosophy and often ignores the historical background to conflict. When one considers the conflicts mentioned above, such disregarding of innocent human life is never justified. A military commander or a drone supervisor, under orders, decides that the death of innocent people (and the loss of homes) is justified as collateral damage because it will probably lead to the killing of an alleged terrorist leader. Speaking personally, in war it's not possible to justify the killing of innocent humans on moral grounds. In reality, it's the consequence of perceived necessity.

An evolutionary perspective

What are the odds of a nuclear device being deliberately exploded somewhere on our planet in the next decade? Or during the next century, or over the next thousand years, or even over the next hundred thousand years? Also, what are the odds of an accidental nuclear explosion taking place over such periods?

A good pointer to these odds is that small, early versions have <u>already</u> been used twice to incinerate Hiroshima and Nagasaki and their entire human populations. And, we've also <u>already</u> had near misses/accidents, as mentioned above (detailed in 'Command and Control' by Eric Schlosser). In 2016, Belgium discovered (or revealed) highly dangerous, numerous cracks at one of its nuclear installations. Short-term survival instincts are not suited to nuclear technology, with its vastly long-term and unprecedented, colossal effects. Furthermore, where are the enemies to fire at? The most likely enemies in the West are religious or other fanatics in small groups, shown to be already embedded in and already *citizens of* a European city and holding passports. One reason that our alpha males use only ridicule and sneers against opponents of nuclear weapons is that reasoned arguments are not available. Also, mega weaponry gives our primate, alpha leaders seats at top, alpha tables. *In their unthinking, instinct-driven, alpha behaviour, this could even be sufficient reason to have such weapons, even when there's no one to fire them at.* In any case, reason is a human activity and fearful alphas are propelled by innate, mindless, basic instincts.

Going further back in recent history

Ethnic cleansing of indigenous North America peoples.

Continuing back, beyond the recent history of violent aggression, there was the ethnic cleansing of indigenous North Americans, that continued. The attitude of the colonialists is exemplified by the following quotations by their leaders. Quotations like these show the ease with which powerful humans can justify evil by projecting evil onto the *weaker* (<u>not</u> less worthy) humans, such as indigenous Native Americans and indigenous Australian Native Aborigines, and wherever weaker people populate land that more powerful people want.

'The only true method of treating savages is to keep them in proper subjection and punish, without exception, the transgressors'. '..... Indians) more nearly allied to the Brute than to the Human creation'.
Sir Jeffrey Amherst, Commander in Chief, British Forces North America

'The more we can kill this year, the less will have to be killed the next war, for the more I see of these Indians the more convinced I am that they all have to be killed or be maintained as a species of paupers. Their attempts at civilization are simply ridiculous.'
Lieutenant General William T. Sherman, September 1868.

'It is probably true that the majority of our wild Indians have no inherited tendencies whatever towards morality or chastity, according to an enlightened standard. Chastity and morality among them must come from education and contact with the better element of the Whites'.
W. A. Jones, Commissioner of Indian Affairs, 1903.

These racist quotations are not from illiterates. They are from high-ranking (alpha male), powerful and 'well-educated' (in 'alpha' schools) humans. There are numerous books describing the history of the Indian wars and the conquest of the American West. 'Today is a good day to fight' by Mark Felton affected me deeply. It covers the half-century 1840 to the 1890s and adds to the evidence regarding an important aspect *not* of American white, or British or European, behaviour, but of *human* behaviour regarding power, territory and survival. It seems that all nations evolve cultural myths: <u>progress is a culture like 'ours'</u>. In his book, Felton refers to the Hollywood version of the American West where the 'whites represent righteousness, civilisation and progress, while the Indians are the bogeymen waiting in the shadows to do foul deeds to the settler or soldier, a people trapped in a prehistoric world of sun worship, ritual mutilation and subsistence hunting and gathering'. Away from Hollywood, the US Army regularly committed atrocities, in cold blood slaughtering men, women and children in peaceful villages. There were <u>371 treaties</u> between indigenous people and white Americans (mostly Europeans in origin).

Every single one of the 371 treaties was broken by the US Congress.

I will end this section with another quotation from 'Today is a good day to fight', this time from a non-combatant, the editor of the Aberdeen Saturday Pioneer, 1891. Is this not pure, non-human, primate instinct?

'The Pioneer has before declared that our only safety depends upon the <u>total extermination</u> of the Indians. Having wronged them for centuries, we had better, in order to protect our civilization, follow it up by one more wrong and wipe these untamed and untameable creatures from the face of the earth. In this lies future safety for our settlers and the soldiers who are under incompetent commands. Otherwise, we may expect future years to be as full of trouble with the redskins as those have been in the past'.

L. Frank Baum, editor. And at the same time, this man was the artistic, creative author of 'The wonderful wizard of Oz'.

Wars - what have we learned?

And what else have humans learned from this slaughter of millions of humans by humans? The answer seems to be nothing at all, probably because the *causes stem from biology*: basic instincts, still alive and healthy after millions of years. Even *after* the Nazi Holocaust, there have been numerous massacres. One example is in civilised Europe, when we had an attempted holocaust in pursuit of a 'Greater Serbia' and an attempted total elimination of every Bosniak (mostly Muslims targeted) and Croat, elimination of entire towns and villages with associated concentration and death camps and deportations (about <u>2 million</u> humans). There are numerous accounts of all the above atrocities, but an exceptional account of the Bosnian slaughter is given by an award-winning journalist Ed Vulliamy in his book 'The war is dead, long live the war. Bosnia: the reckoning'. The evidence for the existence of long, long-lasting impulses innate to humans (and other primates) is overwhelming.

Unhappily, perhaps there was one lesson learned – a *biological* one, billions of years old about territory and foreignness. The 'Wandering Jews', no longer <u>un</u>attached to any particular nation outside the Holy Land and with their foreign religion and foreign language, foreign clothing and foreign lifestyle, are now firmly attached to Palestine. They now have their own, non-alien, official religion and have learned to be like everyone else in defence of their territory, given (or rather taken, assisted by terrorist acts) to them by powerful non-owners. It's an extreme human tragedy.

Extending beyond my close family's lifetime, we have a recently published record of humanity's worst atrocities. Matthew White, in 'Atrocitology: humanity's 100 deadliest achievements', gives detailed accounts of the worst human slaughter and catalogues these events in various ways such as religious, ethnic cleansing and civil wars. In his Introduction, he lists three important lessons from his studies:

1. Chaos is more deadly than tyranny;
2. The world is very disorganised in terms of power structures, leaders and wars;
3. War kills more civilians than soldiers.

In this last lesson, he points out that 'The World Almanac and Wikipedia meticulously list the number of American soldiers, sailors and marines killed in each of America's wars, while ignoring civilian deaths among merchant seamen, passengers, refugees, runaway slaves and, of course, Indians and settlers along the frontier.'

Over 20 years ago, I had the pleasure of a sabbatical in Lille, northern France and my wife and I were deeply affected by the war graves and memorials of the First World War nearby. Some years later, I was driving to a meeting in Nottingham and saw a field of poppies that instantly and shockingly brought back our visit to the Flanders memorials. I wrote down my impressions.

On the way to Nottingham (1995)

Near the end of June
summer
seen from inside my car

Seeds
from other summers
blooming now
bendy, tough stalks
scattered
some alone
but mainly patches
blazing red
bobbing
each to its own drum beat
amidst the seeding grass
stroked even by the golden breeze

Bloody reminders
day trips
Flanders
shocking
tidy fields
filled with crosses
young names
old dates

And not bobbing
then or now
bodies neatly
quietly below

And where no body left
blown away
to compost
other poppy fields
walls of names
smoothed even
by the breeze and rain
and the fingers
of the loving
and unlearning

VIOLENT AGGRESSION: ADDICTIVE DRUGS AND THE 'WAR ON DRUGS'

Introduction

Addictive drugs destroy lives and families in several different ways and on a global scale. The 'war on drugs' is itself a global disaster, with the economy of entire nations being based on illegal drugs: notably Afghanistan, various South American countries and Mexico. Despite more than a trillion dollars having been spent fighting the war, according to the United Nations Office on Drugs and Crime (UNODC), illegal drugs are used by an estimated 270 million people and organised crime profits from a trade with an estimated turnover of over $330 billion a year – the world's largest illegal commodity market. (The Alternative World Drug Report. Drug and Alcohol Review Volume 33, Issue 2, page 215, March 2014. The Alternative World Drug Report: Counting the Costs of the War on Drugs edited by S. Rolles, G. Murkin, M. Powell, D. Kushlick and J. Slater, United Kingdom http://www.countthecosts.org/)

Oddly, this 'war on drugs' *excludes* the drugs tobacco (nicotine addictive) and alcohol (often addictive) that also cause mega costs in terms of cancer and numerous other health and social problems (e.g. car crashes). One possible reason for them being excluded could be their longevity and financial profits. They have been 'big (and profitable) business' for centuries. Action on Smoking and Health (ASH) estimates that tobacco smoking will kill a *billion* people in the 21st century. In the UK, the total *annual* cost to society of alcohol-related harm is estimated to be £21 billion. The UK NHS alone incurs £3.5 billion a year in costs related to alcohol. Few other health harms have such high overall costs when the impact on productivity and crime are included as well as the costs of alcohol-related car and other accidents (Alcohol treatment in England 2013-14 National Treatment www.nta.nhs.uk/uploads/adult-alcohol-statistics-2013-14-commentary.pdf). Undoubtedly, addictive drugs remain a major problem and the hugely expensive, crime-promoting 'war on drugs' has failed: other approaches are needed urgently, essentially by less punitive and more remedial approaches.

Counting the costs of the 'war on drugs'

The cost is undermining development and security, fuelling conflict, threatening public health, spreading disease and death, undermining human rights, promoting stigma and discrimination, creating crime, enriching criminals, increasing deforestation and pollution, and wasting billions on drug law enforcement (www.countthecosts.org). The global 'war on drugs' has been fought for 50+ years, without preventing the long-term trend of increasing drug supply and use. Beyond this failure, the UN Office on Drugs and Crime has also identified the many serious yet 'unintended negative consequences' of the drug war. These costs result not from drug use itself, but from *choosing a punitive enforcement-led approach* that, by its nature, places control of the trade in the hands of organised crime, and criminalises many users. 'Count the Costs' points out that the 'war on drugs' is a policy *choice*. There are other options that, at the very least, should be debated and explored using the best possible evidence and analysis. We all share the same goals – a safer, healthier and more just world.

Apart from the irresistability of addiction and the related destruction of individual lives, there is the potential huge profit, attracting criminal gangs who may even effectively control a country. The associated problems are massive in terms of the destruction of social structures. The question arises naturally: is this 'war' worth it in terms of social disruption, crime and lives lost by murder? The RAND corporation (non-profit, think tank for public policy) released a study in the mid-1990s that found that using 'drug user' treatment to reduce drug consumption in the United States is <u>seven times</u> more cost effective than using law enforcement efforts alone. It could potentially cut the consumption of illegal drugs by a third. In 2011, the Obama administration requested approximately $5.6 billion to support demand reduction. This included a 13% increase for prevention and almost a 4% increase for treatment. The overall 2011 counter-drug request for supply reduction and domestic law enforcement was $15.5 billion with $521.1 million in new funding

('A Regional Strategy for Drug Wars in the Americas'. Center for American Progress. March 2010). Key beneficiaries of the war on drugs are military, police and prisons budgets, and related technological and infrastructural interests.

'Addictive drugs and the war on drugs': Mexico as a specific example

Mexico can be used as an example to illustrate the huge dimensions of the problems regarding costs in many tens of billions of dollars, social destruction and loss of lives. The neighbouring USA is an enormous market for these Mexican drugs. Although Mexican drug cartels, or drug-trafficking organisations, have existed for several decades, their influence has increased since the demise of the Colombian Cali and Medellín cartels in the 1990s ('Mexico's Drug War'. Council on Foreign Relations; Cook, Colleen W., ed., October 16, 2007. 'Mexico's Drug Cartels'. CRS Report for Congress. PDF. Congressional Research Service, p.7). Mexican drug cartels now dominate the wholesale illicit drug market and control around 90% of the cocaine entering the United States. Analysts estimate that wholesale earnings from illicit drug sales range from $13.6 billion to $49.4 billion annually (Colleen W. Cook, ed. (October 16, 2007). 'Mexico's Drug Cartels'. CRS Report for Congress (PDF) Congressional Research Service; Fantz, Ashley (January 20, 2012). 'The Mexico Drug War: Bodies for Billions'. CNN News; BBC News. 26 March 2010). By the end of Felipe Calderón's administration (2006-12), the official death toll of the Mexican Drug War was at least 60,000! Estimates set the death toll above 120,000 killed by 2013, not including 27,000 missing (William Booth, 'Mexico's crime wave has left about 25,000 missing, government documents show'. The Washington Post, 30 November 2012; 'Counting Mexico's drug victims is a murky business'. National Catholic Reporter, Claire Schaeffer-Duffy, March. 1st, 2014).

'Alternative World Drug Report'

The hugely important Alternative World Drug Report was launched to coincide with the publication of the UN Office on Drugs and Crime's 2012 World Drug Report. It exposed the failure of governments and the UN to assess the extraordinary costs of pursuing a global war on drugs and calls for UN member states to meaningfully count these costs and explore all the alternatives. After 50 years of the current enforcement-led (alpha male) international drug control system, the war on drugs is coming under unparalleled scrutiny. Its goal was to create a 'drug-free world'. Instead, as referred to above, despite more than a trillion dollars spent fighting the war, according to the UNODC, illegal drugs are used by an estimated 270 million people and organised crime profits from a trade with an estimated turnover of over $330 billion a year – the world's largest illegal commodity market. The report estimates that enforcing global prohibition costs at least $100 billion a year. These shortcomings partly reflect the problems implicit in *self-reporting* on a system *by those who oversee, enforce and champion it* (The Alternative World Drug Report. Drug and Alcohol Review, Volume 33, Issue 2, page 215, March 2014. The Alternative World Drug Report: Counting the Costs of the War on Drugs edited by S. Rolles, G. Murkin, M. Powell, D. Kushlick and J. Slater, United Kingdom http://www.countthecosts.org/).

Ever-expanding drug law enforcement budgets have squeezed supply while demand has continued to grow. The result is inflated prices and the creation of a profit opportunity that has fuelled the emergence of a vast illegal trade controlled by criminal entrepreneurs. This has a range of negative impacts on local and global economies. Estimating global spending on drug law enforcement is difficult (due to poor data, inclusion criteria etc.), but it is likely to be well in excess of $100 billion annually. In terms of achieving the stated aims of enforcement, this spending has been extremely poor value for money, causing displacement, rather than eradication, of illegal activities, falling drug prices, and rising availability. Enforcement spending incurs opportunity costs in other areas of public expenditure, including other police priorities and drug-related health interventions.

Possible explanations of wars

Wars in the last few millennia have been described and explained in detail by historians. Commonly quoted causes are the expansionist ambitions of neighbours, a desire for territory or energy, such as oil, hatred of foreign neighbours or of another 'race', such as Jews, misguided religious fervour or a desire by the alpha males for seizing of others' resources. But surely, the basic cause is *biology*, notably innate, *primate* instincts regarding competition, territory, fear and suspicion of the foreign and notably those instincts associated with the alpha-male leaders, including power, money and obedience to them. Human instincts are typically inhibited when faced with the expression of overriding primate ones, especially where nations are concerned. Typical of the world's leaders is their constant use of language to instil fear and arouse basic instincts about territory and foreigners: the war on terror, the war on drugs, the war on crime, the war on...

A quotation from George Orwell's '1984' is literally true for alphas: *'Power is not a means; it is an end'*. That is an objective, possibly of us all, but especially of the alpha male. George Orwell did not need any lessons on alpha males or other primate instincts. His intuition was entirely accurate. Bertrand Russell, in his book 'Power' (1938), states that he is *'...concerned to prove that the fundamental concept in social science is Power, in the same sense that Energy is the fundamental concept of in physics'*. In this book, Russell also notes the inequality in the distribution of power, which he thinks is *'...partly due to external necessity, partly due to causes which are to be found in human nature'*. So, once again others have got there well before me – in this case two of my heroes, Bertrand Russell and George Orwell, and likely many more.

It's important to bear in mind that instincts are not expressed independently of environmental influences, of which *frightening* change is one such influence. Also, the creation of agriculture with mass food production and unprecedented increases in population have resulted in a material and human environment that has not previously existed. Evolution equipped us for individual and small-group survival in a different environment, i.e. trees.

As for the 'war on drugs', the uncontrolled availability of the major groups of addictive drugs is unquestionably harmful to the individual and to society. A key defect of the 'war' is that it is punitive and led by *law enforcement* officers. These alpha 'experts' are *predisposed* towards a punitive and prohibition-led approach. The 'Alternative World Drug Report' offers other approaches. One approach would be to eliminate criminality from drugs and perhaps for the pharmaceutical profession to make drugs available under controlled conditions. Advice and counselling could be made available. Non-punitive measures are already working for smoking reduction, i.e. the addictive drug nicotine and the cancerous chemical products of combustion. Alcohol awaits successful approaches. Given the addictive nature of many drugs, together with their availability from criminals, then the current, disastrous consequences of the current policy have always been inevitable.

A word about war from Immanuel Kant (Konigsberg, Prussia, 30ᵗʰ September 1784)

Once again, a bright, novel idea that struck me forcibly as being important and so far, unrecognised, has proved not to be original; in fact, it's at least 230 years old. In 'An answer to the question: what is enlightenment?' published by Penguin Books as part of a series, 'Great Ideas', Kant refers to war. I quote: 'We have to admit that the greatest evils which oppress civilized nations are the result of war – not so much of actual wars in the past or present as of the unremitting, indeed ever-increasing *preparation* for war in the future. All the resources of the State, and all the fruits of its culture which might be used to enhance that culture even further, are devoted to this purpose'. In the UK, with our many tens of billions of pounds (approximately £100 billion) spending on only Trident over the next decade or two, the situation is crystal clear. We have nobody to fire it at, but our alpha males gain a seat at the top table. And if we did fire it, it would deny the teaching of the state religion of the UK, i.e. Christianity.

Violent aggression: slavery, human rights and racism

Slavery and human rights

> '...a persistent and organised system of hostile measures against the rights of the owners of slaves in the southern states' would annihilate' property worth thousands of millions of dollars.'
> **Jefferson Davis, the first President of the new Southern Confederacy, addressing Confederate Congress**

> '...immediate cause of the late rupture and the present revolution'...was 'African slavery as it exists among us – the proper status of the Negro in our form of civilisation'
> **Alexander Stephens, New Confederacy Vice President and racist.**

The above quotations are good examples of the southern USA's vicious approach to slavery: money is more important than human rights and Negro slaves are not human. They also cast light on the needed cultural and widespread acceptance of slavery that existed among the whites. Shortly, below, I mention a public dispute I had with a Baptist minister when in Florida in 1961. He taught that Negros had no souls.

An especially evil practice was lynching as a form of 'extrajudicial authority'. This occurred regularly in the Southern states from the early 1800s. Later in early 19th century, with widespread photography, *postcards were taken of crowds of people picnicking under hanging bodies showing people who were proud of what they'd accomplished.* The following protest song about lynching was not popular at first, but became famous when sung by Billie Holiday who sold more than a million copies. It was originally a poem by the Jewish schoolteacher,

Abel Meeropol who wrote under the name of Lewis Allan. The poem/
song was prompted by Allan (Meeropol) seeing such a postcard.

Strange Fruit
> Southern trees bear a strange fruit,
> Blood on the leaves and blood at the root,
> Black bodies swinging in the southern breeze,
> Strange fruit hanging from the poplar trees.
> Pastoral scene of the gallant south,
> The bulging eyes and the twisted mouth,
> Scent of magnolias, sweet and fresh,
> Then the sudden smell of burning flesh.
> Here is fruit for the crows to pluck,
> For the rain to gather, for the wind to suck,
> For the sun to rot, for the trees to drop,
> Here is a strange and bitter crop.

A famous variation on lynching was when 14-year-old Emmett
Till was dragged out of his bed by two white gunmen who took him
away in a truck, beat him, tortured him, shot him in the head and
dumped his body in the Tallahatchie River. His 'crime' was to have
whistled at a white woman in her store in Mississippi.

Later, April Shipp, a quilt-maker, spent four years working
on a quilt called Strange Fruit. It carries the names of over 5,000
lynched men, woman and children, lovingly sewn in gold thread on
black fabric. The fabric also carries two nooses. April wanted all
their names remembered. She said that she cried every day that she
worked on her quilt of names.

Other extreme examples of cruelty
Associated with *modern* slavery up to today with few exceptions, are
continuous cruelty, ill treatment and violent repression as above. Slaves
have been bred like cattle, with children separated from parents and
enduring extremes of vicious punishment for perceived wrongdoing,

especially disobedience. Particularly in the Caribbean it has been an experiment in human terror. With exceptions, the following punishments were common in *modern* (not classical) slave economies.

- Largely peaceful rebellions have been put down savagely with dismembered bodies left to hang
- Shackles and branding with hot irons
- Flog, then cover with molasses to attract insects and flies
- Put shit in slaves' mouths
- Slit the nose
- Burn cheeks
- Rape women slaves
- A recommended extreme punishment was to pull the living body of a slave in opposite directions until the body split

Slave economy of American South and numerous other slaughters. After the ethnic 'cleansing' of the indigenous, 'Indian savages' came the massive contribution of the slave economy to the American South with its vicious, evil legacy of racism. And there is much more, elsewhere. Millions died in Stalin's Russia and about the same number also died of starvation as a result of Mao's repression in China (see section on the 'State' later), and back to the Irish famine of 1847 with Britain's (or rather our leaders') shocking indifference. Beyond these awful examples we go to modern, continuing slavery – dealt with at more length later. Unlike other forms of slavery (e.g. ancient Rome or Greece), but like the Jews, this was 'racial' and illegitimately 'justified' on the grounds of racial inferiority.

Land theft. On a smaller scale of atrocity, worldwide, we have numerous crimes such as the 'clearances' in Scotland (and many other places), when common land was systematically and 'lawfully' taken over by the rich via misuse of the law (documented in 'The poor had no lawyers' by A. Wightman). In England, some monarchs claimed *all* land as their own personal property and gave to their allies or took from their enemies. And these monarchs also gave titles and other patronage. Partly as a consequence, today in England and

Wales we have, like Scotland, virtually no common land. Indeed, even school playing fields have been sold off by recent right-wing UK governments. The Victorian English social commentator G. K. Chesterton (in 'What's wrong with the world', 1910) quoted an Old English rhyme that has immortalised this 'easy aristocratic habit':

> 'You prosecute the man or woman
> Who steals the goose from off the common,
> But leave the larger felon loose
> Who steals the common from the goose.'

We know that the above criminal list goes back as far as history itself. Such criminal behaviour is so frequent and widespread as to show that it is *characteristic of humans* when in extreme situations of national/group stress <u>or</u> when desiring wealth or territory: money equals safety and survival.

Rohingya people. Relatively unnoticed until now (2017) among the numerous current vicious wars is the plight of the Rohingya people in Myanmar. Since August 2016, nearly 700,000 people – mostly Rohingya – have fled Myanmar to nearby Bangladesh. The Rohingya people are trapped in a dehumanising system of state sponsored discrimination and racial segregation. As Oxfam has said, this is apartheid – a crime against humanity as defined by international law. Since August 2017, reports of killings, rape and massacres have flooded in, as satellite images show numerous villages have been burned to the ground by the 'security' forces. More than 600,000 Rohingya people have crossed over to Bangladesh. They are living in terrible conditions; many are without shelter or clean water. **Note**. Wickepaedia has a useful history of the Rohingya people.

Slavery in 2018. Slavery has been a blot on the story of human rights from time immemorial to the present day. It is surely significant as a *characteristic of humans* that about 30 million slaves still exist worldwide today. The 'Not for Sale' organisation is an extraordinary example of an individual making a huge difference to what seemed an intractable problem. In 2001, David Batstone discovered that his favourite bay area (California, USA) restaurant had been the centre of a local human-trafficking ring. He realised this was part of a growing international issue affecting every industry and corner of the Earth. Batstone wrote the book 'Not For Sale' in 2007, and a new organisation was born. Also, 'Free2Work' is an offshoot that provides consumers with information on forced and child labour for the brands and products they wish to buy.

Slavery was not always associated with racism until modern times. An account of slavery in modern America is given in the book by James O. and Lois E. Horton, 'Slavery and the making of America'. It includes a chronology of significant dates and events related to slavery, starting with 1619 when a Dutch ship brought 20 Africans, the first ever to be sold to British colonists in Jamestown, Virginia. Wikipedia also gives a comprehensive list of significant dates. Recently (2014), a personal account of slavery has been made into a film. 'Twelve Years a Slave' was first published in 1853. Solomon Northup was born a free man (of slave ancestors) in NY State and, aged 33, he was kidnapped in Washington DC and transported to New Orleans where he was sold into slavery. He gives a personal, first-hand account of his life, including vicious, inhuman punishments by slave masters.

Human rights. Different states at different times have established widespread human rights, only later to be lost. Notably, in the 6th century BC, Cyrus the Great abolished slavery in Persia and established unprecedented human rights and religious freedoms. In 449 BC, came the Law of the Twelve Tables that stood at the foundation of Roman law. The Twelve Tables came about as a result of the long social struggle between patricians (alpha males) and plebeians (the 'plebs') and established basic procedural rights for all Roman *citizens* as against one another. Broadly speaking, during this time and also earlier (the Axial Age – see the section on 'Religion'), several philosophical developments arose in different parts of the world in what now seems to have been independent attempts to rise above magic, superstition and the multitude of religious dogmas. These were Confucianism and Daoism in China, Hinduism and Buddhism in India, monotheism in Israel and philosophical rationalism in Greece. It was the period of the Buddha, Socrates, Confucius, Jeremiah, and the mystics of the Upanishads – Mencius and Euripides (see Karen Armstrong's 'The Great Transformation'). Often in history, such developments are forgotten only to be rediscovered maybe centuries later.

Thomas Paine (1737-1809) was an English and American political activist, philosopher, political theorist, revolutionary and author of several highly influential pamphlets regarding the American and French Revolutions and human rights in particular. His ideas are alive today. He inspired the American rebels in 1776 to declare independence from Britain. His prolific ideas reflected the then current Enlightenment ideas of transnational human rights. His pamphlets included *Common Sense* (1776, American independence from Great Britain) and *The American Crisis* (a series, 1776-83, pro-revolution). Paine wrote *Rights of Man* (1791), which was in part a defence of the French Revolution against its critics. His pamphlet *The Age of Reason* (1793-94) advocated deism based on the belief that reason and observation of the natural world is sufficient to determine the existence of a Creator. It rejects organised religion and religious knowledge as a source of authority and also rejects belief in supernatural events such as miracles and the absence of error in the scriptures. Paine also wrote the pamphlet *Agrarian Justice* (1795), discussing the origins of property, and introduced the concept of a *guaranteed minimum income*.

Despite these progressive, liberal examples, over the centuries and to the present time, human rights have beeen continuously and widely attacked. Slavery has been widespread with persistent attempts to outlaw it on an almost yearly basis, all more or less unsuccessful in practice until modern times. In the United States, Abraham Lincoln signed the 1863 Emancipation Proclamation which declared that slaves in Confederate-controlled areas (southern) were to be freed. Most slaves in 'border states' were freed by state action; a separate law freed the slaves in Washington DC. In December 1865, the US abolished slavery with the Thirteenth Amendment to the United States Constitution. It affected about 40,000 remaining slaves.

Nevertheless, to repeat, shockingly it's estimated that the world still has around 30 million slaves today. In 2014, there were about 13,000 slaves in the UK (Reports by Anti-Slavery International and the UK Home Office).

Recent evidence about modern slavery in the West. University College London.
Recently, extraordinary documentary evidence has emerged about the profits of specific individuals and the influence of slavery on many economies, notably that of the UK. Rather like the recent banking crisis – 'too big to fail', the slave economy was also deemed too big to fail.   Historians at University College London (UCL) unearthed detailed 'Slave Compensation Archives' at the UK National Archives in Kew: (http://www.independent.co.uk/news/uk/home-news/britains-colonial-shame-slaveowners-given-huge-payouts-after-abolition-8508358.html);   (http://www.theguardian.com/world/2013/aug/27/britain-slave-trade).

The UK government (*including 37 slave-owning members of the UK House of Lords*) decided that the abolition of slavery required compensation to the slave owners, but not to the slaves! To facilitate the recompense, slaves became legally defined as *property*. There were about 800,000 slaves across the world and 46,000 slave owners and managers, of which 3,000 of the latter were in the UK and who disproportionately owned about 50% of the slaves. These owners were widely distributed throughout the UK. The records show the names and addresses of everyone compensated for their loss of property (yes, *property!*) with a total in today's money of about £17 billion. Modern slavery surely ranks close to the Holocaust in terms of evil but would also appear to be the biggest 'scam' in history in terms of the rich compensating the rich criminals (largely *themselves*) and not the victims.   Unsurprisingly similar, the recent financial crash is being dealt with by having little effect on the rich, but via reduction of welfare for the poor.   There is a current propaganda campaign against the UK unemployed.   The system of slavery was also supported by a massive propaganda campaign falsely presenting the owners as benevolent bosses of simple, ignorant savages.   According to the historian, Edward Long, these African slave 'savages' were inferior in many ways: skin colour, nose shapes and lip shapes.

Even if black Africans were intrinsically inferior in some way, which they were not and are <u>not</u>, how does that justify their evil, extremely violent suppression?   Why was modern slavery so vicious?   Personally, I have no answer to offer.   The evidence, as already stated, is that <u>all</u> modern humans left Africa only around 60,000 years ago; we are all Africans and skin shade is about the sun – avoiding cancer if the skin is dark and getting enough vitamin D if the skin is light. And it was not always so extremely bad for slaves.   In classical Greece (there was about 1 slave to each 2 free citizens), slaves were not treated with such extreme violence.   Even though many Greek slaves worked under bad conditions in the economically important silver mines, many could become educated and work as cooks or nurses and they could become skilled craftsmen.   Freedom was possible, although exceptional, and it was possible (although very rare) to attain citizenship.

In the UK, slavery drove the economy for around 200 years.   It's clear that the huge sums of compensation also affected the overall culture of the UK and the life of the individual recipients.

UCL academics showed how slave money shaped UK industrialisation and also financial services per se; this is thought to be an aspect of why the UK is today a tax haven.

Many 'great estates' came from slave cash, and also benefitted were great public institutions such as the British Museum.   Beneficiaries of slave money infiltrated UK elite society. Membership of the UK House of Lords has long been facilitated by donations to political parties, including today: money has always spoken decisively. During the 'compensation' debate and subsequently, there was much propaganda and airbrushing away of the slavery aspect of wealth with the owners and their offspring presented as 'merchants', 'developers' and 'entrepreneurs'. If any evidence were needed to refute ideas of intrinsic superiority of the elite, the consequences of 'compensation' provide it. Among many, 'compensation' money benefitted the father of former Prime Minister Gladstone, numerous other families including ones that became Earldoms (the Earl of Harewood) and an ancestor of the previous UK Prime Minister, David Cameron. I have personally seen a newspaper aerial photograph of the estate of David Cameron's father and by any standards it is huge. Slave money bought land, built estates and stately homes that became 'heritage' sites, and also bought national titles.

And the slaves received <u>*nothing*</u>.

It should be emphasised that slave owners came from across UK society. Once again, it seems highly likely that the owners were *not* inherently evil people in the conventional sense, but nevertheless they and their estate managers did do great evil. Nor did their descendants inherit evil. But they did inherit money. Again, given the appropriate circumstances, this is what <u>all</u> humans are capable of as a race – <u>all</u> of us.

Racism
The Holocaust is an extreme example of racism at its worst (also see below 'Lessons'). Its factory-efficient, racist slaughter of the Jews is disgusting beyond measure and involved the power phenotype at its most extreme and also, in many cases, the extreme *obedience* to power. Many ordinary individual German, French, Polish and Slav people went along with it, together with collaboration by their states.

For example, the French 'government' negotiated for the removal to death camps only of 'foreign' Jews. In a 'Sign for Cain', psychiatrist Fredric Wertham gives an extensive account of human violence, including details of a pre-Hitler, deliberate and systematic killing of large numbers of German mental patients. In 1939, about 275,000 mental patients were killed. The indications of suitability for killing became wider – 'superfluous people', misfits, undesirables, the aged and infirm. Jewish mental patients, old and young, were excluded at first because they did not deserve the 'benefit' of psychiatric euthanasia. Eventually, they were rounded up and exterminated. Shockingly horrendous is the fact that numerous leading psychiatric institutions and eminent psychiatrists took part in this 'medical' holocaust – people who were established professionally *before* Hitler came to power.

The scale of Nazi atrocities has recently been revealed to be several-fold worse than previously thought: there were an unprecedented 42,500 *sites* as ghettos, killing centres and forced labour camps from 1933 to 1945. Not only is the scale of the atrocities unprecedented, but the nature of them is unprecedented: the factory-efficient mass killing and the extreme cruelty. It was beyond being inhuman. Speaking personally, I have been shocked and disgusted at what humans have done to humans. Any reader who has ignored reading about the Holocaust can be forgiven: it is appalling. Even during the week that I rewrote this section, I watched a TV documentary about the efficiency of the slaughter and of the extreme gratuitous cruelty. One 'small' item physically sickened me. It was the knowledge by inmates of 'Block 11' at Auschwitz. Everywhere, conditions were appalling, but in this block the worst cruelty and torture went on. In one cell, people were locked in and *left in the dark to starve to death*. Which inhuman 'human' thought of this? And why did so many other humans take part and so many not speak out against it? It's beyond sick. Surely this is not simply inhuman, and it is definitely not animal like: it's an extreme form of pathological human behaviour carried out by alpha males _and_ *their mindless followers.* Several countries collaborated over the Holocaust – notably Polish, French and Slovaks.   Later, I refer to how the surviving Jews deserved for the rest of the world to buy some of the 'Holy Land' (despite the erroneous history) for them in recompense for the Holocaust.   But we did not, instead 'we' (the powerful West, especially my own country, Britain) gave them territory that we did not own and created the problems we now have in the Middle East. If the land was holy once, it is not holy now.

From the Holocaust to modern Syria. An individual postscript to the Holocaust was revealed recently (2014) by the Jerusalem-based Nazi hunter, Efraim Zuroff.   Although shocking, it's worth noting as an example of extreme individual pathology.   Alois Brunner, the world's most wanted Nazi war criminal, who sent around 130,000 European Jews to the gas chambers, died aged 98 in Syria in 2010. He was described by Zuroff as a sadist and a fanatical Nazi.   Zuroff quoted Brunner's evil comments to a German magazine in 1985: 'My only regret is that I didn't murder more Jews'.   He fled to Syria in the 1950s and was reported to have worked as a *special advisor on torture* to the previous Syrian government, led by Hafez al-Assad, the father of the current President, Bashar al-Assad.   A young Syrian doctor who fled Syria for Germany recently told the UK press that 'Most political prisoners had been so badly tortured, there was nothing we could do for them, as doctors we felt helpless'.   Thus, Brunner's evil influence lives on, continuing from the previous President of Syria to the present one.

But at least Jews surviving the Holocaust kept their culture. Slaves often did not.   'Modern' slavery, the huge numbers aside, brought about the devastating and deliberate destruction of the ethnic culture and people were bred like cattle and frequently treated much worse.   The destruction of culture and personal humiliation had effects that were widespread and long-lasting.   Among the worst effects of slavery, reinforced by racists, is the totally false idea of racial inferiority.   It is clear that humans have only one race – the human race.   As mentioned elsewhere, there is more genetic variation *within* broad ethnic groups (Africans, Arabs, Chinese, Europeans and people of the Middle East) than there is *between* them.

Personal experiences of racism

Many white readers will not have encountered full-blown racism. I have lived in Bristol, UK where slavery (and tobacco) had been the cornerstone of the local economy. I have often shopped on Blackboy Hill and Whiteladies Road, leading down to the docks. The main beneficiaries of such trade have long lived in luxury in rich Bristol districts such as Clifton and Leigh Woods alongside other notables such as the Bishop(s). On an academic visit to Tanzania, I once visited Zanzibar and went down stone steps through a tunnel leading down to a dock where slave ships had carried slaves. Shockingly, and still stuck firmly in my memory, those granite-like stone steps were deeply worn down by the <u>bare feet</u> of fellow humans: many thousands of people over centuries. In the early 1960s, while working at the University of Florida I had a newspaper debate with a local Baptist pastor who taught that black people had no souls. In such ways, the elite justified the oppression of fellow humans. As it was common *not* to ill-treat animals, any logic in the oppression was absent. A similar false logic is used to justify the removal of 'welfare' from the poor and jobless of any colour: they are automatically and mindlessly labelled as lazy and work-shy, even when there are few or no jobs available.

During the same period at the University of Florida – the <u>19</u>60s and not the 1860s – I witnessed an extraordinary example of racial bullying. I give it because it was not extraordinary in that place at that time. There was a need to appoint a technician on a research grant. After interviewing three candidates, I appointed a black man as a technician. He was clearly and by far the most intelligent and capable. Subsequently, I was told that he was the first black man *ever* to be appointed as a technician at *any* institution in the State of Florida. Some black people did carry out such duties but were classified as laboratory helpers/washers-up and paid poorly as such. The first day he turned up for work in our laboratory an attempt was made by local police to arrest him! This was his crime. He drove to the campus police station to pick up his university permit to park. But he did not have permission to park without a permit! A policeman, carrying a gun and behaving with extraordinary insensitivity, discourtesy and crudeness, arrived in our laboratory and attempted to arrest him! Without intervention, our new colleague would literally have been behind bars within the hour. Unquestionably, the policeman's intention was vicious bullying and intimidation. And only a decade before my arrival in Florida (1961) it was common for mob *lynchings* (i.e. murder by hanging, with *festive gatherings to take place)* as punishment for assertions such as looking at a white woman in an 'unacceptable' way.

Possible explanations of racism and slavery
Racism, and notably the Holocaust, can be explained biologically to some extent e.g. by Jews being perceived as foreign, with associated negative basic instincts about *foreignness* and also territory (Holy Land – their holy land, intended for them by God). They also had a foreign, alien religion and a foreign language (Hebrew and Yiddish). They adhered to their 'foreign' dress customs. Everywhere, they were foreign in every sense. Nevertheless, the extreme systematic horror of the Holocaust indicates the dimensions of the potential for human evil and has no simple explanation. Slavery was strongly influenced by the slaves' monetary value, notably in the southern USA economy and in the Caribbean (many UK owned), but definitely worldwide too. Slavery has not always been associated with racism. It's hard to explain the frequent, but not continuous, systematic cruelty to slaves – possibly to humiliate and subjugate them into submission and obedience. But humans with power often express cruelty: consider the almost routine cruelty associated with wars.

Hierarchical status of slavery, human rights and racism
Throughout human history, probably post hunter-gatherers and definitely for the last several thousand years, we have had hierarchies of humans in terms of power and rights. In Europe we commonly

speak of 'upper' and 'lower' classes. Characteristically, at the top are the rich alpha males and we tend to think that, where they exist, the least powerful are the slaves. In fact, in the modern world there are humans living in ghettoes in numerous cities, e.g. in the USA, who are ignored, having no rights, immersed in drug addiction, crime and extreme poverty, and who are far worse off than, say, Greek slaves. As stated elsewhere, it is now normal to have a relatively small proportion of a population with a disproportionate ownership of the wealth. This is dealt with in more detail under the section 'Causes of human problems', but also briefly here.

Selecting from data mentioned earlier, the richest 1% of people own nearly half of the global wealth (The Credit Suisse Global Wealth Report October 2014). 'Taken together, the bottom half of the global population own less than 1% of total wealth. The richest decile holds 87% of the world's wealth, and the top percentile alone accounts for 48.2% of global assets' (around £70tn). The report found that the UK was the only country in the G7 to have recorded rising inequality in the 21st century. Oxfam (Report Jan 2014) warned that the richest 85 people across the globe share a combined wealth of £1 trillion; that is as much as the poorest 3.5 billion of the world's population.

Approximate hierarchy of power (money and rights) for humans (2017)

World's top alpha-male elite of ~85 people own ~£1tn ie ~
£12bn per person
↓
Top 10% i.e. 700x10^6 own ~ £60x 10^{12} ie ~ £900K per person
↓
Bottom 3.5 billion own ~ £1tn i.e. ~ £300 per person
↓
Slaves with no rights, no income i.e. nil £
↓
Destitute in slum property or homeless, addicted, mentally
and physically ill: no income i.e. nil £.

Violent aggression: religion

Introduction

There have been and continue to be vicious and widespread atrocities by numerous religions, including all the major ones, in the name of God and directly *against* the teaching of their prophets who advocated altruism. Typically, they were carried out by humans impelled by mindless and heartless primate instincts, with religion being merely the superficial reason – 'It is God's will'. In recent times, Buddhists, Sikhs, Muslims, Hindus and Christians have slaughtered each other. Even within religions we have slaughter. The 'Catholic' IRA has basically been at war with the Protestant government of Northern Ireland. I was in the very street in Birmingham, England when a bomb (attributed to the IRA) exploded in a pub, murdering numerous innocent people. I witnessed the altruism of a young policeman who ran *towards* the location of the bomb blast, not away.

As bad as it gets: the 'Holy' Inquisition

One of the worst examples of all time, which bears some comparison with the extreme evils of the Holocaust, was the 'Holy Inquisition' of the hugely powerful RC Church in the Middle Ages. The Church had political *and* religious power. Humans were tortured, burned alive or mutilated in a cold-blooded, deliberate way in the name of God. The Inquisition is surely a horror story of the most extreme kind. 'Witches' were burned alive as a result of clerical allegations or of 'evidence' of witchcraft such as giving birth to a deformed child. This was not unrepresentative extremism: *this was the official Church in action.* A Pope authorised the building of underground torture chambers. Popes financed the so-called 'Crusades' against Muslims that ruthlessly slaughtered entire populations of men, women and children. Surely, claiming this as the will of God is committing pure blasphemy in the Church's own terms.

In the West, and going back in history, the Christian Church's supremacy over beliefs was such that even publicly referring to the possibility of the Earth not being the centre of the universe was dangerous and potentially life-threatening, as in the case of Galileo. What was threatened was the absolute truth described by God in sacred books and as controlled and interpreted by God's clergy – contributing to social control and 'cohesion. Such 'glue' aided biological survival. *Ideas* that contradicted the Church's dogmatic teaching (which would be seen as heresy) could be, and were, met by torture and burning alive as mentioned above. One example, striking for me personally, is Girolamo Savanorola, a Dominican Friar, first tortured on the rack (to extract a 'confession'!) and then burned alive on May 23, 1498 by the Church authorities for heresy

I mention it because I have sat uncomfortably in the square, Piazza della Signoria, in front of the Palazzo Vecchio in Florence, where he was burned to death. For some time, he had denounced the corrupt Borgia Pope as well as the powerful Lorenzo de Medici and Florentine corruption in general. In Christian terms this should have been applauded. In primate terms, it was not wise. In some ways he was similar to modern 'whistleblowers' who are typically (always?) ill-treated. Sometimes there are extreme, modern equivalents such as Syrian government detention and torture centres and USA Guantanimo Bay and other detention and torture centres. Adding to the biological aspects of this behaviour is that I have had and still have personal friends and acquaintances who are Cistercians, Dominicans, Jesuits or regular priests. They are/were as humane, altruistic and intelligent as one could imagine. They barely survive intellectually in organisations demanding intellectual obedience and in the Middle Ages would have been in deep trouble.

Appropriate circumstances for such violation of humans included religious over-obedience by laity as well as an extreme primate, alpha-male leadership by government. The vicious, revengeful World War 1 settlement, connected to the crash in the German economy and the collapse of printed money. Germans felt they needed 'strong leadership' and, almost inevitably, a scapegoat. They were over-obedient, accepted mass conformity of irrational ideas about Jews, with uniformed mass rallies and were over-reverential to an exceptionally extreme, racist leader, Hitler. I have met potential 'Hitlers' in the UK (and elsewhere) who are widely regarded as 'nutters' and to be avoided. And who could have anticipated the behaviour of the Zionists to the Palestinians? Are there not reflections of Jewish history here, with many Palestinians excluded from their own home? And it's not easy to claim that Jews are genetically pure or claim the purity of anyone else for that matter (see earlier and also 'The Y chromosome pool of Jews as part of the genetic landscape of the Middle East'. Am J. Hum Genet. 2001 Nov; volume **69**, pages 1095-112. A. Nebel *et al.*). Interestingly, Jewishness in a religious sense is officially conferred by the mother, i.e. via the X chromosome: probably because of the uncertainty of the father and the certainty of the mother.

INACTION OF OFFICIAL RELIGIOUS CLERGY TO ALL THESE WIDESPREAD EVILS

The indigenous religious clergy of oppressors and of oppressed are typically but *not always* inactive.   Occasionally, religious leaders verbally condemn evil in general terms. The Quakers are often a noble exception and so are numerous, brave people including individual Christian priests in the Poland of Hitler's Holocaust. The official clergy have even supported oppression, even slavery (clearly accepted as far back as the Bible's Old Testament and beyond) or the Holocaust (the Jews killed Christ – so providing a spurious justification of collective punishment by Christians).   We had papal-sponsored 'Crusades' against Islam to retain the 'holy' places when the population of entire towns was slaughtered – men, women and children. To repeat this blasphemy (according to the teaching of Christianity, an insult to God) – holy *places* were the motive for slaughtering entire populations of *men, women and children*. It seems clear that the need for the survival of a religious institution in a particular society override the teaching of the founder. This is enlarged on later under 'Religion' as a social institution. The biological explanations given above for the abuse of women apply equally to women's place in many religions. When the bugle blows, they may not obey (see earlier 'abuse and discrimination against women'.) The lowly place of women in the RC Church is mirrored in other religions.

Throughout it all were numerous instances of individual humanist and religious people fighting and organising to protect fellow humans, but few (if any) examples of 'official' indigenous, religious hierarchies objecting to such specific evil. Denouncing evil in general is another matter. But 'official' religions *could* play a positive role as described later under 'Religion'. The current efflux of refugees, notably from the horrors of Syria and coming West, is a case in point. Only recently (September 2015), led by Germany and initially opposed by the UK and others, has there been significant movement regarding accepting them in west European countries.

Critically involved have been mass, individual protests about this injustice. And only *after* these protests do religious leaders speak out about the need to help when it is now politically OK to do so.

What would Jesus (or very probably any of the great sages) say about the efflux of refugees?

What would Jesus say about people who could help but do not?
Unquestionably, Jesus would demand that we help them in a practical way. The answers to both questions are indisputable because in the New Testament Matthew's gospel (chapter 25) shortly before his execution, Jesus described how, as the Messiah, he would return to judge mankind. Those who help the needy (with whom he explicitly identifies personally) are welcomed into Heaven. Those who do not are cursed and sent into the eternal flames of Hell. This demand from Jesus has been almost lost by the 'official' church in the need for clergy-controlled pious, so-called sacred practices (church services) and the overriding need for *institutional* survival – 'now is not the time to speak out'. Typically for official bureaucracies, <u>it never is.</u>

Violent aggression and lessons learned. The Holocaust as exemplar

We are all capable of such things given the appropriate circumstances and history

(This section can be read partly as an extreme account following that on 'Wars - what have we learned?')

To take extreme cases, the lesson of the Holocaust is *not* that Germans are intrinsically evil or congenitally hate Jews, or that almost everyone intrinsically despises slaves and endorses slavery. In September 2016, Germany gave a generous lead regarding help to the millions of refugees, notably from Syria. To repeat something from earlier about another atrocity, the ethnic cleansing of indigenous people by early 'Americans' and the subsequent use of African slaves was, in fact, committed mostly by European settlers such as the British, French, German, Russian and Dutch.

Appropriate circumstances for such violation of humans included over-obedience to an extreme primate, alpha-male leadership. The vicious, revengeful World War 1 settlement, was connected to the crash in the German economy and the collapse of printed money. Germans felt they needed 'strong leadership' and, almost inevitably, a scapegoat. They were over-obedient, accepted mass conformity of irrational ideas about Jews, with uniformed mass rallies and were over-reverential to an exceptionally extreme, racist leader, Hitler. I have met potential 'Hitlers' in the UK (and elsewhere) who are widely regarded as 'nutters' and to be avoided. And who could have anticipated the behaviour of the Zionists to the Palestinians? Are there not reflections of Jewish history here, with many Palestinians excluded from their own home? And it's hard to claim that Jews are genetically pure (see earlier and also 'The Y chromosome pool of Jews as part of the genetic landscape of the Middle East'. Am J. Hum Genet. 2001 Nov; volume **69**, pages 1095-

112. A. Nebel *et al.*). Interestingly, as mentioned earlier, Jewishness in a religious sense is officially conferred by the mother's Jewishness.

A modern tragedy is that the Jews in Israel have instinctively learned the lessons about power, might and territory and the benefit of having even more powerful friends. Instead of the 'wandering, foreign Jew', with no powerful ally and very 'suspiciously' little allegiance to his nation or place of residence or indigenous religion, but rather to a foreign, mythical Jerusalem, the Jews now have their 'own' territory and regard it in the conventional, primate way. Jews who integrated, for example, into USA society have ended with the same social statistics as non-Jewish Americans. The Palestinians, who had their land given away by powerful non-owners (British 'Protectorate') and have a religion alien to the Jews are learning the same biological lessons regarding survival. The Israelis are teaching them these lessons. They are branded by Israelis as terrorists, although with relatively few weapons.

(Later under 'Background ideas on evolutionary biology' there is a section on cultural myths, of which Israel has its fair share.)

Zionist terrorists are similar to other terrorists

It should also be remembered that the initial Israeli cabinet contained numerous members who were undoubtedly terrorist by any definition. The main Jewish-Zionist terrorist organisations were the Zionist Hagana, Irgun and the Stern Gangs. Today, the opponents of Israeli occupation who use force are also and predictably described as terrorists. Palestine is one of the most intractable problems that the world faces, and I will now spend a little space considering it from a biological perspective.

It needs to be said that numerous, dreadful atrocities were committed by the above-mentioned early Zionist terror groups. Menachem Begin (later the sixth Prime Minister of Israel) planned the destruction of the King David Hotel and the massacre of Deir Yassin. Ex-Prime Minister (seventh) Yitzhak Shamir was originally a member of Irgun, which was headed by Menachem Begin.

Shamir later joined the 'Stern Gang'. Shamir 'justified' the various assassinations committed by the Irgun and Stern gangs on the grounds that 'it was the only way we could operate, because we were so small. So, it was more efficient *and more moral* (my italics) to go for selected targets'. No, it was not more moral: it was biologically impelled to possess territory. Humanly, it is always immoral to kill innocent people.

The selected 'moral' targets in those early days of the founding of the State of Israel included the bombing of the King David Hotel and the massacre of Deir Yassin. The latter was an especially dreadful massacre. A combined force of Irgun and Stern members massacred 260 Arab residents of the village of Deir Yassin in April 1948. Most of the victims were women and children. Chaim Weizmann (first President of Israel), referred to the massacre as this 'miraculous simplification of our task', and David Ben-Gurion (first Prime Minister) said that 'without Deir Yasin there would be no Israel'. This last statement is a pure expression of religious fundamentalism. It infers that nothing matters more than the creation of Israel. But yes, *there are things that matter more*, for example *not slaughtering any innocent people* such as Palestinian Muslim Arabs or German Jews or indeed any innocent people whatsoever - none.

There are numerous parallels that can be drawn regarding the behaviour of other groups in defence or acquisition of land throughout history. Opponents, often victims, of dreadful atrocities think of and describe the perpetrators as evil and deserving of nothing. As I write this, the UK is dealing with the aftermath, decades old, of murders, beatings and indiscriminate bombings by the Irish IRA: decades of violence, bombings and also discussions leading to the current peace. Psychiatrists have surprisingly classified those convicted as *not* psychotic and *not* psychopathic murderers. It seems likely that these IRA 'terrorists' considered themselves as doing noble work, fighting for their land that was wrongly taken away from them centuries ago. In this case, unlike Zionists, they did so without recourse to claiming God's support. It seems obvious that primate instincts about territory (acquisition or loss of) play a major role. Yet nobody can truly justify killing innocent people because it might help towards gaining land, 'sacred' or not.

It is dangerous to recruit God to support the taking of land

The Zionists (*not* all Jews) believe that they have God on their side. To me, this is dubious theology, since any God worthy of the name could easily bring about the taking of land without bombings and slaughter. God does not need nationalist gangs. Nevertheless, the Old Testament has numerous instances of God slaughtering his enemies and creating plagues, famines and tsunamis against the enemies of his chosen people. This is collective punishment. And sometimes against his own people to test their faith. It seems obvious to non-Zionists that the case of Israel is an extreme example, among many, of the instinctive power of territory and of environmental forces – in this case, forces heavily reinforced by deep-rooted, religious beliefs. The behaviour of early (and current) Zionist terrorists who bombed, killed and slaughtered innocent people is explained by primate instincts regarding territory, amplified by the Holocaust and by the 'religious' belief that God has promised them specific land. Zionists believe that their God puts Zionist land before anything; certainly, before the rights of other inhabitants.

The Irish Republican Army (IRA) had similar ideas, but without God being involved. And for numerous groups throughout history, it is *as if* territory is sacred. As mentioned earlier, territorial instincts are entirely explicable in terms of *biology*: that is, territory is a space where the inhabitant knows where it is safe or dangerous or where to hide or where there is food etc. In the case of current Zionists, they did not know the land in that sense: much of their energy for land acquisition came from their religion.

I wish to point out that it is not supportable that the Jews or any other large group are genetically very different to other human groupings (see earlier). The behaviour of Zionism is surely entirely explicable in terms of being post the dreadful Holocaust, coupled with territorial instincts reinforced by conflicting religions. God has promised them this land and God seems indifferent to how they get it and keep it. God, to many Zionists, is somewhat indifferent to the needs of people other than Jews. To the outsider, this is bad and unbelievable, and many see Jews with suspicion, wrongly regarding them as racially different. But, to repeat, there is overwhelming evidence that there is only one human race.

After the Holocaust, what could be done in justice?

When the United Nations Relief and Works Agency (UNRWA) began operations in 1950, it was responding to the needs of about 750,000 Palestine refugees. Today, some 5 million Palestine refugees are eligible for UNRWA services. Nearly one-third of the registered Palestine refugees, more than 1.5 million individuals, live in 58 recognised Palestine refugee camps in Jordan, Lebanon, the Syrian Arab Republic, the Gaza Strip and the West Bank, including East Jerusalem. A healthy humanity would have negotiated and paid for land for the Jews after the dreadful, indelible stain on humanity that was the Holocaust. They truly deserved some land. To extend USA President Kennedy's association of himself with Berliners, we are all Jews, we are all Palestinians. And in biological terms, *we are all African*, since we are all descended from anatomically modern humans who first left Africa only about 60,000 years ago.

Have the alpha-male world leaders thought **_now_** (2018) of raising the many billions of dollars needed to *buy* (with cash and not weapons) land and build and equip self-managed, sustainable human settlements for the displaced Palestinians? The so-called defence spending of the countries most involved could be used at least partly. The amounts ($ billions) are surely adequate: USA (596 – i.e. around 600 billion $)), UK (55), France (51), Saudi Arabia (87). The total for only these few countries is about $0.8 trillion, i.e. **$800 billion**! And could Israel help? Even a tenth of only the arms spending of the interested countries equals about $80 billion. Also, imagine if humans could find a way to live peacefully, then a *world* armaments budget of £1.7 *trillion* would be decimated. Another potential source of finance is the approximately **$20 _trillion_** stashed away in tax havens referred to earlier, owned by individuals.

Q. It is technically possible, so why not?

A. We and our alphas are still impelled by ancient, pre-human instincts

Note: If we divide the world arms budget of $1,700 billion by the world population of about 7 billion, then we have available $242 per inhabitant of our new, common and peaceful planet. If ever proof were needed of our species' sickness, then the continued, colossal spending on world destruction is it.

Even as recently as 28th May 2014, President Obama was reported as addressing graduates of West Point military academy and delivering a new US foreign policy. He said that the US must lead the world, because if 'we do not' then 'nobody else will'. But this new policy included more collaboration with allies and offered funding for the training of allies in the fight against opponents he labelled terrorists. He was advocating an alpha-male approach with the USA as his chosen alpha country. If highly intelligent and educated Barack Obama (with his highly intelligent and educated wife) talked in this way, then the need for widespread, *individual* involvement is ever more urgent. Did President Obama not consider *why* 'terrorists' exist? One reason is that 'they' are frequently designated/invented as such, often by the USA. Does he think of it as simply an expression of spontaneous, mindless evil? Could it not be *partly a consequence* of historical oppressive behaviour by powerful colonialists: for example, the Western partitioning of Africa and of the Middle East into incompatible units: similarly, for the creation of Israel?

CAUSES OF HUMANITY'S PROBLEMS

Contents

INTRODUCTION: AN OVERVIEW

Having considered humanity's key problems earlier, what are the main causes? Broadly, current human society is sick. Evidence suggests that the *disease* is a sense of not belonging: isolation and being disconnected with the attendant malfunctioning of the brain and consequently of the mind. Before going on to ponder how we can reduce humanity's problems, we must now consider these basic causes of our problems. The human needs listed earlier are not being met. We have needs to 'belong' to a community, to be part of the natural world and to make sense of the universe. These needs are not being met in many parts of the world. Ultimately, this leads to *diseases* of the mind. The *symptoms* are the adverse social statistics, e.g. petty crime, murder, rape, the proportion of citizens in prison, mental illness, drug addiction, together with such as obesity, disease and lack of community life. Humans evolved for small-scale life within 'nature' led by alpha males who belonged *within* the group. Now we are poorly equipped for large-scale life controlling nature and predated upon by alien alpha males driven by non-rational, primate instincts.

I now continue by giving further, brief consideration to the historical and currently widely accepted causes of our problems, namely the Devil and sin. After this, other specific causes of our problems will be considered: malfunctioning social structures, the inappropriate expression of basic instincts, the existence of unprecedented destructive powers and of unmet needs.

The Devil and sin as causes of humanity's problems

In the New Testament of the Bible, the Book of Revelation refers to the Four Horsemen of the Apocalypse. The four riders are seen as symbolising Pestilence, War, Famine and Death, connected with the Divine Apocalypse and the 'Last Judgement'. As a Roman Catholic child, I attended a conventional Catholic church and also conventional Catholic schools, all totally dominated by the extremely hierarchical, uniformed, alpha-male clergy. I was taught that God loves me and controls everything around me. There were temptations and tests and also rewards for me if I behaved well. On my side was also a guardian angel who looked over me and saints in Heaven and also Jesus's mother Mary, whom I could ask to petition Jesus on my behalf. There were pious practices that pleased God or his saints and stood me in good stead in seeking divine intervention for my desires. In the Bible's Old Testament there are numerous accounts of God's violent and collective punishment against peoples who misbehaved or who mistreated or opposed his chosen people. On a grand scale were tsunamis, plagues, floods and harvest failures. God would support wars against the enemies of his chosen people.

It is now clear beyond any doubt whatsoever that such events have natural causes, often predictable from scientific _laws_, based on empirical evidence about earthquakes, volcanoes, pathogenic microbes (including plant pathogens) and global weather patterns. These provide entirely satisfactory explanations without recourse to divine intervention. In addition, God's support of war is morally dubious. It is now clear that innocent people are *always* harmed in wars, even when conducted by 'targeted', manless drones, and any God worthy of the name would have always known that. And does God believe in morally unsustainable collective punishment?

God's powers were somehow curtailed in a way I never understood as a child. God was thwarted by the Devil and his fallen angels. They were behind many of humanity's problems. The Devil's task was to lead me into sin by all sorts of temptation – in adolescence mostly, almost entirely by attraction to 'sins of the flesh'. Another major sin, punishable by spending eternity burning in hellfire, was missing Sunday mass. Although it was never denied,

I was never taught that, according to Jesus, the key sin was ignoring the needy.

The Devil was the cause of the world's problems, together with the sinful misuse of our own 'free will'. These explanations of interventions by God and the Devil, nuanced by whatever religion or sect provides such teaching, are no longer necessary. There are physical, chemical and biological explanations that are rational and satisfactory. My purpose is to refer to such scientific explanations of behaviour that is propelled by instincts and often inappropriate in our modern world.

Empirical evidence for the non-existence of the Devil and also for the falsehood of the conventional idea of God

I have referred earlier, under 'Basic needs', to the need to belong and to the strong empirical evidence directly and proportionately linking income inequality to adverse social statistics of crime (sins) and disease. There are numerous studies and I have referred to Paul Krugman in 'End this depression now!', Joseph E. Stiglitz in 'The Price of Inequality' and in 'The Great Divide' and for my current purposes, especially 'The Spirit Level' by Richard Wilkinson and Kate Pickett with its clear graphics. Comparing the most unequal societies with the most equal, there are *several-fold* differences in: mental illness, including alcohol and drug addiction, imprisonment rates, clinical obesity, life expectancy, infant mortality, petty crime and in rape and murder rates. And, to repeat my message from earlier, the USA stands out as having the worst social statistics. Surprising to me, the incidence of each of these bad social and crime statistics is in proportion to inequality – it's not simply a difference between top and bottom nations. Similar correlations exist from related sociological work on 'connectedness'. Even the successful functioning of entire nations is correlated with open, pluralistic, inclusive social structures, as opposed to exclusive, exploitative ones. Clear evidence showing this is described in 'Why nations fail: the origins of power, prosperity and poverty' by Acemoglu and Robinson.

Conventional religious teaching about God and the Devil claims that they intervene directly in human affairs. God rewards and facilitates behaviour considered morally good by the particular religion or punishes evil. The Devil commits evil or tempts humans towards it. Apart from those who believe in the literal truth of the Bible or other sacred text, God is unnecessary as the immediate cause of tsunamis, floods, epidemics and earthquakes: science offers satisfactory explanations. But how can the Devil be involved in such direct, *proportional,* straight line relationships between individual human wrongdoing (sins such as petty crime, murder or rape) and income inequality? It cannot be. Similarly, how can God's wrath be used to explain such a correlation or even explain God's behaviour to the most equal with their relative lack of evildoings? The answer must be that it cannot be done. The Devil cannot possibly be compatible with a linear relationship between social evils (many are formal sins by numerous religions) and inequality. The relationship must have a biological cause. Similarly irrational, is the broadly accepted, anthropomorphic description of a male God, constantly intervening in the world, needing constant praise and reminders of his power (as if he might forget) and requiring 'his' clergy to deliver (and control) his messages, often from hugely expensive, prestigious, awe-inspiring, mostly empty buildings.

Over several millennia there have been many thousands of religions teaching different ideas about God yet claiming exclusiveness for their particular one. And many (possibly all) religions have splinter groups with diverse teachings about God, e.g. Catholic and Protestant Christians, Sunni and Shia Muslims, numerous Hindu sects etc. etc. etc. This state of affairs is self-evident and indisputable and is incompatible with an all-powerful, all-loving, all-knowing, God Creator. Such a God could not do or allow such a state of affairs in 'his' name. In the case of Christianity, apart from any other considerations, there is the contradiction of an Old Testament jealous, vengeful God of power, tsunamis and pestilence and the New Testament Jesus suggesting that God be referred to as 'Papa' or 'Dad' or Father, depending on the translation. In addition, for Christians, there is Christ's clear, major concern for the poor and needy. Especially in the Bible's New Testament Matthew's gospel, there is the crystal-clear, explicit and *absolute* imperative to help the ill, naked, thirsty, hungry, imprisoned and strangers (acronym – '*in this*'). Apart from these contradictions, the linear relationship between sin (such as petty crime, murder, rape) and inequality for numerous nations is incompatible with the conventional idea of God or the Devil. Similarly, the same relationship with health and equality is incompatible with direct intervention by God or the Devil. This empirical, sociological data is incompatible with divine or devilish interventions. The idea of an anthropomorphic, male God needing constant praise and constant reminders of his powers, intervening in the world and 'doing things' in proportion to inequality is not supportable; and this is the same for the idea of the evildoing, tempting Devil.

Some readers may wonder why I even mention such things. But it is necessary. Even today, possibly a majority of humans believe in such explanations. About 40% of Americans (USA) believe that biological evolution never happened (other countries have a similar figure): similarly, for the literal truth of the Bible (or other sacred book), e.g. God's word stating that the Earth was created in six days, several thousand years ago. Richard Dawkins gives details of this in 'The Greatest Show on Earth'. On the day (January 2014) I write these words, a UK politician publicly claimed that the UK's problem of disastrous floods is due to God punishing us (my personal and accurate addition – *especially those living in low-lying areas*) for our liberal approach to homosexuality. A week ago, from the day I write this, in a newsagent shop near my home, a man (a stranger to me) was looking at the front pages of newspapers with pictures of horrific floods and asked me pleasantly why this is happening. His own explanation was God's punishment. When I asked him why God could not restrict his punishment solely to the wrongdoers and not issue a collective punishment, he thought it was a mystery. There are numerous people with such views and they may even be in the majority. They 'believe' what their alphas tell them.

Biological determinism: free will, crime and punishment

'Free will, a pleasant illusion'
Dick Swaab in 'We are our brains'

There is evidence of a correlation between individuals who doubt free will and such people having scepticism about retributive punishment. Thus, free will sceptics treat lawbreakers in a manner similar to a microbial infection or a natural disaster. They do not seek revenge, but protection against further harm. Those who do believe in free will tend towards retribution and suffering for the transgressor (in Shariff and Vohs, Scientific American, June 2014, page 62 and with other references). The USA criminal system is notorious for its punitive approach to crime and harsh imprisonment conditions. Unsurprisingly, this approach, as well as being anti-altruism, has been shown to be relatively ineffective in deterring future crime.

Determinism is defined as a philosophical doctrine that all events, uncluding human actions, are fully determined by preceding events, and so freedom of choice is illusory. If deterministic fears were justified, then Australia should be a special case. It was colonised by officially judged criminals from Britain and should today be populated by a disproportionate number of antisocial inhabitants. The truth, seen by anyone who visits Australia or who meets Australians, is virtually the opposite. It is widely recognised that Australians in general are unusually community-minded, tolerant and liberal people. Even the idea of crime can be, and often is, environmentally influenced. The 'crimes' of working-class, usually poor, British people transported to the 'colonies' commonly included trapping rabbits on the land of uncaring, wealthy landowners to feed their hungry families. Given the current attractiveness of Australian society, it could be that this is because those who were deported were partly the selected cream of society – lively, intelligent, risk-taking and unwilling to accept hunger and injustice. This is not to say that Australians are incapable of primate behaviour towards 'others'. They, British deportees, led by their aristocratic masters, treated the original inhabitants, the Aborigines, as inferior and grossly abused them: there was ethnic cleansing. The point I'm making is that colonising Australia with genetically programmed 'criminals' should have led to exceptional and widespread crime. It did not. Australia is at least 'normal' in this respect. My personal experience in Australia and with Australians has been consistently and exceptionally positive. Post-Darwin, there have been various theories put forward about improving the human race by reducing the birth rate of the 'inferior' (poorer) classes and increasing that of the 'superior' (middle, upper and rich) classes. Colonisation of Australia with almost entirely 'criminal', 'lower classes' has not resulted in the expected consequences. Also, for humans to be classified as superior or inferior simply by their wealth is a mistake – maybe not for primates. Surely, humans to be classified as such requires consideration of their kindness, intelligence, humanity and altruism.

Given that the definition of crime can be subjective and often determined by the rich and powerful, then genetic links are dubious. But possible genetic tendencies to violence, aggression or antisocial behaviour or otherwise (passivity) seem likely. For example, objective, actuarial statistics show that young male car drivers have far more accidents than older men. Doubtless, risk-taking influenced by testosterone plays a role. And for primates, having young risk-taking men willing and able to fight would have been useful. Also, it is now clear that brain development is strongly influenced both by nutrition and the social environment. Abuse of a child, and especially of its mother, results in defective brain development. Socially induced aberrant behaviour resulting from chronic childhood abuse clearly occurs. As described below ('Reducing the long-term harm...'), the logical, rational consequences for society are to pay much more attention to early child development and to approaches for repairing damage: similarly, also for crime.

Moral norms can change and evolve with time and new knowledge. In 'The Better Angels of our Nature', Steven Pinker meticulously documents a humanitarian revolution over the last few centuries. Deeply institutionalised practices such as slavery and extremely cruel punishment by the state and/or Church such as the burning or lethal hanging of witches and torture and burning of heretics was rejected on moral grounds. Pinker attributes this partly to the effects of the Enlightenment's widespread and open dissemination of literacy and learning. He shows that cultural change regarding reducing harsh violence is possible and has happened.

My own contribution to the determinism/free will debate is to leave determinism to a new God who has changed everything to a non-probabilistic world. In our world determinism is a theoretical possibility lurking in the complexity of children's brain development, socialisation and inherited and acquired behavioural tendencies. Nevertheless, knowing that only a God could predict individual behaviour, aberrant or not, should not obscure the fact that human development and environmental circumstances have massive influences on behaviour. What is determined, or rather predictable, is the *probability* of broad patterns of behaviour by a proportion of a population.

Inappropriate or malfunctioning social structures
Government and the rights of citizens

The social reformer, Thomas Paine (1737-1809) contributed to the foundations of both the French and the American republics. I recommend any reader to read any book by Thomas Paine. He was an early advocate of old age pensions and of progressive income tax. In the Conclusion to the first part of his book 'The rights of man', he refers to two modes of government prevailing in the world. The two modes were:

1. 'Erected on the base of Reason, Government by election and representation'
2. 'Erected on the opposite base of Ignorance, Government by hereditary succession'

He also considered the concept of 'Mixed Government' and stated that *'The moving power in this species of Government is of necessity Corruption'*. He states that 'However imperfect election and representation may be in 'Mixed Governments', they still give exercise to a greater portion of reason than is convenient to the hereditary part: and therefore it becomes necessary *to buy the reason up'* (my italics). Now, over 200 years later, we have empirical evidence about the bad social consequences of exclusive structures. Early in his book, he describes their evils. I quote: 'It was not against Louis XVI, but against the despotic principles of the government that the Nation (France) revolted. These principles had not their origin in him, but in the original establishment, many centuries back; and they became too deeply rooted to be removed, and the Augean stable of *parasites and plunderers too abominably filthy to be cleansed by anything short of a complete and universal Revolution'* (my italics). I can only point out the obvious – that such root and branch revolutions do not always work, even when the abuses were extreme as in the *'ancien régime'* with its oppression and injustice suffered by the French population. The Russian and Chinese Revolutions could not be regarded as ultimately successful and also had terrible loss of life, although others on a smaller scale were successful, e.g. the Cuban Revolution.

The Declaration of the Rights of Man, made by the Assembly, started with the following three key clauses (from a total of 27) and with Paine's intellectual approval:

1. Men are born and always continue free and equal in respect of their rights. Civil distinctions, therefore, can be founded only on public utility.
2. The end of all political associations is the preservation of the natural and imprescriptible rights of man; and these rights are Liberty, Property, Security and Resistance of Oppression.
3. The Nation is essentially the source of all sovereignty; nor can any individual or any body of men, be entitled to any authority which is not expressly derived from it.

Automation and loss of paid, inclusive, social employment

This section overlaps somewhat with an earlier one under 'Imminent problems' (page 99) where the unmanageable speed of social change, notably automation, was raised.

The USA Council of Economic Advisors' (CEA) economic report for 2016 concludes that the surge in automation could put workers in non-supervisory roles that make *less than $20 p.h.* out of work. Two recent, favourably reviewed books, both by eminent experts give details of this potential crisis. I found them both to be rational, evidence-based and shocking. In 'The Rise of the Robots' by Martin Ford, detailing the problems arising, one of his suggestions to ameliorate what could be a catastrophe is for a guaranteed basic income. Ford suggests that if we don't recognise *and adapt* to the implications of advancing technology, we may face a 'perfect storm'. That is, coincidentally a rapid rise in inequality, technological unemployment and climate change occur roughly in parallel and may amplify and reinforce each other. To these could be added overwhelming, mass migration currently occurring from war and dysfunctional states. It already seems that the world, as now structured, cannot adjust to the current migration crisis. Despite Ford's good intentions and excellent analysis, I believe that his suggestion for a guaranteed basic income is dubious. We need social work for dignity and self-fulfilment. It would be less socially effective than maintaining and enhancing *human*, social employment such as increasing *social* jobs via parks and sports fields, libraries, art galleries, hospitals, social centres, youth clubs, nurseries and *humanising* prisons and remand centres.

In '*The Future of the Professions*' by father and son Richard and Daniel Susskind, they discuss and justify the idea that unprecedented disruption faces all of the *professions* (not solely low paid workers as per the US CEA, above) and that they should respond urgently. They argue that technology can also be used to enable the public to do far more for themselves. Thus, technology not only can enable the legal profession to improve what it does now, but also to reshape justice for the benefit of the public: similarly for other professions. Both books underline the potential problems from technology delivering a speed of change that is unmanageable. Especially in 'The future of the professions', the Susskinds emphasise the exponential growth of computer power. I used to teach kinetics regarding growth and death (from a biocide) of a microbial culture. For example, exponential growth of *Escherichia coli* can result in a *doubling* of the population about every 30 minutes, so that an initial population of about a million per millilitre will be around a *billion* per millilitre after 10 generations and after 5 hours at which time, depending on the growth medium and conditions, growth will typically have stopped due to running out of oxygen or other nutrient.

In the case of the exponential growth of computer power, 'Moore's Law' predicted that it would double every 2 years. In the case of bacteria, growth stops, often because of running out of an essential nutrient. Even in a strongly agitated culture flask, there is a limit to, for example, the oxygen concentration. If this did not happen, we would soon have the earth coated with bacteria and then a metre deep and then 2 metres and so on until it reached the moon! In the case of exponential increase in computing power, Gordon Moore made this prediction in 1965 and broadly it still holds! Experts predict (it's still a prediction) that this will continue for some unpredictable period with vast consequences. These commentaries on virtually inevitable change are rational and intelligent. Unfortunately, our alphas are largely impelled by instincts for short term survival. For alpha politicians, the need of winning the next election always looms large. Without any sarcasm whatsoever, the most likely imminent concern is the need to manage today's news.

Another key problem is an overall society structure incompatible with human needs. This will be dealt with later under kinds of State. Suffice to say, community and belonging are *essential* needs and rapid change, however idealistic, is no guarantee of social harmony.

Luddites

The current situation is reminiscent of the Luddites who were 19th century English textile workers (or self-employed weavers) who worried about losing their jobs permanently. They protested against newly developed labour-reducing technologies, primarily between 1811 and 1816 (www.nationalarchives.gov.uk › Education › Power, Politics & Protest). They have been castigated as reactionary and being against 'progress'. This raised and still raises the question of priorities. Human work or increased profit? It would appear that nobody is addressing this imminent danger with any seriousness. International capitalism is hardly ever challenged, even to soften the blows, possibly with one exception. The French try and often succeed in reducing the speed of change in a particular industry. The consequences of unmanageable change through IT and AT as above may turn out to be massive and maybe quicker than currently seems likely.

Inequality, lack of social power and not 'belonging'

(See earlier section on Humanity's key problems – 'Growing inequality')

In the financially rich West, a significant proportion of the population are poor and many Western cities, including the USA with its 'top' economy, have of the order of 20% of the people living in squalor and deprivation. And there are also the working poor in the USA, the UK and elsewhere living documented lives of quiet desperation. A recent (December 2014) UK report confirms the shocking situation for the *working* poor of the UK. At the same time, ultra-rich individuals have salted away between 10-20 trillion dollars in tax havens. This is a substantial fraction of the world's total Gross National Product of about $80 trillion (GNP: the value of all final goods and services produced in a given year; data from International Monetary Fund, World Bank and CIA World Factbook). (Also, see below re 2014 Credit Suisse and Oxfam Reports.) These estimated figures for the wealth of the elite constantly change upwards and will likely do so as the book progresses. The question of *how* this has happened is documented in various publications, e.g. 'Treasure Islands: tax havens and the men who stole the world' by Nicholas Shaxon. The question of *why* this is so, why does it happen, is addressed earlier (under 'Basic needs'), partly in biological terms, in relation to the primate-behaving, alpha males who have a special role in sensing and responding to danger and commanding the best of naturally curtailed local resources available to a small group. This has changed to modern human leaders commanding almost unlimited resources, including entire Earth-damaging weaponry, access to powerful communications, the computer power to steal from financial markets and for citizen surveillance, and living a lifestyle foreign to those who are led. Those who are 'led' can see the elites as separate, foreign and 'other', or even as predators with consequential, inevitable negative behaviour.

Two detailed reports cast more light on social inequality. First, the Credit Suisse Global Wealth Report October 2014 states that the richest 1% of people own nearly half of the world's wealth. It shows inequality accelerating, with NGOs saying it indicates that economic recovery is 'skewed towards the wealthy'. 'Taken together, the bottom half of the global population own less than 1% of total wealth. In sharp contrast, the richest decile hold 87% of the world's wealth, and the top percentile alone account for 48.2% of global assets,' said the annual report, now in its fifth year. To repeat from earlier, the report, which calculates that total global wealth has grown to a new record, $263tn, more than twice the $117tn calculated for 2000, found that the UK was the only country in the G7 to have recorded rising inequality in the 21st century.

Secondly and in a similar vein, again repeating, Oxfam (Report Jan 2014) warned that the richest 85 people across the globe share a combined wealth of £1 trillion, as much as the poorest 3.5 billion of the world's population. The Oxfam executive director, Winnie Byanyima, said: 'It is staggering that in the 21st Century, half of the world's population – that's three and a half billion people – own no more than a tiny elite whose numbers could all fit comfortably on a double-decker bus.' Oxfam also argues that this is <u>no accident</u>, saying *growing inequality has been driven by a 'power grab' by wealthy elites, who have co-opted the political process to rig the rules of the economic system in their favour.* The report found that over the past few decades, the rich have successfully wielded political influence to skew specific policies in their favour on issues ranging from financial deregulation, tax havens and anti-competitive business practices to lower tax rates on high incomes and cuts in public services for the majority. Since the late 1970s, tax rates for the richest have fallen in 29 out of 30 countries for which data is available, said the report. This 'capture of opportunities' by the rich at the expense of the poor and middle classes has led to a situation where 70% of the world's population live in countries where inequality has increased since the 1980s and 1% of families own 46% of global wealth – almost £70tn. A closely similar report was published by Oxfam in January 2018

Apart from, but related to, the money, numerous authors and journalists have exposed in great detail, the <u>immediate</u> causes of much of the suffering – the 'how'. Notable examples in the West, and bravely so, are John Berger, William Blum, Joanna Blythman, Noam Chomsky, Robert Fisk, Michael Lewis, George Monbiot, Michael Moore, John Pilger, Jeremy Scahill and Nicholas Shaxson. But the <u>basic</u> causes are surely biological. Consciousness allows other humans to be seen as a threat because of their differing beliefs and ideas: 'them and us'. It's not surprising that the humans who see beyond their instincts and the short-term survival needs of their group are at odds with a society strongly influenced by these basic primate instincts. As stated previously, one deep-seated biological purpose of hierarchies is to facilitate a rapid, concerted response to danger. Consequently, those who seriously oppose the leadership are inevitably attacked. And there is also a strong tendency to obey. So, it's not only the alpha males who attack dissenters.

Whilst alpha-male coordinated responses to danger, including obedience-conditioning, have been biologically effective, the need for dissent comes when the leaders are going in the wrong direction. In the human world, there are the prophets who were and are commonly killed, e.g. Old Testament prophets, New Testament Jesus and modern prophets such as Mahatma Ghandi, Martin Luther King and numerous so-called 'whistle-blowers' who are typically (almost always) badly treated. In addition are the artists and poets who are normally sidelined and relatively poor, apart from the poets and artists who support the current fashions (ART) and sometimes can be rich as a consequence. The 'value' of individuals, professions and social groups as seen by society, can be judged broadly by the salaries they receive. By and large, free spirits such as artists, poets and actors are not paid highly, if at all, although sometimes their work attracts attention after death. The irony is that generally they are the ones who articulate human, altruistic behaviour: they are behaving as humans. Sadly, the world is largely controlled by unrestricted alpha males, driven by primate instincts, who are constructing a disconnected, competitive, winners-and-losers, femininity-suppressing world.

Replacement of the family and local community by the state and the market

'It's the economy stupid'

Election slogan for politicians

This slogan is no longer valid. The effects of economic improvement no longer reach those at the bottom. From the perspective of 2018 for example, the past ten years in the USA and in the UK has seen little or no improvements in workers finances. Predictions for the next decade are similar. Somehow, the 'top' have techniques to acquire a disproportion of the world's wealth. It does not 'trickle down'.

Yuval Harari, a researcher of world history, in his superb, beautifully written book 'Sapiens – a brief history of humankind' states that 'the most momentous social revolution that ever befell humankind: the collapse of the family and the local community and their replacement by the State and the market'. He goes on to say that '...from the earliest times, more than a million years ago, humans lived in small, intimate communities, most of whose members were kin'. He defines an intimate community as 'a group of people who know one another well and depend on each other for survival'. Harari describes how the functions of such communities were handed over to *states and markets*. Clearly, behaviour patterns leading to small group intimacy, interdependence and 'belonging' evolved over millions of years from earlier, pre-human small groups. We are inadequately prepared for the market, state control and the consequent desert-like housing estates, inhuman, soulless work and a great degree of social isolation. These changes took a mere two centuries or so. The phrase 'fish out of water' comes to mind.

INSTINCTS OFTEN INAPPROPRIATE IN OUR MODERN WORLD

Instincts regarding self and non-self, us/them, the foreign

It's important to remember that instincts are not equivalent to 'gentle reminders'. They exist to *propel* us down well-trodden paths to survival.

The phenomenon of sensing self and non-self (us/them) goes back to life's origins. Instinctive survival behaviour, coupled with consciousness, offers at least partial explanations for humanity's problems. It is safe to be with 'us' and we know instinctively that 'they' are unsafe and potentially dangerous. Consciousness allows us to see humans in different cultures as 'other' and 'not us', not only because of skin colour and appearance but also because of intellectual or religious differences. We can also wrongly see other humans as different species or races. This gulf is supported by cultural ideas which damn other religions or races as evil and/or the poor who are condemned also as evil or responsible for their own plight. For example, 'evangelical' Christians point out that in the Bible it is taught that God looks after his own; hence the poor are clearly not God's own. This is despite the consistent teaching of Jesus about the paramount importance of helping the needy. Indeed, Jesus taught that helping the needy (ill, naked, thirsty, hungry, imprisoned, strangers) was an absolute requirement for entry to Heaven (New Testament, Matthew's gospel). Nor did this passage say that it's necessary to do such things in his name in order for those actions to be good. His message is transparently clear – just do it.

It seems that the more intense the sense of belonging and loyalty to one's own group, then the greater the reciprocal lack of commitment and latent hostility to groups perceived as 'other'. In an 'us and them' world, 'they' do not count. A bird predator does not have sympathy or empathy for a worm that it's about to pull out of its soil habitat and eat. One of the first steps towards the reduction of widespread violence and violation is for us all to see all humans as part of 'us'; just the one race and all part of nature. Genetics provides evidence that this is indeed so and, paradoxically, so do virtually all the religious and philosophical <u>prophets</u> of each culture in terms of teaching altruism (see later in the section on religion – Buddhists, Muslims, Christians, Sikhs). Recently, the historian David Cannadine (in 'The Undivided Past') has given an historical look at six major forms of solidarity and identity that define humans: religion, nation, class, gender, race and civilisation. He has questioned the idea that humans can be uniquely partitioned into an 'us' or 'them' in each of the six categories and draws detailed attention to interactions across the boundaries that have always existed. Elsewhere I've mentioned that the likely origin of widespread Jewish persecution was because Jews were widely perceived as foreign with associated negative basic instincts about foreignness and also territory (<u>their</u> Holy Land). They also had a foreign religion, foreign language (Hebrew) and adhered to their 'foreign' dress customs. Almost everywhere, they were seen as foreign in every sense with the virtually *biologically* inevitable arousing of suspicions against them.

Instincts related to territory
The desire to protect or expand territory runs very deep and likely back to microbes. This has been described earlier: microbes live preferably on a surface where they create their own environment and enhance their chances of survival in various ways. One's own or possibly one's neighbour's territory is where we know safety, shelter and find nutrition and other resources. Obviously, this powerful instinct is at the root of numerous wars. Making matters more intense is that a challenge to one's territory typically comes from a foreigner – 'the other'. In other sections reference has been made to the early plight of the Jews, including their attraction, not mainly to their domicile, but to an alien 'Holy <u>Land</u>'.

Power phenotype contributing to our problems

The power phenotype in humans: instinctive behaviour of the powerful and of the powerless

> *'Few, save the poor, feel for the poor'*
>
> **Latitia Landon.**

> *'Power tends to corrupt and absolute power corrupts absolutely'*
>
> **First Baron Acton: Letter in 'Life of Mandell Creighton' (1904)**

> *'When the power of love overcomes the love of power, the world will know peace'*
>
> **Jimi Hendrix**

In the famous quotation from Lord Acton, the word corrupt is probably inaccurate. It may be a case of the acquisition of power altering behaviour and producing the 'power phenotype'. As mentioned earlier, phenotype is the word used in biology to describe an organism's characteristics as influenced by its environment. Thus, white humans exposed to the sun become tanned to protect against damage by UV light. Leaves on a plant tend to face the sun. Humans achieving power exhibit a power phenotype mode of behaviour. Clearly, the tendency for the powerful to be relatively indifferent to the needs of the weak seems to occur cross-culturally and throughout history: the same applies to accepting a rich lifestyle, taking the best and with few exceptions. It arises from the fact that a primate group benefits from a healthy leader whose 'taking of the best' is strongly limited by Mother Nature, including competitor males.

Alas, idealistic political activists have been unaware of the power phenotype. Indeed, many socialist idealists and also aristocrats refer to the 'upper' and 'working' classes as if they were genetically different. It resembles the way that royalty (and often the rest of us) can believe in royal blood. Such a belief stabilises against change – i.e. royalty 'truly' is intrinsically superior to the lower class. In fact, we are all genetically the same in the sense that the differences between large human groups (e.g. African, Asian, European) are less than those within each group. Humanitarian ideals and desires so often are dissolved by primate instincts. Instincts can be like a tsunami. Frequently, idealistic, altruistic revolutions against old corrupt social arrangements and leaders are replaced by leaders who either exhibit the same deeply ancient power phenotype or are swiftly replaced by others who do. Having a clearly identified leadership has helped us survive evolution: alpha-male hierarchies have been biologically vital and sometimes, but not always, are now.

Group behaviour under threat
I'd like to repeat something from earlier, under the Introduction section, on instincts from our ancestors. Human <u>group</u> behaviour although rich and varied is also remarkably constant when the group is under threat from other groups. This constancy occurs across cultures and historical periods and thus again would appear to be genetically predisposed, together with learned behaviour. For example, a human group with much territory theoretically could be generous towards human neighbours with little. In practice, an almost universal response to a serious territorial threat is for young men to defend their territory to the death. Similarly, groups with the greatest power commonly take whatever they want. For millennia, towns have had fortified walls, and standing armies exist everywhere. Also, during relatively stress-free periods, the group may:

a. learn obedience to elites, usually male;
b. bond with their group in numerous ways; and
c. acquire hostility to potential aggressors (foreigners) and thus be predisposed to a rapid response when, for example, their territory is (perceived to be) threatened.

Much of human culture involves conditioning for obedience to social elites – forming the social adhesive. And beneath it all is the need for control to bring about this behaviour and to maintain it. Again,

> *reinforcing obedience to leaders/rulers increases the chances of a rapid, concerted response to the next threat.*

The instincts behind this typical behaviour have served our ancestors well in the sense that they survived evolution and we humans were able to evolve with our consciousness. The addition of human consciousness to the primate mind does not appear to involve loss of the basic instincts, although the possibility of choice of behaviour appeared in a unique way. Thus, consciousness potentially reduces the conditioned tendency of behaviour and allows the possibility of a more flexible predisposition to modes of behaviour. But the instincts are still there, constantly predisposing and unobtrusively influencing apparently 'conscious' actions. Clearly for humans, many personal and group problems are the result of the tension that exists between instinct and the choices available through consciousness.

It's clear that people (*and* organisations and nations) with power typically tend to take it for granted, seek more of it and assume the right to a disproportionate share of wealth and all good things. The longer with power, the more extreme are these power characteristics. The wealth of current alpha-male dictators and despots, worldwide, appears to know no bounds. There are numerous studies on the subject of large-scale financial malpractice. In his book 'Treasure Islands', the respected journalist and well-reviewed author Nicholas Shaxson analyses the specific mechanisms by which super-rich individuals (alpha males) are able to hide away trillions of dollars in so-called tax havens. There were reports (in 2014) of similar practices by mega-rich Chinese living in communist China. Shaxson argues that *tax havens are the main single reason for why poor individuals and poor nations remain poor.* He also points out that my own country

Britain and also the USA are the world's two most important tax havens. Such 'havens' are toxins, which he regards as being at the heart of the global economy and they have been so for some time.

This behaviour of the so-called ('so-called' because they *belong* with other alpha males) 'leaders' also seems to have existed over historical epochs and in different environments. Although badly regarded by many people today, such behaviour will have helped ancestral group survival: better to have one concerted response to threat than disconnected responses. It's worth repetition that the leader had a special role in sensing danger and facilitating an effective, rapid and concerted response: <u>survival trumps everything</u>. For the primate (alpha-male) leader to have the best food, most attractive/ strong (as they are likely to have healthy babies) sexual partners, and most secure sleeping place helped the leader's and hence the group's survival. This 'selfish' behaviour of leaders has helped our predecessors through evolution – healthy leaders help group survival. As noted earlier, this selfish behaviour was once limited by nature. The leader could not eat too much or have more than one sleeping place, which was with his group. It was self-limiting. And he belonged with his group.

Such behaviour has continued in human societies and may account to a large extent for the common (almost universal) excessive 'greed' of powerful leaders and why they take it for granted. Today, it is <u>not</u> self-limiting and sometimes it seems limitless. Thus, it seems to occur in political, artistic and virtually all 'successful' human organisations, including religions. Religious leaders are not noted for the poverty of their circumstances, even if the originators of the religion were indeed poor. Church leaders commonly live in palaces as does the Head of the UK Anglican Church (the Queen who has several palaces) and the Archbishop of Canterbury. Happily, the new Pope Francis has moved out (he never moved in) of his Vatican apartments (2013) and shows signs of being well aware of the dangers associated with power. Hence, the power phenotype could well be instinctive and latent until the individual has power, although most people have some power. Consider the widespread negative behaviour towards the disabled or the bullying of those perceived to be weak in schools and elsewhere. Individuals with such bullying tendencies may even become leaders.

The powerless may also act from *instinct in terms of obedience*, although this is typically reinforced with sanctions by the powerful for the non-obedient. The widespread phenomenon of <u>not</u> seeing that the Emperor is naked could well be instinctive. It certainly assists in maintaining rulers/elites. Political behaviour in a society that is under threat is typically associated strongly with primate behaviour – behaviour becomes territorial/nationalistic (or ideological), hierarchical, competitive, wishing to follow strong leaders, and there is relative indifference to (or the sacrifice of) the weak. Behaviour characteristic of the powerful is reinforced by the culture of the powerful within the overall social culture. We are led by leaders exhibiting primate instincts and we frequently respond instinctively, often as obedient.

Royalty and top alphas
As a reminder to the reader, when in the presence of royal and religious hierarchies, there are strict rules of behaviour that reinforce their supremacy and their power. Similarly, the dress of the powerful often involves numerous special symbols and medals indicating power. Bowing, walking backwards, not being spoken to unless addressed by them first and extreme titles are normal. Thus, the Pope is called 'His (always a male) Holiness' and lives not only in the Vatican Palace (the current Pope Francis is an exception) but is Head of the Vatican State. Traditionally and ceremonially, he is often carried about on a bejewelled throne. The UK monarchy (which does allow women) also has specified modes of address such as 'Your Royal Highness' and similar. In England, the Archbishop of Canterbury lives in Lambeth Palace, whilst the Head of the Anglican Church, Her Majesty the Queen, who lives in Buckingham Palace or in Windsor Castle, has other palaces elsewhere, some of which are also the homes of members

of the royal family (Balmoral, Sandringham, Holyrood and Clarence House), and she often appears in royal robes covered with symbols of power (as do her relatives). She is reputed to be the wealthiest woman in her kingdom. Speaking personally, and as someone not in favour of monarchy, the incongruity is increased when the Queen seems to me to be a reasonably sane, pleasant person! She is certainly a unifying force in a divided UK. It's clear that the Queen (*and most others*) sees no issue whatsoever with her lifestyle and being the Head of the Anglican Church and representing Christ in the UK. Not seeing that the Emperor has no clothes on is a form of social schizophrenia that helps maintain the *status quo*.

Royal genes

Until recently, ideas of God's approval of such systems were prevalent. There was the entirely mistaken, yet long-lasting idea of 'breeding', of royal 'blood', i.e. the inheritance of special, royal and superior values, blessed by God. Even as recently as 2011 there was media mention of the bride-to-be of a UK royal prince being a 'commoner', as are her parents. This has been stated as the reason why she arrived at a ceremony in a car and not a horse-drawn state carriage. Similarly, we can witness clearly identifiable associations of the powerless (or the lower class) such as black-only 'Christian' churches and jazz, initially a mainly black art form. As well, broad differences between the powerful and the rest are easily visible through language, accents and dress code. From an evolutionary perspective, there were thought to be advantages in having a visible upper class or elite who share common values, education and religion – primate advantages. Identifying the leadership of a society was 'thought' (it's likely instinctive) to help that society in its response to change and, vitally, danger.

Royalty anachronistic

During the evolution of primate society, keeping the (large, strong) leader healthy and nourished, mating the healthiest females and making important decisions contributed to the (small) group's survival.   And the taking of disproportionate resources was necessarily restricted by the circumstances. The alpha male could eat only so much food.   Indeed, eating too much food, becoming fat and overweight would be a drawback leading to the loss of the leadership position. The vital need for unequivocal leadership gave rise to blood relationships and definitely reduced uncertainty about leadership at times of crisis. The continuation of the above practices when political power is largely separated from the royal classes is anachronistic and confusing.

Obedience to top alphas enhanced by conditioning between threats

Having alpha-male leaders results in coordinated, rapid responses to danger only if the leader is followed. A human 'class' system facilitates visible recognition of who are and who are not leaders in a culture. Furthermore, a relatively small elite can share common values reinforced by a common elite education and lifestyle. All of this requires much control, often exercised by the alpha males with their characteristic power phenotype (their instinctive right to obedience and the best of everything). Social structures, e.g. religion, official 'Art', the media, cuisine, clothing and fashions, contribute to the social 'glue' and commonly involve alpha males exhibiting power phenotypes. In the 'natural' primate world, the taking of the best resources by the leading apes was necessarily restricted in terms of shelter and food. Today, it is relatively unrestricted and causes communal pathology.

Influencing much of this biological behaviour is the idea, or rather the instinct, as discussed above, that a group (or an individual) that is different to one's own is potentially dangerous. 'Otherness', in itself, appears to be perceived as a danger. When leaders are seen as 'others' by those who are led (and *vice versa*) it inevitably leads to social ills. Thus, society will have groups with specific interests in terms of sports, newspapers, clubs, types of holidays, eating habits, religions, etc. There will be variations associated with regions or climate variations but within any one of these interests commonly there will be identifiable aspects associated with the powerful. The fact that these will vary from time to time does not alter the basic tendency. Thus, the rich and powerful (the upper class) can be visible in terms of the kind (and often big expense) of exclusive education, sport (e.g. polo), exclusive clubs (no blacks, no women, no Jews), exclusive religions (whites only), 'posh' art/music (e.g. opera) and so on that they choose. It is wrong simply to see these arrangements as fundamentally evil: they stem from the ancient, pre-human need to survive.

To repeat, at the base of survival is the need to respond in a rapid and concerted way to danger; a response facilitated by visible hierarchies and leaders. The bigger the danger, the less reasoned thought.

Modern human societies with their complexity would appear to need a more inclusive leadership. If a representative democracy is desired so that we all 'belong', then leadership should come from a group representative of the people. Currently, in Western democracies, the elected leaders are overwhelmingly white, middle-class men, typically leading relatively rich lives, differing from the rest. We have confused the *method* of achieving democracy with the *objective* of representative democracy itself. One subsection of society should not be so over-represented. In addition, the voting system is heavily influenced, even *determined,* by the activities of public relations advisors and costly advertising. And after an election, the winners naturally reward their financial backers with favours. The 2012 presidential election in the USA cost several *billions* of dollars, with massive TV advertising, influenced by PR people commonly attempting to discredit the opponent, thus disuniting society.

In the UK, there is a current move to increase the number of women in company boardrooms. Part of the motive appears to be fairness. But another possible outcome, should the increase happen, could be that decision-making will be after a wider consideration of options and of the perceived business environment. The current male-dominated, highly macho financial services industry may have been less dangerous with more women participants: *but only with women who maintained feminine qualities.* However, the biological basis for leadership and for the power phenotype has nothing directly to do with 'fairness' but to do with short-term group survival/profit. Fairness may help indirectly. Instincts evolved for the short-term survival of pre-human, small groups curtailed by 'nature' millions of years ago.

Another aspect of social obedience: the naked Emperor
'The Emperor's New Clothes' is a children's story in 'The Complete Fairy Tales' of Hans Christian Andersen (Wordsworth Library Collection). Two 'con men' persuade an *Emperor* to buy new clothes which they say are invisible to those unfit for their positions – namely, if they are stupid or incompetent. When the Emperor appears in public 'dressed' in these new clothes, everyone at first pretends to see them, so as not to be seen as stupid or incompetent. 'But he has nothing on!' a little child cries out at last.'

Given the existence of numerous studies by brilliant authors (including Nobel Laureates), drawing our attention to objective, scientific data about the causes of human problems (inequality, lack of connectedness, exclusive social structures), then how is it that people generally act as if this data did not exist? In particular, how is it that politicians and other social leaders are evidently oblivious to this work?

I suggest again that our basic instincts are a significant cause of our problems: not evil, not the Devil, not stupidity but instincts such as the power phenotype and the instinct to obey our elite. Added to which are unmet personal and social needs and exclusive social arrangements. In today's society, it's unwise to point out that our Emperors are often naked. 'Whistleblowers' are typically, almost always, punished. Religious prophets who teach that the 'State' is doing wrong or teach ideas seriously in opposition to the cultural and/or religious norm are often killed, e.g. the Bible's Old Testament prophets and New Testament Jesus. May I repeat something from earlier? At the end of his life, Jesus taught (Matthew **25**, 24) that when he returned as the Messiah he would pass judgement on mankind (he did not mention sacred doctrines or holy texts). He described the criteria for entry to Heaven (or Hell) as responding or not responding to human need. This was closely similar to the teachings of the Axial Age sages. I recently saw the Dalai Lama on television addressing a music festival at Glastonbury, UK and emphasising the need for compassion and praising the joy he saw at the festival. Altruism/compassion is also closely similar to sociological findings regarding what people in differing cultures thought was good or bad behaviour: namely, it's good to help people in need and bad not to. *In other words, humans* _already_ *know what is good and bad behaviour and it accords with the ideas of people recognised as exceptionally wise in different cultures and times.*

Mindless obedience can facilitate the general acceptance of leadership and helps when the leadership is good and harms when it is bad. The power phenotype and social obedience are two sides of the same coin. Such behaviour reinforces and makes explicit the social power structure so that *the chance of obedience to survival strategies dictated by the leader(s) is increased.* That is the very purpose of hierarchies. It facilitates social control. It is a mistake to see hierarchies as evil or bad: they have been a biologically necessary part of earlier evolution and can definitely still be useful – as is the instinct to obey. Both instincts help rapid, coordinated responses to danger. Thus, 'whistle-blowers' are highly likely to be seen as 'not-us', regardless of whether their cause is true and just. Cohesive group behaviour is more likely to help survival than non-cohesive behaviour. Instincts are all about survival, not moral or immoral human behaviour.

'Blowing the whistle' about a moral issue is a *human* activity; group antagonism to 'disloyalty' stems from *primate* instincts. But with our human brains/minds, the leadership function of a rapid response to imminent danger can be carried out by a small group of

varied personalities. Response to less imminent danger is also likely
to be most successful if coordinated by a small leadership group of
varied people so that the initial assessment of danger and proposed
response is more likely to be correct. Today, there are numerous
recorded instances of individual leaders wielding virtually unchecked
power and causing disaster.

Behaviour characteristic of power clearly exists across cultures
and historical periods. Powerful humans consistently exhibit a
power phenotype of behaviour. It would seem clear that this has an
evolutionary origin in terms of providing leaders with the capacity
to take decisions and *facilitate a rapid and concerted response to
danger*. Also, the group that was led accepted that the leader took
the best of everything such as food and shelter. Competition is
deeply entrenched in evolution; it is a characteristic feature of
human societies and serves to distinguish explicitly the winners
(strong) from the losers (weak). Furthermore, the tendency for the
powerful to be relatively indifferent to the needs of the weak seems
cross-cultural and happens throughout history. It is a particularly
striking anomaly in countries where the state religion teaches the
primacy of serving the needy – a kind of social schizophrenia. The
current world financial crisis, mentioned previously, illustrates
this. Trillions of dollars have been 'found' from tax revenue to
rescue banks and other financial institutions, even in countries
that 'cannot' afford to nurture the weak and poor – and even in
countries whose state religion teaches the opposite. And the
banking leaders clearly think that they deserve to receive not only
salaries in multiples of millions, but also bonuses of millions and
sometimes billions – an extreme example of the power phenotype!
It is *as if* (not really 'as if') ordinary people across the world had
put their collective wealth all in one place, 'the market', and a tiny
number of humans, with special knowledge and sophisticated IT,
siphoned off this wealth for themselves.

A reminder of striking examples of vicious behaviour linked to obedience: what humans are capable of

'All that is necessary for the triumph of evil is that good people do nothing'
Adapted from Edmund Burke, Irish orator, philosopher and politician

The Holocaust, slavery and the 'Holy' Inquisition are examples of widespread, long-lasting atrocities carried out by humans that required widespread obedience. Slavery had a financial component and despite its cruelty, had far fewer atrocities (slaves cost money). But even so, it required the widespread ignoring of moral teaching and received *widespread* acceptance. The Holocaust was racial and involved extraordinary organisation and detailed recording of the extermination of humans by humans. Extreme cruelty and bullying was widespread and not just German, but Polish, Slav and other nations were involved. *Once it becomes socially acceptable to demonise Jews as sub-human, then it seems that a large majority go along with it*, especially if the gross punishment of dissenters was likely. Not only were most of the population tacitly accepting the Holocaust, but other nations kept quiet for too long, and notably so did 'the official' Churches when it is their job to speak out. They did not, although numerous individuals did so and helped many Jews, despite the risk of death. A typical response to individuals 'speaking out' or 'blowing the whistle' is for the powerful to punish them. The German education system was changed by Hitler into indoctrination (see the section on 'Education' later) that enforced obedience and anti-Jewishness.

And the 'Holy Inquisition' was also not the consequence of one evil race or group but humans acting from instincts in a way that lower animals do not. Slavery created wealth for the few. The Holocaust and the Inquisition were pathological, human aberrations of primate instincts. So now we know, not simply what evil Germans and Poles and the 'Church' are capable of, *but what all we humans are capable of, collectively and individually.* Humans can individually carry out these depraved acts. It can also be a most extreme form of inappropriate collective obedience to alpha-male power. So, when individuals scoff at the possibility of more of such acts taking place, they are entirely wrong. On a smaller scale they happen all the time, worldwide. And inappropriate, mindless obedience to alpha males is part of it.

An extreme example of evil coming from an alpha male
The Jews, with their foreign religion, alien beliefs, religious leaders with strange clothing and strange habits, foreign language and devoted to a foreign Holy Land were predictably viewed with suspicion in their temporary homes. It is not necessary to offer any explanation other than biology. Nevertheless, without a Hitler *and* the extreme conditions that led to Hitler's rise to power (e.g. the vicious 'settlement' of World War 1), it seems unlikely that the Holocaust would have happened. Evidence has emerged of Hitler's successful public relations campaigns involving thousands of pictures taken weekly depicting him as the strong leader and later as the 'normal' man. Mass rallies were brilliantly stage-managed, with *hundreds of thousands* of uniformed men saluting and honouring him in unison as he stood above everyone as the great leader. Given the context of post-World War 1 and his maniacal, totally ruthless personality, he succeeded in gaining power (see 'Hitler; a short biography' by A. N. Wilson). It's easy to label him as a 'one-off'. I suggest that, *given similar circumstances,* any city could give rise to several Hitlers, and this also applies to mass behaviour. Archives show films and stills of great crowds of German civilians lining the streets as he passed in an open car. They were cheering and waving and saluting a strong leader who would lead them out of their painful past. It is surely not uniquely German to witness a mass following of a 'strong' leader after catastrophic military defeat and a vicious post-war settlement preceded by a history of strongly

obedient militarism. Today, Germany is one of the most humane and liberal of European states. The Germans are not genetically distinct from the rest of Europe or of mankind in general. We are all Germans and some of us are potential Hitlers, given appropriate circumstances.

Why is the existence of basic instincts so underappreciated?
It's unclear why the analysis of leading thinkers regarding the detailed causes of human problems never refers to basic instincts. May I repeat something from earlier? For example, we have truly brilliant thinkers and activists such as Noam Chomsky, George Monbiot and the journalist John Pilger. By any standards they are remarkably good humans and intellectually brilliant: they clearly possess genius. They refer to and superbly analyse pathological social structures, but do not mention explicitly the powerful, basic instincts I've summarised immediately above, including the instinctive behaviour of alpha males and the obedience of their followers. Unquestionably, they and others, often bravely and at great personal cost, emphasise and support the creation of caring, humane communities but frequently imply that the *problems they analyse so beautifully are the result of nasty, greedy people being nasty and greedy.* Nevertheless, this exposure of nasty greed is surprisingly and shockingly largely ignored.

Q. Why is it ignored?
A. Probably because of our instinct to obey/go along with the world views of our alpha- male leaders being so rightfully powerful. And disobedience/whistleblowing is punished and can also be a social disgrace. It is the Hans Christian Andersen's story of 'The Emperor's New Clothes mentioned earlier.Surely, for longer lasting improvements we must face the fact of the existence of *innate impulses often <u>determining</u>* non-conscious, pre-human impulses. (Reminder: The

Oxford English Dictionary's definition of instinct is 'innate propensity or impulse'.)

An important reminder: *we are human*

Alpha behaviour stems from primate instincts, sometimes facilitated by human intelligence. Much of the language about elites is referring to alpha behaviour impelled by basic instincts, i.e. it is *ape-like* and socially useful in an ape society. Humans additionally have behaviour characterised by rationality, altruism, culture, art and literature. Humans have leaders across history and cultures who express such features and with altruism being pre-eminent. Prominent *human* leaders were the Buddha, Confucius, the Taoists (Lao-tzu and Chuang-tzu), Mohammed, Jesus and the Greek rationalists. Note: for those unfamiliar, Taoism also Romanised as Daoism, is a religious or philosophical tradition of Chinese origin based on the writings of Lao-tzu and Chuang-tzu which emphasizes living in harmony with the Tao ("the Way"), advocating humility and religious piety. The roots of Taoism go back at least to the 4th century BCE.

In the case of my Christian country, the UK, Jesus is logically a role model yet only nominal lip service is paid to him. Virtually universally, cultures hold up models of 'getting on', of 'succeeding', of 'progressing in life' as achieving power and financial riches, i.e. of being successful primates. These are the ingrained messages and 'posters' of success placed in front of us all, including our youth. I've referred elsewhere to a local (Balsall Heath, Birmingham, UK) poster placed by local Muslims during Ramadan – 'Be one with the poor'. This is possibly the opposite to 'Get rich and powerful as quickly as you can'. But it's in close accord with *all* the cultural leaders mentioned above.

Unprecedented, destructive powers contributing to our problems

For the first time in world history, associated with the power phenotype, organisms (human animals) have God-like destructive and society-controlling powers on a worldwide scale. Notable is weaponry of unprecedented powers, environmental destruction and digitally encoded information technology. Global capitalism (the '1%') operates *separately* from local societies and cultures. Digital communications place massive power in the hands of the very few to manipulate individual corporations, financial markets and to facilitate widespread social surveillance. Worldwide, and true to their instincts, the alpha males defend their wealth, mega salaries and bonuses as being necessary 'to attract the best'!

Unmet needs contributing to our problems

Society is sick from stress

Animals imprisoned in unnatural, municipal zoos have elevated levels of stress hormones and exhibit stressed behaviour. Modern humans exist commonly in a zoo of our own making and the 'primates' are in charge with all their primate instincts intact. We are sick. As mentioned earlier, we are all familiar with the idea of individual illness – physical or psychological. When humans have a high temperature and cough up blood or we have 'sores' on our skin, nowadays we do not think that these *symptoms* are the basic disease. We think about an infection by pathogenic microbes or possibly sores caused by an allergic reaction. Unequal, disconnected human societies show increased *symptoms* of social malaise such as low life expectation, high rates of mental illness, obesity, petty crime, murder, drug addiction, lack of community life and large prison populations. Societies tend to treat these symptoms but not the *disease* (also see earlier, Michael Marmot's 'The Status Syndrome: How your social standing directly affects your health and life expectancy').

The core of the disease is unmet needs, notably people not belonging, not being socially connected and even being victims of their alpha-male leaders and being in a society with extractive, non-inclusive economic and political structures. I have already referred to much strong empirical evidence linking these intertwined symptoms with inequality, lack of connectedness and not 'belonging' (see earlier references: 'The Price of Inequality' by Joseph E. Stiglitz, 'The Spirit Level' by Wilkinson and Pickett, and also www.ted.com/talks/lang/en/richard_wilkinson.html, 'End this depression now!' by Paul Krugman, and 'Why Nations Fail' by Acemoglu and Robinson). Could it be that 'not belonging' and being 'disconnected' is the main modern social disease? I hesitate to use the word alienation since it is the elite that are the aliens. The above lines of empirical study have converged. Evolution has not prepared humans for an alienated, disconnected world with alpha males being not only alien, but frequently *predators* upon us.

Inequality: requirement for a degree of social power
The 'Spirit Level' by Wilkinson and Pickett (referred to above) gives extraordinary evidence that clearly demonstrates a tight correlation between the incidence of these symptoms and the size of income inequality between the top and the bottom in society. There are numerous straight-line graphs showing the *quantitative* relationship between inequality and social problems of every kind.

Thus, inequality with its broad consequences of a lack of power, community and a sense of not belonging, is a social <u>disease</u> with pathological, social consequences (<u>symptoms</u>). This could well go back to very basic biological roots: the recognition of self and non-self or 'them and us'. We do not care about 'them' and we do care about 'us'. The extreme adverse social statistics of many modern societies, notably the USA and the UK at the worst end, are symptoms of social disease(s). The numerous examples of quantitative data correlating inequality with, for example, crime of various kinds should have profound social consequences. It is not only the efficiency of the police service that causes Scandinavia to have a several-fold lower incidence of crime and prison populations than the worst societies. Basically, it is the having of a more equal society: similarly, for homicides and mental illness and similarly for lower infant mortality rates not being due solely to the efficiency of the medical services.

For better health and less crime, reduce inequality and increase belonging and community bonds.
Alas, this is easier said than done, yet we must attempt the task. Another way to look at the graphs in the 'Spirit Level' (authors Wilkinson and Pickett) is to see the y-axis as degrees of power. Money is power, so degrees of wealth show degrees of power. Being relatively powerless in one's own society results in these symptoms. The less the power difference, the less the incidence of the 'symptoms'.

Brain function
From a different perspective and involving the relative roles of our left and right brain hemispheres, Iain McGilchrist in 'The Master and his Emissary' (pages 434-437) has important things to say, related to the above. He points to much evidence showing that the bias of the brain's left hemisphere towards seeing the world as a <u>mechanism</u> has led to *'destruction and despoliation of the natural world, and the erosion of established cultures on a scale which I scarcely need to emphasise; but this has been justified in terms of its utility to bring about human happiness'*. He points out numerous quantitative, objective, scientific papers highlighting that above a low, minimum level, 'increases in material well-being have *little or nothing* to do with human happiness'. These large-scale studies covered numerous cultures and included individuals' age, sex, race, income, geographical location, nationality and education. He quotes Robert Putnam in 'Bowling Alone' that happiness is best predicted by <u>'the breadth and depth of one's social connections'</u>. Being connected is to belong. McGilchrist goes on to emphasise

the integrity of mind and body and quotes (page 436) much work linking the lack of 'social connectedness' with the incidence of numerous diseases. Surprisingly, these include colds, heart attacks, strokes, cancer, depression and premature deaths of all sorts. So, not being connected and not belonging results in crime and numerous adverse social ills and at the same time numerous medical diseases. (Also, see above, Michael Marmot, 'The Status Syndrome: how your social standing directly affects your health and life expectancy'.)

Inclusive political structures

From yet again a different perspective, 'Why nations fail: the origins of power, prosperity and poverty' by Acemoglu and Robinson shows with crystal-clear clarity the positive effects of *inclusive* political institutions and national policies and the consistent negative effects of non-inclusive, *extractive* political institutions and policies. The main focus of the book is relating inclusive or extractive political institutions and policies with outcomes in terms of national power, prosperity and poverty. They point out the strong synergy between economic and political institutions.

> 'Extractive political institutions concentrate power in the hands of a narrow elite and place few constraints on the exercise of this power. Economic institutions are then often structured by this elite to extract resources from the rest of society. Extractive economic institutions thus naturally accompany extractive political institutions. In fact, they must inherently depend on extractive political institutions for their survival'.

Two clear examples were:

a. the plantation system in Barbados based on the exploitation of slaves, which could not have survived without political institutions that suppressed and completely excluded slaves from the political process; and

b. the economic system impoverishing millions for the benefit of a narrow 'communist' elite in North Korea, which required the total political domination by the so-called 'Communist' Party.

The positive message of their remarkable book, based on numerous, detailed studies of different nations across history and geography, is that *inclusiveness* makes things better. They show how powerful elites seek to rig the rules and influence/control governments virtually everywhere for their own benefit at the expense of the many. Inclusive political institutions and political policies are hugely beneficial. Extractive policies for the few are socially bad/disastrous. From the perspective of this book, it shows the importance of the unrestricted elite power phenotype adversely affecting the fate of nations and also that it need not always be so.

A subtle form of exclusiveness is also 'natural'. It's natural to feel comfortable with people one knows: people with similar values and a similar background – 'us'. This makes for a cohesive group. An example is the former leadership of the UK (Prime Minister Cameron). The UK parliamentary cabinet and its smaller 'inner' cabinet were exceptionally homogeneous socially. This cabinet had *several* members educated at the *same* 'top' school, Eton. (**Note:** There are several thousand secondary schools in the UK.) There was 'natural' cohesion about their views on many things, including society. Biologically, Eton *predetermines* alpha-ness. Alphas are reassured by most of them having had a 'top' education (Eton), particularly when many have gone on to a 'top' university – in the UK, Oxford or Cambridge. Thus, they are alpha males *by definition* and easily identified. In a pre-human, arboreal world, any identifiable alpha was better than none. In our world, currently in the UK, to some extent, they are predetermined as candidates for alphahood. Broadly, but not always, they share little in common with non-alpha citizens. Doubtless, in their education they truly benefit from small classes, a pleasant environment, well-paid teachers and eventually from a comfortable personal salary and personal wealth. But they probably also acquire and conform to an alpha accent, alpha dress code, an attitude to non-alphas, alpha sporting interests, alpha attitudes to culture generally, to alpha vacations and become aware of being different to non-alphas. This is a drawback if one is leading the nation. It leads to unrepresentative 'in' groups – 'cliques'.

A British journalist, Yasmin Alibhai Brown, has pointed out that the UK's most powerful institutions and individuals are Conservatives (The 'i' 18 January 2016, i@independent.co.uk). They are the present UK government, the royal family, leaders of the UK armed forces, newspaper proprietors and most editors, the Institute of Directors, the CBI, shareholders of commercial broadcasting companies, Oxbridge chancellors, our ambassadors, key government advisors, peers, those appointed to quangos and public service boards who *share core beliefs* about wealth, privilege, capitalism, militarism, individualism, and self-interest. She points out that this might explain why the police, governments and secret services have spied on, infiltrated and tried to discredit or criminalise those fighting economic injustice, racism, environmental devastation and state surveillance. In other words, those who dare to oppose the alphas. It's not surprising that the alpha leaders are unsympathetic to any change in the *status quo*, including any redistribution of wealth or property. The instinctive behaviour of the alphas regarding the taking of the best (which was useful for arboreal life, controlled by Mother Nature) is reinforced by their alpha education and their circle of alpha associates.

Lack of suitable habitat

All over the world, numerous humans have none or inadequate homes *or wider social facilities*. Also, where there is housing, the arrangements do not always favour community building. There is often a lack of effective city and urban planning. In the UK, there is currently a housing crisis, partly a lack of housing and partly the unaffordable cost of it. In cities across the world, numerous humans are *living* on the street. In India, increasing national wealth has not been devoted to eliminating this scourge: this, while a new, multi-$*billion*$ space programme is being considered. In Indonesia, I have seen people cooking food on the street that is there home. Even where there are houses, the arrangement is not always adequate. In the UK and the USA, for example, housing for the poor ('social housing') is often erected without adequate planning and inadequate attention to humanizing the arrangements. In London, the recent destruction by fire of Grenfell Towerfire with much loss of life was avoidable. Inflammable cladding materials should not have been used but were used. Worldwide, homes for citizens are not a high priority, even though they are for humans. This will be dealt with in more detail later under 'Reducing Humanity's Problems'.

Causes of our problems: conclusions
After millennia of philosophy from the greatest minds about society, crime and punishment we now have detailed, factual, quantitative relationships between inequality (a lack of power) and crime, illness and general social ailments. Another strand of complementary sociological research shows similar links between social connectedness and health and also happiness. In addition, we now have strong empirical evidence about the socially good consequences of inclusive economic and political institutions. Thus, inequality, disconnectedness and non-inclusive social structures point to the same conclusion. Exclusive social structures exaggerate the power phenotype. Belonging is essential for health and happiness, both of the individual, the community and the nation: they are intertwined. To put it another way, as so clearly described by Iain McGilchrist in 'The Master and his Emissary' and by Dick Swaab in 'We are our brains', <u>mind, body and environment (including social) are really and truly interrelated</u>. And, making matters worse, we

have unprecedented God-like destructive powers in the hands of our alpha males, instinctively and mindlessly taking it all for granted and who are now unsuited for such a task. President Donald J. Trump and the people behind him are notable examples.

We have had a plethora of religious teaching about evil, sin and the Devil. Now we have empirical, reproducible evidence linking sins (many are formal crimes) to sociological data. On the other hand, the widely ignored insights of the world's greatest religious prophets about the crucial need for altruism is certainly at one with the biological need for us all to 'belong' and thus tempers the short-term instincts for individual and small-group survival. This is discussed separately under 'Religion' as a social structure. Broadly speaking, current society is sick – to repeat, the *disease* stems from not belonging. It is isolation and being disconnected with the *inevitable adverse consequences for our minds*. The *symptoms* of the sickness are the adverse social statistics of crime, e.g. petty crime, murder, the proportion of citizens in prison, mental illness and drug addiction, together with such as obesity, diseases and a lack of community life. Humans evolved for small-scale life within 'nature' led by alpha males who belonged. Now we are poorly equipped for large-scale life, controlling nature and predated upon by alien alpha males who are driven by non-rational, primate instincts. In general terms, the world currently has a substantially primate, obedient and conforming, alpha-male-led, 'us and them', territorial, competitive, frightened of the foreign, anti-feminine culture. Likely, improvement is *almost* impossible.

The causes of our major problems originate not from the Devil or God's intervention: they are diseases of the mind due to the inappropriate expression of primate instincts, too little expression of human instincts regarding altruism, femininity, rationality, art and creativity in general. In addition, we have pathological, exclusive social structures at least partly related to alpha-male primate instincts which are incompatible with our *human* evolutionary development.

HOW WE MIGHT TACKLE HUMANITY'S PROBLEMS

Improvements via <u>broad</u> approaches
Recognising the influence of biological
evolution on our problems broadly
With a view to answering needs, harmonising
primate instincts and expressing the human

Contents

INTRODUCTION

As already emphasised, the world currently has a substantially primate, obedient and conforming, alpha-male led, 'us and them', territorial, competitive, frightened of the foreign, anti-feminine culture that under-expresses human instincts. Likely, change is almost impossible. Even so, not all nations are equally dysfunctional, and the most equal societies offer hope (e.g. Scandinavia). Without being unrealistic and over-idealistic, there are obvious and useful things that we can do which are not being done by the most dysfunctional. We all need somehow to control the influence of our instinct to obey and, perhaps via social media, suggest improvements in society and expose wrongdoing.

What are the causes of our problems? The causes of our problems are not God's punishments and/or Satan's temptations or human evil. This is dealt with earlier under 'Evidence for the non-existence of the conventional God or Devil'. In summary, it's not possible to satisfy their existence with a direct, straight-line relationship between 'sins' such as mugging or murder or rape and income inequality. Is God somehow handicapped in unequal societies and Satan enhanced? Is their behaviour determined by the man-made environment? Science has helped by casting a bright light on the *biological* basis of our problems, notably the biology of ancient, so-called 'God-sent' biblical punishments such as pestilence, famine, volcanoes, earthquakes and tsunamis. A major contribution to the causes of wars are our basic, thoughtless (literally), impulsive *instincts* regarding territory, fear of the foreign and those associated with alpha males and obedience to them. We humans must attempt to provide for unmet human needs, the expression of human instincts and to control the inappropriate expression of primate instincts.

Repeating from the earlier section on instincts, it is *not* a case of 'primate' always being bad and 'human' always being good. When faced with a real threat, one's first basic instinct may be the correct way to behave for physical survival. In the case of human instincts relating to arts and religion, their benefits can be perverted, e.g. through being swamped by our basic instincts destroying our creativity. For example, the extreme bureaucratising of the arts in Russia's 'Stalin' era resulted in official, authorised ART. And as for the myriad of religions claiming the ear of God, then their social adhesive properties can be outweighed by their disruptive potential, especially when they exist in the same place. And much of their varied teaching regarding God's role in controlling the world has negative effects. And if altruism is indeed an instinct, then it is commonly swamped by more basic ones. Only the very basic, almost universal altruistic teaching of the prophetic originators of the major religions deserves support. What does *not* deserve support is the later, primate constructions of male, hierarchical religious institutions competing with other religions for numbers, wealth and ownership of the one, authentic, commoditised version of the 'truth'. They commonly and closely resemble commercial corporations in their behaviour.

Non-violent direct action

In recent years in the USA, an extraordinary social revolution has started through the direct action of *individuals* motivated by unprecedented inequality, widespread poverty and anti-human social arrangements. It's called 'Occupy'. Thousands of sites are 'occupied' in various ways including by tent camps. One such occupier was the Jesuit and peace campaigner Daniel Berrigan before his death. I became friends with him at a conference and later when I invited him to speak at meetings in the UK. I found him to be a wonderful, utterly 'normal', fully human person. He was an additional reason to support 'Occupy'. Noam Chomsky in 'Occupy' (an inexpensive Penguin Special, £5 in 2016) has basically written a handbook for Occupy and its ideals. In a beautiful introductory note by the editor, Greg Ruggiero, he points out that Occupy is 'in no rush to produce leaders or issue a closed set of demands' and goes on to say that 'Occupy embodies a vision of democracy that is fundamentally antagonistic to the management of society as a corporate-controlled space that funds a political system to serve the wealthy, ignore the poor' I loudly say 'Amen' to that. I will refer to Chomsky later under the section on 'Commerce, Finance and Capitalism'.

Initially as an 'outsider' to this area, but writing this book and reading widely, I have found Noam Chomsky somehow intriguing. I could not put my finger on it until today when I decided to put it into this section. He has his name to several books where he answers questions and others edit his answers and produce books. 'Occupy' also has question and answer pages. It's an efficient way to get his important ideas in print. It occurs to me that he is very like my hero, Socrates! In fact, Socrates wrote little or nothing, but questioned alpha males relentlessly and, like Chomsky, was recorded by someone – Plato. Also, Socrates' normal, unpretentious and fearless manner of 'speaking' and exposing the truth (notably as recorded in his 'defence') is similar to Chomsky's style. No wonder I (and so many others) admire Chomsky. As for George Monbiot, he's a poet/genius.

I should add that I have never met either person face-to-face or had any direct contact with them. I recently (2017) attended a beautiful talk/song/poetry session with Monbiot and Ewan McLellan.

Earlier, I referred to the activist organisation Avaaz (Avaaz. org), with about 40 million members, giving us an excellent example with numerous, specific successes regarding social evils. Similarly, for Amnesty International (www.amnesty.org.uk). And 'Occupy' is increasing by the day, motivating numerous people to become socially involved by direct, *non-violent* action (www. occupytogether.org/). New organisations are appearing like wild flowers, exposing and campaigning against injustice, such as '38 degrees' (action@38degrees.org.uk), SumOfUs.org (us@sumofus. org), Truthout (messenger@truthout.org) and globalcitizen.org. How to make things better? These organisations could all formally cooperate, at least on the level of campaigns. It seems that Avaaz is the best organised regarding internet campaigns and delivering millions of individual protests. Why not all coordinate forces and also share resources?

Link between inequality, lack of connectedness, exclusive institutions and social harm

Given that so many human societies are so violent and often dysfunctional and commonly at or close to war with others, then how best to improve matters in a rational, reasonable way? In addition to non-violent, direct action, I support the social scientists who showed the empirical, evidence-based link between inequality, lack of connectedness, exclusive institutions and social harm. I also support those proposing gradual, incremental and do-able improvements regarding our needs, modifying our expression of primate instincts which are inappropriate to human life, and encouraging more expression everywhere of human instincts; altruism, art, creativity and human culture. History shows us, without doubt, that the basic teaching about altruism by the philosophical, humanist and religious 'prophets' is mostly ignored and/or replaced – in the case of religions, by 'pious' practices devised and controlled by the clergy/priests demanding obedience. These clerical, pious practices are often described as the 'spiritual' side of religion as opposed to the 'social' side so strongly advocated by the major prophets. Exceptions include the unclerical humanism and Quaker movements.

This change to pious practices resembles the early magicians who predicted such as eclipses and tides and whose power lay in controlling the signs and hence society at large. It was cohesive. It was important social glue. The basic teaching of altruism by the prophets is remarkably similar and owes nothing to magic. At differing times and in different cultures, their intuitions coincided. *It seems that a major, universal problem is the overriding effects of our basic instincts, resulting in basic human needs remaining unmet, i.e. being connected and belonging.*

THE NAKED EMPEROR FABLE

Why are many more people not like the boy in the fable who shockingly points out that the Emperor is naked? The answer is found in our basic instincts about our alpha-male leaders. Any proposals for social improvement should be compatible with the objective facts regarding the existence of instinctive primate behaviour patterns that are predisposing. Similarly, there should be compatibility with our human instincts and all our basic needs, even a focus on them. As I proceeded through the major social structures (see later), it became apparent that it's hard to find *any* structure that does not, more or less, exhibit *all* of the basic 'primate' characteristics. Certainly, they are exhibited by all the main social structures. *Consequently, as a kind of audit, I explicitly apply the following questions only to the first specific structure – the state.* Numerous individuals behave differently and at times so do a few organisations. 'Even' the major religions commonly exhibit strong primate characteristics, despite their origins with founders who taught altruism as their core value. It must be emphasised that instincts in common with primates cannot be considered as always bad, that an instinctive response to danger is always wrong. These reactions are *not* always wrong. And, rock-like, instincts exist.

Nevertheless, given recognition of their existence, attempts can be made to diminish instinctive *behaviour* without rational foundation and with negative consequences, and encourage the use of reason. As a modest example, the typical negative male attitude to women is slowly being modified in some parts of the world and, for example, salary differentials reduced. Also, the positive influence of feminine qualities is being recognised. Hostility to others is often not justified and frequently fermented by over-anxious elites. I will consider the extent to which essentially human instincts are expressed in terms of community, belonging and culture. Overall, as well as providing the basics such as food, shelter and security, do the major social structures contribute to community (belonging) inside and also outside the social structure? Do they help satisfy the need for human culture broadly?

Community, belonging and local power

As I have examined all these structures, what has struck me with force is the need for community and belonging. These are obvious needs, but now proven by empirical social science. All the social structures should reinforce the sense of belonging and community and the sense of it being 'us'. It would seem that when our leaders become 'them', the consequences are always bad. Maybe, human belonging and connectedness are deeper than instincts; *perhaps they are an absolute requirement.* If absent, they are replaced by personal and social pathology.

It has become clear that progress cannot be made via existing social structures led by leaders strongly exhibiting the power phenotype. As mentioned earlier, Al Gore, the former Vice President of the USA (and Nobel Peace Prize Laureate), in an otherwise admirable book (as I see it) 'The Future' about analysing and improving the human condition, starts and ends by suggesting that *only* the USA can lead the world to a better future. I don't think so. He is relying on the same inappropriate alpha-male primate instincts that contributed to our condition and picks a nation to lead us that is at the very top of the inequality league! And a nation with atrocious social statistics resulting from a most unequal and diseased USA society. The evidence is against this conclusion. It seems self-evident that the very forces of biology that have brought us to this sorry situation are unlikely to lead us out of it. The USA is an alpha-male state with its very visible and indisputably alpha-male instincts and colossal arms expenditure, equal to that of the next eleven highest nations. This is especially true now that the alphas have:

a. unprecedented powers of various sorts (including nuclear) in their (frequently) primate hands;
b. modern information technology; and
c. the speed of social change is becoming unmanageable, notably regarding the diminishing numbers of jobs.

It's important to re-emphasise that the USA is the world's most unequal state, for which there is reliable data, with the attendant and numerous adverse social statistics which they possess (see earlier and 'The Spirit Level' by Wilkinson and Pickett). The UK is not far behind with adverse social statistics moving closer to those of the USA. Some new, <u>non</u>-evolutionary-based proposals are needed. For some strange reason, it seems impossible for politicians in the most unequal societies to recognise their adverse social statistics as *symptoms* of a social disease.

'HUMAN RIGHTS' APPROACHES TO REDUCING HUMANITY'S PROBLEMS

Alas, throughout history, idealistic political activists have been unaware of the *biological* nature of the power phenotype or at least of its overriding influence. It comes from instincts existing well before humans, millions of years ago. It supports the *status quo*: the lower classes deserve to be where they are because they are inferior. Indeed, many modern socialist idealists and also aristocrats have referred to the 'upper' and 'working' classes as if they were genetically different. Marx refers to class war. It resembles the way that royalty (and often the rest of us) can believe in royal blood. There is no blood specifically 'royal', nor is there upper or lower 'class' blood. In fact, we are all genetically the same in the sense that the differences between large human groups (e.g. African, Asian, European) are less than those within each group. Humanitarian ideals and desires so often are dissolved by primate instincts. Instincts can be like a tsunami. So often, almost always, revolutions against old, corrupt social arrangements and leaders are replaced by idealistic plans and leaders. Alas, alas, these leaders, on acquiring power, either exhibit the same deeply ancient power phenotype, or are swiftly replaced by others who do, notably Stalin. Social roots are deep: mammals have existed for around 200 *million* years. Taking power and passing new laws are not sufficient to make large changes. And the existing powerful leaders, associated with these deeply entrenched structures, do not stand by watching and quietly idle. That is why an organisation such as 'Occupy' is so attractive.

Any idealistic plan must somehow face the reality of these powerful biological instincts. Not doing so contributed to the short life of many proposals for human rights. Earlier, in the section on slavery ('Violent aggression: slavery, racism and human rights'), I referred to various attempts to establish human rights by decree. Notably, there was Cyrus the Great who abolished slavery in Persia and established unprecedented human rights and religious freedoms in the 6th century

BC. In 449 BC came the Law of the Twelve Tables that established basic procedural rights for all Roman *citizens* as against one another. In the 'Magna Carta' (Great Charter) of 1215 and in later revisions, it is laid down that no free man is to be imprisoned, dispossessed, outlawed, exiled or damaged without the lawful judgement of his peers. No person is above the law, even the monarch.

In modern times, Thomas Paine (1737-1809), referred to earlier, authored several highly influential pamphlets regarding the American and French Revolutions and human rights in particular. His pamphlets included 'Common Sense' (1776, American independence from Great Britain) and 'The American Crisis' (a series, 1776-83, pro-revolution). Paine wrote 'Rights of Man' (1791), which was in part a defence of the French Revolution against its critics. His pamphlet 'The Age of Reason' (1793-94) advocated deism. Paine also wrote the pamphlet 'Agrarian Justice' (1795), discussing the origins of property, and introduced the concept of a *guaranteed minimum income*. The French Revolution (1789) led to the 'Declaration of the rights of man and citizen'. There was 'The Communist Manifesto' (Marx and Engels, 1848) and recently the United Nations 'Declaration of human rights' in 1971 (Link to the Universal Declaration of Human Rights: http://www.un.org/en/documents/udhr/index.shtml; this declaration was based on that of King Kyros the Great.)

Just as early Christians saw the second coming of Christ as imminent and this therefore influenced their actions, so early communists thought that capitalism would inevitably and soon be destroyed by its internal contradictions. In the Communist Manifesto, class struggle is emphasised – 'The history of all hitherto existing society is the history of class struggles'. Sadly, the communist ideals of 'from each according to his talents; to each according to his needs' were formed in ignorance of our biological instincts. They remain admirable objectives, but their achievement requires *awareness of biology and of our common identity*. And, influencing much of this biological behaviour is the idea, or rather the instinct, that a group (or an individual) different to one's own is potentially dangerous. 'Otherness', in itself, is instinctively perceived as a danger, including perceptions of 'upper' and 'lower' classes. When leaders themselves are seen as 'others' or even as predators by the led (and *vice versa*) it inevitably leads to social ills: it's a pathology.

NOT ALWAYS 'LEFT' SOCIALLY GOOD AND 'RIGHT' SOCIALLY BAD

Social reformers seeking a more egalitarian society are typically on the 'left' and display typical altruistic tendencies. It's obvious that 'left' wing social policies and the associated altruism are always socially good and right-wing policies (short-term survival at any cost) are always socially bad. *As mentioned earlier, although obvious, it's not true; not always.* It's definitely not a simple matter of left always being good for social justice and right always being socially bad. Responding to basic instincts can often make sense. When one has neighbours visibly preparing for war, it could make sense to attempt conciliation and negotiation whilst also preparing for the worst. Individuals regarded as right wing can also express humane, altruistic instincts. Also, the consequences of left-wing power are not always altruism and community. When human instincts conflict with the primate, *it's the primate ones that triumph.* Thus, the 'power phenotype' frequently occurs as soon as the left gain power: primate instincts have such deep roots.

> *What is desirable is not the same as what is possible.*
> *It's a creative judgement.*

The initial aims may be egalitarian and altruistic, but the results of the attempted changes commonly fall short. It seems that the more extreme the attempted changes towards a more egalitarian society, then the less likely is success. Exceptions include the elected 1945 Labour government in the UK, when *nearly bankrupt* from World War 2 and following on shortly after World War 1 when so many of *all* the social classes were slaughtered. It led to the UK welfare state with a universal health service, free school dinners and free milk for all children and free, fully-funded higher education and subsidised social housing. After these two recent major wars, the UK was exceptionally united. <u>Virtually everyone belonged</u>. The

UK Health Service was featured as a national triumph during the opening ceremonies to the 2012 Olympics in London. Alas, heavily influenced by right-wing thinking, the more recent trajectory of UK social movements is towards that of the USA with its world's worst social statistics (of nations with available statistics – see Wilkinson and Pickett's 'The Spirit Level').

Another exception was the Cuban Revolution that resulted in huge improvements in social justice also including a universal health service, still today highly regarded. It's tempting to speculate that in both these cases, success was because internally the countries were especially united – everyone 'belonged' and a 'them and us' attitude was at a minimum. The UK was exceptionally united after the two recent wars with horrendous loss of life to all social classes. Cuba was united after suffering many years under an extremely corrupt regime and then further united by the USA invasion and by the constant *USA embargoes and 'dirty tricks' over decades and continuing.* For example, in April 2014, the Associated Press (AP) exposed a secret 'dirty tricks' campaign by the US Agency for International Development (USAid). The 'Cuban Twitter' was intended to foment opposition to the Cuban leadership via encouraging social media-based flash mobs that had occurred naturally in other countries. According to AP, a surveillance dimension existed with the building of a vast database of political dissidents and indications that other countries may also be targeted.

Rapid change commonly ends in chaos: especially in disunited nations

But most examples are sadly different to the two examples above. Marx, Engels and many others (see 'The Communist Manifesto' as well as Marx's 'Das Kapital') had thought and hoped that once the workers assumed control of the means of production and distribution, then great progress in social justice would follow – simple. If only! The Russian Revolution by the 'left' rapidly led to Stalin coming to power and did not result in such progress and cost about 30 million lives. And the Chinese Maoist Revolution, also with the loss of about 30 million lives by avoidable starvation, is now still struggling towards social justice and apparently is slowly moving towards conventional capitalism and with a leader, Xi Jinping, appointed for life.

The roots of human society are deep and widespread and go back to primates and beyond and are supported by instinctive behaviour.

To change society in a radical way, such as the workers controlling production and distribution of goods (even if that is desirable), requires the elimination of the existing, deeply established alpha-male-led culture with its powerful, vested interests. Maybe even the elimination of our evolutionary background is necessary, although of course impossible. The Russian and Chinese Revolutions could hardly be described as successful or evencomparable to what happened in the UK in 1945 regarding social justice. And, sadly, the new revolutionary leaders soon exhibited extreme forms of the power phenotype. It thus seems that starting any major social change with a united community offers the best prospect of success. It seems that the existence of actual and felt belonging, of community, is a basic human need and a prerequisite for social justice.

The 'right' are not known for easily giving up power to produce an egalitarian society. Commonly, the aims of the left change rapidly to the ruthless defeating of the 'right' with full expression of right-wing, primate instincts against 'them', the right-wing enemy. Thus, *the power phenotype appears on the political left as well as on the right*. Altruists may start a revolution with pure intentions of helping the dispossessed and then, on attaining power, the deeply rooted power phenotype appears, often personified by different, more ruthless leaders who do not personify altruism. Marx, Engels (see 'The condition of the working class in England') and many others study, work, debate and encourage a revolution, and soon a Stalin is often in charge. It's deeply sad. Bertrand Russell visited Russia at an early stage of the 1917 revolution with high hopes and soon returned saying that it was finished as far as social justice is concerned. Even if it had 'worked', tens of millions of lives are a crazy, immoral price to pay. Such means cannot justify some hoped for, theoretical ends. Marx, Engels and other progressive social thinkers were unaware of the alpha-male power phenotype, lurking in all males and possibly all females.

2014 saw events commemorating the start of the so-called First World War: another example of hoped for ends 'justifying' bad means. The general UK public view of it is that the war was a colossal waste of human life, with tens of thousands machine-gunned in a single morning, partly blamed on incompetent generals. This view is being revised by right-wing historians. Nobody can argue about the unprecedented loss of life caused by the use of modern armaments. But they argue that it was a necessary loss to hinder or stop German expansionism that might eventually have threatened the British Empire, i.e. the ends of protecting the Empire justify the means of colossal loss of life! It's similar to the current use of the phrase 'the economy' to justify the devastation of the innocent poor who rarely benefit (if at all) in proportion to improvements in 'the economy'. The Victorian mill workers suffering poor conditions, long hours, poor pay and squalid living conditions did not benefit from Empire-gained, cheap raw materials (see earlier re Corn Laws and low wages for low-level workers). The ultra-rich mill owners 'naturally' had their alpha-male lifestyle and splendid, palatial homes and badly paid servants. Nevertheless, it seems that their wealth was at least partly spent locally, employing builders, gardeners and servants, rather than removed from the local economy and hidden in secret tax havens, as for the ultra-wealthy today.

A similar state of affairs existed for the 19th-century seafaring economy with large profits and poor pay and lethally dangerous working conditions. Such was the state of many ships that numerous seamen refused to go to sea. In 1855, a group of seafarers calling themselves 'The seamen of Great Britain' wrote to Victoria the then Queen, complaining that courts had found them guilty of desertion when they complained about going to sea in dangerous ships. Around the same time, an inspector of prisons reported that nine out of twelve prisoners in the jails of South-West England were seamen, imprisoned for twelve weeks for refusing to sail in ships they considered to be unseaworthy, or without enough crew. In one case in 1866, the whole crew was jailed when they refused to set sail on an old, unsafe ship. In the one year 1873-4, 411 ships sank around the British coast, with the loss of 506 lives. Overloading and poor maintenance made some ships so treacherous that they became known as 'coffin ships' with shipowners, like factory owners, mostly indifferent to the plight of their workers. Imagine if today we had 411 airliners crashing with massive loss of life! The Merchant Shipping Act of 1876 made load lines (Plimsoll line) compulsory, but the position of the line was not fixed by law until 1894, *decades* after the serious problem was identified.

Karl Marx, Frederick Engels and others identified and publicised many of the problems of the poor working class over a century ago. As mentioned above, communists thought that capitalism would inevitably *and soon* be destroyed by its obvious internal contradictions. In 'The Communist Manifesto', class struggle is emphasised – 'The history of all hitherto existing society is the history of class struggles'. Alas, the ideals of the phrase, 'from each according to his talents; to each according to his needs' were formed in ignorance of our biological instincts. Alpha-male social structures, and alpha-male 'class', have had a lengthy existence. The first animals appeared around 200 million years ago. Perhaps modern ideals were partly realised in early hunter-gatherer groups where everyone 'belonged'. They broadly remain desirable objectives, but their achievement requires awareness of the relevant biology and of our common identity. A persistent tendency is towards: 'we' are the upper, alpha-male class; 'they' should be the obedient working class.

A quotation exemplifying this attitude is as follows and was spoken by Bishop (i.e. a 'follower' of Jesus!) Samuel Horsley in a speech in the UK House of Lords:

'The people have nothing to do with the laws but to obey them'.

REDUCTION OF INEQUALITY: BENEFITS OF SOCIAL INCLUSIVENESS

Over the decades, I've been reading, studying and learning as I've written down ideas for this book. This includes philosophy, sociology and theology from before and after I became an agnostic. Debate and differences of opinion are normal in all spheres. Recently, there has been much social research on the bad consequences of social inequality (referred to earlier). It definitely bears repetition. For the first time in my experience there are now *straight-line relationships* between income inequality and adverse social statistics: similarly, for the consequences of being unconnected and lacking a sense of community. I was shocked. Put aside for the moment, if you will, intuitive ideas from the greatest philosophers and theologians and advice from eminent sages. Here we have empirical, quantitative data. There are several-fold differences in numerous social ills between the most unequal (USA, with the UK rapidly moving towards this wrong end of the line) and the least unequal (Scandinavia and Japan). To reduce crime, increase health and longevity, help people 'belong'. Help them become more equal! Likewise, healthy communities where people are connected have a similar effect. And there is the extraordinary book 'Why Nations Fail' by Acemoglu and Robinson that shows how nations are hugely influenced positively by *inclusive* economic and political institutions. There are numerous scientific papers and books available about these positive influences. I repeat the recommendation given earlier: 'The Spirit Level' by Wilkinson and Pickett provides clear, graphic evidence linking income inequality (which could also be seen as a lack of 'power') with ill health, crime and other adverse statistics. How can the evidence be so *linear*, directly relating income inequality to bad social statistics for numerous countries? For me, I repeat one possible overall answer – the idea of belonging. Because of differences in wealth, and not simply the people at the top and bottom (it's *in between* – it's linear), they lead different lives and no longer belong to the same society except in name. In ape society and possibly early human society, the alpha male hunts with his group, eats with his group, returns with his group to where he sleeps, grooms and is groomed by his neighbours and is a vital part of his group. *Broadly, they all belong.* In modern society, many of the leaders not only live a different lifestyle to the rest of us, and hence do not belong; indeed, they can be predators upon us!

FACILITATE EXPRESSION OF HUMAN ATTRIBUTES

My purpose in this section is to present broad suggestions about society which are intended to focus on:

a. *answering human needs* including the expression of human instincts and mitigating primate instincts expressed inappropriately in a human world. Worldwide, human needs are not being met and some instincts, naturally curtailed in the earlier primate world, are pathologically unrestricted in the modern world; and also

b. *considering new social arrangements* that reduce the role of alpha-male leaders strongly/completely driven by innate impulses that are relatively independent of the thinking parts of the brain, especially instincts regarding territory, foreigners, women and their own alpha powers. And it seems clear that for communities, 'small is good'. Size matters.

1. Change ideas of *admirable* social success from primate towards human qualities
If we consider world-wide, accepted ideas of social success, they predominantly include such as: wealth, property and land, numerous followers, formal qualifications, titles and high formal status. They might be considered as linked to power, broadly primate. For example, even in religions such as Christianity, the hierarchy are distinguished by alpha titles (His Holiness, Very Reverend, Reverend) and alpha residences such as Bishop's Palaces and even be huge and awe-inspiring such as the Vatican Palace. The latter was recently the cite of a paedophile ring and of mafia activity re the Vatican Bank, yet has never been a refuge for the homeless or been a place of permanent help such as for Sikh temples with four doors open for that very purpose. That is, until recently through Pope Francis.

To move society towards being more human, then somehow socially recognise the importance of people with human qualities of: integrity, generosity, sensitivity, altruism and artistic insight. Broadly, these characteristics are not linked to power.

2. Healthy child development

Particularly in Western, 'developed' societies, high importance should be given to child development. In the UK in recent times, there have been numerous, comprehensive studies strongly supporting this priority:

a. the damaging effects on child development of social and emotional deprivation, leading to adverse social behaviour in later life with high financial costs; and
b. the human benefits of early intervention and also the large cost benefits.

Given the importance of this subject, I hope that the reader will allow me to comment on a few key papers.

One such paper in this area is by Robin Balbernie (Director of the 'Parent Infant Partnership' UK), underlining the effects of specific neurological changes correlated with behaviour as in the title: 'Circuits and circumstances: The neurobiological consequences of early relationship experiences and how they shape later behaviour' (Journal of Child Psychotherapy, vol 27, Issue 3, 2001). Another report is 'Early intervention: smart investment, massive savings' ('The second independent report to Her Majesty's government' July 2011). It was coordinated by Graham Allen MP. It recommends that the UK's 'Late reaction culture' be transcended by an 'Early intervention' one. The front page of the report shows images of CT scans illustrating the negative impact of neglect on the developing brain. The scans compare the developing brain of a healthy three-year old child with that of three-year old children following severe sensory-deprivation neglect in early childhood and showing abnormal development. 'Being taken in – the framing relationship' by Sarah Sutton clearly describes, with examples, how neuroscience and child development studies offer descriptions of how minds are wired or 'miss-wired'.

Another UK Parliamentary Committee (2015) issued a report entitled 'The 1001 Critical Days. The importance of the conception to age two period'. This report accepts and emphasises the earlier findings above. I quote from 'The 1001 Critical Days':

'From birth to age 18 months, connections in the brain are created at a rate of one million per second!

The earliest experiences shape a baby's brain development and have a lifelong impact on that baby's mental and emotional health. A foetus or baby exposed to toxic stress can have their responses to stress (e.g. cortisol) distorted in later life. This early stress can come from the mother suffering from symptoms of depression or anxiety, having a bad relationship with her partner, or an external trauma such as bereavement'.

An extraordinarily magisterial article was also published recently by the WHO (World Health Organization. Published by Elsevier Ltd/ Inc/BV 2014). It was republished in the Lancet (www.thelancet.com, vol 385 May 9, 2015). The authors were Anthony Lake (Executive Director of UNICEF) and Margaret Chan (Director General of the World Health Organization). Its apt title is 'Putting science into practice for early child development'. I quote: 'The debate between nature and nurture as determinants of early child development is over. Today, we understand that the two are inextricably linked. The degree of their interdependence – and the impact of this interplay on the developing brains of children – is even greater than we previously imagined. This knowledge has tremendous implications for how we design and deliver early child development interventions'. Another important quotation: 'We are just beginning to understand how environmental factors – including the quality of parenting – might *modify the expression of genes, and possibly affect not just one, but multiple generations*' (my italics). This growing area of inquiry is accelerating change in the way we think about development in early childhood and early childhood development interventions.

As separate fields of study begin to come together, aiming to translate scientific evidence into practical action, some key recommendations are emerging:

First, early intervention is essential. Neuroplasticity begins to decline after early childhood. It becomes progressively harder to offset the effects of early childhood deprivation on the brain. Interventions are most effective during the period of most dynamic growth and what happens in these early years affects a child for life.

Second, to be most effective, interventions must be <u>intersectoral</u>, going beyond education to encompass health, nutrition and protection. The healthy development of a child's brain depends on multiple positive experiences. Nutrition feeds the brain; stimulation sparks the mind; love and protection buffer the negative impact of stress and adversity. And distinct interventions are mutually supportive, achieving the strongest results when delivered together.

These ideas about child development, emphasising multiple factors, should be a priority for all nation states: a safe and happy home, good nutrition and education. Dare I mention the word 'love'? It would seem obvious that the hard-to-define word 'love' leads to the good factors mentioned. A very relevant book is 'Why Love Matters: How affection shapes a baby's brain' by Sue Gerhardt. Leaning on experimental work, she explains why love is essential to brain development in the early years of life, particularly to the development of our social and emotional brain systems. The book presents the multidisciplinary discoveries that indicate how our emotional lives operate. Sue Gerhardt considers how the earliest relationship shapes the baby's nervous system, with lasting consequences, and how our adult life is influenced by infancy. She shows how the development of the brain can affect future emotional well-being and looks at specific early 'pathways' that can affect the way we respond to stress and lead to conditions such as anorexia, addiction and antisocial behaviour.

Consequently, and unquestionably, a healthy approach, in

keeping with evidence, could be first to *socialise* the young child and early on include reading stories, dance, drama, poetry, sculpture. *Socialising is belonging*: playing music, creating art, participating. Later on, it would help if we saw formal education more as a part of the important *human* development of a person, the individual (see earlier section on 'Importance of early development: non-human primates to human primates' for references). Healthy child development facilitates later healthy adult behaviour. Sadly, progress remains generally slow in developing detailed plans for the above broad proposals. In numerous countries, including the UK and the USA, the individual is not the focus.

3. Answer basic human needs

We should incrementally improve the way society answers basic *human needs*, especially the reality of belonging and of togetherness/connectedness for citizens and also the need of inclusive social structures. Facilitating the expression of *human* instincts is key: altruism, creativity in its numerous forms, rationality (evidence-based reasoning) and human culture. Building housing that creates a sense of community, with communal facilities. Allowing and encouraging workers to participate in decisions in their work. Numerous commercial enterprises have done this and currently do so. Controlling the expression of primate instincts when inappropriate – which is difficult given the instant, embedded consequences of fear.

4. Broad proposals: social media

A new, potent force for good is the spontaneous expression of protest or of idealism by large numbers of relatively leaderless *individuals* via social media (as described previously). This is a new development utilising social media and is in its infancy. For the last year or so I have witnessed large-scale uprisings *as they happen* – mainly young people, men and women, protesting peacefully in public against injustice, poverty and brutality. Using smartphones, they directly broadcast what is happening, including *instant* sight of events such as unprovoked police brutality that cannot be lied about or explained away. Given the existence of this instantaneous 'free reporting', the media seems more willing to show such things on television. History teaches us about the typically, almost universal, bad consequences of violent revolution. Rather, it seems best if each major social institution is reformed gradually, involving such mass, instant publicising of injustice, wrongdoing and corruption.

Furthermore, as referred to earlier, and this bears repetition, there are now spontaneously formed organisations unlinked to governments or business that publicise injustice and global crime. For example, mass movements of *individuals*, e.g. Avaaz. The movement 'Occupy' (OccupyWallSt.org; support@occupywallst.org) 'embodies a vision of democracy that is fundamentally antagonistic to the management of society as a corporate-controlled space that funds a political system to serve the wealthy, ignore the poor ...' (Editor Greg Ruggiero's note in 'Occupy' by Noam Chomsky). In 'Occupy' (A Penguin Special), Noam Chomsky has a beautiful quotation about another social activist, Howard Zinn. Zinn's primary concern 'was the countless small actions of unknown people that lie at the roots of those great moments that enter the historical record'. Again, at the risk of over-repetition, 'Occupy' is an evolving social movement, hoping for a new kind of democracy not led by primate alpha males. It is hoping to change society by individual action. It's harder for the elite to attack individual leaders if we are millions and have no or changeable leaders. I recommend reading the inexpensive Noam Chomsky book 'Occupy'. I have referred above to Avaaz, 'Occupy', 38 degrees, SumOfUs, Truthout (messenger@truthout.org) and Amnesty. They are doing wonders for humanising a primate society and exposing social ills. There are many more, appearing everywhere as I write and which deserve support as best we can. Likely they are major forces for humanising society._Interestingly, and importantly, many (but not all, alas) brutal dictators and despots do not like their brutality exposed. This is a hopeful fact.

It would help to have mass publication of situations where workers do not receive a living wage and/or have no adequate shelter.

This could include different industries in different places and also their suppliers who exploit their own workers. Too often, suppliers in developing countries treat workers in a manner similar to or worse than Victorian mill owners; possibly for the same biological reasons, i.e. the powerful vs the powerless. The UK Office for National Statistics (ONS) reported that in 2014, almost a quarter of jobs outside London paid less than the 'living wage' with the proportion increasing over the last four years. State supplements to such inadequate wages come out of taxes. Thus, the UK government is seducing companies to come to the UK by offering low or no tax arrangements and also allowing them to pay less than the minimum wage, topped up by the UK taxpayer. Why? And why is this not well known? In summary, numerous large companies pay little or no tax and pay only about 80% of a wage needed to provide a 'living' wage. Surely, this is a deliberate policy? I watched on live TV the UK Chancellor of the Exchequer say that he was trying to create a low tax, <u>high</u> wage economy. Yet he is (and has done) clearly creating a state-supplemented, low-wage economy for the employees and a low/no tax economy for the multinational companies. Is it because his motives are not at all bad, but he thinks that not doing so could be a catastrophe? In other words, not doing so would lead to mass unemployment, and that these multinationals are 'contributing' about 80-85% towards the workers' so-called living wage and welfare covers the other 15-20%. It's wrong that rich, profitable, multinational companies such as Google should not pay genuine, living wages. Currently, in 2018, Google is being sued for several billion Euros due to unpaid taxes in Ireland.

Similarly, it would be helpful to publicise industries that allow no representation by workers, but maintain them solely as mechanical units of production to be treated as disposable machines – harming or eliminating any feeling of belonging. There was publicity about a report giving numerous such examples of the ruthless exploitation of powerless migrant workers building the facilities for the soccer World Cup in Qatar ('The dark side of migration: spotlight on Qatar's construction sector ahead of the World Cup'). In 2012 there were numerous injuries and deaths of workers who lived in unsanitary, squalid conditions, working 10 hours a day, 7 days a week and in the summer at temperatures reaching 45°C and too often *deprived* of their pay. Between January 2012 and January 2014 over 500 Indian migrant workers on Qatar building sites died (Indian Doha Embassy). During 2012 and 2014 about 400 Nepalese workers died in a similar manner. This is happening in *one of the world's richest countries!* Would it not be good for Amnesty, Avaaz, Occupy and similar organisations closely to cooperate using social media for their common goals?

5. Mitigate α-male phenotype and other basic instincts

We should try to reduce our instinctive obedience to alpha males, our fear of the 'foreign', including the fear of femininity, and our territorial instincts. Facilitating the expression of *human* instincts, notably altruism and also poetry, literature and drama, art and artefacts, music, painting and sculpture is vital, especially in young children. Libraries and galleries can exhibit the work of *local* schools and of *local* people generally. School children can visit institutions for the elderly and also hospitals. Society can encourage artistic expression in the *workplace*: paintings, tapestries, music, choirs. Artistic creations exhibited by the workers would help cultivate a sense of belonging and also give pride. A largely unreleased and unpublicised social force, a humanising influence, is that of the feminine aspect of women: not from macho women, but typical women. This femininity can be helped to exert its influence beyond the home. Hopefully, an actual catastrophe is not required to bring about such achievable changes. It's less men versus women, as macho versus feminine.

'Localism' is commonly a force for unity. I'm familiar with an area in South-West France. The local commune is truly local. When a street light is persistently dysfunctional, a visit to the mayor personally is needed. Regular parties/meals are arranged, with older people collected and brought to the meal. Children are given gifts, and all are paid from local taxes. The commune is very proud of its schools, playing fields and public baths. Doubtless, money could be saved by pooling resources centrally from different communes, but the commune spirit maintains their own facilities. Money does not rule! Similar arrangements exist in Scandinavia where tax is more often seen as a personal contribution to communal life and much less seen as an evil imposed by an alien state. This is partly because the state is not alien and the pursuit of money is not regarded as God's command.

Deconditioning of primate instincts
In addressing inappropriate, innate, instinctive impulses, we should encourage conditioning to enable conscious thought. But facilitating the expression of *human* instincts and managing primate ones is easier said than done. 'The Chimp Paradox' by the psychiatrist Steven Peters describes the author's behavioural approach to controlling inappropriate impulses and facilitating human ones. He has worked especially with individual lite athletes and also some organisations and with spectacular success in applying his ideas – notably numerous Olympic Gold Medallists. He *explicitly* confronts our evolutionary, biological history and offers an 'easy working model' of the brain for discussion purposes. The model comprises the 'human' part, the emotional 'chimp' and an information-storage part. Peters contrasts how the human and the chimp interpret input of information. The chimp interprets with feelings and impressions and then uses *emotional* 'thinking' to plan action. In contrast, the human interprets by searching for facts and establishing the truth. Then there follows logical thinking, leading to a plan.

He suggests that we should not ignore, but attempt to live with the chimp. He offers what might be called deconditioning approaches to controlling and managing inappropriate 'chimp' impulses. Superficially, the book might appear to be a kind of airport book, offering an easy way to self-fulfilment or a quick way to riches. It's not that. In terms of facilitating the expression of human attributes and managing 'chimp' ones, this book faces the real, biological issues and offers ways to move forward. The question arises as to whether the principles can be applied more widely. The evidence suggests that they can. Peters' approaches should be applied and propagated throughout education, large organisations and especially political structures. It would help society in general if powerful alpha-male leaders familiarised themselves with Peters' approaches and were 'deconditioned'.

A fantasy
It could help if Peters gave up his day job, gave up coaching athletes and was employed by a new United Nations with overriding world powers to coach world leaders who would be required to gain Peters' approval before taking up office as part of a small, Belbin-like leadership group of around five (see management literature re Meredith Belbin). The ones that he failed to decondition would be excluded from leadership positions forever. (Some hope!)

Table of chimp and human broad traits
('The Chimp Paradox' by the psychiatrist Steven Peters)

Traits of emotional (chimp) thinking
Jumps to an opinion
Thinks in black and white
Paranoid
Catastrophic
Irrational
Emotive judgement

Traits of logical (human) thinking
Evidence-based
Rational
In context and with perspective
Shades of grey and balanced judgement

6. Ideas of original cultural sages

We ought to pay attention, not to religious institutions, but to the *original* insights of religious prophets/sages – i.e. regarding altruism – e.g. instigating a genuine 'living wage' and not a 'minimum wage' or less, with a couple of low-paid jobs. There should be in evidence human instincts of <u>widespread</u> art (from children and local people, and not so much 'ART') *everywhere*: in the workplace, schools, homes, public places, galleries, on transport, the street, libraries.

7. Belonging and local power

We should encourage anything and everything to increase a sense of human belonging and connectedness (considered under sections on 'Government' and elsewhere). Facilitating the *bringing together* of the alpha-male leaders and the led is of paramount importance. We need to make any parliament's composition representative of the nation as a whole. Providing homes, humanising the working class and other housing estates, supporting small communities. Marx and other thinkers of the Industrial Revolution concur with modern thinkers regarding the need for the workers to be involved in their work.

We must work towards: humanising the workplace by encouraging human participation by the workers in major decisions and also in 'local' matters affecting them directly. Facilitate workers' unions. Allow union representatives to sit on company boards. Consider the current UK Lewis's and the original Quaker Cadbury's owners' approach (see later re Cadbury's origins in 'Commerce and business) to workers being treated as fellow humans. In the UK, the next 'City of Culture' is Coventry and the city is emphasising the developing of street communities: reducing streets of strangers.

The state to encourage 'localism'. Currently in the UK, local people, as for factory workers, have little or no say in anything. For biological reasons, this will inevitably cause aberrant behaviour. Wherever possible, delegate decisions on minor spending to local street/locality level. Encourage street/local, elected committees to spend and/or advise on local spending. Increase local control.

8. 'Misinformation Machines'

It's imperative that laws are passed worldwide and perhaps by UN, regarding fake 'think tanks' and fake 'citizens' groups', funded by mega-rich corporations and industries that attack any evidence that harms profits. 'Dark money' describes the <u>undisclosed</u> funding of organisations who advocate politically on behalf of other organisations preferring to remain in the shade. The media should be forced to expose the funding of fake think tanks and the origins of the 'dark money'. Previous examples include the tobacco industry funding deniers of the lethal and disease-causing effects of tobacco-smoking against overwhelming evidence. A current example is the denial of the dangers of global warming by so-called think tanks funded by energy companies. The Murdoch-owned Fox News might be difficult to change, but reputable news outlets such as the BBC should not use the idea of 'balance' to publicise 'opinions' and assertions from commercially funded and fake 'think tanks'. All news agencies should ban 'think tanks' funded by vested interests. The individual and social consequences of delaying recognition of these dangers was catastrophic regarding tobacco and is likely to be similarly catastrophic when it comes to global warming. Global warming is referred to under 'Humanity's Key Problems'. Dare I ask this question about defence? Is the global mega expenditure on 'defence' partly the consequence of advocates for the defence industry and the 'revolving door' between politics and industry?

I will not attempt a comprehensive account of global warming, but a brief account follows. Numerous <u>independent</u> sources accept the imminent dangers of global warming – simply 'Google' global warming. The World Wide Fund for Nature (WWF) is an international non-governmental organisation founded in 1961, working in the field of wilderness preservation and the reduction of humanity's footprint on the environment. It was started by eminent, reputable naturalists and ecologists. It reports that a mere 2°C rise in temperature will put 30 per cent of species at high risk of extinction, marine food chains will collapse, and ecosystems could completely disappear, while shortages of food and water are predicted to trigger massive movements of people, leading to migration, conflict and famine. In 2013, the planet passed a dangerous milestone when atmospheric levels of carbon dioxide exceeded 400 parts per million, prompting the scientific community to advocate renewed vigour in efforts to combat climate change. However, current commitments by the world's governments fall *far short* of the greenhouse gas reductions needed to limit global temperature rise to 2°C by 2020. We need to take urgent measures to slow down and reduce the extent of the climate crisis. Global temperatures have been rising for over a century, speeding up in the last few years, and are now the highest on record. This causes negative impacts such as the melting of Arctic sea ice, prolonged heatwaves and rising sea levels. Bangladesh, among others, is in danger of being submerged. Compiling the necessary environmental laws will be difficult, but possible. Climate change is here, despite the irrational, evidence-denying assertions by President Donald J. Trump and the deniers now in his cabinet.

9. Femininity

This is linked to item 1. We should positively encourage and support femininity, not only women's advancement and rights. Femininity softens macho, masculine behaviour. Tackle the repression of women, especially the tendency for men to suppress them from 'public speech'. Feminine characteristics are invaluable in any new and needed approach to society. The very reasons that have probably held back women from developing a public voice – i.e. their often unwillingness to jump when war bugles sound in a nuclear world, make feminine characteristics important in a new, human world. It seems significant that it's a woman, Angela Merkel, who is leading Germany in a kind, altruistic way regarding accepting a disproportionate number of refugees from Syria and elsewhere during the current crisis (September, 2015). Sadly, in 2017 she experienced low poll ratings as a consequence.

10. Facilitate widespread creation of truth, justice and reconciliation commissions

Commissions, such as that in South Africa post-apartheid, empower conflict-affected communities to participate in processes of justice, healing and reconciliation. Perhaps linked to such commissions, we should encourage world-sponsored acts of financial and territorial help. Sadly, sadly, it seems too late for Palestine but, in passing, one wonders if a generous purchase of Palestinian land for the Jews would have helped subsequent history. Similarly, and *not* too late, the descendants of slavery today could at least get some focussed help regarding education at all levels and help to improve basic living and community conditions in deprived areas.

11. Support George Monbiot's manifesto ('The Age of Consent')

Monbiot's main projects (www.monbiot.com) are partly about democracy on a global level and are practical and rational. He is also distinguished by his rational approach to:

a. seeking a new world order in which current major institutions are replaced on a large-scale; and
b. every _individual_ is exhorted to do something _immediately_.

His proposals are summarised in his book 'The age of consent: a manifesto for a new world order' and broadly consist of four main projects. These are:

1. A democratically elected World Parliament;
2. Democratise the UN General Assembly and give it the powers currently possessed by the Security Council;
3. Create an International Clearing Union that automatically discharges trade deficits and prevents the accumulation of debt;
4. Create a Fair Trade organisation that restrains the rich while emancipating the poor.

Personally, I would wish to add a campaign of social education regarding:

a. the existence of instinctive, non-conscious, innate behaviour tendencies that can be destructive; and

b. that sin, God and the Devil are less plausible causes of evil than are these sometimes inappropriate, innate, instinctive and deeply rooted behaviour tendencies. Similarly, unmet essential human needs lead to 'evil' behaviour.

George Monbiot is calling for the globalisation of democracy. Given that people do not consist of various races, but just one – the human race – his ideas have an added genetic logic in bringing humans to an acceptance of our common humanity. Also, they will help give much needed power to the powerless. I will again repeat one caveat that also applies to Noam Chomsky and the numerous intellectuals and prophets who have analysed our problems and offer solutions. Chomsky and Monbiot join the Axial Age sages (Greek philosophers, the Buddha, Confucius, Daoists), modern humanists and also Jesus at the end of his life, two days before his execution (see Matthew's gospel, 'the Day of Judgement'). All advocated the need for kind _behaviour_ (help others, especially the needy) rather than the adherence to 'sacred' creeds and doctrines which so deeply divide the human race. In the case of Jesus, he gave response to need as an absolute requirement for entry to Heaven (and not responding sent people to Hell) and he identified himself with the needy. Burning in Hell for all eternity as a punishment for missing mass or reading a sacred book or other 'sacred' duty was not mentioned by Jesus.

How is it that for Christians 'the cross' and 'guilt' (Jesus, the Christ (God), died for our sins, so we are guilty for killing God) have taken over as key concepts? Jesus did not emphasise (or even mention) the 'cross' as central, but massively he did emphasise love and altruism. After all, the cross was at the end of his life. Answer: this came about to enhance clerical control for _biological_ reasons. Jesus died for our sins and redemption can come only by pious practices *controlled by the clergy*. They call such practices the 'spiritual' side of religion (as opposed to the 'inferior', social side). This can usefully help social coordination and *control* which can be needed biologically for response to social threat. It's not that Jesus's execution was insignificant, rather that he constantly emphasised love and altruism as did the other great religious leaders mentioned above. Another trick: the image of the Buddha as a fat man with eyes closed. In fact, as do many people, he meditated as an aid to reducing the impact of his basic instincts. He advocated kindness: good, human, altruistic behaviour '....there is no need for temples ....my philosophy is kindness'.

Q. Why do so few people accept and follow the above rational ideas?
A. Because instincts developed over millions of years impel us towards primate (and earlier) survival behaviour of mindless obedience to mindless leadership. In addition we are manipulated by two factors:

1. <u>Fear</u> stimulating these instincts regarding territory, the foreign or our alpha leaders.
2. Right-wing, 'primate' media (in the West, typically owned by right-wing media barons living in tax havens) relentlessly fermenting the same basic, primate instincts.

SUMMARY OF POSSIBLE BROAD SOCIAL IMPROVEMENTS

With a view to answering needs, harmonising primate instincts and expressing the human. Not restricted to religions.

1. Education worldwide re the above-mentioned causes of our problems and of our needs. <u>Science</u> helps by casting light on:

    a. the old problems of pestilence, famine, volcanoes, earthquakes and tsunamis; and

    b. advancing human brain and personality development; and

    c. the biological and genetic basis of many problems.

Educate re the scientifically proven need for belonging/ connectedness, for inclusive social structures and for an understanding of our place in the universe.

Education re basic, *common* teaching of humanism and the originators of major religions regarding altruism.

Educate re our common humanity. There is only one race and it's in serious danger.

2. Focus on child development, based on established empirical evidence and on the humanisation of society: <u>socialise</u> children (e.g. as in Scandinavia), and early on include reading stories, music, art, dance, drama, poetry, sculpture, cooking. See formal education more as a part of the important <u>human</u> development of a person. Encourage anything to increase that sense of human belonging and connectedness.

3. Positively encourage and support femininity and human rights.

4. Promote the widespread deconditioning of leaders and the led: attempt to reduce the irrational fear of the foreign, increase the use of reason (evidence based) mre territory and obedience to alpha males.

Start with leaders, e.g. Prime Ministers and Presidents, Cabinet Ministers, Head Teachers, Heads of Public Hospitals, and Military Commanders. Use techniques described in 'The Chimp Paradox' by Steve Peters.

5. Facilitate the expression of specifically human instincts – altruism, creativity, rationality, widespread art (by children and local people, not so much monied 'ART') everywhere: in the workplace, schools, homes, public places, galleries, libraries, on transport and in the street.

6. Pay attention to original and common insights put forward by the major religious prophets – altruism. For example, a genuine 'living wage' and not a 'minimum wage' or less, with workers forced to have two or more low-paid jobs.

7. Facilitate the *peaceful*, mass exposure of injustice via social media including the already existing mass movements. It's proposed that progress will come mainly from mass demands from *individuals* for structural changes. Reduce the instinctive (hence mindless) obedience to elites, e.g. via these non-violent mass movements of *individuals*. Currently this is very promising.

8. Facilitate the bringing together of the alpha-male leaders and the led. Small communities, reduce inequality. Make Parliament *representative*. Needed are parliaments and senates whose actual constitution represents the *community mix* and parliamentarians and public servants who serve the people and whose members live lifestyles *at least similar* to those who are served. Social focus on community, belonging, inclusiveness and creativity.

9. As advocated by numerous USA presidents over 200 years, the connection needs to be *broken* between politicians, political parties and corporations/ 'big business' with their 'big money'. No donations, no buying influence by buying laws. In the USA there seems little

hope of this happening soon with President Donald Trump in the White House.

10. Increase direct, individual and personal involvement in social processes and structures, *including work*. Encourage commercial enterprises that involve their employees as participating fellow humans and not as disposable objects. Humanise the workplace. Remove anti-union legislation.

11. Encourage a 'media' that informs, educates and entertains in the absence of over-powerful, individual media 'moguls' personally determining a commonly 'over-primate' media culture. Separate the media, including the UK BBC, from interference by corporations and political parties. Given the example of the USA over centuries, likely impossible as things stand now.

12. 'Provide homes, humanise the working class and other 'habitats' (estates). Design these dwellings to encourage and facilitate communities.

HOW WE MIGHT TACKLE HUMANITY'S PROBLEMS

Improvements to specific social structures
(i) The State: Parliaments, Military, Justice/Law, Education
The USA and UK as special Cases

Contents

Approaches to the audit of each of the specific social structures

Questions and comments for improvement of social structures and of their impact on society

1. Focus on the original intentions of how the structure serves society.
2. Improve the answering of human needs and assisting social expression of human instincts of altruism, creativity and art.
3. Humanising of social structures *per se* and their impact on society.
4. Reducing the influence of inappropriate primate instincts: territory, the foreign, anti-feminine, blind obedience to alpha-male leaders.

Questions for each structure

Given the undoubted reality of basic instincts and needs, human progress requires that all are taken into consideration. In 'auditing' each social structure, these basic questions can be asked regarding the expression of primate and/or specifically human instincts. The audit starts with the state and government and then military, law and formal education. Starting with child development, education has crucial, lifelong consequences. And then follows commerce and then religion.

> *Given that all the main structures exhibit all the key primate features then, as an illustration, <u>only the state</u> is considered explicitly with each specific question.*

1. Is any particular institution characterised by being in competition with and hostile to other similar organisations?
2. Does it protect its 'territory' at all costs and attempt to expand its influence?

3. Is it characterised as having a male-dominated hierarchical structure, with obedience to those at the top levels?
4. Are the conditions of work and rewards for individuals related to their position in the hierarchy or to their gender?
5. Is the differential in rewards between the top and bottom large? Are the rewards at the bottom adequate to provide shelter and nutrition?
6. Are women as a group treated as unequal in terms of power?
7. Are non-members (foreigners, 'not us') characteristically treated with suspicion? And in terms of human instincts and needs:
8. Does each social structure contribute to our needs for *community and* connectedness, i.e. belonging and assisting our understanding of the universe?
9. Is each social structure *inclusive*?
10. Do the institutions affecting our basic physical needs actually help provide them (such as shelter, food and health)?
11. Does the institution itself, and also for society, specifically facilitate the expression of the human instincts of altruism, belonging and human culture in broad terms?

At the end of this section are comments specifically on the USA as the world's super (alpha) power. Although the UK is highlighted generally, there are also comments at the end of this section specifically on the UK as it moves rapidly towards being an increasingly unequal society, close to the USA in inequality. In terms of the listed primate characteristics, notably regarding territory, fear of the foreign/different, including women, alpha-male leadership and associated obedience, <u>every state and their substructures</u> exhibit all of these characteristics to varying degrees. This applies whether the state is capitalist, socialist, religious or a sub-category.

The State: Parliaments, Military, Justice, Law and Education. The USA and UK as special cases

Introduction

Questions and comments for improvement

1. Is the state characterised by being in competition with and hostile to other states?

Worldwide, the answer is a definite yes. The UK has the added burden of being a major world power but no longer with a large empire and finding it difficult to adapt. Similarly the USA, as the world's most powerful nation, is clearly exhibiting power-phenotype behaviour with its military interventions worldwide (see the later section on the USA). Broadly speaking, the attitude of any state to the rest of the world is at best suspicious and at worst hostile. It is obvious that the behaviour of states in general is strongly influenced by primate instincts. Currently about one third of nations are at war. See www.warsintheworld.tk for details of specific countries, regions and the numerous groups involved in conflicts. It is truly shocking. Inter-state spying and surveillance is widespread and possibly global.

2. Does it protect its 'territory' at all costs and attempt to expand its influence?

The answer again is a definite yes. Self-evidently, territory is of huge importance to every nation. A notable example was the situation in Ukraine, with the annexation of the Crimea. Disputed territory is a component of almost every conflict, together with precious resources

3. Are the states' official subunits characterised as having a male-dominated hierarchical structure, with obedience to those at the top levels?

Definitely yes, probably with no exceptions.

4. *Are the conditions of work and rewards for individuals working for the state related to their position in the hierarchy or to their gender?*

Yes, for all states and for both questions.

5. *Is the differential in rewards between the top and bottom large?Are the rewards at the bottom adequate to provide shelter and nutrition?*

States vary in the differentials of income for citizens. For those with the largest salary differential, rewards at the bottom levels barely provide shelter and food. The 'working poor', even in the UK and especially the USA, barely survive, often needing two or even more jobs. The Pulitzer Prize winner David Shipler in 'The Working Poor' details their plight in the USA, often referring to unmarried women with children. He also gives an insight into the plight of employers with tiny profits and in intense competition from overseas. In more equal countries such as in Scandinavia, the bottom levels do receive adequate incomes. Even the direct employees of many states typically have large salary differentials compared with people at the bottom who have no security of employment (so-called zero hours 'contracts'), minimum (not living) wages and experience hostility to any union representation. Essentially, in the most unequal states, employees of the state and of corporations at the bottom end of the pay scale, generally have few, if any rights.

6. *Are women as a group treated as unequal in terms of power?*

Unquestionably and almost universally, women as a group are not treated as being equal to men. This inequality varies between nations and also exists among state employees.

7. *Are non-members (foreigners, 'not us') characteristically treated with suspicion?*

I have been unable to find studies that I can quote but, obviously, nations vary in their hostility towards and suspicion of foreigners. The main, obvious causes of suspicion are skin colour and religion, especially when linked to a shortage of jobs. My personal, anecdotal opinion and experience from living in various European countries and in the USA supports a 'yes'.

8. And in terms of auditing the existence of *human* instincts and needs:

Does each state and its structures contribute to our needs for community, connectedness and belonging, for cultural expression and to assist our understanding of the universe?

Where the state and the nation are the same, then being a citizen of the state or being an employee can contribute to our human need to belong. Where the state and the nation are not the same, such as when state boundaries result from colonialist interventions or war, with little or no regard for cultural identity, then the feelings of belonging are diluted, if they exist at all. Such is the complexity of modern societies with large populations, that the state has an essential coordinating function – a 'central nervous system'. In itself, this adds to feelings of belonging – *our* railway, *our* roads, *our* hospitals, *our* schools, *our* universities, *our* galleries and libraries. Those keen to reduce the size of the state greatly, 'should' be aware of the *essential* need for belonging.

It is common but variable worldwide for the state to provide, directly or indirectly, libraries, art galleries, museums and public parks as well as schools and hospitals for universal public benefit. This accords with our human instincts of altruism and of culture. Where the elite use health, educational and recreational services (private) that are different to the rest, then this contributes to a lack of togetherness. In extreme cases, it leads to a separate, alien lifestyle. Inevitably, when led and leaders live different and separate lifestyles, society is harmed.

As for our understanding of the universe and our place in it, then the state religion, if there is one, can contribute greatly in this biological sense. But multiple religions can lead to conflict. Depending on the state education system, history can contribute to our sense of belonging.

As well as having intrinsic worth, cultural studies can contribute to the feeling of belonging to humankind as a whole. Consequently, the state should provide a wide-ranging education including the humanities together with music and drama. Scientifically based explanations of natural phenomena can contribute to our understanding of the universe as well as having their own intrinsic worth. Numerous worthwhile results in terms of localism and belonging can flow from exhibiting pupils' (and staff's) artwork and poetry on school premises and in local libraries and galleries.

9. *Are state structures inclusive?*

This varies greatly across the world. Acemoglu and Robinson in 'Why Nations Fail' have shown that inclusive economic and political structures correlate with successful states, and exclusive ones with failure. In the latter, the coalescence of economic and political power leads to the elites ruling for their own benefit at the expense of the many. In the recent UK cabinet of David Cameron, we had an unusual coincidence of our cabinet having a high proportion of members (male) having attended *the same* top private boarding school (Eton). In primate terms, this could be useful in that having had a common education and lifestyle, they were familiar with each other's ethos and world view and were more likely to be loyal and familiar. Of course, they could not have had the same awareness of citizens' needs and aspirations as those who shared a common lifestyle. Also, it could have been less important except that Parliament was, itself, unrepresentative of the diverse UK population with gross over-representation of middle-class men with UK only backgrounds (see below).

10. *Do the institutions of state affecting our <u>basic</u> physical needs actually help provide them (such as shelter, food and health)?*

It is reasonable that the state should facilitate the availability of land for housing including that for the poor: similarly for food. In the UK, we currently have a housing crisis, but compared with many parts of the world we are not doing badly. Nevertheless, over 900,000 people were given emergency food in the UK during 2013-14 according to the Trussell Trust (the largest UK food bank charity). Also in the UK, we benefit from a universal national health service, the NHS. It is currently being visibly downgraded because 'we' cannot afford to provide for the increasing proportion of elderly people as well as the increase in cost of care generally. Nevertheless, it is still a wonderful aspect of UK life. Alas, there are numerous states without a universal health service, notably the top *economy*, the USA. I repeat my suggestion that the introduction of a universal health service in the UK after World War 2 and when the UK was bankrupt, was because we were a united nation with a socially minded government. I suggest that to do so today with our present government would never happen.

A *huge factor affecting all UK expenditure is as follows.* Relatively unpublicised is the cost of attempting to continue the UK as a major 'world power'. The 'Trident' programme of submarines armed with nuclear weapons that are on permanent patrol at sea is one example of unsustainability. Together with the costs of aircraft carriers, associated planes and other weaponry, various estimates are around £150-200 *billion*. Ministers repeatedly state publicly that they are needed to procure us a seat at the 'top table' (this is primate, alpha-male 'speak'). In 2014, the then UK Prime Minister David Cameron referred to the situation in North Korea as justifying this expenditure! He means that if North Korea attacks the UK or its allies, then we can retaliate *after* the destruction of (parts of) the UK by 'us' destroying North Korea. If any reader is unaware, it's aptly called MAD (mutually assured destruction). Also, there is obvious and massive US pressure to go ahead. It was widely reported (pre-'Brexit', pre-Donald Trump's election) that we will no longer be the USA's main partner if we do not go ahead. It's hard not to think that the UK has secret treaties with the USA involving Trident and other weaponry as well as their numerous UK (and other European) bases. It was announced decades ago that the UK could not actually fire any nuclear weapon. It would have to be

NATO, i.e. the President of the USA. It's interesting and significant that the UK Labour Party does not target this as an unrequired expense: doubtless they fear right-wing newspaper attacks about 'Trotskyites' or the 'loony left' or being 'soft' on defence.

Note: Growth forecasts for the UK released by the International Monetary Fund (IMF) show that the total bill for Trident's replacement could be £167bn. The new figures estimate that the programme would run between 2028 and 2060. But the Campaign for Nuclear Disarmament (CND) claim the true figure could be around £205bn once the *cost of decommissioning* has been taken into account.

Another factor affecting UK expenditure is government reluctance/refusal to increase taxes. VAT and National Insurance is roughly equal for everyone. Why not tax the rich more than the poor?

11. *Does the state and its subunits specifically facilitate expression of the human instincts of altruism and broadly human culture for the state structures* <u>*per se*</u> *and for society generally?*

'It's the economy, stupid' is a well-known American aphorism for electioneering. There is little doubt that the economy is key to winning elections in 'democratic' (more on democracy later) societies and for maintaining order in non-democratic ones. But the economy should not be the main objective of politics. Rather, the well-being and happiness of the citizens is what leads to a successful society in human terms: the economy can provide much of the basic *means* if profits are distributed fairly. In recent decades, increases in the economy have *not* led to proportional increases in the benefits to the middle and even less to the lower classes. Increasingly common is for capital to be removed rapidly from local economies and into tax havens. It's interesting that, above a low, subsistence level of finance, there is almost no correlation between the level of personal finance and the level of happiness/well-being.

Modern financial techniques/manipulations coupled with ever-increasing, astronomical computational power have led to disproportionate, massive rewards for those controlling such power

– the 1%; or is it the 0.0001%, i.e. about several thousand out of about 7 billion? Despite the 'economy' being the watchword of politicians, improvements to the 'economy' do <u>not</u> mean improvements for all. Adding to the harm is the fact that the looted money disappears *from the local economy* into so-called tax havens. Indeed, the disproportionate enrichment of the few has led to rising social ailments which are increasingly visible (in the UK as I type).

Conformity to primate instinctive behaviour
In relation to the various characteristic, primate behaviour patterns, political systems worldwide typically conform quite closely: they are in competition with and suspicious of other nations, territorial, typically alpha-male hierarchies which demand obedience to them, and there is inequality for women. In terms of my own country, the UK, we are now (May 2017) led by one alpha, secretive female – Teresa May. The USA is led by alpha-male Donald Trump who recently (May 8th 2017) 'terminated' (fired) the Head of the FBI. The FBI had been investigating Trump's possibly corrupt dealings with Russia during the recent US elections. Doubtless, this investigation will be affected. Much of the world, especially the 'undeveloped' world, is led by single alpha males/royalty or otherwise. In this way, little has changed *in terms of decision-making* since the appearance of tree-dwelling *Hominidae* (great apes) 20 million years ago. What have changed are the circumstances, such as we are no longer arboreal, and populations have risen from around 30-50 to many millions. Also, there is much empirical evidence to show that important decisions for a human organisation are best made by small groups (around five people) with *varying* personalities. Such groups are best equipped to recognise the nature and dimensions of the problems facing the organisation.

Perhaps I should point out that my personal, direct experience of politics is as a voter in the UK. Also, I have observed politics when my family and I lived in Austria, Canada, France, Switzerland, the USA and when I had professional dealings in Africa and Indonesia.

Naturally, in preparation for this book, I have read a great deal on political systems. I still see myself as an amateur, but one with my eyes open and able to see the nakedness of the Emperor: at least in terms of this book.

I join those who say that the present system of nation state, world politics does not work. That is an understatement. As referred to earlier, Anthony Storr (in 'Human Aggression') described humanity as the cruellest and most ruthless of species (apart from some rodents). About a third of all UN countries are at war and the other two-thirds prepare for its possibility at unaffordable expense. Colossal sums of money are spent worldwide on 'defence' and weapons manufacture and sales fuel several economies. Ruling elites commonly profit from such spending. I have referred earlier to many trillions of dollars hidden away in 'tax havens' by individuals. This is about 20% of the world's gross domestic product: another calculation is that about half the world's wealth is owned by about 85 individuals. At the same time, much of the world's population lives in dire poverty with inadequate food and without clean water. We ignore the needs of, and commonly slaughter, 'others'. Why so much war and why does the affluent minority not do more to help the poor within and across countries? Even as I write these words (2014), news organisations report the UK government's opinion that 'we' (i.e. 'them') cannot afford the current arrangements for old people. It seems we have a real financial crisis brought about mainly by a segment of the ultra-rich alpha males who siphoned billions out of our local economy to tax havens.

'We' in the UK also wish to maintain the military might of a *former* time with our empire and colonies. And nuclear submarines, *without anyone to fire at*, give 'us' (the alphas) a perceived seat at the 'top table' at the cost of cuts in numerous socially beneficial services – many tens of billions of pounds. It's hard not to suspect that our alpha politicians are constantly offered ever more powerful and ever more expensive weaponry by our alpha weapons manufacturers and / or backers. Our alphas are able to gather with the alphas of other nations and express their alpha instincts at alpha meetings in alpha buildings and staying in alpha hotels. On top of this, we are seriously harming the planet by our activities. The costs of being at the nuclear 'top table' are astronomically too high. And who do we fire these weapons at?

Even if we could decide on a desirable way forward, can humanity and individual countries achieve it? As described earlier, part of the reason for our plight is biological, instinctive behaviour. Yet nations are run as if instincts did not exist. To repeat, instincts (innate impulses) evolved to enable the short-term survival of small groups of tree-dwelling animals without human consciousness, living within and curtailed by nature. Broadly, they were about alpha males and hierarchies, fight or flight, the vital importance of territory and hostility to and fear of 'otherness', including the suppression of females. The frequent and widespread occurrence of war, atrocities, famine and other catastrophes across all broad human cultures and historical periods, indicate that they are a consequence of our human make-up. Possibly, it's a consequence of primate instincts and human consciousness interacting, although it's known that perception of danger reduces or even eliminates our thought processes and pushes us towards instinctive behaviour.

The power phenotype greatly influences the behaviour of the alpha elite and could well cause a permanent state of something close to paranoia, despite the existence of 'consciousness'. The world is dangerous and the alpha males are aware of this. Given the colossal amounts of material recently leaked or discovered about the security apparatus of numerous nation states, revealed retrospectively, it seems that they are permanently suspicious of each other even when apparently friendly: typically, correctly so. The leaks about the *comprehensive, worldwide surveillance* carried out by the USA's National Security Agency (NSA) show that this activity is far beyond any previous estimate. These exposures came from Edward Snowden, an American computer specialist, former employee of the Central Intelligence Agency and former contractor for the NSA. US surveillance includes friends as well as enemies and is extraordinarily widespread. Recommended reading about this is 'The Snowden Files' by an eminent, award-winning foreign correspondent, Luke Harding.

Given that fear adversely affects the reasoning parts of the brain, <u>could it be that the ruling elites are commonly paranoid/near-paranoid?</u> This could contribute to a partial explanation of the state of the world regarding inter-group violence. True paranoia is a state of false and permanent fear of imagined threats. In terms of nation states, the fear may often have a real basis. And this is in addition to the other negative behaviour patterns (in the modern world) of the alpha males.

Historical political systems
I will restrict myself to an evolutionary perspective. I propose, very briefly and broadly, to consider the various political systems that have existed, including early ones. Given the *theoretical* possibility of choice, I would like to consider what kind of society we seek and how to achieve it. What works best and what criteria can we use? How can we mitigate inappropriate instincts and satisfy our needs, such as the need to belong? Importantly, we can consider which nations achieve the greatest degree of well-being and happiness as well as *sufficient* wealth.

Early human societies
In early human society, such as with hunter-gatherers, it's thought that all or a high proportion of the entire group after working together would meet each evening and consider group needs and plans and generally 'bond'. In existing 'hunter-gatherer' societies, such a system exists today, more or less. This natural system has the advantage of utilising the insights and knowledge of the entire group. That *everyone* '<u>belongs</u>' around the communal fire and/or meal hardly needs saying. This approach is in accord with the need to bond and reinforces a sense of community and belonging. Likely, the small group size (about 20-40) of early human communities facilitates this. There is obviously little

chance of its widespread occurrence today without an extreme global catastrophe or exceptional cooperation to create small 'communes'. It's interesting to consider the possibility that man-made ideas about political structures could be less useful than, say, simply having an evolutionary-derived, small-sized group to live within. Nevertheless, large populations create their own problems.

Later, non-democratic societies

Tyrants

For millennia, the deep need for easily identified leaders to coordinate a rapid response to danger has led to dictators and tyrants who impose their will by force. Acceptance of the power phenotype (including the instinct to take the best of everything) permits such arrangements and commonly leads to the virtual looting of a nation's wealth by its elite. Changing these systems obviously involves disruption and potentially violence.

Royalty

A system less disruptive than tyranny, when changed, involves having a 'royal' family with power inherited automatically and with a supporting legal framework. Thus, the evolutionary-based power phenotype has added legal justification. Unsurprisingly, it was taught that God approved of such royal arrangements and actively inspired the monarch. Not many years ago, at an Anglican Church ceremony and using the Book of Common Prayer, I saw an illustration of God sending rays of approval down towards the monarch. Similarly, at the consecration of a UK Queen or King in Westminister Abbey, holy oil is used to bless the royal forehead as a symbol of God's approval. Even today, over 60 years since Arthur Kornberg identified and isolated the enzyme that makes DNA, and since James Watson and Francis Crick published its structure (using much material from the unpublished work from King's College: Maurice Wilkins, Rosalind Franklin, A.R. Stokes and H.R. Wilson), the idea of royal blood as opposed to the blood of commoners still exists. The London Times (June 26th 2012 – *not* 1912) reported a 'leak' about the Queen updating the 'Order of Precedence' in the royal household. It clarifies who is required to curtsy or bow to whom and when. *Even in private*, within the royal palaces, these protocols exist and are adhered to. Thus Kate, married to Prince William, is ranked lower than '*blood* Princesses' and should curtsy to them except when her husband, Prince William, is present at which times she assumes his status! Such practices of bows, curtsies and walking backwards from the monarch served a function of social conditioning at a time before democracy and parliament and before the science of genetics. There is no royal gene and no blood type named 'royal'.

Religious

Possibly the worst, most evil political system ever, was when religion and politics dangerously merged in medieval times. The Roman Catholic Church, especially in Spain, instituted the Holy Inquisition with its dreadful tortures, burnings and hangings in the name of God. A current political structure with strong religious connections to the evangelical right in the USA is based on ideas of freedom and individualism and the idea of freedom from the state, often called the 'neo-liberal state'. This is characterised by having strong, individual private property rights, rule of law, institutions of freely functioning markets and free trade. This important structure is described and analysed in 'Neoliberalism' by David Harvey who exposes its devastating consequences for most people everywhere. A point that puts it at odds with the human need to belong is that neo-liberalism is deeply anti-democratic. Also, neo-liberals/conservatives are intrinsically authoritarian. Consequently, it would also seem at odds with the idea of a widespread sense of belonging and the empirically demonstrated need for the gap between top and bottom to be relatively small. Also, the nation that most advocated neo-liberalism for many years currently has the most unequal society on Earth (for which there are reliable statistics) and the one with the worst adverse social statistics – the USA.

Somehow, in modern times, there has been a successful 'con trick' that has been widely accepted: all that matters for a country is its economy and its military might, i.e. survival in primate terms. In fact, what matters most for humans is community, trust, freedom from crime and a sense of belonging facilitated by people, leaders and those who are led, living a common lifestyle. In other words, we need happiness and well-being. It has become clear that increases in the 'economy' benefit very few.

Other kinds of modern states: definitions based on those of the University of Idaho *(http://www.webpages.uidaho.edu/)*
Socialist
Most generally, socialism refers to state ownership of common property, or state ownership of the means of production. A purely socialist state would be one in which the state owns and operates the means of production. However, nearly all modern capitalist countries combine socialism and capitalism. Notably, the UK instituted a National Health Service for everyone shortly after World War 2. The University of Idaho claims that itself and any other public school or university is a 'socialist' institution, and those who attend it or work for it are partaking in socialism, because it is owned and operated by the state of Idaho. The same is true of federal and state highways, federal and state parks, harbours etc.

Communist
Broadly speaking, communism refers to community ownership of property, with the end goal being complete social equality via economic equality. Communism is generally seen by communist countries as an idealised utopian economic and social state which the country as a whole is working towards; that is to say that pure communism is the ideal that the People's Republic of China was working *towards*. Such an ideal is often used to justify means (such as authoritarianism or totalitarianism) that are not themselves communist ideals. Fundamentally, communism argues that all labour

belongs to the individual labourer; no man can own another man's body, and therefore each man owns his own labour. In this model 'profit' actually belongs in part to the labourer, not, or not *just*, to those who control the means of production, such as the business or factory owner. Profit that is not shared with the labourer, therefore, is considered inherently exploitive.

Fascist

Fascism is similar to a tyranny – most generally, 'a governmental system led by a dictator having complete power, forcibly suppressing opposition and criticism, regimenting all industry, commerce, etc., and emphasizing an aggressive nationalism and often racism'. (*http://www.webpages.uidaho.edu/*). Unlike communism, fascism is opposed to state ownership of capital, and economic equality is not a principle or goal.

Cautionary note regarding socialism, communism and fascism

However well meaning were the intentions of the leaders and theorists of the Russian Revolution (Marx, Engels, Trotsky and many others), the country ended up as a catastrophe and is currently a dysfunctional state by any definition. It started with relatively kind, individual humans responding to the dreadful plight of the European working class. For example, Frederick Engels studied the terrible conditions of the English working class and published 'The Condition of the Working Class in England in 1884'. There was the beautiful, logical 'Das Kapital' (Karl Marx) and 'The Communist Party Manifesto' (Marx and Engels) with its logical (but wrong) prediction of the eventual (soon) triumph of the proletariat. Soon after the Russian Revolution started, it rapidly acquired a dictator in Stalin, vast concentration camps and eventually tens of millions of people died. All facilitated by the earlier, authoritarian social structures of the Czars. How one man could achieve such huge harm needs some explanation. In 'Stalin' by Oleg Khlevniuk, is detailed how Stalin maintained control and the appalling consequences. The Bolshevik party was the huge, overall structure with a top tier of about 53,000 positions and a step lower were officials running regional bodies with around 350,000 posts (1952). Stalin was ruthlessly in control and used terror routinely. Khlevniuk details fatal torture, death camps and prisons. _Every_ year, over a 20-year period of Stalin's rule, *a million people* were shot, incarcerated or deported to barely habitable areas of the Soviet Union. Stalin exercised extraordinary control over the main levers to power, the so-called State Security and the Secret Police. Khlevniuk states that this was a key reason for his 'success' (my inverted commas). In addition, there were periodic famines or starvation. In 1932-33 alone, 5-7 million people lost their lives from starvation, all largely the result of political decisions to break peasant opposition to collectivization. And today, unsurprisingly, the USSR resembles a failed state.

China, with Mao Zedong as a dictator, also suffered the death, mainly by famine, of about 20-40 million people (1958-62, numerous studies by various authors) as part of 'The Great Leap Forward'. This was an economic and social campaign by the Communist Party of China from 1958 to 1961. The campaign was led by Mao and was intended rapidly to transform the country from an agrarian economy into a socialist society through rapid industrialisation and collectivization. However, it is widely considered to have caused the Great Chinese Famine. Historian Frank Dikötter asserted that 'coercion, terror, and systematic violence were the foundation of the Great Leap Forward' and it 'motivated one of the most deadly mass killings of human history' (Dikötter, Frank (2010). pp. x, xi. ISBN 0-8027-7768-6).

The modern European fascist states (20th-century Germany, Italy, Portugal, Spain) were also human disasters with vicious, ruthless leaders taking over. The 'Church' also played a major role, often negative via its silence, in all of the European fascist countries. It (the institution) maintained its authority on religious and moral issues and was opposed to the threat of 'godless communists'.

Fascism, holiness and heroism

Mussolini, the Italian father of fascism, wrote that: '...Fascism [is] the complete opposite of...Marxian Socialism, the materialist conception of history of human civilization can be explained simply through the conflict of interests among the various social groups and by the change and development in the means and instruments of production....Fascism, now and always, believes in holiness and in heroism; that is to say, in actions influenced by no economic motive, direct or indirect. And if the economic conception of history be denied, according to which theory men are no more than puppets, carried to and fro by the waves of chance, while the real directing forces are quite out of their control, it follows that the existence of an unchangeable and unchanging class-war is also denied – the natural progeny of the economic conception of history. And above all Fascism denies that class-war can be the preponderant force in the transformation of society. After Socialism, Fascism combats the whole complex system of democratic ideology, and repudiates it, whether in its theoretical premises or in its practical application. Fascism denies that the majority, by the simple fact that it is a majority, can direct human society; it denies that numbers alone can govern by means of a periodical consultation, and it affirms the immutable, beneficial, and fruitful inequality of mankind, which can never be permanently levelled through the mere operation of a mechanical process such as universal suffrage...'

Q.   Why were the Russian, Chinese and fascist regimes such catastrophic failures?

A.   Any approach to social reform, however idealistic, however well meaning, however ruthless, that ignores the following would seem bound to fail:

   a.   the basic, biological consequences of population size;

   b.   the deep-seated evolutionary roots of instincts;

   c.   essential human need to express *human* instincts and 'to belong'.

These long-established social structures were not able to respond to radical changes at the speed demanded. It was 'natural' that the humanitarian, idealistic initial leaders would be replaced by leaders 'strong' enough to remove all traces of the deeply rooted, previous evil regimes. This almost inevitably meant ruthless, inhuman behaviour. In addition, the new alpha-male leaders exhibited all the behaviour patterns of the alpha male. And in addition to the instinctive obedience of the masses, the new alpha males, in virtually all of these situations, achieved control of the so-called security services, notably the secret police. They used these services ruthlessly. They became the 'alphas' and in charge.

Democratic societies
('Government by the people': Oxford English Dictionary)

Audit and suggestions for improvements. In the West, a system developed where elected politicians represent the people. An early version, commonly given as an example, was in Athens (BC) where city people would congregate in an open space and could contribute their ideas and citizens (not including slaves or women) could vote. An early influence was the widespread practice of Greek communities having their own theatres as part of a public space. This space was also used for public discussions/debates and votes on matters of importance.

In an early, prehistory human society, people in a group would know one another intimately. Even in Athenian society, people broadly would or could know one another. Although numerous political systems have existed in complex, large societies, democracy is widely accepted as best, or as least bad. Not surprisingly, all political systems for complex societies, including democratic ones, can become corrupted by the powerful, who have the desire and the means to bias the system towards their own goals. For example, in the USA <u>billions</u> are spent on advertisements and on other methods to influence the voters' perception of which party or person to vote for, or in negative campaigns, whom to malign and not vote for. It's been called 'one dollar, one vote'. Millions are spent elsewhere for the same purposes.

A right-wing press, with right wing owners are already pre-disposed to right-wing policies. Significantly, as mentioned earlier, in April 2014, a US Supreme Court ruling *struck down* an overall cap on federal election contributions. So, money continues to talk. The 'Golden Rule' has often been 'Those that have the gold make the rules'.

The scale of corrupt practices by mega-powerful corporations has been highlighted by George Monbiot ('How did we get into this mess?' and www.monbiot.com). It's not simply large donations to election funds, bad and corrupting to democracy as they are, it's the creation of fake think tanks and fake spontaneous protests funded by major corporations, from such as energy or tobacco. These fakes respond instantly to any news that might affect their profits such as illness caused by tobacco or harm from global warming or news of an unwelcome scientific finding that they refute speedily and vehemently. This is discussed in more detail under the earlier section on 'Humanity's Key Problems', including the extraordinary decision by President Donald Trump *to include these very people in his first cabinet!* In tennis terms, it's game, set and match for the corporations. This is despite the numerous early presidents of the USA recognising the dangers of corporations corrupting the political process. The following centuries-old quotations are particularly apt regarding the current financial crises in Western democracies. I ask the reader to bear with me in repetitions of these quotations from early presidents of the USA of a couple of centuries ago, all of whom had the *exact opposite* intentions to Donald Trump. I wish heavily to emphasise how these earlier Presidents were aware of the dangers of corporate money influencing democracy.

Advice and comments from early leaders of capitalist USA.
Given the current composition of President Trump's 2017 cabinet, including leaders of the fake 'think tanks', these quotations are striking. The USA now has 'government by the corporations', rather than 'government by the people'.

'I hope we shall... crush in its birth the aristocracy of our moneyed corporations which dare already to challenge our government in a trial of strength, and bid defiance to the laws of our country.'
President Thomas Jefferson, 1801-09

'There is an evil which ought to be guarded against in the indefinite accumulation of property from the capacity of holding it in perpetuity by corporations. The power of all corporations ought to be limited in this respect. The growing wealth acquired by them never fails to be a source of abuses.'
James Madison, 1809-17

'In this point of the case the question is distinctly presented whether the people of the United States are to govern through representatives chosen by their unbiased suffrages or whether the money and power of a great corporation are to be secretly exerted to influence their judgment and control their decisions.'
President Andrew Jackson, 1829-37

'I am more than ever convinced of the dangers to which the free and unbiased exercise of political opinion – the only sure foundation and safeguard of republican government – would be exposed by any further increase of the already overgrown influence of corporate authorities.'
Martin Van Buren, 1837-41

'These capitalists generally act harmoniously and in concert to fleece the people, and now that they have got into a quarrel with themselves, we are called upon to appropriate the people's money to settle the quarrel.'
President Abraham Lincoln, 1861-65

'As we view the achievements of aggregated capital, we discover the existence of trusts, combinations, and monopolies, while the citizen is struggling far in the rear or is trampled to death beneath an iron heel. Corporations, which should be the carefully restrained creatures of the law and the servants of the people, are fast becoming the people's masters.'

Grover Cleveland, 1885-89

'I again recommend a law prohibiting all corporations from contributing to the campaign expenses of any party. Let individuals contribute as they desire; but let us prohibit in effective fashion all corporations from making contributions for any political purpose, directly or indirectly.'

President Theodore Roosevelt, 1901-09

'The fortunes amassed through corporate organization are now so large, and vest such power in those that wield them, as to make it a matter of necessity to give to the sovereign – that is, to the Government, which represents the people as a whole – some effective power of supervision over their corporate use. In order to insure a healthy social and industrial life, every big corporation should be held responsible by, and be accountable to, some sovereign strong enough to control its conduct.'

President Theodore Roosevelt, 1901-09

Nevertheless, despite these crystal-clear warnings, given the positive human need to belong and given the instinct for needing leaders, my focus will be on democracy. In any event, in complex, huge, modern society, leadership and social coordination of some sort is inevitable, as it is and was for earlier primates. The neo-liberal idea of doing away with the state is incompatible with complexity, including large populations. The state provides the central nervous system to coordinate the complexity. And being ruled by representatives of the people can help the human need for belonging. But the rulers need to be *truly* representative. Leaders should belong to the same community as the led.

Furthermore, billions of years of evolution have not produced humans hard-wired for individualism, but rather for community life.
Coping with fake 'think tanks' and fake citizens' uprisings (funded by 'dark money') is a newly recognised problem, now made vastly worse by the very perpetrators and organisers of such fakery being appointed to President Donald Trump's inner cabinet. It's widely reported (The Guardian, Julian Borger, 30.1.17) that the January 2017 pronouncements by President Trump about banning migrants were drafted by the ideologically driven, extreme right-wing group around Trump. There was no consultation whatsoever with Departments of Justice, State, Defence or Homeland Security who could have weighed up its implications for US foreign relations. Furthermore, it was announced that Steve Bannon, the former executive of the far-right Breitbart news website, would take part in national security principals' meetings. They make key decisions on defence and foreign policy. On the other hand, the director of national intelligence and the chairman of the Joint Chiefs of Staff would *not* automatically attend. Subsequently, (February 2017) Bannon was firmly established as a key Trump advisor, only to be sacked in 2018! Steve Bannon was also part of a network exposed in the UK 'Observer' 7th May 2017 by journalist Carole Cadwalladr. She described how a 'shadowy global operation involving big data, billionaire friends of Trump and the disparate forces of the (UK) 'Leave' campaign heavily influenced the results of the UK EU referendum and helped 'Team Trump in the USA Presidential election. A centre spread linked the organisations ('Cambridge Analytica' and 'AggregateIQ, both largely owned by Robert Mercer

– described as a 'secretive' billionaire hedge fund manager) and other people, including Donald trump, Nigel Farage, and Arron Banks. It was headed as 'The great British Brexit robbery: how a secret network of computer scientists hijacked our democracy'. A year later, the psychological profiling IT tools used to target the electorate in these campaigns, that were created by a Canadian, Christopher Wylie, were further exposed in the Observer 18th March 2018. An article, again by Carole Cadwalladr explained how the Cambridge Analytica psychological profiling tool worked.

If one's voice is not heard, one does not belong
The voting system is one of the possible means by which we can achieve a representative parliament (e.g. in the UK or the USA Senate or Congress). The current system of constituency voting (the 'means') is confused with the ends (representative parliament) and leads to a non-diverse, non-representative parliament. The results are partly and *mechanically* representative in that a constituency has elected someone to represent them, but the resulting *parliament* is unrepresentative of, for example, the UK, since it is comprised of overwhelming white, middle-class males with women and several other groups grossly under-represented.

Primate instincts lead to a 'winner takes all' world. A human parliament should have more *voices* than at present. A parliament that is representative of the UK would mean broadly proportionate numbers of such as women, ethnic minorities, youth and people of *diverse* views from diverse geographical areas. Also, it is obviously inappropriate in terms of representation if the representatives live lifestyles that are vastly different to those they represent. Voting methods should change to bring about these desirable ends. Also, many countries have a second 'House' that acts as a kind of break, a chance to think again. In the UK, this is the House of Lords.

What state(s) has worked or is working best or worst?

I have referred to much evidence that strongly links unequal societies with bad social defects, proportional to the level of inequality. Also, I have emphasised the established human need for belonging. Instead of discussing the pros and cons of different political systems, another approach is to look at which societies 'work' best. In terms of the absence of negative social indices, it is entirely clear. Overall, in relation to life expectancy, infant mortality, obesity, mental illness, level of trust, children's educational performance, rape, homicides and imprisonment rates, then the 'best' societies are Japan and Scandinavia (see 'The Spirit Level', Wilkinson and Pickett). The worst performing states are the USA (by far) then Portugal and then the UK (which is swiftly becoming less equal and showing the negative social indices). The differences between best and worst in these adverse indices are several-<u>fold</u> and not merely several per cent. The question arises as to how more equality could be achieved. <u>Unfortunately, society, even if it wanted change, is not constructed by an intellectual decision</u>; rather it happens for historical, geographical and cultural reasons.

Nevertheless, progress could be made by numerous, small adjustments peacefully worked towards by a mass movement of <u>individuals</u>, involving answering needs and harmonising instincts. Happily, this has already started.

Note on Plato.

Plato, a student of Socrates, taught that the state should be ruled by 'the wisest and the best' – 'The Guardians' – with no personal wealth, living communally and the recipients of a special education with a focus on philosophy. They were to consist of two groups, the Rulers and the Auxilaries. A third group was comprised of the money-makers who were to receive a rounded, less philosophical education. He taught that the root of all evil in a society came about because of flaws in the education of the Guardians. Slaves were unspecified as Plato took their existence with few rights as natural. This approach has a logic, is rational and was advocated by a great philosopher, Plato. Nevertheless, and naturally, Plato was ignorant of modern findings in biology and sociology. We don't feel we belong if our 'Guardian rulers' live, and have lived, a different lifestyle to us. An exclusive education with a focus on philosophy does not inevitably lead to happy, healthy humans in a happy, healthy community. Also, experience with 'money-makers' is that they consistently seek ever more money and characteristically exhibit the power phenotype and take it all for granted. If Plato thought, even intuitively, that an education with an emphasis on philosophy would eliminate instincts, then he was wrong. The 'wisest and best'?

Biology tends to suggest that a democracy led by one's own has more merit. It can lead to belonging. The problem comes when such an arrangement is subverted. An extreme example, condemned by early USA presidents (see the quotations above), is when rich individuals or rich corporations 'purchase' laws that are favourable to themselves. This is all facilitated by ideas of having *'one's place in society'* firmly fixed, with God placing the rich at the top and the poor (serfs and peasants, with slaves barely having a place at all) at the bottom. In the UK, many (not all) stately homes and 'heritage' mansions were given as gifts by some monarch for favours rendered or were purchased from the proceeds of slavery or the industrialisation of mills and mines. But biology supports an uncorrupted democracy.

Justice – crime and punishment – a comment.
Under the section on 'Biological Determinism' the point was made that if deterministic fears were justified, then Australia should be a special case, being colonised by so-called 'criminals' from Britain. Similarly, the ethnic cleansing of native peoples in pre-USA was not by 'Americans', but mostly by European colonisers. The instigators of apartheid injustices in South Africa were not

native peoples but Dutch colonisers. The owners of slaves in the southern states of the USA and the Caribbean lived all over the world including widely throughout the UK (see earlier, 'Slavery'). There is a clear link between the possession of power and the capacity to assign blame to one's opponents and noble motives to the behaviour of one's own nation.

Broad ideas on bridging the gap between politicians, civil servants and general citizens

1. For all politicians of all parties, it would be a good idea to hold weekly seminars by specialist non-party political speakers on potential improvements for the nation's physical and mental health, the economy, Local Authority work, the elderly, defence, foreign relations etc.

2. Invite speakers (world leaders, Nobel Laureates) from <u>other</u> nations to describe exceptional successes in a particular area of national life. Examples could be from economics, sociology, town planning, brain/child development. Similarly, seminars for cabinet ministers and civil servants from major Departments from world leaders: Health, Exchequer, Security.

3. All politicians to spend one week per annum living with and understanding the lives of the poor.

4. The same would apply to civil servants regarding their departmental work, e.g. <u>with a focus on the patient</u>. Deparment of Health workers spend (per annum) in specialist clinics one day, GP practice one day, health centre one day, general hospital two days.

Humanising Parliament

Suggestions for improvement by answering human needs, assisting the expression of human instincts, reducing the influence of inappropriate primate instincts and humanising the organs of parliament and their impact on society.

Looking at the UK, and similarly for other states, the purpose of parliament is to rule our country and should bear in mind our instincts and our basic needs for protection, safety, food, shelter and a sense of community. It should be *representative* of the people and also able to optimise not only the nation's survival chances, but also its *health and happiness*. Also, empirically demonstrated is the need for society to have inclusive political and economic structures. Currently, the UK Parliament consists mainly of well-to-do, middle-class, white men. The current existence of hunger and the shortage of homes in the UK suggest that much improvement is possible. The UK is closely behind the USA in terms of inequality and associated bad social statistics. I suggest that the current lack of a truly representative parliament contributes greatly to the UK's problems and elsewhere too. In addition, there should be some way for minorities to be heard: not being heard means not belonging. Hence, it follows that in a democracy the parliament should be representative of our society as it actually is. It's <u>not</u> a question of evil or unintelligent people being our Members of Parliament. It's a question of having a parliament, the membership of which is broadly *representative* of the UK population mix. An important consequence of such changes would be a less strong emphasis on war and weaponry. In the case of the UK, it could accelerate the adaptation from (former) world leader with our (former) empire to our realistic present, relatively impecunious state.

What follows is unlikely to happen quickly, if at all, because the changes proposed require action by those already in power and visibly expressing the power phenotype. But maybe, and hopefully, small steps can accumulate. Also, I am not the best qualified person to suggest the most effective changes. But I can see some obvious and much-needed changes. Others can surely improve on the following. We now have strong, objective, evidence-based proof that we need to belong, be connected and have inclusive social structures. We should act upon this empirical evidence.

Composition should be representative of national mix

Clarifying the confusion between means and ends is necessary. The basic need to belong supports the notion of being ruled by:

a. a representative parliament – truly representative of the national mix. e.g. the current *composition* of the UK (and of other nations) Parliament is not representative.

b. The basic need for survival supports the idea that our parliament is also aware of our broader environment; and

c. is able to interpret changes, especially danger and respond accordingly; and

d. the need to humanise society is answered by adjustments favouring those fostering the human characteristics of altruism and culture.

This should assist in a more accurate interpretation of our environment and of world changes. The voting system should be changed so as to produce the following approximate, final, *representative mix* of *citizens*, based on UK geographical constituencies. Computer algorithms would need to be devised to produce a truly representative parliament. A minor departure from strict adherence to these ideas would be that minorities should have at least a voice and that specific, useful expertise would help. The present large number of UK MPs is expensive, but *if* they are truly representative, then they are a vital link between the 'people' and the parliament and worth the money.

1. 50% women, and of those at least approximately that percentage of mothers as occurs in the general population. For those with young children, full generous expenses, including nursery costs should be given to ease the living arrangements. Similarly, that percentage of fathers as occurs in the general population and with similar expense arrangements where necessary.

2. 40% who have lived in and experienced other cultures directly – eg for at least 1 year.

3. A fraction equal to that of those whose parents or themselves came from a different culture (e.g. India/Pakistan, Africa, Caribbean, China, North and South America, Middle East). My guess would be about 15%.

4. At least 40% aged over 60 years, having obvious life experience, and at least 50% of whom are grandparents.

5. Somehow, elect 3 people from the homeless, i.e. at some time having lived 'on the street' for at least a year.

6. Not representing a geographical constituency, but elected by their 'constituencies' and with half-time appointments:
   i) 3 poets, 3 writers, 3 classical musicians, 3 folk/jazz musicians.
   ii) Elect 3 gay and 3 lesbian representatives. This, in addition to those gay but not explicitly or not known to be so.
   iii) A 'voice' given to youth by having 5 elected representatives for the under 25s.

7. A cabinet minister for children should be appointed to represent the interests of babies and infants.

8. Ex officio CEOs of the leading 10 charities.

9. An approach of 'winner takes all' is not a way to have a representative leadership. It's pure primate. Any group getting, say, 5% of a vote should get one representative to have their voice at least *heard*.

The cabinet

Commonly, across the world, the Leader/Prime Minister/Monarch selects a group to advise/decide on major issues consisting of the ministers of major offices, e.g. Health, Defence, Economy, Foreign Affairs. Usually, there is a smaller 'inner cabinet'. As mentioned previously, the last UK cabinet was led by a predominance of exceptionally wealthy people, several with a finance background and with similar schooling. The inner cabinet had several men from the same, 'top' school (Eton). It was not possible for them truly to represent the actual UK population, for example regarding decisions on taxation. In order for the people to belong to our society and to feel that they belong, there is a human need for our leadership to be representative of us, to live a broadly similar style of life, including holidays, food, education and medical care. Major decisions, notably that of declaring war, surely should be taken at least by a small group in the first instance and then ratified by the whole cabinet and then by Parliament. The small group should not be composed solely of the Prime Minister together with military personnel. In 2017 we had a Prime Minister attempting to avoid a parliamentary vote about *how* we leave the EU. It was widely report ed that Mrs May wished to make the decision herself, advised by a tiny, unrepresentative group who could fairly be described as zealots.

As well as Parliament in general, the cabinet should have a broad seminar programme given by leading world authorities, and perhaps a second meeting to meet personally those already giving seminars to Parliament as a whole. It could help overall unity if representatives of other parties were invited to the seminars and meetings.

Members of Parliament remuneration

If Members of Parliament are to be representative of and serve those they represent and thus visibly add to the sense and *reality* of community, then they should broadly share the normal life of the people they represent. It is not the unanswerable question of what an MP's salary should be. It is what *represents a standard of living within the norm for those they represent,* e.g. no more than twice the median UK salary, and with <u>full, generous help with expenses</u>. As most of them spend much time away from home, disrupting family life, they need appropriate, strong support. Expenses should be covered generously, including for accompanying wives/partners. Good quality accommodation *should be provided* to avoid the worsening situation in London over property prices. Accommodation should not be based on party lines: social mixing should be encouraged, partly by the architectural arrangements. Pensions should be seen as generous. The attraction of the job and the scope of candidates could be widened on deselection/loss of an election: up to a year's salary could be retained in the first year out of office and when jobless. But, above all, conditions of employment must facilitate MPs having a lifestyle <u>similar to those they represent</u>.

Financing of elections

Advice and comments from early leaders of capitalist USA

Given the current composition of President Trump's cabinet, the reader is recommended to re-read the strong warnings from numerous Presidents given earlier. Below is an example – an early warning from Thomas Jefferson from over 2 centuries ago.

> *'I hope we shall... crush in its birth the aristocracy of our moneyed corporations which dare already to challenge our government in a trial of strength and bid defiance to the laws of our country.'*
>
> **President Thomas Jefferson, 1801-09**

These early leaders of the modern USA clearly recognised the inappropriate political power of corporations. The first quotations, from presidents so long ago are reminiscent of the recent banking crisis, bailed out by the UK taxpayers. The conduct of elections in the West grossly favours those with access to the most finance. Especially in the USA today, as then, elections are to some extent a battle of public relations experts, often unscrupulous and costing <u>billions of dollars</u>. They find out what worries the voters most and present the candidate as if answering the need. And wealthy, powerful donors naturally, corruptly and undemocratically expect 'payback' in terms of influencing later spending decisions and laws. The 'Misinformation Machine', highlighted by George Monbiot previously and under 'Key Problems' adds sophistication to the corruption. The failure by US presidents, over centuries, to curtail corporate finance influencing elections and government is a shocking measure of corporate power. It is also destructive of democracy. The dictionary definition of democracy is not 'money rules'.

Elections *intended to produce democracy* should not be determined by how much a candidate has to spend. Note the advice of these early presidents above. It would be more democratic to fund the election modestly by taxes for any candidate and not allow other spending and advertising. Have cost-free, personal appearances on public TV and radio to present policies: a focus on policies. There are permanent, right-wing-financed campaigns against such changes. 'It is wrong to use hard-working taxpayers' money to fund an election' has become a mantra. But it's acceptable for powerful, wealthy interests to do so. Also, it's acceptable to top up the 'minimum wage' with hard-working taxpayers' money as welfare to save the wealthy industrialist, e.g. Google from paying a living wage. Earlier, I referred to a recent (April 2014) US Supreme Court decision *striking down any cap on funding* for federal elections! To make matters more biased against the average person, there are specialist lobbyists for powerful interests. A notorious example is that approximately 125 people lobby for *each* elected member of the US Congress. This inevitably introduces massive bias – a so-called '$1/1 vote'. See the tables below of lobbying costs and the number of lobbyists.

Pope Francis. The current Pope, Francis, advocates elections free of financial corruption. 'Because many interests come into play in the financing of an election campaign and then they ask you to pay back. So, the election campaign should be independent from anyone who may finance it.' Pope Francis, quoted in *Ansa en Vatican*, March 10, 2015; available on the web at:

http://www.ansa.it/english/news/vatican/2015/03/10/pope-calls-for-free-election-campaigns_35296d5c-c578-4ea4-babe-e9cb9f520bb1.html

According to the internet company 'Statista' ('Statistics and studies from more than 18,000 sources') total lobbying spending amounted to 3.24 **billion** US dollars. The same company reported that in 2013, the total number of unique, registered lobbyists who had actively lobbied amounted to 12,353. Spending by the top 20 lobbying industries in the United States in 2014 varied from pharmaceutical and health products being the top, with spending amounting to around $230 million in 2014 and the bottom industry of retail with sales at $57 million. The total costs of the fake 'think tanks' and similar corrupt structures is largely unknown, but it's likely to be at least in the many millions.

The candidates

Who are the candidates? At present, it's virtually impossible for candidates to be known by the electorate except through what PR people tell us. Brief, objective and verified biographies of candidates should be published together with policies that they favour. This could be in more detail than normal party 'handouts'. In a previous Parliament, the UK had a Prime Minister (David Cameron), the son of a very rich member of the financial community, with a 'top' educational background, obviously intelligent, first specialising in PR and then acting as an aide to politicians, becoming one and rising to the top. In many ways it's similar for the leader of the opposition and other politicians. Then, as is the case for royalty, on entering office the politician *instantly* acts as spokesman or woman for the specific cabinet function: foreign relations, the economy, crime and punishment, defence, energy and so on. If Prime Minister, then he or she commonly speaks on everything or anything. On the first day in office this pretence occurs. The actual knowledge base of a minister appears to be irrelevant.

In terms of citizens with specialist knowledge, professors come to mind. In academic life, a professor may have started with his basic degree, performed well, studied for a doctorate in his subject (3-4 years), spent a period as a post-doctoral fellow (1-2 years) and then spent years researching and teaching in a narrow area before being promoted, if ever, to professor, typically with the approval of, and occasionally turned down by, numerous external assessors. Even then, he or she may speak cautiously, knowing how restricted his/her knowledge is. In the 'Last Days of Socrates', Socrates mentions how the Oracle of Delphi states that nobody is wiser than Socrates. This, Socrates attributes to the fact that he is well aware of his ignorance. On the contrary, a politician of any party rarely shows his ignorance: he is an alpha person. <u>This falsehood tends to keep the electorate in a state of fairy-tale infancy</u>. Of course, the civil servants brief ministers. But who are they? Maybe civil servants should be more visible, not taking decisions, not debating publicly, but their advice could be made more visible generally. And civil servants are moved between departments where their expertise may be lacking. The civil service often speaks of 'generalists' as if a 'generalist' is genetically programmed (or by magic) and identified to deal with any topic – if only! Also, ministers appoint advisors and experts and frequently it's clear that the appointment is for party political purposes, i.e. the expert already agrees with the minister's view (this is open and formalised in the USA). There should be a great deal more transparency as determined by a balanced group of non-politicians.

Taxes
Currently we have the scandal of many of the world's rich looting much wealth via complex financial arrangements and avoiding tax, and corporations are also avoiding tax on a massive scale.

Respectable economists and study groups estimate that around \$20 <u>trillion</u> (Yes, \$20 trillion!) is removed from the local economy and hidden away by *individuals* in untouchable, secret

accounts. And the response to current severe financial problems is mainly to cut down on social benefits, wages, the health service and education for the poor. Neo-liberals sneer at such humane benefits as 'big government'.

In the mainstream Western media, the option of trying to take it back off the ultra-rich is not even mentioned. This is presumably because 'they' are too powerful, such as the media owners. The magnitude of the problem is astonishingly illustrated as follows. In an election discussion, Donald Trump responded to an allegation about his not paying tax by *boasting* that 'It's because I'm smart'! The far right has managed to change the meaning of tax to theft by big government. Without 'ordinary' people, multi-billionaires would not exist, and neither would human society. The government should propagate the true idea that taxes are our contribution to our community. We are *actually* all in this together.

Humans are intrinsically social individuals:
isolation leads to pathology
Parliament should legislate and prioritise living wages that enable all citizens to pay for nutrition and shelter. Thus, a realistic 'living wage' is a minimum. These ideas are not proposed mainly for justice or democracy. Not doing so leads to gross inequality with the attendant consequences of social disorder and disharmony. Currently in the UK, massive, profitable companies are seduced to the country with little or no tax paid and wages that are not a living wage but the 'minimum wage' and this wage is topped up by the state from welfare. Is this not crazy? And is it not welfare for the corporations?

The Second House
In the UK, the second house is the House of Lords, with some peers appointed for their lifetime. Britain has had monarchs who claimed ownership of all the land, took it from adversaries and gave it to supporters and similarly gave out titles such as Lord or Earl. Some of these titles still exist and the holders are called hereditary peers.

Some bought titles, some from huge profits from the abolition of slavery (dealt with earlier under slavery). Attempts are made from time to time by prime ministers to adjust the numbers to accord with party proportions, current at the time. On the principle that rapid change commonly does not work, I would suggest that hereditary peerages cease after two more parliaments or with the death of current holders.

Note: It's interesting that, centuries later, President Vladimir V. Putin of Russia has in place similar arrangements as the English monarchs to enrich his supporters. Investigative reporters from the New York Times (The New York Times International Weekly, 5th October 2014) detailed the financial manipulations, involving Bank Rossiya, which transferred funds from state enterprises to President Putin's supporters.

UK peers offer the real advantage of not being so close to the party system and its disciplines, i.e. pressure to vote as 'the party' wishes. And it offers experienced and specialist membership, often of people who are successful in the outside world. In some ways it is successful, although expensive. Possibly most importantly, it broadly supports the *status quo* regarding inequality and the consequential social harm. As a system it needs changing in terms of being <u>representative of the people</u> and also being able to optimise not only the nation's survival chances, but also its *health and happiness*. Clearly, the second house should not be in competition with the House of Commons. Its function is partly the same, namely to represent the people and enhance their safety, their other needs and aspirations, including community building – but to do so by creating 'a pause for thought' where they consider things could be done better or not at all. They cannot have the ultimate power to decide. In addition, the House of Lords could have a bias towards people who are experienced and successful in various fields of endeavour. Suggestions to change in accordance with such needs are as follows.

Elected membership should be somewhat similar to the

Commons, except for a total of 100 members (not the current 1000) and seen as a *half-time job* for those elected. Also, members should <u>take an oath</u> to vote independently and <u>not</u> be allowed to take any party whip, nor to have 'party' help before or during the election, paid for from taxes. To summarise, their function is to <u>act as a break</u> where thought necessary, to have unrushed second thoughts and have a <u>representative membership</u> with a bias towards non-parliamentary experience.

    a.   50% women and of those at least 40% mothers, no longer with children in education. Thus, older and more experienced. Similarly, 50% men of whom 40% fathers, no longer with children in education.

    b.   40% who have lived in and experienced other cultures directly.

    c.   A fraction equal to that of those whose parents or themselves came from a different culture (e.g. India/Pakistan, Africa, Caribbean, China, North and South America). An estimate would be about 15%.

    d.   At least 50% aged over 50 years and at least 40% of whom are grandparents.

    e.   No more than 10% from former MPs.

    f.   5 full professors from different disciplines from UK universities.

In addition:

Ex officio the last 3 former prime ministers; the last former Chief of the Armed Forces; chairmen/women of the leading 5 charities; 3 eminent economists; 3 environmental experts; 5 Nobel Laureates of which at least 2 should be from science, all nominated by the Royal Society; the President of the Royal Society, the Poet Laureate, the President of the RSA (Royal Society for the encouragement of Arts, Manufactures and Commerce).

Royalty

Royalty would fit perfectly with primate instincts if they still were the 'alpha male' or 'alpha female' when King/Queen. But they are not: they are merely presented as such with appropriate symbols and submissive behaviour rituals. Today, royalty is an anachronism. Yet, in the UK it surprisingly often works reasonably well, compared to other aspects of state. It would seem clear that a dramatic removal of royalty is probably not possible, in the same way that dramatic social changes are defeated by the depth and complexity of our social roots. Nevertheless, it would seem highly desirable to eliminate the more anachronistic elements. For example, the Queen as the Head of the Protestant Church with her wealth and numerous (five) palaces is Christ's representative in the UK. It would seem appropriate that this should change. The main problem is not only the high expense of royalty; it's that the function of the Head of State is confused by having a large royal family, all with the trappings and symbols of status and power, inappropriate in a democracy (or any other rational, human grouping) and implying a bogus genetic superiority – blue blood. The current loss of importance of the lineage of royalty was illustrated when recent (2014) DNA evidence called into question various claims to the throne, notably the Tudors. DNA analysis of the Y-chromosome (passed only through the male line) of the recently discovered remains of Richard III (15th century) did not match that of a living aristocrat supposed to be related to Richard III through the male line. Mitochondrial DNA (passed only through the female line) did indeed precisely match that of two female descendants alive today. If only DNA analysis was available 500 years ago!

Humanising royalty

Suggestions for improvement by answering human needs, assisting the expression of human instincts, harmonising basic instincts and humanising the organs of royalty.

The function of monarchy is to be the Head of State in a

parliamentary democracy and to maintain impartiality regardless of which party is in power. The UK monarchy today has few powers, mostof which are related to the change of government. Even so, the Head of State function should bear in mind our instincts and our basic needs for protection, safety, food, shelter and a sense of community. Despite her numerous palaces, the Queen could speak out about gross social injustice. Also, her role as Head of the Anglican Church is questionable. Just as 'early' Christians were happy about the Emperor Constantine becoming a Christian with the consequent increase in safety and material power for the Church, so the Protestant clerical hierarchy will predictably oppose 'losing' the Queen as its head. It's unlikely that any mention would be made of Henry VIII's brutal influence on the leadership of Anglicanism. The alternative would be for the Queen to give up her throne – which is likely a step too far!

Some suggestions.
    a. The Queen ceases to be Head of the UK Protestant Church. These duties could be taken over by the Archbishop of Canterbury.
    b. Gradually and significantly reduce the importance of royal activities, especially by royal relatives. Increase the role of eminent, widely admired 'ordinary', representative citizens, half of whom should be women, to represent our country when necessary, e.g. poets, philosophers, artists, scientists, Olympic athletes, heads of charities, former military chiefs (unlikely to yield many women). Reduce finance to royalty on a planned, long-term basis.
    c. Have only one state palace, used for state and public occasions. If this is unacceptable to the monarch (e.g. it may be unpleasant to live solely in a state palace), provide separate, smaller, private and safe accommodation elsewhere. Use the remaining palaces for useful public activities or sell them.

d. Set up a joint parliamentary/Lords committee to discuss such changes, including the question of why the monarch needs any substantial private wealth at all. The current Queen is reputed to be the wealthiest woman in Britain. *In any event, the transition should be arranged with generosity, respect and humanity.* The overt hostility and personal abuse shown to royalty by a small minority should be strongly discouraged. It has a very *negative effect of entrenching* them and likely slows down the process of gradually eliminating royalty. On the other hand, spokespeople for the monarchy are typically and counterproductively over-subservient in their extreme deference.

e. At present, the Queen does indeed act as a unifying, positive figure in UK life. The Queen definitely comes across as 'okay' and not just as seen by our right-wing press. This is a big plus in our national life, however anachronistic. When the succession comes around things may change. Would UK citizens prefer the elected President Trump as Head of the UK state? I don't think so, certainly not by me.

Civil service
Answering needs, harmonising primate instincts and expressing the human

The civil service should consist of public service motivated people, with diversity as at present, and offering different specialities and disciplines. The same need exists as for the elected representatives; actually to represent the people and not receive salaries allowing a lifestyle that is remote from the majority of citizens. Changes could result initially in issues over the recruitment of civil servants, e.g. no more than three times the UK median salary as a maximum although with excellent pensions. The cost of living in London (2018) grossly distorts life, especially unprecedented housing costs. Possibly, there could be generous, non-pensionable *allowances* for those living in London and other expensive places. Money-oriented people would not be attracted to such a system. Also, as now, consultants could be recruited on a temporary basis but not based on their allegiance to the current party in power, but based on their expert knowledge needed in the short term. The civil service's bureaucracy is also influenced by history. In the UK, with a relatively recent history of being a huge power with an empire, offering numerous resources, we are still adapting to the new reality. But the political structures inevitably lag behind the reality, with expensive consulates and embassies remaining all over the world.

In making appointments to the UK civil service, we should achieve approximately the following *representative 'mix'* with an emphasis on experience, <u>exceptional ability,</u> not judged solely on examination performance, but success and specialist knowledge. This mix will contribute to the culture of the civil service.

a.   50% women and of those at least 50% mothers. For those with young children, full generous expenses should be given to ease the living and nursery arrangements. Similarly, 50% men of whom 50% should be fathers and similar expense arrangements should be in place where necessary.

b.   A third who have lived in and experienced other cultures directly.

c.   A fraction equal to that of those whose parents or themselves came from a different culture (e.g. India/Pakistan, Africa, Caribbean, China, North and South America). My guess would be about 15%.

d.   At least 40% aged over 50 years and at least 50% of whom are grandparents.

A postscript on politics: blunders by UK governments of different kinds

How does any government rate regarding competency? How good is any government at 'running' the country? 'The Blunders of our Governments' by Anthony King and Ivor Crewe describes hardly believable UK blunders over the last three decades. Why the UK is somewhat worse than other nations is less obvious. I agree with a comment by Baroness Shirley Williams emphasising the adverse effects of frequent shuffles of ministers. How can a minister understand the complexities of his/her ministry if rapidly moved? Answer: it's not possible. And the pretence carries on.

There is the often unmet need to allow Parliament sufficient time to consider and make legislation effective, and the need to *listen, read, attend seminars and deliberate*. Frequently, the government fails to anticipate the problems of *implementing* policies. King and Crewe claim that these defects have little to do with party leaders or members or partisan ideologies. Surprisingly, in the UK, Conservative or Labour governments seem to err in the same way and are about equally blunder prone. They thus emphasise that *systemic* defects are rooted in the institutions and broad culture of Whitehall and Westminster. The following points suggest that blunders are inevitable.

Frequently, the backgrounds of MPs do not include <u>any</u> 'normal', non-political work and can be of a virtually exclusive political nature, e.g. as per the previous Prime Minister, David Cameron. This creates a tendency towards being exceptionally partisan since their habitat has always been partisan. MPs are typically ambitious and will naturally prioritise their own re-election, i.e. their <u>survival</u>. Given the existence of the 'power phenotype', survival and re-election are of even greater importance than it is for 'non-alphas'. Short-termism/ survival, i.e. winning the next election (<u>and keeping their job</u>), is therefore probably near or at the top of an MP's agenda. Pleasing their alpha-male leaders is the route to personal 'success'. Even more short term for any party is the importance of influencing next weekend's newspapers.

Thus, keeping their eye on the 'ball' is keeping it on the next election. So, the 'ball' is all too often <u>power</u>. This can explain why so much time by ministers is allotted to meetings with commercial and media barons who may influence the outcome of an election by offering money or positive publicity and support, e.g. the media mogul Rupert Murdoch's numerous meetings with UK prime ministers. In addition, it has been admitted in the UK that both the governing party and the opposition attempt to influence the BBC on a daily basis. <u>As part of any plan to improve politics, this must be greatly curtailed or eliminated</u>. This state of affairs raises important questions about the narrow ownership of the media.

Summary of the causes of 'blunders'
Politicians are not characteristically stupid, rather they are *ignorant,* with narrow backgrounds and personal ambitions. They are fully occupied with being alphas, influencing the media (especially senior politicians), rising up the ranks of their party, winning the next election for their party and for themselves, and with helping constituents. Typically, they have little time for reading and otherwise keeping up with new knowledge. In the UK, ministers are moved too frequently for them to master their brief.

Military: power phenotype
Audit and suggestions for improvements with an emphasis on the UK

Answering needs, harmonising primate instincts and
expressing the human

Introduction
In a world that now includes nuclear weaponry, bioterrorism and other means that provide us with a massive capacity for human and environmental destruction, we are again led to the question as to what extent human group behaviour is indeed influenced by our primate instincts and to what extent by our conscious, human reason and/or human intuition. Another question is about the method by which we humans achieve an effective, speedy and concerted response to threat, i.e. the influence of leadership, power and obedience.

As stated earlier, <u>all</u> 'successful' (large, powerful) human institutions are indeed characteristically primate. That is, they tend to be hierarchies (typically, but not necessarily, male dominated) concerned with survival (commonly short-term), the expansion of power, territory and degree of control, so that concerted responses to threats (and opportunities for increased power) can be made with speed. Furthermore, leaders and hierarchies can help condition groups to appropriate learned behaviour. An obvious social structure bearing the marks of our primate past with crystal clarity and answering 'yes' to all of the earlier questions is the military: Chief of General Staff, Field Marshall, General, Brigadier General, Colonel, Major, Captain, Lieutenant, Sergeant, Corporal, Lance Corporal, Private – about 12 levels (closely similar to the RC Church). Similar structures exist for navies, air forces and specialist units.

Here, the hierarchical structures constitute an obvious example of survival behaviour, with 'training', in addition to martial arts, being a clear example of extreme obedience conditioning. Commonly, as with the clergy of some religions, individuals are stripped of personal identity in terms of having a shaved head, uniforms and a subservient demeanour (standing to 'attention') when in the presence of superior officers. Clearly, this is so that in the heat of combat the probability of *obedience* to higher authority is increased yet further. And, of course, such concerted primate behaviour, honed specifically to conflict, tends to work well in terms of survival. The world is a dangerous and violent place and groups feel less vulnerable with a formal, military capability in a state of readiness. Typically, the military, <u>as an institution</u>, is essentially primate in behaviour, although such arrangements are rational in order to fulfil such a purpose. The parallels with religious institutions continue: seminaries for religious 'novices' offer similar intensive conditioning, but with less justification than for the military. The religious prophets did not ask for blind obedience: they taught kindness and the need to help others. Also, in well-developed military structures, the leadership is not simply a primate, kill-or-be-killed organisation. Many human attributes are expressed. Within it, individuals typically belong, and often show extraordinary, human acts of conscious selflessness and bravery in helping their comrades (mates).

The intense obedience and mental conditioning, universal in much military training, is illustrated by a BBC documentary I personally heard and recorded, including an interview with the then current Commandant of the elite US Marine Corps. The following comments were made about the Marine Corps. 'They (recruits) come from a soft and liberal society and we cannot have that'; 'We strip them of their identity'; 'We make them homogeneous'; 'We don't put clean water into dirty water, we empty first'. It hardly needs saying that it would be foolish and dangerous to abandon the armed forces and their training. But who gave permission for such indoctrination? Such an ideology of mindless obedience (to a questionable philosophy) is not necessary and is harmful to society. In unstable societies, the military often take over the reins of political power and control political life with an increase in 'primate' characteristics. The above frightening comments I heard from the Commandant of the US Marine Corps could well have come from George Orwell's '1984'. Here is a quote of almost identical content from Orwell's '1984': 'Power is in tearing human minds to pieces and putting them together again in new shapes of your own choosing.' Here are two more from '1984':

1. 'Orthodoxy means not thinking – not needing to think. Orthodoxy is unconsciousness.'
2. 'Power is not a means; *it is an end.*'

Obedience to orders

An ugly consequence of such conditioning can be, and commonly is, willingness to obey orders to kill or torture even one's own kind. As I type these words, Syrian tanks are bombarding Syrian cities and snipers are shooting unarmed civilians and even children. The throats of children are being cut open to terrorise. Refugees escaping into Turkey and even within Turkey are shot by Syrian forces 'loyal' to the President. One questions whether this is 'primate' in any sense, but rather some form of aberrant, sick, human behaviour. It's hard to escape the impression from broadcasts by the Syrian President (or his spokesmen) about 'terrorists' (translation = his opponents), that he truly believes he has a form of divine right to rule. Opposition to his rule is *de facto* illegitimate. It's the power phenotype at work as extreme as it gets. This situation also illustrates the need to belong. The Alawite Muslim sect to which the President belongs is a minority within the country, yet dominates the civil service, politics and the military – a recipe for strife. Before the protests were met by brutal violence, Alawites accounted for around 12% of Syria's population: around 70% of Syrians belong to Sunni Islam (as do almost 90% of all Muslims in the world).

And now, after beautiful, peaceful protests by the youth for a greater say in affairs, we have a dreadful war with atrocities on both sides and so-called religious fundamentalists as active participants who have a philosophy of condemning women to subservience and leaving them with no formal education. From my perspective (2017), Syria with Aleppo destroyed, even obliterated, now looks like a terrible choice between two evils. And, as discussed elsewhere, we have the dreadful example of the Holocaust with widespread involvement and social acquiescing in the obedience to 'orders' to torture, mutilate and murder fellow humans.

National security and the state – paranoia
It seems likely that the power phenotype in modern society contributes to a permanent state similar to paranoia for the leaders. That is, our alpha-male leaders being constantly aware of potential dangers from competitor states spying on them, acquiring superior arms and making alliances with other states. This would contribute to the current dysfunctional, world scene and likely the historical situation as well. Unlike the past, we now have unprecedented arms and also capacity via IT to monitor the world's information exchange. In terms of interstate tensions, alpha males have an

instinctive and special role in responding to danger. In the pre-human, primate, 'natural' world, an unnecessarily violent attack on a perceived enemy would not have the widespread consequences of today. It was then best to be safe than sorry. Today, this precautionary attitude (or instinct) is supported and probably exaggerated by modern espionage and secret services providing information about competitors' armaments and defences. The 'Snowden' leaks prove that this is so, as described in 'The Snowden Files' by Luke Harding. It is a shocking but believable account of virtually unlimited surveillance by the USA National Security Agency aided by the UK (GCHQ). The book also describes the attempts by the government to stop any leaks. The New York Times and the Guardian cooperated with government regarding what was thought to be genuinely dangerous leaks, but published much evidence of *illegitimate* government spying on its citizens and on the rest of the world under the umbrella of 'security'. 'They' (our alpha males) are spying on 'us' on a grand scale. According to Newsweek (May 2014), the then latest contribution to the 'spying scandal', as well as the US spying on everyone, involves Israel's comprehensive spying on the USA. 'They' are vacuuming up vast amounts of personal information about 'us' apparently because 'they' can, and it might come in handy. Being 'handy' could also mean the capacity to expose embarrassing/criminal behaviour by any organisation or individual and/or use it to blackmail. Several news outlets in the UK routinely threatened public figures with the possibility of exposing such behaviour, discovered illicitly. As each nation learns more about its competitors/enemies, then the tendency is for each to increase its expenditure on defence. It thus becomes a vicious circle. Therefore, it could be that it is 'normal' for each nation to be led by alpha males, relatively ignorant of the outside world, but advised by a security service in a state of near or actual paranoia.

Humanising the military

Answering needs, harmonising primate instincts and expressing the human

Audit and suggestions for improvements
Bearing in mind our instincts and our basic needs for safety, food, shelter, a sense of community and the need for inclusive political and economic structures, the main task of the military is to protect their country. It would be in the national interest if the armed forces were fully integrated into normal society. We need armed forces for basic safety. If we are to have a sense of belonging – all being in it together – the armed forces should not be alien and their sometimes dangerous work seen to be carried out by 'others'.

1. We should, <u>at least to some extent,</u> consider a citizens' army, navy and air force. In addition to regular forces (as a job), at the age of 18 all youth should have a form of two years' National Service, serving either mainly in the armed forces <u>or</u> mainly doing community service. They would learn about all aspects of their nation. <u>All</u> should have instruction/ training and visits regarding the operation of the military, navy, air force and 'special forces'; the emergency services of the police, ambulance and fire services; and also in the operation of the UK social services for 12 months followed by actual service. All could learn some useful activities such as painting/decorating, cooking, food production and apply their skills to helping elderly people in homes, child care, nurseries, orphanages, prisons.

   Similarly, all citizens could have one week per annum devoted to helping the needy, as required by the main religion of every nation, including the UK – perhaps rotating through different social agencies and during different years.

2. Conscientious objection to specific conflicts or activities should be respected. Such objections should be recorded at the start of service and the objectors could spend the first year of the above two-year programme as for everyone else and then the second year in an aspect of social services.

3. Everyone must have the right to refuse to do things they consider morally wrong.

4. Members of the UK armed forces have faced difficulties when injured in combat and needing rehabilitation into working life. This includes mental health issues after violent combat. In 2016, there were numerous examples of injured UK service people not receiving what they needed and deserved. This is now recognised as a scandal in the UK. Injured service people should receive generous, sustained help as a first call on national income.

5. In peacetime, military personnel should assist in civilian duties. We should reduce the idea of the military being separate and not spoken about. The involvement in the security arrangements for the London Olympics 2012 worked exceptionally well and clearly contributed to the idea of us all belonging. Similarly, military involvement in the UK floods was very helpful, well appreciated by everyone and aided integration.

6. We should pay the military relatively high wages for this dangerous job of defence. The costs of this could have the beneficial side effect of reducing the tendency to have an over-large military – the UK can no longer afford imperialism.

Justice and the law

With a view to answering needs, harmonising primate instincts and expressing the human

Audit and suggestions for improvements
A nation's legal system does not and cannot operate independently of the general culture. The culture is formed by all the components of a society and its whole informs each and every part. It resembles a complex biological system with numerous reversible biochemical reactions and in varying equilibria depending on how the whole is operating. Where the power lies in a culture is obviously important and extreme power can push the equilibrium to a harmful state of imbalance. For example, we have the following extreme examples. Europeans burned witches and non-believers in the reigning religious belief of Christianity. This was in total defiance of the indisputable, New Testament teaching of Jesus. If one considers new or greatly altered nations, for example when the British colonised Australia (with *so-called* UK criminals), they designated the original inhabitants as inferior (to UK criminals?) and so 'justified' gross injustice to them. Similarly, when Europeans (mostly) colonised North America, they 'justified' their ethnic 'cleansing' of the indigenous people by designating them as savages and subsequently also 'justified' slavery (see earlier) by asserting that the blacks from the Caribbean were inferior. The situation in South Africa was similar with the Dutch suppressing the indigenous blacks under the cloak of inferiority. This particular crime was especially ironic, given that *all* anatomically modern humans left Africa only 60,000 years ago to populate the entire world.

Suggestions for improvement in the justice system
1.   Justice is a vital need for a healthy state. As a national service, its composition should be as for the political structures, that is, representative. We should attempt to ensure that the legal

profession is representative of the national population as a whole: similarly for the judiciary. As for Parliament, salaries for the government's legal employees should be within the scale for the population as a whole and with generous expenses.

2. Justice must be equally available to all and hence free of charges.

3. The composition of any national police force <u>should be broadly representative</u> of the population mix and with top salaries within sight of the national median. Local police forces should also have a mix broadly representative of the local population. Police and recruits should be instructed about the vital importance of their work in contributing positively to the overall *social* health of their community. The police role is more important than simply solving crime. Efforts should be made to integrate the police into the local community with police housing within the community and visits to schools on a routine basis.

Keeping one's eye on the ball for all professions.
The 'ball' is the nation's health, happiness and security. Money is a requirement, the *means*, but is not the *objective*. 'Belonging' and being part of the same nation and culture could be enhanced and sustained if the leaders shared or at least 'tasted' the life of those they led. I suggest that a universal policy should apply of experiencing the life of those who are led. All lawyers, police, MPs, all civil servants, all local authority staff and all military and security services personnel (ambulance, fire, police) could spend a week each year living in a poor or other appropriate area on the minimum wage and also half a day or an evening each month helping out in an appropriate, normally alien situation, e.g. a soup kitchen, hospital, hostel or prison. Senior medical staff could work as juniors in hospitals in departments that are different to normal, e.g. biochemistry or radiology or even occasionally as cleaners. The effect on each hospital's community

spirit could be great. In the UK, the military's recent experience in helping with floods and with the previous Olympics was entirely helpful and rewarding socially. The experience of otherwise senior staff in lowly temporary positions could well lead to improvements suggested by these temporary staff. Similarly, those in lowly jobs could offer insights to their 'visitors'. I suggest that it would require a couple of years to plan and then implement. It could also help to ameliorate the exceptional and instinctive attraction to power of the alpha males.

Formal education

Audit and suggested improvements

With a view to answering needs, harmonising primate instincts and expressing the human

Education: Educo (-ere) (Latin) lead forth, draw out, develop

Before addressing education *per se*, a truth must be recognised that exists in politics generally and in its subunits. What is *desirable* is not the same as what is *possible*. A creative judgement is always involved.

How do we best encourage the healthy, full development of children? Surely, this is a major duty of a well-functioning state with aims of health and happiness. By the nature of the instincts associated with being an alpha, they tend to be preoccupied with alpha projects, often associated with defence. It seems likely, that because of the vast expense of modern weaponry, this accelerates development of ever more expensive weapons and defences.

How do we improve the 'humanising' aspects of education and also enable the controlled expression of primate instincts? This applies especially to the formal education of young humans. Early human development is crucial for obvious reasons, but also because of the difficulty of later remedying early harm. Given the plethora of assertions about education, it should be based on empirically established facts about human development – infant, child, adolescent and later human needs. Official education should use objective knowledge of human natural development to inform specific approaches. Thus, this section starts with a consideration of what is known about early human development before discussing modern institutional approaches to formal education. It's now clear that influences on development start *before* birth. An earlier section has emphasised the hierarchy of schools that exists in a nation and worldwide. This results in a kind of *a priori* identification of alphas *via* the position of one's school in the hierarchy. In the <u>pre</u>-human world, any form of alpha is preferable to none. At the least, for tree-dwelling apes, one alpha increases the chances of a rapid and coordinated response to change and danger.

Importance of early development:
non-human primates to human primates
Child-rearing
Bonobo mothers carry and breastfeed their babies for about two years. What a safe, happy, socialising way to spend this first two years! Unsurprisingly, human brain development/nerve circuits make major advances during this same period. Ape communities are small, as were early human ones. Probably all healthy human adults, including some mothers carrying babies, would have some involvement in hunting or gathering. It also seems likely that children aged over about two years or so would be 'looked after' by the elderly or infirm and other children unable to hunt/gather or simply allowed to play with other children. Is this the 'natural' way to rear and socialise human children, evolved over millions of years? And does departure from small communities and ancient patterns of child-rearing contribute to the problems of modern, 'advanced' societies? Jared Diamond in 'The World Until Today' offers much evidence that makes it seem likely.

In the UK in recent times, there have been numerous, comprehensive studies and continuing research and these were considered under the earlier section 'Reducing humanity's problems' (summary of broad approaches), especially on:

a. the damaging effects on child development of social and emotional deprivation, leading to adverse social behaviour in later life with high financial costs; and
b. the human benefits of early intervention and also the large cost benefits.

The above information clearly demonstrates that physical, brain and emotional developments occur in an interactive social setting. Also known is the necessity of loving nurturing for healthy human development. Interference to brain development by any method affects subsequent behaviour. It's remarkable that the normal brain influences many, perhaps *all*, aspects of behaviour and is itself influenced by its social environment. 'Why love matters – how affection shapes a baby's brain' by Sue Gerhardt gives much empirical evidence that loving relationships are vital to healthy early brain development.

Various countries, notably in Scandinavia, have successfully pioneered an educational process of socialisation as a first priority, with an introduction to such as art and poetry *before* starting formal lessons a year or two after most other countries. Consequently, based on empirical evidence, early years/infant education should be about socialising, experiencing nature, 'playing' and 'negotiating' with other children, learning games, drawing and painting, stories, poetry, music, dance and singing. This leads on to listening and to learning how to read. Thus, acquiring skills in making relationships and exploring the world facilitate the *'leading forth, drawing out and development'*. In these early years, the crucial characteristics of any teacher must surely be empathy and altruism and these should inform the appointment of teachers. In such terms, humane attitudes to disadvantaged or disabled children are essential and should be emphasised in the training of teachers.

Is creativity in children and adolescents enhanced by formal education, often consisting of learning/memorising facts selected by others, starting early and for many years?

It's worth remarking on the fact that modern, conventional education can often be mostly learning facts *selected by others* and then examined, most importantly during adolescence, when humans are in a most variable phase of their lives. Can this enhance and develop creativity? Clearly, children are more likely to adapt to this process if they've had a healthy, natural process of early development. The fact of a syllabus being selected by others seems unavoidable. Even so, an *open* culture allowing questioning and diversity is an important aspect, not only in early education. A *closed* culture, such as in a rigid, sectarian, political or religious society, can have a quite different influence on developing children. Facilitated exploration of the world and rational questioning at an early stage of life should be established as a good preparation for later life. Not all nations are equally effective in educating children and less successful nations can learn from the most effective, e.g. Scandinavia.

University

The survival of any organism in any environment is strongly affected by its continuing knowledge and awareness of that environment. *Closed/secret* human communities enable the continuation of practices shown to be unhelpful/harmful in the wider world, e.g. secretive religious sects. A university is a gateway to the wide world (universe) and beyond, past and present. For millennia, kings and emperors in advanced cultures have created centres of learning and have attempted to assemble all known knowledge in one place. Associated with and integral to such places have always been scholars. It's interesting and significant that advanced centres of knowledge and learning are one of the few social structures that have <u>existed for millennia</u>. It thus seems likely that such long-lived structures play vital social roles.

(**Note:** In the same way, cities at the crossroads of different cultures have typically learned and flourished).

The Western term 'university' was used by the Italian University of Bologna, founded in 1088, and is thought to be from the Latin *'universitas magistrorum et scholarium'*, meaning 'community of teachers and scholars'. The designation as oldest university is somewhat contentious. The first university is often said to be at Bologna, while the first 'true' one is thought by some to be the University of Paris because it was the first to cover *all* known subjects, i.e. the universe of knowledge. So, *diversity* is an intrinsic characteristic of such institutions and contributes to their longevity. Thus, a university is a place embracing the universe of knowledge – a 'Citadel of Reason'. Its ancient, <u>human</u> purpose is to *uncover the truth* in any or all subjects. Such a purpose is essentially human. Derived from their function is the idea of 'academic freedom', widely recognised internationally and in 1988 several hundred university rectors (and continuing) worldwide signed the 'Magna Charta Universitatum', emphasising this freedom.

Top-down (alpha males) management of
scholarship is intrinsically dodgy
The notions of scholarship, of revealing the truth, are hard to equate with top-down 'management'. Being an employee obeying the 'management' is not the same as being in a community of scholars. This is not to say that large, complex establishments do not require organising to be effective. Today, there are numerous examples of political leaders attempting to *use* universities for many purposes. One example is to help the economy directly via commerce. The future is always tricky to predict, and politicians and governments are ill equipped to do so. Typically, and understandably, they have their eyes fixed firmly on winning the next election, rising in the party and helping their constituents. There are also examples, especially of lower-grade UK universities being turned into corporation-like institutions with male executives showing their alpha status *via* having long titles, expensive suits, white shirts and pointy, shiny black shoes as the outward signs of alpha-hood. In my experience, women executives conform less. All such signs are indicative of a top-

down power structure. Why is such a *uniform* so common? My guess is that the university 'executives' are copying the alphas/executives of top corporations, such as in financial services. But authentic academic 'alphas' are different to the conventional alphas of evolution. They are *less* identified by conventional power, such as the status of Professor or Dean or Vice-Chancellor. They are characterised, not by attire copied from business, but by stimulating, up-to-date under-/ postgraduate courses and/or by revealing the truth about Mother Nature (or by adding to or disseminating the Universe of Knowledge such as philosophy or history or art or mathematics or science), *via* lectures, seminars and publications in widely accessible journals. Some may, indeed, choose to wear suits.

Privatisation of higher education

Recent publications and conferences have drawn attention to the marketisation/privatisation of UK higher education (Stefan Collini 'Speaking of Universities', 2017 and 'Sold Out', 2013). Marina Warner, former UK Conservative Minister for Universities, has stated that 'cuts are the tools of the *ideological* decision to stop subsidising tuition and to start withdrawing from directly supporting research. What we are in effect moving towards is the privatisation of higher education' ('Learning my Lesson', 2015).

Here is a case study of why a top-down approach is dangerous. A spectacular example is that of 'Silicon Valley', California, mentioned later in more detail ('USA as a special case', see below), which has lessons for us all, including the UK. After World War 2, the US government supported fundamental research in computing, notably Information Technology and Artificial Intelligence, and also in molecular biology. This led indirectly to numerous, profitable companies. Not only did the government <u>not</u> start these, but broadly, government top-down approaches to novelty have a very bad record. It was mostly the US academic scientists who started the companies; they sometimes left their universities, sometimes not. And the California Bay Area universities, mostly owning the 'intellectual property', adopted very, very generous terms to encourage their staff not to 'moonlight'. It was common, even in my time (post 2000), in Palo Alto, to find an evening group in a restaurant, all with laptops out, friendly, cheerful and talking and working and later joined by partners for dinner. Many had relatively modest wages but shares in the company. It seemed a very human, communal experience to me. I became familiar with the very <u>non</u>-top-down system when I became CSO of a Palo Alto biotech company. In 2018, California state has an economy that is the sixth largest among the world's nations based strongly on IT and molecular biology. In the UK similar developments are occurring, but slowly and not with widespread success. Cambridge University has an annual turnover of around six billion pounds sterling, mostly with the same scientific base as Silicon Valley. Commercialisation of advances in molecular biology, casting light on life itself, have minimal interference with academic research. Revealing the truth about an aspect of molecular biology can have an immediate commercial value: similarly, for computer/digital revelations.

In all nations, any barriers to entry into higher education should be scrutinised and eliminated unless needed. In the UK, after World War 2 *when the country was bankrupt*, the government introduced a *free* national health service, *free* school meals and also *free* higher education with no fees and *free*, living allowances. Today, UK students leave university with massive debts of tens of thousands of pounds. Unquestionably, part of the current situation is the attempt, expensively, to maintain the UK in its earlier state as an imperial world power, partly represented by having large military and nuclear weaponry. The weapons have no one to fire them at, but our leaders constantly reiterate that such weapons buy them 'seats at the top table'. Behaving in accordance with our actual resources and perhaps without nuclear weapons could help *hugely* with higher quality services for health, housing and education. If our alphas lived even approximately in the style of the life of those they lead, then this would be much more likely to happen. As well as this, the UK has joined the USA in advocating low taxes. Imperial arms spending and low taxes lead *inevitably* to lack of finance for social services for the poor.

Appendix to Education

An extreme example of the indoctrination of youth to mindless obedience

(Information from the USA Holocaust Memorial Museum, Washington, USA)

As well as learning from the best, we can also learn from the dreadful consequences of extreme, pathological indoctrination as exemplified by the Nazis. Because of its importance, I quote at some length. I have long wondered at how Hitler and his fellow Nazis achieved such power and obedience. I have also long wondered at how such extraordinarily uniformed parades of tens of thousands of 'goose-stepping' troops could be cheered by many tens of thousands of civilians giving identical Hitler salutes; and with their leader, above them, also saluting. What follows, gives a partial explanation of how Hitler achieved such indoctrination to an inhuman ideology. It is a pathological opposite to healthy child development.

> *'These boys and girls enter our organizations [at] ten years of age, and often for the first time get a little fresh air; after four years of the Young Folk they go on to the Hitler Youth, where we have them for another four years. And even if they are still not complete National Socialists, they go to Labour Service and are smoothed out there for another six, seven months . . . And whatever class consciousness or social status might still be left . . . the Wehrmacht [German armed forces] will take care of that.'*

Adolf Hitler (1938).

> *'In 1939, membership in Nazi youth groups became mandatory for all boys and girls between the ages of ten and eighteen.'*

Bildarchiv Preussischer Kulturbesitz

From the 1920s onwards, the Nazi Party targeted German youth as a special audience for its propaganda messages. These messages emphasised that the Party was a movement of youth: dynamic, resilient, forward-looking and hopeful. Millions of German young people were won over to Nazism in the *classroom and through extracurricular activities*. In January 1933, the Hitler Youth had only 50,000 members, but by the end of the year this figure had increased to more than 2 million. By 1936 membership in the Hitler Youth increased to 5.4 million before it became mandatory in 1939. The German authorities then *prohibited or dissolved* competing youth organisations.

Education in the Nazi state
Education in the Third Reich served to indoctrinate students with the National Socialist world view. Nazi scholars and educators glorified Nordic and other 'Aryan' races, while denigrating Jews and other so-called inferior peoples as parasitic 'bastard races' incapable of creating culture or civilisation. After 1933, the Nazi regime purged the public school system of teachers deemed to be Jews or to be 'politically unreliable'. Most educators, however, remained in their posts and joined the National Socialist Teachers League. 97% of all public school teachers, some 300,000 persons, had joined the League by 1936. In fact, teachers joined the Nazi Party in greater numbers than any other profession. In the classroom and in the Hitler Youth, instruction aimed to produce race-conscious, obedient, self-sacrificing Germans who would be willing to die for Führer and 'Fatherland'. Devotion to Adolf Hitler was a key component of Hitler Youth training. German young people celebrated his birthday (April 20) – a national holiday – with membership inductions. German adolescents swore allegiance to Hitler and pledged to serve the nation and its leader as future soldiers.

Schools played an important role in spreading Nazi ideas to German youth. While censors removed some books from the classroom, German educators introduced new textbooks that taught students love for Hitler, obedience to state authority, militarism, racism and anti-Semitism. From their first days in school, German children were imbued with the cult of Adolf Hitler. His portrait was a standard fixture in classrooms. Textbooks frequently described the thrill of a child seeing the German leader for the first time. Board games and toys for children served as another way to spread racial and political propaganda to German youth. Toys were also used as propaganda vehicles to indoctrinate children into militarism.

Youth organisations
The Hitler Youth and the League of German Girls were the primary tools that the Nazis used to shape the beliefs, thinking and actions of German youth. Youth leaders used tightly controlled group activities and staged propaganda events such as mass rallies full of ritual and spectacle to create the illusion of one national community reaching across class and religious divisions which had characterised Germany before 1933. Founded in 1926, the original purpose of the Hitler Youth was to train boys to enter the SA (storm troopers), a Nazi Party paramilitary formation. After 1933 however, youth leaders sought to integrate boys into the Nazi national community and to prepare them for service as soldiers in the armed forces or, later, in the SS. In 1936, membership in Nazi youth groups became mandatory for all boys and girls between the ages of 10 and 17. After-school meetings and weekend camping trips sponsored by the Hitler Youth and the League of German Girls, trained children to become faithful to the Nazi Party and the future leaders of the National Socialist state. By September 1939, over 765,000 young people served in leadership roles in Nazi youth organisations which prepared them for such roles in the military and the German occupation bureaucracy. The Hitler Youth combined sports and outdoor activities with ideology. Similarly, the League of German Girls emphasised collective athletics, such as rhythmic gymnastics, which German health authorities deemed less strenuous to the female body and better geared to preparing them for motherhood.

Their public displays of these values encouraged young men and women to abandon their individuality in favour of the goals of the Aryan collective.

Military service

Upon reaching the age of 18, boys were required to enlist immediately in the armed forces or into the Reich Labour Service, for which their activities in the Hitler Youth had prepared them. Propaganda materials called for an ever more fanatic devotion to Nazi ideology, even as the German military suffered from defeat after defeat. In the autumn of 1944, as Allied armies crossed the borders into Germany, the Nazi regime conscripted German youths under the age of 16 to defend the Reich, alongside seniors over the age of 60, in the units of the 'Volkssturm' (People's Assault). After the unconditional surrender of the German armed forces in May 1945, some German boys continued to fight in guerilla groups known as 'Werewolves'. During the following year, Allied occupation authorities required young Germans to undergo a 'de-Nazification' process and training in democracy designed to counter the effects of 12 years of Nazi propaganda.

Recognising the influence of biological evolution on the USA

With a view to answering needs, harmonising primate instincts and expressing the human

In addition to the proposals described above about increasing humane characteristics and decreasing the inappropriate expression of basic instincts by nation states and their institutions, the USA and the UK deserve special, additional mention. The USA is currently the world's most powerful and financially rich nation and is clearly exhibiting the power phenotype. It is an alpha state. The UK, a century or so ago a leading world alpha power, is adjusting slowly to the loss of one of the world's greatest empires. It is swiftly moving up the inequality, straight-line graph and closer to the USA and *simultaneously* exhibiting the correlated higher crime and numerous other bad social statistics. It's where I live and so did my parents and grandparents and far beyond, with one grandfather being French.

Out of all the nations that have useful data, the USA is the most u̲nequal and exhibits the correlated *highest crime and other antisocial statistics* (per head of population). As mentioned earlier, there are numerous studies about the bad social consequences linked with inequality. 'The Spirit Level' by Wilkinson and Pickett, mentioned earlier, gives clear graphs showing these straight-line correlations for Western-type, rich nations. With its top economy, the alpha USA deserves closer scrutiny regarding GDP, crime and happiness levels. As a nation, it clearly and strongly exhibits primate instincts inappropriately. In addition to the ideas expressed earlier about humanising governments in general, it seemed appropriate to consider the USA specifically.

Personal experience
I ask the reader to allow me some personal reflections on the USA for reasons that will become evident. I do not believe that the USA can be described as one single culture. I have lived in the USA on several occasions, starting in 1961 in Gainesville, Florida with my family when I went to work for a year with an eminent pharmacokineticist at the University of Florida. Immediately on arrival, we saw the rampant commercialism that was on display everywhere and the crudeness of the advertising, including that aimed at young children (subsequently reformed). We saw for the first time, motels with residents having little or no social interaction. We saw 'drive-in' churches where, again, social interaction was nil or low. We saw multiple 'MacDonald's, without crockery and using solely cardboard plates, reducing/eliminating local cafes, and we saw 'drive-in' food outlets. A crossroads in central Gainesville had petrol stations on each of three corners and a beautiful old house on the fourth corner. During our time in Gainesville, that house was knocked down and replaced by a fourth petrol station. The TV, wireless and newspapers

were broadly parochial and commercial: after all, the companies were financed from advertisements. This is not evil, but has inevitable consequences for the content which is obviously required to *please the sources of revenue*. News agencies are rarely charities. There are exceptions such as the high-quality New York Times with a reducing circulation and numerous small circulation specialist cultural publications. This commercially directed bias for sources about the outside world has obvious consequences.

They could not be compared in any way to *the then* relatively independent standards of the BBC (being eroded in 2017 as I revise), managed by an independent trust and relatively separated from commerce and government: similarly, for the trust-controlled UK Guardian newspaper. Commerce was triumphant, and racism was conspicuous (see the earlier section on 'Racism'), notably in the police. Even on our first night, as my wife and I lay on our bed, hot and humid, we wondered how we could possibly have come to this awful, inhuman place! But we were wrong. We quickly came to love Americans. Hence, I must point out this wonderful, human side to USA life, later reinforced by numerous subsequent visits. Hopefully, this will reduce the perception of bias as I go on to describe the objective, dreadful social statistics and racism in the USA.

(**Note**: It's noteworthy that the UK right-wing government is changing the rules (December 2016) for public appointments. It will be easier for ministers to pick political allies for senior appointments at the BBC and for government regulators.)

During this first visit, our individual experience of ordinary Americans, black and white, turned out to be superb. They were then and also later, during other lengthy visits to other USA locations, overwhelmingly kind and generous. Obviously, this cannot be extrapolated to the entire USA. But it is uniformly our personal experience. This is so at odds with the world's view of the USA and its violent foreign policy that I would like to expand on it a little. My wife and I had four children below the age of five during our first visit to Florida. The climate in the summer is dreadful, with heat and high humidity and I had a very demanding laboratory job. Without the kindness, humanity and practical help of *numerous* Americans we could not have coped.

My favourite places on Earth (apart from wherever my family is) include the small coastal towns of the Wirral in North West England, the Welsh Black Mountains around Hay on Wye and Brecon, the seaside around Dundee in Scotland and the Scottish Isle of Skye. But despite being strongly British and loving the British values of tolerance, free speech and fairness, probably my favourite place of all is Half Moon Bay (about 20 miles long), west of Palo Alto, California, USA. The town in the centre of the bay is itself called Half Moon Bay and somewhat resembles the Cotswolds in the UK, but without any atmosphere of being quaint or posh. At the risk of being seen as an exaggerated idealist, this small, humane village has lots of *owner-run* shops, cafes and bookshops with wall spaces for numerous postcards advertising social groups of numerous kinds, mostly book-reading, music, dance and poetry groups. Without exception, all were staffed by kind, concerned and idealistic people. It's a place inhabited by highly developed humans. They have somehow legally prevented large national supermarkets from being within the town. When the locally owned grocery store was burned down, the entire town helped out in various ways. Whether this area with the beautiful seaside attracted such people or whether it was its proximity to relatively humane San Francisco, it is a truly human place.

I feel at home there and during my stays at Stanford University my wife and I went there most weekends. Further up Half Moon Bay at the northern end is a small fishing village, Princeton, with the most beautiful beach I've ever walked on, just a short walk north of the village. This narrow beach has wonderful, endless waves and is normally almost empty. 'The Mavericks', known to surfing enthusiasts worldwide, is a few miles offshore. If you meet anyone, as happened to me on numerous occasions, it's as if you are already a friend. On one occasion, a stranger approached me and, without me even speaking, her first sentence was 'What do

Europeans think of us?' I recall that it was around the time of an invasion or a bombing by the US military. When we parted company, we hugged as friends! I have no idea as to how she had recognised that I was European.

Unquestionably, of all the other numerous countries that we've lived in (Austria, Canada, France, Switzerland), the kindest, most open people we encountered by far were Americans. Although this impression is based mostly on American academics and scientists, this is not exclusively so. Obviously, we shopped, and we travelled, and we had neighbours. I have lived in the USA on several occasions, mostly to work in universities and also industrial companies as a consultant. Nevertheless, we had little close, personal experience of the numerous Americans at the very bottom of the income ladder. We had some personal contact with Mexican immigrants running a cafe at Stanford University who were all helpful, kind humans who, as a collective, supported each other in every way, especially a recent immigrant Mexican family that we knew. Then and today (2018), there was and is a distinct difference regarding large sporting events such as American football. They were entirely peaceful and well organised compared to the UK, e.g. regarding soccer. UK professional soccer matches are heavily guarded by numerous stewards and numerous police in attendance: violence is ever close to the surface.

During my first visit to the University of Florida, together with another visiting UK scientist, we organised regular 'Brown Bag' (many staff carry sandwiches in brown paper bags) lunch-time seminars. The seminars were wide in scope and were a novelty to the institution. Typically, the attendance was often around a *hundred+* and the discussions were lively. But looking back, it's surprising and interesting that there were no visible consequences to our advertising titles such as 'The President should be impeached' or 'The US health service is an inhuman disgrace'. Nobody in authority ever spoke or wrote to us about our possibly dangerous views. Similarly, when a local politician wanted to rid the state system of communists (it was not long after the McCarthy period), he ordered that all curricular be investigated for communist material. Shortly afterwards, he extended his campaign to eliminating gay people (how he was to identify gays and communists remained a mystery). As part of this, all professors had to be investigated and I was called to attend a meeting with someone (I now forget who). I had a surreal conversation, fixed in my memory, with a university secretary which included at least five repetitions about my attendance: 1. 'Dr Brown, you're required to attend...' 'Thank you, but sorry, I am not going.' 2. 'Dr Brown, you don't understand, but you have to.' 3. 'I'm sorry, Miss X, but I'm not going.' These exchanges were repeated several times and then Miss X actually gasped audibly and exclaimed, 'You mean that you are not going to attend.' I replied that this was correct.

Again, looking back, it is surprising that nothing whatever happened to naïve me or my English friend. This episode was not a joke. Friends left, or tried to leave, Florida who were not communists but could not trust this extremist McCarthyite politician who might destroy their careers with unsubstantiated allegations. I had no visible consequences from my behaviour. I believe that ordinary, local *university* administrators helped my survival. Looking back, my being an active, Mass-going Roman Catholic family man with a wife and four children may have suggested to them that I was not a communist and not gay. At that time, even locals thought that Florida politics was deeply corrupt, notably the determined attempts to exclude blacks from voting. We organised debates and seminars on all these contentious topics.

In the context of this book, with an emphasis on the effects of evolution on current human society, what can be said regarding this disparity between at least one, large group of 'ordinary' and remarkably kind Americans and their government's ferocious, alpha foreign policy driven by pure primate instincts?

Origins of the USA

First of all, I wonder if the USA has *ever* been actually united as a whole: belonging is a 'must' for social health. As mentioned earlier, it was <u>not Americans</u> that slaughtered the relatively weaponless indigenous Indians whose country it was. It was the colonialists of numerous kinds who did the exterminating. Early European possessions in North America included Spanish Florida and New Mexico, English colonies of Virginia, Bermuda and New England, French colonies of Acadia and Canada, a Swedish colony of New Sweden, and the Dutch with New Netherland. In the 18th century, Denmark-Norway revived its former colonies in Greenland, while the Russian Empire claimed part of Alaska.

(**Explanatory Note**: The Acadians are the descendants of French colonists who settled in Acadia during the 17th and 18th centuries. The colony was located in what is now Eastern Canada's Maritime provinces (Nova Scotia, New Brunswick, and Prince Edward Island), as well as part of Quebec, and present-day Maine to the Kennebec River.)

As more nations gained an interest in the colonisation of the Americas, competition for territory accelerated. Colonialists faced the threat of attacks from neighbouring colonies, as well as from indigenous tribes and pirates. Thus, the birth of what became the USA was a brutal stealing of territory from indigenous native peoples and also their slaughter by a *variety* of foreign <u>European</u> nations who sometimes fought also each other. And there was the lucrative and massive slave trade referred to earlier, with mega profiteers from worldwide, including the UK.

It would thus seem clear that the modern USA grew out of ethnic cleansing, widespread strife and with peoples <u>dis</u>united by many widely different origins, cultures and languages. I wonder if such an environment resulted in two different sets of consequences.

1. Crime and antisocial behaviour as responses to that stressful environment by mainly basic instincts and leading to the current dreadful social and crime statistics. These are worse than those of any of the countries who originally populated the USA.

2. Specific, small-group social structures of cooperation as mainly human responses. For example, at Stanford, there was (and likely still is) a 'Newcomers Club' not exclusively for university staff, that actively and swiftly sought out newcomers and welcomed them into numerous social activities. In Florida, decades earlier, there were numerous *spontaneous* acts of friendship and help from individual staff and postgraduate research students with whom I worked. Many remain my good friends to the present day.

Given the origins of the USA, and given its current alpha state, exhibiting the power phenotype, it's not surprising to see consequence one above. The USA is at the top end of the graphs linking inequality to numerous, awful social statistics. One statistic of current interest relates to homicide. In a graph of homicides per million people versus inequality (Wilkinson and Pickett's 'The Spirit Level'), the USA is off the otherwise straight line *at the top worst end* with all the other countries (rich countries) following a linear relationship. For example, the most equal, Japan, has about 5 homicides per million, while the USA as the most unequal has around 64 per million citizens, i.e. about a 12-fold difference. The next highest rate to the USA is Portugal with about half that of the USA. AlterNet provides exceptionally shocking facts and figures about income inequality in the USA (AlterNet July 15th 2015). One fact that struck me with force was that solely Wall Street *bonuses* in 2014 equalled *twice* the amount that *all* minimum wage USA workers earned combined!

The USA's pro-gun lobby is notoriously powerful and contributes to the level of gun ownership and may partly explain the statistic and also the recent shootings (2018). In 2015, President Obama drew attention to this bizarre surfeit of guns. Unsurprisingly, gun ownership in the USA is the highest in the world at 112 per 100 residents in 2014. The next highest is Serbia with 69 per 100 residents. Also unsurprising is that data regarding *firearm-related* deaths shows not the USA as the highest at 11, but Honduras at 65, Venezuela 51 and El Salvador 47 per 100,000 population per annum. These dysfunctional states, not included in the 'Spirit Level' data, endure the massive problems of mafia-like drug cartels, related murders and general social dysfunction.

Are there links between GDP, crime and national happiness?
For modern economies, the USA has the worst crime figures (and is the least equal in terms of income per head). Possibly an examination and comparison of GDP (the USA has the world's highest), adverse social statistics and happiness levels could reveal something about the world's nations as discussed later (under 'Commerce'). Are they linked in any way? Happiness is increasingly considered a measure of social progress and a subject of public policy. It is hard to quantify. The first World Happiness Report was published at the 2012 United Nations High Level Meeting on Happiness and Well-Being. The initial World Happiness Report reviewed the scientific understanding of the measurement and explanation of subjective well-being, and presented a wide range of internationally comparable data, including a ranking of national average life evaluations, based on Gallup World Poll data from 2005-2011 for 156 countries. The current authoritative (2015) ranking of countries by happiness (below for the top ten) is based on: GDP per capita, social support, healthy life expectancy, freedom to make life choices, generosity, perceptions of corruption and dystopia (dystopia: dysfunctional, bad society).

Wilkinson and Pickett's 'The Spirit Level' (Figure 2.2 in the book) shows a graph of income inequality versus an index of health and social problems for 21 rich countries (Western democracies). It's a straight line, with one, the USA, somewhat off the line at the top, at the worst end (most unequal and most problems). In sequences, going down the line from the worst towards the 'good' end are USA, Portugal, UK, Australia, New Zealand, Italy, Greece, Ireland, France, Canada, Switzerland, Spain, Germany, Netherlands, Austria, Belgium and then the most equal and with the least health and social problems – Denmark, Norway / Finland / Sweden and Japan.

Ranking of health and social problems
From 'The Spirit Level', Wilkinson and Pickett
(Least problems at top of ranking, most problems at bottom)
↓ More unequal, more health and social problems.
↑ More equal, less problems.

1. Japan
2, 3, 4. Norway, Finland, Sweden (roughly equal)
5. Denmark
6. Belgium
7. Austria
8. Netherlands
9. Germany
10. Spain
11. Switzerland
12. Canada
13. France
14. Ireland
15. Greece
16. Italy
17. New Zealand
18. Australia
19. UK
20. Portugal
21. USA

World Gross Domestic Product

The world Gross Domestic Product (GDP), according to the International Monetary Union (2014), is $77.3 trillion. The ranking of the GDP of the top ten world nations is listed below in $ trillion. The USA is top with $17 trillion. Figures from the World Bank, The United Nations and the CIA Fact Book for 2014 are closely similar. The ranking lists feature different countries and it's dangerous to extrapolate far. Nevertheless, it's noteworthy that of the GDP top ten countries, none (zero) feature in the top ten for happiness (see table below). It seems that 'small is beautiful'. Another happiness feature that I speculate is important is the degree to which geography facilitates, even forces, communities to be small, e.g. Scandinavia (fjords, ravines, hills) or extreme cold weather, as in Canada, especially in the early colonial days. The index of happiness (below) is topped by small countries whose territory is separated by ravines and mountains or in one way or another is - facilitating small, local communities. I also speculate that such conditions may partly explain why geographically large Canada has a relatively high ranking (12th out of 21, compared to the USA at 16th) regarding freedom from health and social problems (above) and for its relatively high happiness ranking (15th out of 85 countries) below. Canada has extreme winter weather and when colonised (over centuries) had small communities facing harsh weather conditions. Such conditions predispose local cooperation for mutual survival.

This is so despite the fact that, like America to the south, Canada's history is partly a story of wars, with the indigenous peoples being removed from power and territorial wars being fought between mostly France, England and Spain. I have been unable to find any other ranking data with a correlation between GDP, country size and happiness or with geographical or climate features favouring small communities. One would predict that happiness would be multifactorial and anomalies would exist. It's odd that Japan at the top of the equality index is not in the top ten for happiness. In fact, it's 43rd out of 85 countries (last is Portugal). Nevertheless, it's surely significant that <u>none</u> of the top ten countries in the GDP index feature in the top ten index for happiness. Insofar as money may affect a happiness index position, in recent times in the UK, national wealth increases are not passed down to the socially 'lower' classes with low minimum wages, or even a 'living wage', often described by the alphas as 'unaffordable'. Elsewhere, I have commented on the fact that about a third of the world's GDP is hidden away in 'tax havens' by a few *tens of individuals*.

Dear reader, please do not skip the following shocking facts
Given the context, I briefly repeat some earlier, shocking comments about wealth distribution. Credit Suisse Global Wealth Report October 2014 states that the richest 1% of people own nearly half of the *global* wealth. Similarly, Oxfam (Report Jan 2014) warned that the richest 85 people across the globe share a combined wealth of £1 trillion, as much as the poorest 3.5 *billion* of the world's population. The Oxfam executive director, Winnie Byanyima, said: 'It is staggering that in the 21st Century, half of the world's population – that's three and a half *billion* people – own no more than a tiny elite whose numbers could all fit comfortably on a double-decker bus.'

Oxfam also argues that this is no accident, saying that growing inequality has been driven by a 'power grab' by wealthy elites, who have co-opted the political process to *rig the rules of the economic system in their favour*. The report found that over the past few decades, the rich have successfully wielded political influence to skew specific policies in their favour on issues ranging from financial deregulation, tax havens, anti-competitive business practices to lower tax rates on high incomes and cuts in public services for the majority. See earlier and below regarding several books detailing the negative liaison between politicians, corporations and the military and also the strident views of early US presidents about the dangers of corporations corrupting the political process, e.g. Thomas Jefferson, President of the USA **18**01-09.

Since the late 1970s, tax rates for the richest have fallen in 29 out of 30 countries for which data is available, said the report. This 'capture of opportunities' by the rich at the expense of the poor and middle classes has led to a situation where 70% of the world's population live in countries where inequality has increased since the 1980s and 1% of families own 46% of the global wealth – almost £70 trillion. It's interesting to note that in Denmark, for example, not only are tax rates *higher* than for many countries including the UK, but BBC documentaries have shown that there is widespread support for this. Broadly speaking, the Danes view taxes as their contribution to their fair society. The Personal Income Tax Rate in Denmark stands at 55.60 per cent. The Personal Income Tax Rate in Denmark averaged 61.40 per cent from 1995 until 2014, reaching an all-time high of 65.90 per cent in 1997 and a record low of 55.40 percent in 2010. My personal experience on scientific visits to Denmark is that the Danes are widely proud of their relatively just society. It's hard not to reflect on the boast of USA President Donald Trump that he paid no tax (for years) because 'I'm smart'! And now the USA cabinet *includes* numerous lobbyists and leaders of fake 'think tanks' (e.g. energy companies sponsored) deniers of global warming.

GDP ($ trillion) World Bank (2014)
Note: IMF, UN and CIA World Factbook (2003-2015) list closely similar figures.

1. European Union as a whole 18.5
2. USA 17.4
3. China 10.4
4. Japan 4.6
5. Germany 3.9
6. UK 3.0
7. France 2.8
8. Brazil 2.4
9. Italy 2.1
10. India 2.1

Note: Members of the European Union (EU) are Austria, Belgium, Bulgaria, Croatia, Republic of Cyprus, Czech Republic, Denmark, Estonia, Finland, France, Germany, Greece, Hungary, Ireland, Italy, Latvia, Lithuania, Luxembourg, Malta, Netherlands, Poland, Portugal, Romania, Slovakia, Slovenia, Spain, Sweden and the UK*.

(* UK voted to leave in 2017)

UN World Happiness Report 2012-14
(Most happy at top)

1. Switzerland (7.587)
2. Iceland (7.561)
3. Denmark (7.527)
4. Norway (7.522)
5. Canada (7.427)
6. Finland (7.406)
7. Netherlands (7.378)
8. Sweden (7.364)
9. New Zealand (7.286)
10. Australia (7.284)

Present-day USA dysfunctional politics – a threat to the world
The data regarding the USA strongly suggests a dysfunctional, exceptionally divided state which is internally and externally violent. The political system is corrupt with anti-democratic malpractices regarding voting boundaries, massive lobbying by multinational commercial companies who enjoy numerous tax breaks, sometimes 100%, and pro-corporations' laws. The clear recognition of social danger from powerful, ultra-rich corporations goes back to the origins of the USA (New Constitution, 1789, Bill of Rights, 1791), as the earlier quotations by various presidents show (at the end of this section) and mentioned earlier. I hope that the reader will forgive my repetitions of the the numerous presidents who strongly opposed

the corrupt interference of corporations in the democratic process. An early example I repeat is from Thomas Jefferson, President of the USA (**1801**-09). He said:

> '*I hope we shall… crush in its birth the aristocracy of our moneyed corporations which dare already to challenge our government in a trial of strength, and bid defiance to the laws of our country.*'

Also, President Theodore Roosevelt's wise recommendation to stop financial contributions to political parties is as significant today as it was over a century ago. Nevertheless, a recent USA High Court Ruling *prevents restrictions* on party donations, i.e. 'game' over! The quotations from a couple of centuries ago also show the failure then to curb the corporations, which are now multinational. They have the expertise, corrupt intentions and computer power to avoid tax and even for individuals as well as corporations to hide money in tax 'havens'. Political parties receive campaign funds from ultra-rich corporations that have indisputable influences on political decisions. The game is now truly over. Now, they no longer have to buy influence. They are now within and full members of President Donald J. Trump's cabinet. Government by the people (the definition of democracy) has been replaced by government by the corporations. And news corporations (BBC and Fox News) and political leaders (Mrs Teresa May and all USA leaders) continue publicly to refer to the USA as the world's greatest democracy. The USA has the world's worst statistics (for nations that keep statistics) by far for social ailments such as crime of various kinds, obesity, prison populations. It's great in the sense of powerful. The USA spends as much on the military as the next 11 nations combined (about $600 billion per annum).

Also, Information Technology and Artificial Intelligence add to the massive power placed in the hands of the few, and huge sums of money make corruption easier. Alpha males and alpha corporations are doing what alphas characteristically do – expressing the power phenotype, snatching the best of everything for themselves, and taking it all for granted, as if by right. And to a large extent, the rest of us do what non-alphas characteristically do – either we follow the leaders and obey, or we don't even notice that 'the Emperor is naked'. And, as above, President Trump has put together a cabinet of the very people involved in these corrupt practices! This is referred to in more detail underneath and in the earlier section on 'Humanity's Key Problems'.

When I worked in the USA (Florida) in 1961 and witnessed its gross commercialisation, workers on a non-living wage and experienced the dodgy politics myself, what was extraordinarily shocking was the fact that these flaws were already analysed, clearly and accurately, and already published by numerous **USA** analysts. Yet, it seemed to make no difference! Now, in the 21st century, the widespread rigging by the most right-wing states has been investigated and continues to be analysed by eminent social commentators. Furthermore, such anti-democratic, cheating techniques are being considered by the right-wing Conservative Party in the UK (see later). This is clearly a continuing crisis of democracy and has been developing for centuries, exacerbated by rich, powerful interests hand in glove with the Republican Party and now in government.

Two books about democracy and elections detail the cheating. They are 'Democracy and Justice: collected writings' by Desiree Reiner and others from The Brenner Center for Justice (NYU Law School) and 'The voting wars: from Florida 2000 to the next election meltdown' by Richard Hasen. As in the case of 'Saving Capitalism', mentioned below, the reviewer also makes an exceptional contribution to this ugly story of democratic subversion: Elizabeth Drew reviews both books in The New York Review, May 21st 2015. She states that three overlooked dangers facing the democratic elections (then a year ahead) are voting restrictions, redistricting and loose rules on the large amounts of money being spent to influence voters. The two books amply illustrate the depths of the problems, notably the *successful* attempts to reduce the so-called 'black' and 'Hispanic' vote.

The books give 'chapter and verse' on the crooked behaviour. I quote from her review, based on published statistics: 'The lesson seems to be that once Republicans get total power at the State level, they find a way to rig the rules to keep the other side's strongest constituencies from voting.' Paul Krugman in The New York Review, December 17th 2015, reviewed Robert Reich's book 'Saving Capitalism: for the many, not the few'. His review comes under the apt title, 'Challenging the oligarchy'. The book and the review are illuminating regarding the 'vicious circle of oligarchy' that describes the US over the past generation. In the review, he takes the opportunity to consider the various theories accounting for the rise in inequality and associated social ills. Krugman is a Nobel Laureate in Economics, he writes with reason and clarity and deserves attention both for his ideas on Reich's book and for his own commentary. Needless to say, 'Saving Capitalism' deserves close attention. Reich calls for something akin to, as Krugman puts it, *'an uprising of workers against the quiet class war that America's oligarchy has been waging for decades'*. Krugman refers to 'the increasingly ugly turn taken by American politics' and to the 'rise and fall of the 'theory of skill-based technological change"' (SBTC). Krugman cites the evidence that SBTC does not account for the rising inequality and lagging wages. Nor does the evidence suggest that increasing workers' skills is plausible as a way towards more equality. Reich argues that inequality is fuelled by political decisions that were not inevitable. The role of monopolies is given prominence. As an example, Reich points out that US unionisation is down to 11 % (down from around a third) while in Canada (also previously at about a third) it's at 27%. He sees the unions to some extent as a potential counterbalance to political power. Reich points out (and Klugman agrees) that there's a feedback loop between political and market power. I quote from the review:

'Rising wealth at the top buys growing political influence, via campaign contributions, lobbying and the rewards of the revolving door. Political influence in turn is used to re-write the rules of the game – antitrust laws, deregulation, changes in contract law, union busting – in a way that re-enforces income concentration. The result is a sort of spiral, a vicious circle of oligarchy.'

And now, buying influence is not so necessary since President Donald Trump created his new cabinet out of the corporations.

The banking system

An especially important component in this spiral of oligarchy is the banking system. Banks, corporations and political power contribute to this vicious circle. Secret conspiracies by their nature are hard to prove, until at least some of the secrets are revealed. But when they are revealed by world-leading journalists with excellent personal qualifications and the events are deeply important, then they deserve attention. What follows is new to me and extraordinarily shocking as to the unlimited extent that the alpha males of banking, politics and the military conspire. It is also truly frightening. So, I would like to draw attention to an extraordinary lethal *conspiracy*.

Ellen Brown is an attorney, President of the Public Banking Institute and author of numerous books on public finance. Her websites are http://WebofDebt.com, http://PublicBankSolution.com and http://PublicBankingInstitute.org. In the 'Web of Debt' blog ('Making the World Safe for Banksters: Syria in the Cross-hairs', posted on September 4th, 2013), she writes about the shocking findings of investigations carried out by another eminent investigative journalist, Greg Palast. Greg Palast has been called the 'most important investigative reporter of our time – up there with Woodward and Bernstein' (*The Guardian*). Palast has broken front-page stories for *BBC Television Newsnight, The Guardian, Nation Magazine, Rolling Stone* and *Harper's Magazine*. Palast is the author of the *New York Times* bestsellers 'Billionaires & Ballot Bandits', 'Armed Madhouse', 'The Best Democracy Money Can Buy' and the highly acclaimed 'Vultures Picnic', named Book of the Year 2012 on BBC Newsnight Review. The USA is not short of accurate analysis of her problems and by USA writers.

Making the World Safe for Banksters: Syria in the Cross-hairs (September 4ᵗʰ 2013)

(What follows are direct quotations from Ellen Brown's scary 'Web of Debt' blog.) 'Iraq and Libya have been taken out, and Iran has been heavily boycotted. Syria is now in the cross-hairs. Why? Here is one overlooked scenario.'

(To the reader – please do not skip the following quotation. It's an extreme example of vitally important information about evildoing that is ignored: a $700-plus trillion pyramid scheme with catastrophic consequences.)

In an August 2013 article titled 'Larry Summers and the Secret 'End-game' Memo', Greg Palast posted evidence of a secret late-1990s plan devised by Wall Street and US Treasury officials to open banking to the lucrative derivatives business. To pull this off required the relaxation of banking regulations not just in the US but globally. The vehicle to be used was the Financial Services Agreement of the World Trade Organisation. The 'endgame' would require not just coercing support among WTO members but *taking down those countries refusing to join.* Some key countries remained holdouts from the WTO, including Iraq, Libya, Iran and Syria. In these Islamic countries, banks are largely state-owned; and 'usury' – charging rent for the 'use' of money – is viewed as a sin, if not a crime. That puts them at odds with the Western model of rent extraction by private middlemen. Publicly-owned banks are also a threat to the mushrooming derivatives business, since governments with their own banks don't need interest rate swaps, credit default swaps, or investment-grade ratings by private rating agencies in order to finance their operations.

Bank deregulation proceeded according to plan, and the government-sanctioned and nurtured derivatives business mushroomed into a $700-plus trillion pyramid scheme. Highly leveraged, completely unregulated, and dangerously unsustainable, it collapsed in 2008 when investment bank Lehman Brothers went bankrupt, taking a large segment of the global economy with it. The countries that managed to escape were those sustained by public banking models outside the international banking net. These countries were not all Islamic. Forty per cent of banks globally are publicly-owned. They are largely in the BRIC countries –Brazil, Russia, India and China – which house forty per cent of the global population. They also escaped the 2008 credit crisis, but they at least made a show of conforming to Western banking rules. This was not true of the 'rogue' Islamic nations, where usury was forbidden by Islamic teaching. To make the world safe for usury, these rogue states had to be silenced by other means. Having failed to succumb to economic coercion, they wound up in the crosshairs of the powerful US military.

Note regarding 'derivatives' (*The Washington Post* May 4, 2010)
In its simplest form, a derivative is a financial agreement between two entities that depends on something that occurs in the future, such as the performance of an underlying asset. That underlying asset could be a stock, a bond, a currency or a commodity. Although derivatives have been used effectively for three decades by institutions around the globe, they also have contributed to financial meltdowns, including those at Enron and the American International Group. In 2002, Berkshire Hathaway CEO Warren Buffett issued a warning about derivatives in an annual letter to shareholders. 'We view them as time bombs, both for the parties that deal in them and the economic system,' he wrote. 'Unless derivatives contracts are collateralized or guaranteed, their ultimate value also depends on the creditworthiness of the counterparties to them.'

'*The End-Game Memo*' (see appendix below). In his August 22nd article, 2013 Greg Palast posted a screenshot of a 1997 memo from Timothy Geithner, then Assistant Secretary of International Affairs under Robert Rubin, to Larry Summers, then Deputy Secretary of the Treasury. Geithner referred in the memo to the 'end-game of WTO financial services negotiations' and urged Summers to touch base with the CEOs of Goldman Sachs, Merrill Lynch, Bank of

America, Citibank, and Chase Manhattan Bank, for whom *private phone numbers were provided*. The game then in play was the deregulation of banks so that they could gamble in the lucrative new field of derivatives (*despite the above dire warning by Warren Buffett in 2002*). To pull this off required, first, the repeal of Glass-Steagall, the 1933 Act that imposed a firewall between investment banking and depository banking in order to protect depositors' funds from bank gambling. But the plan required more than just deregulating US banks. Banking controls had to be eliminated globally so that money would not flee to nations with safer banking laws. The 'endgame' was to achieve this global deregulation through an obscure addendum to the international trade agreements policed by the World Trade Organisation, called the Financial Services Agreement. 'Seven countries were named by US General Wesley Clark (Ret.) in a 2007 'Democracy Now' interview as the new 'rogue states' being targeted for take down after September 11, 2001. He said that about 10 days after 9-11, he was told by a general that the decision had been made to go to war with Iraq. Later, the same general said they planned to take out seven countries in five years: Iraq, Syria, Lebanon, Libya, Somalia, Sudan and Iran. What did these countries have in common? Besides being Islamic, they were not members either of the WTO or of the Bank for International Settlements (BIS). That left them outside the long regulatory arm of the central bankers' central bank in Switzerland.' Further details of Greg Palast's explosive 'End-Game Memo' are given as an appendix at the end of this section.

Another especially potent danger comes when a corporation is an armaments manufacturer. Nations need arms to defend themselves (or to be aggressors) and cosy, profitable relationships develop. This is exacerbated by the colossal, *multi-billion dollar* costs of weaponry Some extraordinary and massive blunders in defence projects have been exposed by the 'alternative' organisation called 'AlterNet' (www.alternet.org/ 'Syndication service and online community of the alternative press, featuring news stories from alternative newsweeklies, magazines and web publications').

As I write this, I have an eerie feeling that this also describes trends in the UK, accelerated by a right-wing Tory government. Robert Reich ('Saving Capitalism: for the many, not the few'), mentioned above, calls for several changes to reverse this purchased influence, such as raising the minimum wage, reversing the anti-union laws and changing contract law to allow debtors and workers redress against creditors and employers. He also calls for changes in corporation law in an attempt to make corporations answerable to more than shareholders, such as customers and workers. Paul Klugman is cautious about the possible success of the proposals but hopes there may be synergy between them. He is even more cautious about Reich's optimism that political change will bring about these changes. For any reader interested, Klugman writes regularly in the New York Times (for example, 'Doubling Down on W'. The Opinion Pages, OP-ED December 28, 2015).

What some early US presidents thought about the harmful political influence of corporate wealth
The following is somewhat repetitive from earlier, but again emphasises how very long ago the above problems had already been recognised. If the presidents of the USA from more than a *couple of hundred years ago* (see earlier quotations) saw these problems so clearly, then it would seem that we have little hope of eradicating the mighty influence of large corporations and big money. This is especially so if corporations can continue to fund political parties and undermine democracy itself. Perhaps attraction to money is the biological equivalent of gravity in physics – it's always there. And now we have Donald Trump bringing into his cabinet the very people denounced by these previous presidents. Corporations will need to bribe less and simply make the laws themselves, facilitating the paying of less taxes and with less workers' rights such as a living wage, vacations, pensions or belonging to a union. The latter human rights are frequently sneered at as 'unnecessary bureaucracy' or

'the nanny state'. 'Government by the people' is being replaced by 'government by the corporations'.

As a 'PS' to the banking mega scandal, details have emerged of dozens of Western financial institutions that processed at least $20 billion of Russian criminal cash through Latvia during the period 2010-2014 (Harding and Hopkins, The Guardian, 21st March 2017). The scheme was called the 'Global Laundromat'. Details of the complex, criminal scam have emerged. Politically powerful Russians laundered $ billions of Russian money via UK-registered companies. Also involved was the Deutsche Bank, who lent $300 million to Donald J. Trump.

Election to USA Presidency of Donald J. Trump

The above presidential quotations indicate that the election of Donald J. Trump as President of the USA and the composition of his cabinet are the consequence of events from even *before* the election of Thomas Jefferson (**18**01-09). As emphasised above, Jefferson and numerous other presidents warned against the corrupting influence of corporations on democratic politics. *Buying* laws favouring corporations in terms of taxes and labour laws against unions, living wages, pensions, vacations and reasonable working hours *harms democracy*. (Oxford Dictionary: democracy is government by the people; a principle is that all citizens have equal political rights.) The corporations have gradually and relentlessly increased their power.

The situation is made worse by the mega increases in the power of Information Technology (IT) and Artificial Intelligence (AI). This further facilitates the ever-increasing closeness of corporations, political parties (notably right wing) and the military-industrial complex (mostly right wing). *And now they are in the White House.*

Thomas Jefferson and other early presidents must be turning in their noble graves.

How to humanise and thus improve US society

With a view to answering needs, harmonising primate instincts and expressing the human
Bearing in mind our instincts and our basic needs for safety, food, shelter, a sense of community and the need for inclusive political and economic structures, a major task of the state is to reverse these growing trends of inequality, with their awful correlates of social ills. Also needing reversal is the corrupt integration of corporations and politicians. But numerous segments of the US state are willing partners in the corruption and approve and benefit from it. George Orwell's insights in his book '1984' are worth repeating. 'Power is not a means; it is an end… The object of power is power.' Similarly, Bertrand Russell in 'Power: a new social analysis' argued that the key to 'human nature' is power. He argues that power is 'man's ultimate goal, and in its numerous forms is the single most important element in the development of any society. These ideas are compatible with the evolutionary survival mechanism of having alpha males who facilitate group survival, described at length earlier.

Suggestions
Suggestions are made with much hesitation, given that the USA is so dysfunctional. As evidence, despite Donald Trump's unprecedented abuse during and before the campaign of his opponent, Hilary Clinton, and also of foreigners, immigrants, gays, the left (i.e. racism, xenophobia, homophobia and misogyny), he was elected by a comfortable majority, including support by about 80% of evangelical Christians.

1. <u>All</u> the earlier, detailed suggestions about making political systems truly *representative* apply, are needed and would help. But the current emergency is unlikely to change and is getting worse. Donald Trump is doing the opposite of what's needed. The USA is dysfunctional as the interests of the corporations dominate.

2. Robert Reich's book 'Saving Capitalism: for the many, not the few', referred to earlier, was reviewed by Paul Krugman ('Challenging the oligarchy') in The New York Review, December 17th 2015. I quote Krugman's summary of what the book advocates: '...*an uprising of workers against the quiet class war that America's oligarchy has been waging for decades*'.

3. Reich's suggestions could be less effective than a *coordinated* campaign by the numerous internet groups. How can an 'uprising of workers' be coordinated and how can it be kept non-violent? Using internet groups is realistic. It's urgent that the internet anti-injustice groups come together, e.g. Amnesty International (https://www.amnesty.org.uk), the network Avaaz (avaaz.org), SumOfUs.org (us@sumofus.org), the 'Occupy' Movement (occupywallstreet.org), 38 Degrees (38degrees.org.uk), WeMove.EU, Change.org, Truthout (messenger@truthout.org) and numerous and increasingly others.

4. Humanising the USA by providing a universal health service for all out of taxes is vital. Currently, such a move is described as socialism. In the USA, as a result of relentless propaganda, this word has been separated from social and come broadly to mean evil.

5. Enable the provision of affordable housing with communal facilities, suitable for humans.

6. USA President should seek discussions with other world leaders with a view to *worldwide* cooperation regarding the following current and imminent global problems:
   i) Improvements in health; and
   ii) Housing provision; and
   iii) Coping with the imminent loss of employment worldwide.

Question: Can the USA afford these suggestions?

Answer: Yes, it can. It's about the *priorities* of the 'alphas'. Reduce the USA's 'defence budget'. This is about $600 billion and is by far the largest in the world. *It is broadly equal to the total budget of the next 11 nations.* Why so large? One likely explanation is that it satisfies the instinctive alpha ambitions of the top alpha state with its top alpha leaders: 'sitting at the top table'. In addition, it enriches the alphas of the military-industrial complex, including the mega, mega-rich arms manufacturers.

Another suggestion is an increase in taxation for the rich and ultra-rich. Thus, spend less on armaments, tax the rich more and move towards a more human, happy country such as Denmark with several-fold less bad social statistics such as murder and petty crime.

An example of 'socialism' of a kind in the USA – a commercial model for any country

During my collaboration with colleagues at Stanford University, I was invited to join a start-up biotech company as Chief Scientific Officer. This company was at a very early stage and did not occupy much time, mainly occasional lunch-time meetings. It gave me an insight into the origins of the many hundreds of biotech and IT companies in California, especially in the Bay area. I have referred to this earlier. I was able to compare it with my experience as a board member of a UK Science Park and as consultant to several major pharmaceutical companies. The major feature was the low level of any bureaucracy. Essentially, the US government funded fundamental research at universities on numerous topics including information technology, artificial intelligence, molecular biology and biotechnology. The National Institute of Health (NIH) is an example. When a novel, commercially interesting possibility was discovered, it was developed by the university investigator and with the university having, by UK standards, very generous terms regarding the subsequent distribution of profits. Given that only a small proportion of 'start-ups' succeed, the university avoided the cost of a large department to manage innovation. Also, very generous arrangements to staff regarding distribution of profits reduced the possibility of staff 'moonlighting' to keep control and enhance financial gain.

Alternatively, someone could choose to develop ideas by starting a new, independent company. This was the origin of the company I was invited to join. The process was to visit a legal firm who consulted independent, eminent experts. If they thought that the project was good, then the firm provided legal help free of charge until profit was achieved. When the company became profitable, then the *first* call on payment was by the legal firm who was paid very, very handsomely. A common practice was for workers (not always all) in independent start-ups to be paid modestly but receive shares/partnerships in the company. For example, it was common to be at dinner in a restaurant in the Palo Alto area and see groups of people with laptops working intently and cheerfully. Often, they would be joined by their spouses for a late dinner. In an important sense they were partners in the company, somewhat similar to John Lewis in the UK.

This approach of involving staff in a form of cooperative was highly successful commercially. California, when seen as if a nation state, now has the 6th largest economy in the world. Also, socially, staff definitely belong.

Appendix

Ellen Brown's blog regarding the secret 'End-Game Memo'

I ask the reader not to skip this just because it's an appendix. 'Normal', typical non-alphas may find it hard/impossible to believe what it says. I did, despite being in my 80s. I recommend that the following is read twice. This is the way the world 'works' (or rather doesn't work). <u>This appendix is an exact copy of the blog</u>.

Making the World Safe for Banksters: Syria in the Cross-hairs
Posted on September 4th, 2013 by Ellen Brown in her blog

> *'The powers of financial capitalism had another far-reaching aim, nothing less than to create a world system of financial control in private hands able to dominate the political system of each country and the economy of the world as a whole.'*
> **Professor Caroll Quigley, Georgetown University, 'Tragedy and Hope' (1966).**

Iraq and Libya have been taken out, and Iran has been heavily boycotted. Syria is now in the cross-hairs. Why? Here is one overlooked scenario.

In an August 2013 article titled "Larry Summers and the Secret 'End-game' Memo," Greg Palast posted evidence of a secret late-1990s plan devised by Wall Street and U.S. Treasury officials to open banking to the lucrative derivatives business. To pull this off required the relaxation of banking regulations not just in the US but globally. The vehicle to be used was the Financial Services Agreement of the World Trade Organization. The "end-game" would require not just coercing support among WTO members but taking down those countries refusing to join. Some key countries remained holdouts from the WTO, including Iraq, Libya, Iran and Syria. In these Islamic countries, banks are largely state-owned; and "usury" – charging rent for the "use" of money – is viewed as a sin, if not a crime. That puts them at odds with the Western model of rent extraction by private middlemen. Publicly-owned banks are also a threat to the mushrooming derivatives business, since governments with their own banks don't need interest rate swaps, credit default swaps, or investment-grade ratings by private rating agencies in order to finance their operations.

Bank deregulation proceeded according to plan, and the government-sanctioned and -nurtured derivatives business mushroomed into a $700-plus trillion pyramid scheme. Highly leveraged, completely unregulated, and dangerously unsustainable, it collapsed in 2008 when investment bank Lehman Brothers went bankrupt, taking a large segment of the global economy with it. The countries that managed to escape were those sustained by public banking models outside the international banking net. These countries were not all Islamic. <u>Forty percent of banks globally</u> are publicly-owned. They are largely in the BRIC countries - Brazil, Russia, India and China - which house forty percent of the global population. They also escaped the 2008 credit crisis, but they at least made a show of conforming to Western banking rules. This was not true of the "rogue" Islamic nations, where usury was forbidden by Islamic teaching. To make the world *safe for usury*, these rogue states had to be silenced by other means. Having failed to succumb to economic coercion, they wound up in the crosshairs of the powerful US military. Here is some data in support of that thesis.

The End-game Memo

In his August 22nd article, Greg Palast posted a screenshot of a 1997 memo from Timothy Geithner, then Assistant Secretary of International Affairs under Robert Rubin, to Larry Summers, then Deputy Secretary of the Treasury. Geithner referred in the memo to the "end-game of WTO financial services negotiations" and urged Summers to touch base with the CEOs of Goldman Sachs, Merrill Lynch, Bank of America, Citibank, and Chase Manhattan Bank, for whom private phone numbers were provided. The game then in play was the deregulation of banks so that they could gamble in the lucrative new field of derivatives. To pull this off required, first, the repeal of Glass-Steagall, the 1933 Act that imposed a firewall between investment banking and depository banking in order to protect depositors' funds from bank gambling. But the plan required more than just deregulating US banks. Banking controls had to be eliminated globally so that money would not flee to nations with safer banking laws. The 'endgame' was to achieve this global deregulation through an obscure addendum to the international trade agreements policed by the World Trade Organization, called the Financial Services Agreement.

This is what Palast wrote. 'Until the bankers began their play, the WTO agreements dealt simply with trade in goods –that is, my cars for your bananas. The new rules ginned-up by Summers and the banks would force all nations to accept trade in "bads" – toxic assets like financial derivatives. Until the bankers' re-draft of the FSA, each nation controlled and chartered the banks within their own borders. The new rules of the game would force every nation to open their markets to Citibank, JP Morgan (*added fact*: JPM's CEO earns around $23 million per annum) and their derivatives "products." And all 156 nations in the WTO would have to smash down their own Glass-Steagall divisions between commercial savings banks and the investment banks that gamble with derivatives. The job of turning the FSA into the bankers' battering ram was given to Geithner, who was named 'Ambassador to the World Trade Organization.'WTO members were induced to sign the agreement by receiving threats regarding their access to global markets if they refused; and they all did sign, except Brazil. Brazil was then threatened with an embargo; but its resistance paid off, since it alone among Western nations survived and thrived during the 2007-2009 crisis. As for the others: the new FSA pulled the lid off the Pandora's box of the worldwide derivatives trade. Among the notorious transactions legalised: Goldman Sachs (*where Treasury Secretary Rubin had been Co-Chairman*) worked a secret euro-derivatives swap with Greece which, ultimately, destroyed that nation. Ecuador, its own banking sector deregulated and demolished, exploded into riots. Argentina had to sell off its oil companies (to the Spanish) and water systems (to Enron) while its teachers hunted for food in garbage cans. Then, bankers gone wild in the Eurozone dived head first into derivatives pools without knowing how to swim – and the continent is now being sold off in tiny, cheap pieces to Germany.

The holdouts

That was the fate of countries in the WTO, but Palast did not discuss those that were not in that organisation at all, including Iraq, Syria, Lebanon, Libya, Somalia, Sudan and Iran. These seven countries were named by US General Wesley Clark (Ret.) in a 2007 'Democracy Now' interview as the new 'rogue states', being targeted for take down after September 11, 2001. He said that about ten days after 9-11, he was told by a general that the decision had been made to go to war with Iraq. Later, the same general said they planned to take out seven countries in five years: Iraq, Syria, Lebanon, Libya, Somalia, Sudan and Iran. What did these countries have in common? Besides being Islamic, they were not members either of the WTO or of the Bank for International Settlements (BIS). That left them outside the long regulatory arm of the central bankers' central bank in Switzerland. Other countries later identified as 'rogue states' which were also not members of the BIS included North Korea, Cuba and Afghanistan. The body regulating banks today is called the Financial Stability Board (FSB), and it is housed in the BIS in Switzerland. In 2009, the heads of the G20 nations agreed to be bound by rules imposed by the FSB, ostensibly to prevent another global banking crisis. Its regulations are not merely advisory but are binding, and they can make or break not just banks but whole nations. This was first demonstrated in 1989, when the Basel I Accord raised capital requirements a mere 2%, from 6% to 8%. The result was to force a drastic reduction in lending by major Japanese banks, which were then the world's largest and most powerful creditors. They were undercapitalised, however, relative to other banks. The Japanese economy sank along with its banks and has yet to fully recover. Among other game-changing regulations in play under the FSB are Basel III and the new bail-in rules. Basel III is scheduled to impose crippling capital requirements on public, cooperative and community banks, coercing their sale to large multinational banks.

The 'bail-in' template was first tested in Cyprus and follows regulations imposed by the FSB in 2011. Too-big-to-fail banks are required to <u>draft 'living wills'</u> setting forth how they will avoid insolvency in the absence of government bailouts. The FSB solution is to 'bail in' creditors – including depositors – turning deposits into bank stock, effectively confiscating them.

The public bank alternative

Countries labouring under the yoke of an extractive private banking system are being forced into 'structural adjustment' and austerity by their unrepayable debt. But some countries have managed to escape. In the Middle East, these are the targeted 'rogue nations'. Their state-owned banks can issue the credit of the state on behalf of the state, leveraging public funds for public use without paying a massive tribute to private middlemen. Generous state funding allows them to provide generously for their people. Like Libya and Iraq before they were embroiled in war, Syria provides free education at all levels and free medical care. It also provides subsidised housing for everyone (although some of this has been compromised by adoption of an IMF structural adjustment programme in 2006 and the presence of about two million Iraqi and Palestinian refugees). Iran too provides nearly free higher education and primary health care. Like Libya and Iraq before their 'takedown', Syria and Iran have state-owned central banks that issue the national currency and are under government control. Whether these countries will succeed in maintaining their financial sovereignty in the face of enormous economic, political and military pressure remains to be seen.

As for Larry Summers, he went on to become President of Harvard, where he approved a derivative bet on interest rate swaps that lost over $1 billion for the university. He resigned in 2006 to manage a hedge fund among other business activities and went on to become State Senator Barack Obama's key campaign benefactor. Summers played a key role in the banking deregulation that brought on the current crisis, causing millions of US citizens to lose their jobs and their homes. Yet he is President Obama's first choice to replace Ben Bernanke as Federal Reserve Chairman. Why? He has proven he can manipulate the system to make the world safe for Wall Street; and in an upside-down world in which bankers' rule, that seems to be the name of the game.

A simple way to seeking out the greatest corruption
'Follow the money'

The mega rich, obviously not all, with mega influence and their financing of *bogus* 'think tanks' that misrepresent the ill effects of mega-rich industries are associated with big money industries. These industries are: armaments, finance (aided by IT and AT), energy (oil, gas, petrol), health services (in the USA, not available for everyone), tobacco, alcohol, illicit drugs and 'organised crime' generally.

On the assumption that money is power and that the mega rich alphas are seeking power, at least partly instinctively, via their fake think tanks and spurious publications, then the USA has reached the final stages of the objectives of the financial alphas – political control.

    a. A law has now been passed that the corporations cannot be prevented in influencing politics and politicians with finance and

    b. Their agents, appointed by President Donald Trump. are now in the White House. And characteristic of his personal administration, they are leaving or being sacked in unprecedented, large numbers as I write (March 2018).

Recognising the influence of biological evolution on the UK
With a view to answering needs, harmonising primate instincts and expressing the human

The UK is not only adjusting to its loss of power, wealth and empire, it is also becoming less equal and is increasingly exhibiting the correlated higher levels of crime and numerous other bad social statistics. It's the country where I live and so did my parents and grandparents and far beyond, but with one granddad originating from France. In addition to the suggestions listed previously about humanising the state, the UK deserves special scrutiny regarding the 'economy' and 'security'. Like the USA, the UK is moving in the wrong direction – that is, up the inequality graph which correlates with adverse social and crime statistics. It is two places below the top and most unequal country, the USA (see 'The Spirit Level' by Wilkinson and Pickett). It should be noted that inequality *per se* is not the issue, but the bad correlations are. A good word that integrates the bad effects is 'belonging' or not belonging. Not belonging is associated with numerous antisocial consequences. Mentioned earlier, the idea of not belonging for lower animals, if they could think as humans, would make no sense and be unintelligible. Not belonging equates with not surviving. Another overall word re equality is *power*. Plotting income difference against incidence of adverse social statistics such as theft, murder, rape and prison populations could as well plot relative power. Relative power is crudely measured by relative wealth. Lack of belonging and lack of power are commonly linked.

Once, just before a microbiology conference in Anaheim, USA, a small group of us asked for advice regarding an art gallery or museum to visit. We were told that there was none. None at all? No. A friendly person recommended that we visit a shopping mall. Today in Britain, we are moving in a similar way with cuts for art galleries and libraries and even parks. UK Local Councils are raising cash by privatising parks or sections of parks. A report by The Heritage Lottery Fund estimated that 45% of UK local authorities are considering selling parks and green spaces or transferring their management. It's most likely to affect small spaces, especially those in metropolitan areas, i.e. land is valuable <u>financially</u> as well as socially. If 'we' (i.e. 'them') continue to cut taxes, then the likelihood is that social services of all kinds will be cut. *Primate alpha males do not see parks, art galleries and libraries as important as <u>high-status armaments</u>, armies and <u>seats at top tables with other alphas</u>.*

Our UK right-wing Conservative government is emphasising

the economy (the increase in GDP, with all the extra income going to the 'few', as in the USA) and 'security'. Extra consideration is now given to 'security', notably the ultra-expensive (approximately £200 billion over a decade) Trident with nobody and no place to aim at, but it gives our alpha leader(s) an extraordinarily expensive seat at the 'top table' and much money to the UK arms industry. Anti-terrorism, imperial overseas wars, *overseas bases and their costs*, the military, navy and air force are all enormously costly to the UK in terms of money and social decline. The UK is no longer the world's superpower. As pointed out previously, tax cuts favoured by the 'right' result in reduced social services. As is the case for the USA, there is no link between the UK's position high on the GDP list (6th) and its relatively low position on the happiness index (21st).

The UK Gig economy
What is the so-called 'gig' economy, a phrase increasingly in use, and seemingly so regarding employment disputes (see The Guardian 7th July 2017)? According to one definition, it's a labour market characterised by the prevalence of short-term contracts or freelance work, as opposed to permanent jobs. It can be presented as either a working environment that offers flexibility regarding employment hours, or it's a form of exploitation with very few workplace rights and little protection. In the gig economy, instead of a regular wage, workers get paid for the 'gigs' they do, such as a food delivery or a car journey. In the UK, it's estimated (2017) that *five million people* are employed in this type of capacity and contributing to a rise in employment figures.

The latest attempt to bring a degree of legal clarity to the employment status of people in the gig economy has been playing out in the UK Court of Appeal. A London firm, Pimlico Plumbers, lost its appeal (2017) against a previous ruling that said that one of its long-serving plumbers was a worker – entitled to basic rights, including holiday pay – rather than an independent contractor.

A UK government study (report, July 2017) into the gig economy was chaired by Frank Field MP. In one case, *employees were required to sign a contract forbidding them from challenging their employment status.* Field stated that such contracts were 'too often characterised by poverty wages, chronic insecurity and appalling treatment'. Like other UK cases of a similar nature, the outcome will now be closely scrutinised for what it means regarding the workplace rights of the five million people employed in the gig economy in the UK.

How to win elections – a biological approach

As I type these words, the UK government has granted high social status via a knighthood to the person thought to be largely responsible for the Conservative Party (with David Cameron as leader) win in a previous general election. It was described as being given for his contribution to 'politics'. In fact, it was for successful electioneering, which is somewhat different to 'politics'. I refer to this because the strategy of the Conservatives coincided with a focus on basic, primate instincts (the *'message'*). The strategy comprised of overall survival via 'the economy'; fear of the foreign (Europe); territory (again Europe) and a successful, coordinated attack on the opponent leader's qualities as a <u>leader</u>. The attacks were not refuting his ideas with better ones, they were sneers and ridicule. He was not, <u>definitely not,</u> an alpha male. The Labour Party leader was presented by the almost entirely right-wing press as awkward, odd, clumsy and could not even eat a sandwich decently (pictures of his 'failure to do so' appeared in <u>all</u> the right-wing press) – he was definitely not a leader. The Conservative leader remained closely aligned to the message, relentlessly looking like and speaking as a strong, confident leader. In this campaign, the Conservatives were supported closely in terms of their 'message' by the right-wing, Conservative press. His appearance of being a 'true' leader: height, clothing, upper-class accent, schooling and 'breeding' did not prevent him and previous leaders from making bad mistakes.

These external marks of leadership, which worked well for alpha apes living in trees, are not so effective in identifying leaders in massive human populations living on the ground.

In an even earlier general election, a similar campaign was successful. The right-wing press published articles and pictures of another Labour leader (Neil Kinnock) who was so clumsy that he could not walk along a beach without falling. The coordinated press campaign was relentless and always 'on message'. Of course, if numerous photographers follow someone and _select only_ those occasions and pictures when someone is sneezing, slipping, blowing their nose or awkwardly eating a large, multi-layered burger sandwich, then a coordinated campaign can portray _anyone_ as un-leader-like. Any undecided voter, of which there were about 25% in the last election, pausing over the ballot paper could well be impelled by instinct and go for a 'real', true leader. If there's to be a prize for ruthless, focussed and successful _electioneering_, then the Conservative Party advisor, mentioned above, definitely deserves it. It's noteworthy that _on the very day_ that the current Labour leader, Jeremy Corbyn, was elected as leader by a massive margin, he was subjected to the same _non-rational_, coordinated attacks on his non-leader-like qualities by the Tory press (or rather the mega-rich, non-UK-resident, right-wing, 'press barons' and their unscrupulous PR advisors).

It seems clear that outside Parliament, there is widespread support for Labour taking a new direction. Very significantly, Corbyn's campaign was helped by a surge in new members and supporters who paid £3 to take part in the vote, leading to a near-_tripling_ of those eligible to about 550,000 people. Unexpectedly, throughout the campaign, he addressed packed rallies and halls, so full that he had to give speeches outside the buildings to crowds gathered in the street. Corbyn's ideas are attractive to numerous people outside the parliamentary party and who think that the Labour Party had become 'Tory-lite'. He has apologised for the Iraq war and is strongly opposing cuts to public services and welfare. He began his leadership with a speech to a rally in London in support of refugees. He was not attacked rationally for these ideas, he was subjected to sneers and derision for his non-leader-like *appearance* and because such ideas (opposing a war, opposing welfare cuts and supporting refugees) *are too absurd to consider*. Further consideration to Jeremy Corbyn's treatment by the UK media is given in the section on 'Media' later.

The UK Conservatives, since their election, have been quietly changing the rules of elections. They've altered constituency boundaries in their favour, reduced finance to opposition parties and squeezed out young urban voters. In 2016, they have axed student grants and disenfranchised 800,000 students and young people by contentious new voter registration rules. These changes are being pushed through via an obscure parliamentary committee and without full debate in the UK House of Commons. In 2017, student loans are loaded with an interest charge (~6 %) several-fold greater than normal bank charges. If this all sounds familiar, it's because you've just read the same thing earlier about USA Republicans. Just as US Republicans and rich corporations have got ever closer, rich UK multinational corporations and the Conservative Party have started to do the same: money talks in the UK as in the USA. This is driven by the same *social biology / pathology*.

Currently Europe has a genuine, large-scale refugee crisis with tens of millions of humans displaced. There is also fear of terror attacks and possibly the refugees may harbour some terrorists. They are all foreign, many are Muslims, and the rich and Christian UK will accept only a small number to save itself from misery. Some Muslim countries, such as politically remarkable and tolerant Jordan, have accepted huge numbers of refugees. Jordan is mainly Sunni, but is tolerant of other religions and sects. But even rich Muslim countries are not all helping, in some cases because the refugees belong to the wrong version of Islam, reminiscent of the split in Christianity between Catholicism and Protestantism. Sadly, this refugee crisis continues with little help from official Christian Britain or its official Christian leaders, including the Queen as Head of the Church of England.

Suggestions on how to humanise and thus improve UK society

With a view to answering needs, harmonising primate instincts and expressing the human

As for all nation states, bearing in mind our instincts, our basic needs for safety, food, shelter and a sense of community, there is a proven need for inclusive political and economic structures. These facilitate happy communities and most importantly, healthy, well-developed children. All the earlier, detailed suggestions about making the political system truly representative apply and would definitely help *if applied*. But the current situation with its skewed distribution of power is unlikely to change and is getting rapidly worse. A major task of the state is now to reverse the trends of inequality and the corrupt integration of corporations and politicians, which is accelerating in the UK. But, as in the USA and other states, numerous components are willing partners in the corruption and approve and benefit from it. Nevertheless, a hopeful development is the use of social media by numerous individuals to change things and expose injustice (listed in the section on the USA above).

In other European countries with large immigrant communities, such as Belgium and France, it has been a custom to place them in isolated locations outside major towns in ghettos. It's in such places that radicalisation can take place, breeding antagonism towards the alien original population. These immigrants are foreign with a foreign language, foreign customs, foreign religion and foreign appearance. Primates are frightened of the foreign and tend to treat them accordingly. It's hardly surprising that the foreigners feel unwanted and not belonging: they *are* not wanted and do not belong! A greater degree of integration is needed if antagonism or even terrorism is to be avoided. Help early on with learning the indigenous language and local customs, as well as housing would greatly improve things. Writing as an agnostic, but with a great admiration for Jesus's teaching, it would help if the advice in Saint Matthew's gospel were followed. One criterion for entry to Heaven was listed by Jesus (as the Messiah,

Christ) shortly before his death, as helping strangers/foreigners (other criteria consisted of other basic human needs). The official *Christian* Church of England should speak up, even at the risk of being attacked ('...*when I was a stranger, you took me into your home...*'). After all, it's what Jesus taught, although very shortly afterwards he was executed in an excruciatingly painful way. Abbé Pierre, when asked if he approved of expenditure on public art, said yes, when the last homeless person is off the streets. I wonder what the UK Tory press barons today would make of Jesus in Matthew **25**, 31-46? My guess is that they'd say it's from a hard-left, idealist extremist who doesn't live in the real world.

Create new structures to humanise society

Small-scale ways to accelerate adjustment from a
UK imperial world power

- Ask the UK government to set up a small team to visit countries excelling in child care and in being human in order to learn from them, e.g. Scandinavia. Then endow a Centre for the Study of How to Humanise Society, out of taxes. To include 1 x Professor, 2 x Fellows, 2 x PhD Students, 1 x Secretary, travel costs; housed (heating, lighting, rooms, furniture) in a university and to pay overheads. Publicise worldwide best practice. Site in a Social Sciences setting. Publish papers and other literature and advise government.

    This same team to study the possible extended use of schools in the evenings and vacations for social purposes.

    Costing about £1 million <u>per annum</u>

- Government to endow 5 Regional Poet Laureates, including travel expenses, on 5 (or maybe 3 years so seen as short term) year contracts. Tax-free £35 K per annum + travel expenses of £2K per annum.

    Costs £185K <u>per annum</u>.

- Government to endow 5 Regional Folk Singers, including travel expenses, for 5 (or maybe 3 years, so seen as short term). Tax-free £35 K pa + travel expenses of £2K pa.
  Costs £185K pa.

- Government to endow hostels/rehabilitation centres for homeless and/or addicted people for 10 major cities in addition to existing national structures. Food, sleeping accommodation and advice from part-time medical staff and advisors. Use existing buildings.
  Costs 10 x £2 million, i.e. £20 million pa.

- Government to endow free centres/child-care nurseries on 100 most deprived *working-class* housing estates. To be attached to a new, purpose-built social centre with facilities for meetings, small library and subsidised cafe. Build and equip at start for £2 million. Run by professional nursery personnel with paid help by residents.
  Building costs year 1 approx £200 million.
  Approx. running costs at 3 full-time Nursery Nurses, 2 P/T Helpers, 1 Secretary, heating lighting, maintenance, etc. Approx. running costs £250K pa.
  Totals: Approx. running costs £22 million pa. Approx. capital costs, one-off £200 million.

Q: Could, for example, the UK afford it?
A: At first consideration, it seemed obvious that it was unaffordable and not a priority. The following calculation suggests strongly that it is affordable, but 'they' don't wish to do it.

Take it from the Defence Budget of £45.6 *billion*. The one-off £200 million is about 0.004 % of the budget; the annual £22 million is about 0.0005% of the Defence Budget. See below.

Estimated UK Government spending 2017

Total Spending	£784.1 billion
Penions	£156.9 billion
Healthcare	£142.7 billion
Education	£85.2 billion
Defence	£45.6 billion
Welfare	£113.1 billion

Providing homes

Estimated costs of tackling the UK housing crisis

Habitat for Humanity (UK) reports that nationally over 3 million people are significantly impacted by the high cost of housing and 600,000 children in *London* live under the UK poverty line (Habitat for Humanity: Global Housing Charity Fighting Poverty. https://www.habitatforhumanity.org.uk/ E-mail: hello@habitatforhumanity.org.uk). In December 2016, there were several heavyweight reports that investigated Britain's housing crisis. The Redfern review (www.redfernreview.org/) is an independent review into the causes of falling home ownership. It details the catastrophic slump in home ownership, how real house prices have jumped 151% since 1996, while real earnings have risen only about a quarter as much. The ResPublica think tank (www.respublica.org.uk/) is also an independent non-partisan think tank that seeks to establish a new economic, social and cultural settlement for the United Kingdom. Its report described how 1.2 million people are languishing on housing waiting lists in England, while *more than 6 million* face tenure insecurity and no prospect of ever buying their own home. The Lyons Housing Commission (www.housing.org.uk/), an independent group of 12 housing experts chaired by Sir Michael Lyons, reminds us how, after decades of failure to build the homes the country needs, public concern about housing is the highest it has been for 40 years. This review was welcomed by the BSRIA (The Building Services Research and Information

Association). For this account, I have also relied on articles by Liam Halligan and his BBC Dispatches documentary, 'Britain's home-building scandal' and articles in the 'Spectator'.

A huge problem with housing is that to make a significant impact, the sums of money required are huge (of course, one new home helps one family). Britain's housing stock is worth £6 trillion. A billion or two spent here and there on HomeBuy (2005), Open Market HomeBuy (2006), First Buy (2011) and Help to Buy (2013) has been regarded as a waste of taxpayers' money. During the lifetime of these schemes, fewer and fewer young adults and families have been able to buy. It takes tens of billions to make a difference. Cranking up building to the 200,000 + units a year most experts say we need as a minimum, remains a dream; we don't have the money, the land or the workers to build them.

What is the UK housing crisis about? The housing crisis isn't simply about houses – it's about people. On the one hand, it's about very rich alpha males seeking ever more money. It's about powerful, alpha political parties putting housing low on their list of priorities. On a human level, it's about the family struggling to meet next month's mortgage payment and the young family renting a rundown flat, wondering if they'll ever be able to afford a home of their own. It's about the children living in temporary accommodation, forced to change schools every time they move. The lack of affordable, decent homes is affecting families across the entire UK. Here are some important facts.

UK home ownership is slipping out of reach. On average, house prices are now almost seven times people's incomes. No matter how hard they work, it's becoming more and more difficult for young people to save up and buy a home of their own. In the last decade, UK home ownership fell for the first time since census records began. Massive house prices in London are causing large, unmanageable demographic changes.

Housing costs are hugely expensive compared to income. Many of the people on the housing ladder got there by taking out risky mortgage loans that stretched them to their financial limit. Now that the economy is static for them, people are finding it harder to meet their monthly repayments, often with dire consequences – 28,900 homes were repossessed across the UK in 2013. Happily, this reduced to around 8,000 by 2016 although unhappily, there were 94,100 mortgages with arrears of 2.5% or more of the outstanding balance.

More families are renting from private landlords. There are now more than 9 million renters in private rented accommodation, including almost 1.3 million families with children. Renting can be unmanageable with soaring rents, hidden fees and eviction a constant worry. And it can mean living in dreadful conditions too – one third of private rented homes in England fail to meet the Decent Homes Standard.

Levels of homelessness are rising. The ultimate impact of the housing crisis is the huge numbers of people forced out of their homes altogether. The number of homeless households has risen to more than 50,000. Some of these households, many with dependent children, will then wait for years, sometimes in temporary accommodation. And more than 2,000 people a year will have no roof over their head at all, ending up sleeping rough.

Housebuilding. Housebuilding in the UK peaked at 425,830 in 1968 and the trend has been downward ever since. The UK is in the midst of a housing shortage that numerous credible experts now describe as 'chronic' and 'acute'. While it's widely recognised that we need 250,000 new homes each year to meet population growth and household formation, housebuilding hasn't reached that level since the late 1970s. During the Thatcher era, as fewer council houses were built, an average of 190,900 new homes were constructed each year. That dropped to 160,800 while John Major was Prime Minister as we came to rely ever more on private-sector housebuilders, then fell to 156,000 under Blair.

Land-banking. The idea of 'land-banking' – with the biggest housebuilders remaining on a go-slow to up their profit on each unit – used to be dismissed as a conspiracy theory. That has changed. A quarter of all new homes in the UK are built by the biggest three providers and over half are provided by the top eight. The UK housebuilding market has been described as having *all the characteristics of an oligopoly*' in a little-noticed report from the House of Lords Economic Affairs Select Committee. The Secretary of State has weighed in, as has the veteran MP Clive Betts, who chairs the Commons Select Committee that monitors his department. 'The big developers are deliberately restricting supply, maximising their prices and profits, rather than the numbers of houses they build,' he says. There's increasing evidence, though, that while the planning system remains cumbersome, more and more permissions are being given. Yet the homes aren't being made. Internal government figures show that over a three-year period, while there's been a 46,600 rise in building units granted permission, there's been a 94,300 rise in such units remaining *unbuilt* – with the entire increase in planning permission being absorbed by increased alleged 'land-banking'.

Where can we get the money to deal with the needs for UK housing, health and employment?
Housing cannot be at the end of the queue for finance. It should not be an afterthought. 'The market' clearly is not working. Housing comes *before* vacuous proposals such as expensive high-speed rail to help the slogan of the 'Northern Power House' by reducing travel times. Did a PR advisor, guessing that the weekend papers could be bad news, suggest to a minister that building a faster railway would create short-term jobs and sound good to voters? And for decades, powerhouses of any kind that generate profits rarely allow the profits to dribble down to those below. Homes have an immediate and a long-term humanising effect on society.

The world's most commercially successful enterprise, Silicon Valley, unfortunately has little passenger use of the limited railway. Almost any UK TV news programme has crystal-clear pictures of journalists and conversations in faraway places such as China or Australia. And Skype is available almost everywhere. People in business, or for any reason, can have 'Skype' meetings when located at opposite ends of the world. Saving a small number of alphas half an hour on a train journey should come behind numerous people having homes. And Londoners know how insecure is renting in the UK. People's homes are as basic as it gets. Of course, updating old, dodgy rail stock and lines is a necessary, real and routine need.

Using the UK as an example of existing local, humanising, social structures that must be protected or worldwide created as local, social glue

Communal- anyone can start such a group
Street committees
Book groups
Sewing/embroidery/quilt groups
Gardening groups
Walking groups
Choirs
Fishing clubs
Tenants associations
Bridge/Chess etc. clubs
Dancing clubs
Residents' associations

Communal/Public
Communal spaces/common land (almost gone)/parks (at risk)/ playing fields
Libraries
Art galleries
Swimming pools
Schools
Allotments

Nursery schools
Churches and associated clubs/choirs
Boy Scouts/Girl Guides/Cubs
Markets
Political parties
Pubs, darts, quiz nights
Local shops – not multiples
Cafes/restaurants (<u>privately</u> owned) – discourage 'multiples'
'Evening classes'
Local newspapers
Sports clubs. Indoors/outdoors. Cricket, soccer, squash, table tennis, hockey, darts, bowls, tennis, swimming
Post Offices
Local charities

Summary of possible improvements to The State
With a view to answering needs, harmonising primate instincts and expressing the human

1. Education worldwide re the above causes of our problems and of our needs. <u>Science</u> helps by casting light on:
    i) old problems of pestilence, famine, volcanoes, earthquakes and tsunamis; and
    ii) illuminating the human brain and personality development; and
    iii) the biological and genetic basis of many problems.

    Educate re the scientifically proven need for belonging/connectedness, for inclusive social structures and for an understanding of our place in the universe.

    Education re the basic, *common* teaching of humanism and the originators of major religions regarding altruism.

    Educate re our common humanity. There is only one race and it's in serious danger.

2. Focus on child development, based on established empirical evidence and on the humanisation of society: <u>socialise</u> children (e.g. as in Scandinavia), and early on include reading stories, music, art, dance, drama, poetry, sculpture, cooking. See formal education more as a part of the key <u>human</u> development of a person. Encourage anything to increase that sense of human belonging and connectedness.

3. Positively encourage and support femininity and human rights.

4. The widespread deconditioning of leaders and the led: attempt to reduce the irrational fear of the foreign, increase the use of reason re territory and obedience to alpha males. Start with leaders, e.g. Prime Ministers and Presidents, Cabinet Ministers, Head Teachers, Heads of Public Hospitals and Military Commanders. Use the techniques described in 'The Chimp Paradox' by Steve Peters.

5. Facilitate the expression of specifically personal, human instincts – altruism, creativity, widespread art (by children and local people, not so much monied 'ART') everywhere: in the workplace, schools, homes, public places, galleries, libraries, transport and the street.

6. Pay attention to the original and common insights of the major religious prophets – especially regarding altruism. For example, provide a genuine 'living wage' and not a 'minimum wage' or less, with 2+ low-paid jobs required to survive.

7. Facilitate the bringing together of the alpha-male leaders and the led. Small communities, reduce inequality. Make Parliament *representative*. Needed are parliaments and senates whose actual constitution represents the *community mix* and parliamentarians and public servants who serve the people and whose members live lifestyles *at least similar* to those served. Social focus on community, belonging, inclusiveness and creativity.

8. As strenuously advocated by numerous USA presidents, starting over 200 years ago, the connection needs to be *broken*

between politicians, political parties and corporations – 'big business' with their 'big money'.

No donations from anyone including corporations, no buying influence and even laws. Fund all election expenses by the state publishing objective biographies, statements of policies and organising public debates (TV and radio), uninterrupted by advertisements and chaired by eminent people with impeccable reputations.

9. Increase direct, individual and personal involvement in social processes and structures, *including work*. Encourage commercial enterprises that involve their employees as participating fellow humans and not as disposable objects. Humanise the workplace. Remove anti-union legislation.

10. Encourage a 'media' that informs, educates and entertains in the <u>absence</u> of over-powerful, individual media 'moguls' personally determining a commonly 'over- primate' agenda. A human understanding of the world cannot be left to rich, right-wing moguls.

11. 'Provide homes and humanise working-class and other 'habitats' (estates). Design them to encourage and facilitate communities.

    Facilitate the *peaceful*, mass exposure of injustice via social media including the already existing mass movements. It's proposed that progress will come mainly from mass demands from *individuals* for structural changes. Reduce the instinctive (hence mindless) obedience to elites, e.g. via these non-violent mass movements of *individuals*. Currently this is very promising.

12. Until those in power re-rig the election system in new ways, social media is an effective and growing force for exposing and fighting current injustices. Numerous social movements have a minimum content of primate instinct-driven behaviour. They are typically very human and work on a daily basis to expose injustice worldwide. Surprisingly, the

most powerful dictators/despots/evildoers respond positively to such mass exposure as evidenced by numerous stories of success. Hopefully, these sites will be increasingly active prior to elections, correcting bias and falsehood. Worldwide, the numbers are increasing rapidly. To mention them again, these loose organizations include Avaaz (Avaaz.org), Amnesty International (www.amnesty.org.uk), 'Occupy' (www.occupytogether.org/), '38 degrees' (action@38degrees. org.uk), SumOfUs.org (us@sumofus.org), mail@change.org, Open Britain (contact@open-britain.co.uk), Social Europe (info@socialeurope.eu), Age UK (ageuk@mailer.ageuk.org. uk), WeMove.EU (info@wemove.eu) and globalcitizen.org (https://www.globalcitizen.org/, www.globalpovertyproject. com/global-citizen/ replyuk@globalcitizen.org), Truthout (messenger@truthout.org). They motivate numerous people to become socially involved and facilitate direct, non-violent action, typically by expressing a personal opinion about an evildoer or organisation regarding some injustice. The organisation's alpha male hardly appears – not very alpha. They offer their facilities to allow any individual to start a campaign. The emphasis on non-violence helps to avoid the surfacing of basic instincts. The success of Mahatma Ghandi in bringing about non-violent, humane social change in India comes to mind.

Individuals using social media definitely offer hope. I suspect that biological evolution has never 'seen' uprisings by non-alphas *en masse*. It would not be surprising if non-evolutionary solutions (even partial ones) arose to meet evolutionary challenges. It seems likely that the world needs *non*-alphas to rise up peacefully and assert themselves against their basic instincts.

Union bashing/elimination has the inevitable consequence of dehumanising 'lower class' workers. Inevitable problems arise from preventing workers from contributing as humans and as persons to their work. They should also be afforded the dignity of negotiating their own wages, hours and conditions of work, pensions and vacations. Inhuman working conditions *always* lead to trouble eventually. Workers *are* humans. And who would wish to impose such inhumane conditions? Answer: probably money-obsessed people, over-expressing their primate, short-term, alpha instincts.

Question
Given the numerous, detailed exposures of the corrupt web of Wall Street, corporations and, for example, the Republican Party, why does it all continue and worsen? There have been numerous articles, books and exposés over many years, notably by Noam Chomsky, Greg Palast, George Monbiot, Robert Fisk and John Pilger. In terms of the deeply corrupt financial services, there is Ellen Brown's blog about the secret 'End-Game Memo', described above. It appears that there has been no or negligible effect. Possibly, the uprisings by individuals have been affected by such people, e.g. 'Occupy' in the USA.

Answer:
1. Again, this is due to our ever-present *instinct to obey our alpha leaders* and their instinctive behaviour to acquire more power without limit; *and*
2. 'blowing the whistle' on any 'evildoing' typically results in punishment.

Human survival *requires* that this corrupt web be removed. Individuals *must act as individuals and make their voices heard* via social media using the numerous organisations that already exist. Also, non-alphas and alphas must not always obey their instincts. Non-alphas must not always obey alphas. For our survival, *humans* must take responsibility for their own actions and the powerful, *often inappropriate* expression of basic instincts must be addressed.

HOW WE MIGHT TACKLE HUMANITY'S PROBLEMS

(ii) Religion

Contents

INTRODUCTION

This book is about the influence of evolution on human society. It is intended to cast light on dark areas that maintain the world in its current, often violent state. In this section, focussed on religion, it's not my intention mindlessly to attack religions or to disrespect them. Virtually all, as they visibly exist now, exhibit prominent, primate characteristics and virtually all have humans who are trying to humanise them in line with the original prophets. In my own former religion of Catholicism, I have met, known and been befriended by many wonderful women and men, some are nuns and priests, living according to the ideals of Jesus. If anything I write below appears to contradict this, then it is wrong and mistaken. These people are inspirational, often disregarded by the alpha-male, top clergy, yet they keep faith with the original prophet, Jesus, who taught the absolute primacy of responding to human need. It's significant that Jesus was killed largely by the activities of his co-religionists. From my own, personal experience, other religions have similar, fully fledged humans. The tendency towards the 'primate-isation' of all social structures is an evolutionary, biological one, ever present and inevitably about biological survival, with alpha males leading this *biological* process. We are stuck with these primate instincts that typically overwhelm our human ones of altruism as well as culture and art (but not our money-seeking, big, commercial ART).

> *What follows includes evidence that the <u>founders</u> of the major religions were examplars of fully human, kind, altruistic behaviour. They controlled expression of their primate instincts. Typically, these founders were quickly followed by organisations that resembled corporations in having alpha males in charge, fighting for survival in competition with similar organisations, expanding their territory, ever seeking more money and followers, and suppressing women.*

It could be easy to describe the clerical alpha males as necessarily stupid, or evil or ignorant but it would be wrong to do so. They and their institutions are following their primate instincts, notably associated with the alpha male, religious territory, foreign competitor religions or even 'foreign' enemies and the need for control. The teaching about altruism (often described by clergy as the 'social side' of religion), typically downplayed in favour of the biologically necessary control, is fully human as was Jesus himself, and similarly for other major prophets. The biological, instinctive forces never go away. The need to humanise and return to the founders' teaching is permanent. So often, 'renewal', led by clergy, is to renew obedience to clerical, so-called *pious practices* (the 'spiritual side' of religion). It still amazes me that Jesus was so un̲clerical – help the needy. At the risk of being too repetitive, I (now an agnostic) suggest to any reader, humanist, atheist, whatever, to read the account of the Day of Judgement in Matthew's gospel, i.e. help the needy with several cross-cultural examples: end of story. Religious renewal is actually to return to *altruism* as the driving force. It thus seems that religions and other major social structures are populated by a few alpha males expressing their alpha-male basic instincts, a few humans expressing human instincts including altruism, and a mass of people expressing their basic instinct of obedience.

It could be instructive to consider each major religion *as it actually is now* and compare this with the teaching and characteristics of the founding prophet. In what direction has each religion moved? In my own former religion of Catholicism, the movement has clearly been towards biological survival. There is the clear distinction between the simple lifestyle of Jesus and his teaching, notably at the end of his life and shortly before his execution, on the absolute need for altruism and that of the current Church. We have the Vatican State with its Palace and a Pope called His Holiness and clerical hierarchy worldwide with various titles and wearing 'sacred' vestments or clerical uniforms. They are mostly controlling or carrying out pious, 'religious' practices. Does each religion obey the teaching of their founders in respect to altruism and love, or do they obey the biological laws for biological survival: seek power/money/numbers (converts), be competitive, territorial, fear the foreign/different, be hierarchical, obedient?   Overwhelmingly, the major religions are strongly primate.

In terms of the listed primate characteristics (notably regarding territory, fear of the foreign/different, including women, alpha-male leadership and associated obedience), religions more or less develop all of them. This is despite their typical origins in the teaching of numerous prophets who taught and also practised altruism as their central teaching. As a start, it could usefully provide context to consider the world's religions in terms of their numbers of adherents. The table below shows that the top six most followed religions constitute 94% of the total listed 20 broad religious groups, mostly with numerous subgroups and sects. It's worth noting that secularist, agnostics and atheists constitute the third largest group at about 1.1 billion (15.4%).

NUMBERS OF ADHERENTS TO WORLD RELIGIONS INCLUDING SECULAR, NON-RELIGIOUS, AGNOSTIC AND ATHEIST

'Sizes shown are approximate estimates and are listed mainly for the purpose of ordering the groups, not providing a definitive number' (*Adherents.com*)

Religion	Adherents	percents
Christianity	2.2 billion[3]	31.50%
Islam	1.6 billion[4]	22.32%
Secular[a]/Non-religious[b]/Agnostic/Atheist	≤1.1 billion	15.35%
Hinduism	1 billion	13.95%
Chinese traditional religion[c]	394 million	5.50%
Buddhism	376 million	5.25%
Ethnic religions excluding some in separate categories	300 million	4.19%
African traditional religions	100 million	1.40%
Sikhism	23 million	0.32%
Spiritism	15 million	0.21%
Judaism	14 million	0.20%
Bahá'í	7.0 million	0.10%
Jainism	4.2 million	0.06%
Shinto	4.0 million	0.06%
Cao Dai	4.0 million	0.06%
Zoroastrianism	2.6 million	0.04%
Tenrikyo	2.0 million	0.03%
Neo-Paganism	1.0 million	0.01%
Unitarian Universalism	0.8 million	0.01%
Rastafarianism	0.6 million	0.01%
total	7167 million	100%

References

'The Global Religious Landscape'. The Pew Forum on Religion & Public Life. Pew Research Center. 18 December 2012. Retrieved18 March 2013.

'Major Religions of the World Ranked by Number of Adherents'. Adherents.com. 2005. Retrieved 19 Jun 2010.

'Global Christianity'. Pewforum.org. Retrieved 2012.

God as an explanation of everything

An almost universal, socially convenient and useful explanation of human behaviour and of external events is to ascribe everything to God. It's cross-cultural to thank God for all good things, although not for the bad which is often explained as a consequence of God's anger or of the Devil's work. As mentioned earlier, religion offers God as an entity who makes sense of humans in the universe. Given that religion occurs across cultures, regions, climates and times, then it broadly qualifies as an instinct. Religion plays a major role in human societies and deserves special attention. Another perspective is that religion has played an important role in social control. An extreme punishment for non-compliance can be the threat of burning in Hell for all eternity.

At this point I'd like to draw more attention to the *common* teaching of important religious prophets and humanist writers who advocate altruism as being central. This commonality is not something peripheral, it is core. Let my list below outline some definitions, *which in practice are not followed* and are widely ignored, as the essence of the various religions. Religions are performing now, or have done, violent, harmful, evil acts, sometimes when possessing supreme power and sometimes when present in the same place as competing religions. This is because they have moved from the teaching of the prophets to primate, competing 'ideologies'. Essentially, they have moved towards expressing <u>instincts</u> regarding territory, increasing numbers (converts), competition, fear of the foreign/different (including the feminine), alpha males and with their main objective being biological survival. At different times and places, there are exceptions, and these notably include Quakers and humanists (which is hardly a religion).

Religions commonly refer to 'faith'. The word can frequently be used to summarise religious beliefs but without specifying them in detail. Typically, it's sufficient to name the religion as defining the faith. This leaves the clergy in charge of the detailed specification.

For example, many years ago, when asked, I'd say that I was of the Roman Catholic faith and I 'believed' whatever the clergy said was the 'faith'. Irish Christian Brothers was an order that taught me my faith. A textbook was entitled 'What We Believe'. It was read aloud in class, with pupils reading in sequence to learn what they were supposed to believe. Maybe it should have been titled 'What the Papal Curia wants you to believe'. The use of the words 'belief' and 'faith' can be misleading. What we believe needs enquiry: what I had was indoctrination. In many ways things have improved greatly in Catholicism from several decades ago, now typically with intelligent, knowledgeable teachers. The religious order that taught me has diminished greatly. Catholicism has a different, admirable kind of Pope. Nevertheless, the words 'belief' and 'faith' still require clarification. Elsewhere, I've referred to the Axial Age sages (Confucianism, Daoism, Buddhism, Greek rationalists) and this reference stands repetition. The sages were against religion defined as stating a <u>belief</u> in doctrine but rather they favoured altruistic <u>behaviour</u> as a defnition. And Jesus, very near the end of his life and predicting the 'Day of Judgement' spoke only of helping the needy as the requirement for entry to Heaven. Catholicism has now turned into a corporation.

Broadly speaking, religions, including Christianity, can take several forms in terms of the mentality of the adherents who practise them. What follows is <u>not</u> an attempt to ridicule. It is an attempt accurately to describe actual behaviour. I will describe two behaviour patterns and then consider major religions in terms of whether or not altruism is a central teaching within them.

The numerous views on God

As part of religions' biologically important social glue and control functions, the representations of God become adapted/changed as society changes. This change enables the specific church to continue its function as a useful social adhesive and maintain its own local power and influence. This is truly helpful in basic, biological terms.

Cohesion is required for unified responses to danger. Religion can be an excellent social glue.

Consequently, religions and their Gods are as diverse and variable as the cultures they support. Only some are monotheistic. There are pagan gods and Hindu, Shinto, Muslim, Sikh, Jewish and all their religions with numerous separated sects and subsects. A recent USA presidential candidate is a Mormon. In addition, we have numerous other 'ancient' gods being worshipped in different times and places: India, China, Mesopotamia, the Americas, Rome, Greece and Egypt. Even where the religion teaches the existence of only one God, as in Christianity, Judaism and Islam, numerous sects and divisions occur. Christianity, for example, is fragmented and includes Roman Catholics, Anglicans, Methodists, Presbyterians, Evangelicals, Quakers, Baptists and all with numerous, identifiable subgroups and sub-subgroups. In my own case, as an English RC (now ex-RC; agnostic), broadly we were theologically 'middle of the road' compared to the liberal Dutch Catholics or the west of Ireland ultra-conservative Catholics. The latter were considered by the English to be in the vice-like grip of the 'conservative' and now exposed as corrupt Irish clergy.

An interesting religious development was detailed by David Harvey in 'A brief history of neoliberalism'. Among various detailed developments, he points out how (in his words) 'an unholy alliance between big business and conservative Christians, backed by neoconservatives.... eradicated all liberal elements from the (USA) Republican Party... and turning it into the relatively homogeneous right-wing electoral force of present times'. This happened with no more than about 20% of the population being evangelical Christians. With the recent Republican nominee, Mitt Romney, a Mormon, advocating the elimination of or vast reduction in 'welfare' (as does our current UK Tory government as well as US President Donald Trump), it's not possible to square this with Christ's emphasis on helping the needy. This is especially so in a severe economic crisis. For example, the USA has no state health service open to all, comparable to the European situation. In fact, such a service is routinely denounced in the US popular media as 'socialist (this word seems to be synonymous with evil) medicine'. Those watching the acclaimed opening ceremony of the London Olympic Games will have noticed the pageant on the UK National Health Service, proclaimed as a triumph of the UK state, and hugely cheered by the crowds.

But it's easy to square the 'right's' proposal with a strange version of biological 'Darwinism' in which the weak die off. In fact, Darwin did not *advocate* the survival of the fittest; he *described* the biological process of evolution. Actually, in the broad, adverse biological terms of mental illness, life expectancy, infant mortality, obesity, homicides, imprisonment rates, then societies with the highest difference between the 'haves' and the 'have nots' (the top and bottom – but not in Jesus's terms) in income levels, suffer the most across the board. As mentioned previously, the USA has the worst record among all countries for which there are sound statistics, with several-fold worse data than the best (see Wilkinson and Pickett's, 'The Spirit Level'). Surprisingly, not only poor societies have bad statistics. In unequal societies *everyone* is affected.

Obviously, over time as different cultures changed at different rates, so the religions and other social structures changed accordingly in order to 'survive'. The previous Pope Benedict's UK visit was testimony to the RC Church having adapted in part to the modern world and changing some of its rules (at the loss of some of its 'outmoded' principles) in order to enhance its power. It has been suggested, for example, that some of the characteristics of fundamentalist Muslim perceptions of an over-literal interpretation of the ancient, sacred texts of Islam are because it has not yet entered the modern world. Bernard Lewis (an eminent historian of the Middle East) in 'The Crisis of Islam', written several years before the present unrest in the Arab world, points out the poverty and tyranny that affects almost the entire Arab world. His words were prophetic. Lewis refers to American economic dominance and exploitation as explaining the poverty and also in order to support the many Muslim (so-called) tyrants who serve America's purposes. He also highlights the consequent appalling economic performance of Arab countries. In 2011, the chickens came home to roost with widespread, popular uprisings in Arabia. There were, widespread examples of leaderless masses of young idealistic Arabs successfully protesting in a mostly peaceful way and with, initially, amazing success, which sadly was not long lasting.

An alien, arriving in England and studying how we portray God would observe that the language is anthropomorphic. The official state religion of Anglicanism and also Catholicism portrays God rather like a medieval monarch. He (definitely <u>he</u>), like many monarchs, requires constant praise and constant reminding of his almighty powers. It is as if God had either forgotten or did not know about his powers. In other religions, sacrifices of various kinds were demanded by their God – animal and even human. Does God need sacrifices? More likely, such practices boost the power of the priests in charge of and interpreting God's supposed wishes for these events. Official Christianity also portrays God as head of an animal-like hierarchy in Heaven: God as alpha male, archangels, angels and faithful humans. The enemy's hierarchy is in another eternal place, Hell, with the Devil as alpha male, fallen angels and human sinners. Yet, in the <u>New</u> Testament, Christ suggests that people refer to God as 'Papa', i.e. as a familiar, intimate father.

Also, 'sacred' buildings are created to honour God. Is God honoured by buildings? In Christianity and in many religions, churches (God's house) often evoke awe as well as portraying might and beauty. By any standards, many are beautiful constructions. The 'faithful' are allowed in, and in a hushed way, to marvel at such majesty, all orchestrated and controlled by the clergy. Often, after honouring God in his awesome house, they return home to poor, inadequate, cold homes with inadequate food. The evidence of the Bible is that Jesus and his family did not live in an awesome, majestic building but more likely an ordinary home; after all, the tradition is that he was born in a stable. Maybe Matthew in his gospel had a lapse of memory and forgot to include the building of awesome churches in his list of Jesus's requirements for entry to Heaven. Probably not.

Religions are part of the local human 'ecosystem'. In the UK, the Anglican Church is securely and *safely* woven into the English culture. The monarch is the Head of the Church and bishops are represented in Parliament. The Christian (Roman) church at the time of the Reformation was clearly corrupt and in need of reform. Nevertheless, the Anglican Church owes much to its accommodating the wishes of Henry VIII regarding his being the new Head of the Church. It was partly a consequence of his increasingly tyrannical approach and certainly it was convenient for the break-up of his marriages. It would seem clear that none of this is to do with God. It has all to do with biology and institutional survival.

Football club religion

This approach is common – 'my religion, right or wrong'. The idea of searching for truth is typically abandoned. My father supported Liverpool Football Club and so did I. When Liverpool won a match, it was '<u>we</u> won'. When Liverpool lost, it was '<u>we</u> lost'. It was part of my identity. A different country, a different father and it could have been a different club or even a different national game. The same applies for one's religion: my parents were RC, so I went to an RC primary school and later an RC secondary school. If born on the west coast of Ireland and of Roman Catholic parents, then I may well have been a Catholic of the 'conservative' kind. If born in Holland, likely a Catholic of the 'liberal' kind, and if of Baptist parents in Alabama, USA, then a Southern Baptist with its associated ideology, possibly with racist overtones. Born in certain areas of Pakistan or the Middle East, then Muslim (likely the kind predetermined by my birth – Sunni or Shia). Your religious 'club', as for your football club, genuinely adds to the meaning in your life. You support it through thick and thin. You are a loyal, reliable supporter <u>whatever</u>. Typically, the Church is helpful regarding the poor and deprived. When you move towns, you can join in at once with your local church and its numerous clubs. You belong. *Biologically*, it can be hugely helpful.

This 'loyalty' contrasts somewhat with the attitude of Jesus to his religion and to truth. He was a 'troublemaker' who was *executed by his own Church* (via a Roman bureaucracy that washed its hands of Jesus's proposed guilt). Some of the troubles he 'made' were to seek the truth and teach the primacy of helping the needy. He also believed that he was the Messiah. That did not endear him to the Jewish religious leadership who had a quite different opinion.

'Magic circle' religion

Ancient human societies and contemporary 'primitive' ones have had and still have soothsayers and magicians. 'Magic is the belief that control of the signs implies control of what is signified' (written by a friend on her kitchen wall – Margaret Todd). Another definition is the 'Art of influencing events by occult control of nature' (Oxford English Dictionary). In such societies the magician can play a truly important role in social control and social glue – *vital because social glue is needed to help biological survival.* The belief that such a leader can influence and predict food availability or rain or health or eclipses leads to obedience and the necessary social control. It's now clear that ancient civilisations had the capacity to understand planetary motions and thus predict the seasons, eclipses and other natural phenomena. Such knowledge gave the practitioners obvious power over the uninitiated.

There is a tendency in numerous religions towards a kind of 'magicification' of the religion. In other words, *a focus on the external symbols and pious practices*, that are created by and *controlled* by the clergy. For society, control is biologically necessary for a rapid, coordinated response to change, especially danger. A prominent example is in the status of sacred texts: the word of God *interpreted and authenticated by the clergy.* This makes good biological sense in terms of social control. I refer elsewhere to a RC priest demanding to be assured by me that the candles used in a 'Family Mass' contained the correct proportion of beeswax. Otherwise it was not a valid Mass! Did Jesus forget to emphasise during the 'Last Supper' the absolute necessity for specifying the composition of the candles and the species of wood to make the table and other magical requirements?

A personal example of a non-magical, non-total-control aspect of my previous (and only) religion was when I was invited to dine with the Dominicans at Blackfriars, Oxford. During the meal there was a reading to which, so it seemed to me, apart from the reader I was the only person paying any attention whatsoever. There was ostentatious non-attention and I never found out the reason for this. The reading (I still remember it) was about the distinction between attempting to control Jesus and allowing him to influence us. In other words, as I saw it, it was about <u>us</u> controlling Jesus or us being open to his ideas. To me, it was an excellent reading. Years later (and now), I realised that I'd seen something unique in my experience of the Catholic Church – dissent by 'clergy' (the Dominicans then were very unclerical) from an official requirement from higher authority. They could not stop the reading, but they could pay no attention to it.

Major religions and humanism

Throughout my life, I have studied the theology of Christianity and, much less deeply, other religions. I have attended seminars and meetings about various religions and spoken with many professional theologians. Early in my academic career I was director of the Science and Religion Group of Bath University (a very part-time post). In recent decades, for this book, I've read numerous books on religion and sacred texts. I have a certificate enabling me to teach the Catholic faith. Nevertheless, I do not claim to be an expert. However, I regard my conclusions about altruism being central as broadly reasonable and supportable. I have definitely not selected texts to support the comfortable idea that the major prophets all advocated altruism. What follows are ideas regarding the major religious and humanist prophets supporting the idea of altruism as the highest good or at least following the 'Golden Rule'.

One ancient summary of good behaviour is 'The Golden Rule', namely, 'Do to others what you would have them do to you', also known as the 'Ethic of Reciprocity'. This admirable teaching is referred to across numerous religions and is compatible with humanism. Altruism perhaps goes a step further, in that it proposes that you put the needs of others *before* your own needs. Love is important in probably all religions. I have mainly used the word altruism because its definition is relatively unambiguous – put the needs of others before your own. The word love has many meanings: from having active sex to the pre-eminent Christian theologian Thomas Aquinas' definition of 'an act of the will'. When I first read this in his 'Summa Theologica', I thought that it was wrong and cold. Now I realise that it's right. Love is willing the good of the other – being *committed* to the other's good. In that sense, the word love is fine by me. Charity is another word used to describe basic, truly religious behaviour, as is kindness. The word kind has origins in the idea of family, e.g. kinder/children. The dictionary (Oxford English) describes the word charity as kindness, lenience in judging others, almsgiving. Commonly, these words are stated as first being applied to one's own people, as in 'charity begins at home'. This does not mean that charity should stop in the home. The translators of the various prophets (or their followers) mostly used the word altruism to convey the central teaching. What follows are texts and commentary on various religions regarding these overlapping and interchangeable ideas.

Much material described as important by numerous religions is connected towards the feeling of belonging in the religion, being connected and being repeatedly reminded. This plays an important biological role in social survival. Whilst a 'practicing' Catholic, there were numerous ceremonies (Mass, Benediction, Stations of the Cross, Rosary) and also many clubs that played this role. One definitely belongs and group cohesion benefits from this, as it did for me from numerous gifted, altruistic, 'unclerical' clergy.

Christianity

The primacy of altruism is obvious in the New Testament – respond to the needs of others. The command by Jesus to help strangers goes beyond the home. That is not incompatible with starting in the home. The following quotations support this.

> *'Therefore all things whatsoever ye would that men should do to you, do ye even so to them: for this is the law and the prophets.'*
>
> **Matthew 7:12, New Testament, King James Version.**

> *'And as ye would that men should do to you, do ye also to them likewise.'*
>
> **New Testament, Luke 6:31, King James Version.**

Matthew's gospel 25, The Last Judgement. Shortly and, significantly, just before his own predicted execution, Jesus identified himself with the needy. He describes how when he returns as the Messiah on the Day of Judgement, those who responded to need will have a place in Heaven. To those who ignored the plight of the needy (Christ explicitly *identified* with the needy), they were to be sent to the eternal fire of Hell. Each need was referred to four times. The definitions of need used were normal across all cultures: ill, naked, thirsty, hungry, imprisoned and being a stranger (acronym – *in this*). I am conscious of possibly being accused of selecting a passage to justify my ideas, despite being a religious agnostic. This selectivity is relatively easy for any religion. But this passage in Matthew was about the time just before Jesus's predicted death. It is Jesus describing his return at the Day of Judgement as the Christ, the Messiah and giving the criteria for that judgement. He does not mention any of the sins that were instilled into me as a Catholic child. I doubt that there is any text so crystal clear. Responding to need is paramount. In addition, we have Jesus's statement at the start of his ministry, quoting the prophet Isaiah: 'I have come to give hope to the poor'. Yet responding to need is ignored and sidelined in normal clerical discourse with remarkable frequency. Also missing is the importance of obedience to the Jewish clerical hierarchy. It does not follow that Jesus repudiated all other teaching.

What is clear is that the overwhelming bulk of the teaching I received as a Roman Catholic about *obedience* to Holy Mother Church or to Jewish elders and the synagogue (i.e. the clergy) is missed out by Jesus in this crucial message just before his execution. Missing mass mean hellfire for eternity unless forgiven by Holy Mother Church through her clergy. 'Sins of the flesh' led to a similar fate. I have *rarely* heard a sermon teaching that positively answering the needs of others is central. Likely, it's because the key *biological* need is obedience to the clergy and hence on to wider society's alpha males. I have met, made friends with and been influenced by numerous amazing priests and nuns who did follow this key teaching of Jesus: almost all, probably all, were in some conflict with their superiors or later left the clergy. Whenever I have heard talks teaching the primacy of altruism, it has been by such priests and nuns. Currently, the system is being modified with the new Pope Francis. But the RC structure is hard to change, with the deeply rooted, hierarchical, anti-women, anti-gay, anti-sex clergy controlling and advocating pious practices and creeds, created mostly by the clergy. Such practices are described as the superior, 'spiritual' side of religion as opposed to the 'social' side. But suppose that the Christian religion became truly 'extremist' and truly 'fundamentalist'? Suppose it taught *only* extreme altruism; *only* that we must respond to need? What then?

Society of Friends (Quakers)

(https://www.quaker.org.uk; https://www.quaker.org.uk/about-quakers)

> 'Our life is love, and peace, and tenderness; and
> bearing one with another, and forgiving one another,
> and not laying accusations one against another; but
> praying one for another, and helping one another up
> with a tender hand.'

Isaac Penington, 1667

They are a Christian movement founded by George Fox and focussed on peaceful principles. Central to the Quakers' belief is the doctrine of the 'Inner Light', or the sense of Christ's direct working in the soul. This has led them to reject both formal, clerical ministry and all prescribed (by clergy), formal forms of worship. Quoting from their website: 'In 1647 he came to the belief that people could have a personal experience of God, which he called the 'Inner Light'. He started travelling all over the country preaching to people and converting them to 'Friends of the Light'. He was often punished and imprisoned for preaching his radical vision. This vision included denouncing the need for priests or churches, as they prevented a direct and personal experience of God and expressing the incompatibility of belief in God and warfare.'

Economy. Quakers call for an economic system that has equality, justice and environmental sustainability at its heart. Quotation: 'We work on welfare and inequality, corporate accountability and ethical finance, whilst exploring principles and practical steps towards a 'new economy'.

Peace. Quakers support each other to live out their deep commitment to peace. This includes promoting peace education, challenging militarism, campaigning against war and for disarmament, and supporting the peace movement in Britain.

Social justice. In the UK they work on specific aspects of social justice. Their long-standing work for a more compassionate criminal justice system continues. Housing and housing conditions is another long-standing Quaker concern. It is thus clear that Quakers work for a loving and socially just, altruistic society.

Judaism

Once more, because of the breadth of this book and despite much reading, I am tentative about my knowledge of an important area. Among other aspects, this is regarding all the main religions apart from perhaps Christianity (I was certified to teach the RC faith). And this is to say nothing about the many thousands of non-main religions.

Judaism appears to me as being suspiciously magic-like, attached to its past, its rituals, its powerful clergy and to a *land* promised to them by God. Acquiring this land was un-religiously associated with murderous terrorism by its then truly terrorist leaders who later became political leaders (see earlier).

But the *actual basic* teaching of Judaism clearly has much about altruism. Altruism is an important part, as highlighted by Jesus at the start of his ministry, when he quoted Isaiah: 'I have come to give hope to the poor'. Isaiah was an important, early Jewish prophet, documented by the biblical book of Isaiah and lived around the 8th-century BC. But the current territorial, anti-'foreign', violent Zionism has all the hallmarks of primate instincts. Nevertheless, somewhat buried beneath the needs of biological survival, similar to Christianity and Islam, are numerous indications of the primacy of altruism. The following quotations are entirely compatible with Judaism being essentially altruistic. And, of course, altruism-teaching Jesus was himself a Jew, as were his altruism-teaching apostles.

Judaism has leaders who have clearly followed primate instincts regarding territory and the merciless keeping of it, after receiving it from the non-owners. This is similar for many other leaders of numerous religions who have followed their instincts over territory, the foreign and obedience to alpha leaders. The basic teaching of their prophets is, like Christianity, clearly altruistic. Nevertheless, the victims of the Spanish Inquisition and of the current Israeli violence and occupation might well say, 'So what?'. As I again revise this section (April 2018), Palestinians in the Gaza Strip marched in the tens of thousands to demand their right of return as part of the 'Great Return March'. The Israeli response is reminiscent of the origins of Israel. The Israeli military opened fire on the unarmed marchers as they approached a border fence, killing over 18 and injuring over 1,000. The web site Truthout (messenger@truthout.com) has an article entitled 'In Wake of Gaza Massacre, Israeli Leaders Should Be Prosecuted for War Crimes'. *By Marjorie Cohn, Truthout, News Analysis,* April 06, 2018. It does not take much time to imagine the response of Isaiah, or of Jesus to any massacre.

Quotations from Jewish prophets of a different persuasion

> '*...thou shalt love thy neighbour as thyself.*'
> **Old Testament Bible. Leviticus 19:18**

> '*What is hateful to you, do not to your fellow man.*
> *This is the law: all the rest is commentary.*'
> **Talmud, Shabbat 31a.**

> '*And what you hate, do not do to any one.*'
> **Tobit 4:15**

Islam

The current racist, anti-women and vicious behaviour of some self-styled Islamic groups is obviously aberrant and at least partly the consequence of the humiliation of Middle East peoples by powerful, violent colonialists of a different religion. Middle East countries and much of Africa were *created* by the colonising 'Christian' West. Historically, the West has been involved in violence in Islamic states – notably, Egypt, Iraq and Afghanistan. The behaviour of all sides has often not been representative of their religions' founders.

Similarly, as for Judaism, I am tentative about the primacy of altruism in the basic teaching of Islam as I am not an expert. Some texts propose violence against apostates and non-believers. Nevertheless, there is much support for the idea that Islam is fundamentally altruistic. It is widely believed that Islam rests on 'Five Pillars'. As for numerous religions, including Christianity, the religious practices can be described as partly pious activities to give a sense of belonging and discipline to the followers and also specifically altruism *per se*. The first pillar is the Shahada. Shahada is the Muslim profession of faith, expressing the two simple, fundamental beliefs that make one a Muslim. These are that there is no god but Allah and that Muhammad is the prophet of Allah. The second pillar is daily, ritual prayer – Salat. The main prayer of the week is the midday prayer at the mosque on Fridays. Fasting is important especially during the month of Ramadan (sawm). It commemorates the revelation of the Quran to humanity during Ramadan, the ninth month of the Islamic year. During Ramadan, all adult Muslims (with exceptions) are required to abstain from food, drink and sexual intercourse during daylight hours. Another pillar of Islam is the Pilgrimmage to Mecca (hajj). At least once in his or her lifetime, each Muslim is expected to undertake a pilgrimage to Mecca, the sacred city of Islam. These practices surely contribute to a feeling of belonging and being connected for all Muslims. I can well believe that participating in the hajj must be an extraordinary experience of togetherness and belonging.

Importantly, almsgiving is a central activity in Islam. The Quran explicitly requires it (9:60) and in terms of significance often places it alongside prayer when discussing a Muslim's duties ('Perform the prayer and give the alms.' 2:43, 110, 277). Zakāt ('that which purifies') is the practice of taxation and redistribution, including benefits paid to poor Muslims. It's imposed upon Muslims based on their accumulated wealth and is obligatory for all who are able to take part. It is considered to be a personal responsibility for Muslims to ease economic hardship for other Muslims in order to eliminate inequality among followers of Islam. According to the Quran, there are several categories of people who qualify to receive *Zakāt* funds, notably those living in absolute poverty and those who are restrained because they cannot meet their basic needs. I quote other texts below regarding charity and justifying charity/love/altruism as an absolute requirement of Islam.

> *'None of you (truly) believes until he wishes for his brother what he wishes for himself.'*
> **Translation of Imam An-Nawawi's Hadith thirteen**

> *'The perfect altruism of the earliest Muslim society: a unique example for later generations.'*
> **Abdur Rahman Mahdi, 2006. IslamReligion.com**

> *'...And they give others preference over themselves even though they were themselves in need...'*
> **Quran 59:9**

> *'If you are not altruistic, you are not a Muslim.'*
> **Mohammed.**

Given to me by an Imam while we travelled on a train. I cannot verify it directly, although it is in accord with the reference immediately above.

Now, near to where I am writing in Birmingham, UK is a huge Islamic public poster that I greatly admire. It is about the fasting period of Ramadan and its message is: 'Be one with the needy'. This is identical to the account of the Day of Judgement by Jesus. It's a good definition of love or of altruism which is clearly central to Islamic belief.

Hinduism

Despite considerable efforts on my part, I have found it impossible to achieve a satisfactory, cohesive understanding of Hinduism. I have been unable to answer the question, 'Is it essentially about altruism?' There are numerous, sometimes apparently conflicting, versions of this very ancient, possibly the oldest religion. Scholars disagree as to what is a caste and even suggest that the British colonialists exaggerated their role. However, the emphasis on reincarnation is compatible with Hinduism being a social glue, as if the idea is 'do as you are told and in the next life you'll be rewarded by going up the social ladder', then this is good for social obedience. Also, the social category labelled as 'untouchables' seems incompatible with the concept of altruism, central to other major religions, *or rather to the teachings of their founders.*

In Hinduism, an avatar (Sanskrit 'descent') is a descent of a deity to Earth. The phenomenon of an avatar is observed in Hinduism, Ayyavazhi and also in Sikhism. Avatar is regarded as one of the core principles of Hinduism and depending on the branch, the number of incarnations vary. An early reference to avatar, and to avatar doctrine, is in the Bhagavad Gita. Vishnu's avatars typically descend for a very specific purpose. An oft-quoted passage from the Bhagavad Gita describes the typical role of an avatar of Vishnu as bringing dharma, or righteousness, back to the social and cosmic order. But how is 'righteousness' related to the caste system?

Sikhism

Sikhism arose from Hinduism in the Punjab area of India, some hundreds of years ago. Sikhism also teaches reincarnation. In Sikhism, an avatar is a deliberate descent of a soul to Earth in any form. However, my researches into books on Sikhism and into Sikh texts were less telling to me than the discovery that every Sikh temple has four doors, facing north, south, east and west, so that *anyone* may enter for shelter, warmth and food. This is surely altruism in action.

Buddhism

There are different descriptions of Buddhism, commonly with a focus on personal enlightenment. Buddhists also believe in reincarnation. According to the Buddhist Centre, Buddhism is a path of practice and spiritual development leading to insight into the true nature of reality. But what *is* the true nature of reality? Buddhist practices such as meditation are a means of changing yourself, overcoming basic instincts <u>*in order*</u> *to develop the qualities* of awareness, kindness and wisdom. The current Dalai Lama, questioned live on television, summarised the *core* of Buddhism as 'kindness': he summarised his views by stating, 'My religion is kindness'. Also, he states, 'Every religion emphasises human improvement, love, respect for others, *sharing other people's suffering (my italics)*. On these lines every religion has more or less the same viewpoint and the same goal'. I have a picture of the Buddha on my wall of him meditating, together with a quotation as follows:

> There is no need for Temples
> No need for complicated philosophies
> My brain and my heart are my Temples
> My philosophy is kindness

Other commentators on the 'Axial Age' mentioned below include Buddhism as emphasising good behaviour as central, rather than 'belief' in textual doctrine. I wonder if the current, widespread image of the Buddha as a rather fat man with his eyes closed is similar to the iconic image of Jesus on a cross. Meditation by the Buddha is a *means* to acquire and enhance awareness, kindness and wisdom. It's not the final *objective*. As the current Dalai Lama says, the Buddha essentially taught kindness. In the case of Jesus, he unwaveringly taught kindness and even described the Day of Judgement in terms of exclusively helping others or not. And yet, the Christian clergy have represented his iconic, abiding, universal image as that of suffering and dying on a cross. They also teach that he died for our sins and so true Christians must redeem themselves by obeying clerical commands. For biological reasons, religious institutions tend to forget the core teaching of their prophet and emphasise allegiance to the subsequent institution and its survival. I have also heard that the current Dalai Lama has advocated an election for the next Dalai Lama. This seems to be against Buddhist practice regarding the recognition of a new leader. Clearly, he is not a mindless, clerical leader – but he is the Dalai Lama and he does advocate kindness. Two quotations from Buddhist scriptures follow:

> '...a state that is not pleasing or delightful to me, how could I inflict that upon another?'
>
> **Samyutta NIkaya v. 353**

> 'Hurt not others in ways that you yourself would find hurtful.'
>
> **Udana-Varga 5:18**

Confucianism

Confucianism appears entirely compatible with altruism as the following quotations show:

> 'Do not do to others what you do not want them to do to you.'
>
> **Analects 15:23**

> 'Tse-kung asked, 'Is there one word that can serve as a principle of conduct for life?' Confucius replied, 'It is the word 'shu' – reciprocity. Do not impose on others what you yourself do not desire.'
>
> **Doctrine of the Mean 13.3**

> 'Try your best to treat others as you would wish to be treated yourself, and you will find that this is the shortest way to benevolence.'
>
> **Mencius VII.A.4**

Ancient Egyptian teaching

'Do for one who may do for you, that you may cause him thus to do.'

The Tale of the Eloquent Peasant, 109-110, translated by R. B. Parkinson. The original dates to circa 1800 BCE. This may be the earliest version of the Ethic of Reciprocity ever written.

Zoroastrianism

Adherents are advised: *'...be among those who renew the world... to make the world progress towards perfection'*. Its basic teachings are:

1. Humata, Hukhta, Huvarshta, translated as: Good Thoughts, Good Words, Good Deeds.
2. There is only one path and that is the path of Truth.
3. Do the right thing because it is the right thing to do, and then all beneficial rewards will come to you also.

This is in accord with the other religions' teaching of altruism.

Humanism

From the official website of the British Humanist Association)

'Throughout recorded history there have been non-religious people who have believed that this life is the only life we have, that the universe is a natural phenomenon with no supernatural side, and that we can live ethical and fulfilling lives on the basis of reason and humanity. They have trusted to the scientific method: evidence and reason to discover truths about the universe and have placed human welfare and happiness at the centre of their ethical decision making.' Some further quotations follow:

'Being a humanist means trying to behave decently without expectation of rewards or punishment after you are dead.'

Kurt Vonnegut

'...as human beings we can find from our own resources the shared moral values which we need in order to live together, and the means to create meaningful and fulfilling lives for ourselves.'

Richard Norman

The Axial Age

My concern about not imposing my own subjective ideas on this book is at its deepest over religion. It could be warm and reassuring to be certain that the great prophets all taught kindness/charity/love/altruism as being central. From my personal perspective, this would come from their individual and exceptional intuition, rather than from any God. But is it true? The quotations above suggest yes. A major problem has been that after the death of the prophet(s) there was a rapid move to emphasise the *survival of the institution(s), turning it into something like a corporation.*

In the case of Jesus and in his crystal-clear description of how we should behave altruistically, there is no doubt (Matthew's gospel re the Day of Judgement). But for the others? As indicated above, I have read widely and discussed widely, but recently I found reassurance from someone far more knowledgeable than myself about world religions, namely a leading expert on this subject, Karen Armstrong. Her book 'The Great Transformation' is an account of humanity's early attempts to seek 'enlightenment' and to rise above violence, self-destruction, superstition and magic. I will quote some of her ideas and conclusions. She refers to a period in humanity's history described as the Axial Age by the German philosopher Karl Jaspers. The concept was introduced in his book '*Vom Ursprung und Ziel der Geschichte*' (*The Origin and Goal of History, 1949*). The Axial Age was from about 800 to 200 BC and in four regions of the world there independently arose what Karen Armstrong describes as remarkable movements. Jaspers had argued that they were independent, separate movements: as if they arose spontaneously. These were Confucianism and Daoism in China, Hinduism and Buddhism in India, monotheism in Israel and philosophical rationalism in Greece. It was the period of the Buddha, Socrates, Confucius, Jeremiah (my addition – and surely Isaiah, 800 BC – 'I have come to give hope to the poor') and the mystics of the Upanishads – Mencius and Euripides.

Karen Armstrong believes that the Axial Age was one of the most seminal periods of intellectual, psychological, philosophical and religious change in recorded history. I quote from her book 'The Great Transformation' (my underlines): 'The prophets, mystics, philosophers and poets of the Axial Age were so advanced and their vision so radical, that later generations tended to dilute it. In the process, they often produced exactly the kind of religiosity that the Axial reformers <u>wanted to get rid of</u> ... It is frequently assumed ... that faith is a matter of believing certain creedal propositions ... it is common to call religious people 'believers' as though assenting to the articles of faith were their chief activity. But most of the Axial philosophers had <u>no interest whatever</u> in doctrine or metaphysics. A person's theological beliefs were a matter of total indifference to somebody like the Buddha.

What matters is not what you <u>say you 'believe'</u> but <u>how you behave</u>.

Religion is about doing things that changed you at a profound level. The only way you can encounter what they called 'God', 'Nirvana', 'Brahman' or the 'Way' is to lead a compassionate life ... <u>Indeed, religion *was* compassion</u>' (end of quotations).

The current Dalai Lama in a speech in June 2015 emphasised the central role of compassion. As pointed out earlier, he also answered a direct question on TV by saying 'My religion is kindness'. But such teaching does not lead to easy social, biological control, e.g. questioning, 'What is your faith?' or 'What do you believe?' My old, spontaneous answer was, 'I'm a Catholic' – i.e. anything the Church (the infallible Pope) tells me.

My own childhood, including my official religious upbringing, was almost entirely about 'believing' articles and doctrines of 'faith' and carrying out pious church practices. And centuries earlier, we had the evil horrors of the 'Holy' Inquisition with torture, burnings and disembowelling for one's non-official beliefs. I'm tempted to add to Karen Armstrong's comments by saying that *stating* a belief in a creed is not the same as having it and living it. In the field of religion, surely how one *behaves* is a better statement of one's actual belief, of one's actual faith than anything given by verbal statements. Karen Armstrong also points out that the Axial Age was not perfect. It was indifferent to women, adding to the idea that the suppression of women goes very deep in men's psyche.

So, the idea is well supported that almost all of the world's major prophets and humanists taught the key importance of altruism or at least the Golden Rule of treating others as you would like to be treated yourself.

RELIGION AS A SOCIAL ADHESIVE: HELPS CONTROL SOCIETY AND EXPLAINS THE UNIVERSE

Currently, the actual, basic role of *official* religions is mainly biological. They help glue society together according to the basic rules of biological survival. Official religion contributes positively to facilitating a rapid, coordinated response to danger involving leaders and obedience to them. Also, religions typically have contributed and still do contribute greatly to the human need for community, for artistic expression and for meaning about our place in the universe. The prophets' teaching about altruism applied to society as a whole. Even so, religions do indeed support helping the poor and thus favour the provision of food and shelter. Unfortunately, this support does not work sufficiently. The world, including the UK, currently with food 'kitchens' for the hungry, has numerous hungry people. The day I write this, on the BBC 'news', I learned that India's leaders plan to spend $billions on space exploits despite having about 30% of its population below the poverty level with millions living on the streets. In what sense are the leaders representatives – and of whom are they representative? In Christianity, the clergy claim to represent Christ – a claim giving them remarkable power. Even so, especially for adherents, religions offer belonging and they importantly offer explanations of the universe in terms of a God. And religions can offer a strong social adhesive, having the qualifications mentioned below. In these ways religions help human society in a biological sense. The extraordinary extent to which religions typically exhibit 'pure' primate instincts is also indicated above. That the many thousands of religions, past and present, vary greatly in their official teaching is a separate issue. Biologically and within a culture, they can offer belonging and connectedness, and each can act as a strong social glue. Between cultures with different religions or sects then the opposite is often true.

Many religions commonly opposed the idea of biological evolution and even today, among many adherents to major religions, 'creation' is believed to have occurred a few thousand years ago and within a week.

Biological evolution is condemned as a sinful, anti-God belief by some. It is explained as an irrational 'belief'. For example, understanding how evolution could result in something as complex as, for example, an eye seems impossible. Indeed, brought up as a Roman Catholic, this specific example was given and accepted by me as a 'proof' that God must have directly created life. What was described as random, chance, evolutionary change was stated as being an impossible way to result in something with the complexity of an eye. Comparison was also made with the obviously astronomically low chance of a monkey randomly typing and ending up with a Shakespearean play. As stated, it made sense to me as a child and later. Similarly, people who believed and those who still believe that the Earth is flat can point to the obvious flatness as far as the eye can see. The same applies to the sun orbiting the Earth. It is obvious and mistaken. I refer to the earlier section on the proof of evolution, notably 'The Greatest Show on Earth' by Richard Dawkins. I also add the following.

What is wrong with such statements about evolution and random chance which were given to me as a child? Apart from:

a. the direct evidence for evolution (see earlier) is that they
b. underestimate the consequences of the colossal, hard-to-imagine, timescales, and
c. the huge, astronomical numbers of organisms and offspring involved, and
d. the massive diversity among organisms. Also,
e. although changes can be relatively random, the *selection of survivors is not random*.

Selected organisms are those that are the most appropriate ('fit') for the environmental conditions. In fact, evolution is less a 'selection' than the elimination of the unfit, leaving those best equipped to survive in a particular environment. Commonly, an ecosystem (not simply an individual) becomes 'sick' from environmental change. Biological evolution is about biological survival and is still occurring.

Biological survival again

Survival requires effective, swift and collective responses to danger. As mentioned earlier, this requires control, often by alpha males and their associated hierarchies and also *compliance* by those who are led. Religion helps this by being a social glue with great adhesive powers and also and importantly by providing social control. Commonly, religions play highly positive community roles. In my own case, brought up a Roman Catholic by RC parents, our church was important with its communal ceremonies and festivals, youth clubs, associated Boy Scouts and Girl Guides, 'pious' societies, religious devotions and charities, all offered a sense of belonging. When moving home, the local church provides continuity and the facility for immediately joining in with something familiar. In today's increasingly mobile society such social glue is obviously of great benefit. As well as encountering reactionary, rigid clergy, I also met and benefitted greatly from friendships with humane, kind, altruistic, non-clerical clergy who inspired me. Typically (possibly always), they were at odds with the official Church. I regarded them as the leaven mentioned by Christ in the gospels.

The idea that a God creator acts through a priest gives massive authority to the priest. Ultimate human authority comes from being the interpreter of God's will and the ability, for example, to send adherents to a Heaven or miscreants to a Hell or even to authorise torture or burning alive. In retrospect, given the need for social adhesives, together with social control, then the creation of the idea of God by early humans with primate instincts and human minds would seem virtually inevitable. This would be regardless of other paths to the belief in God as it explains (almost) everything, gives meaning to life and can be the result of deep, personal intuition.

Today, many religious people will thank their God for everything good that happens, whilst ignoring the origin of the bad things, although these can be seen as God's punishment or the work of the Devil. My own life as an academic scientist has allowed me to live for extended periods in several countries in addition to my UK home. Also, I have visited numerous countries for conferences and as a consultant. In every country, it was common to thank God, even if only in a superficial way, for minor good events or blessings. In the past and in sacred books it was common to explain large-scale disasters as God's punishment (often collective punishment), e.g. floods, plagues and earthquakes.

Apart from the immorality of collective punishment (though logical as a primate instinct about the foreign), knowledge of the causes of natural phenomena due to air pressure, sea temperature, earthquakes from forces within the Earth's crust and resulting in tsunamis in the ocean make any reference to God superfluous. Similarly, human diseases are now understood in physical, chemical and biological terms: the nervous, blood circulation and immune systems. Infections and plagues are not collective punishments from God, but are caused by microbes, sometimes through bad hygiene.

To what extent are religions concerned with carrying out the teaching of their founder, and to what extent are they concerned with survival and with characteristic primate behaviour patterns? Intuitively, one might expect religious organisations to be among the least primate of human institutions. Typically, a religious movement starts with a founder leading an exemplary (non-primate) life of peace, love and self-sacrifice and teaching altruism for humankind as a whole. Surprisingly, it soon becomes an institution with an ever-increased capacity for survival (as an *institution – a 'corporation*') via attention to increasing numbers of adherents and power-seeking associated with increased chances of 'survival'. Commonly, being a prophet in the true religious sense was dangerous and often resulted in being killed, e.g. as in the case of Old Testament Jewish prophets, 'New Testament' Jesus and the numerous 'whistle blowers' throughout history.

Institutional structures
In terms of (almost always) male, controlling hierarchies concerned with survival, power, territory and numbers of adherents, the

behaviour of 'successful' religious institutions are, in fact, clearly primate. The answer to all the questions at the start of this section is yes – all the characteristics of primates are present. Calls for loyalty from the 'faithful' by a hierarchy are typically a call for obedience. Almost all statements of religious fidelity (e.g. a 'practising' Christian, 'the faithful') refer to the adherence to Church rules of dress, church attendance, payments and practices designated by the official Church as pious and the explicit statements of belief in creeds. Formerly, when a practising Catholic, I rarely (possibly never) heard a definition of a *practising* Christian as being one who helps the ill, clothes the naked, gives water to the thirsty, feeds the hungry, visits people in prison and helps strangers. Yet, and I emphasise, these are Jesus's criteria for entry to Heaven (Matthew's gospel), the neglect of which leads directly to exclusion from Heaven. In many ways and in terms of formal structures, the major religions are the opposite of the prophets of the Axial Age. They emphasise explicit, controlled statements of faith, belief in precise creeds and doctrines, and predominantly produce male, anti-women, bureaucratic, clerical, corporate 'control centres' leading and having power over the 'faithful'. On the contrary, Jesus, other prophets and the Axial Age leaders emphasised *behaviour* – leading a compassionate life. In Jesus' account of the day of Judgement, 2 days before his predicted execution, the key behaviour (I do not apologise for the constant repetition) was to help the ill, naked, thirsty, hungry, imprisoned and the stranger. This is unambiguous in the extreme.

There are numerically few exceptions to the above characterisations of religions or sects. Although small in number, they are widespread and important: notably the Quakers and Methodists. I once attended a meeting at which numerous Quakers were present and was assured that *every one* of them had served time as criminals in prison! This was because of their Christian views regarding war or nuclear weapons. Also, the Methodists have moved towards structures closer to that of the founder of Christianity and away from the common primate ones. Numerous Catholic priests and parishes seek to follow Jesus's teaching, but usually (maybe always) they are in tension with the hierarchy who emphasise obedience to them. The current Pope Francis is clearly attempting a move towards the teaching of Jesus as opposed to mindless obedience to the Curia.

ROMAN CATHOLIC CHURCH AS THE WORLD'S LARGEST RELIGION

Christianity embraces about 32% of all the followers of religion and has around 2.2 billion adherents. Roman Catholicism is the largest religion at 1.28 billion. It's difficult to select one religion as an exemplar, but the Vatican and the formal, powerful, authoritative institution of the Roman Catholic Church offer an example with millions of adherents worldwide. And, as I was raised as an English Roman Catholic, I have familiarity with it although, as an agnostic, I am no longer a Catholic. Perhaps I should mention that my agnosticism is not about the God taught to me as a child. I am entirely certain that 'he' does not exist – in that sense I'm an atheist. I'm not certain about other possibilities. I was an 'altar boy', helping the priest to 'say' Mass, and eventually as an adult I passed an examination authorising me to teach the Catholic faith. The hierarchy, with special, personal titles (his Holiness, his Eminence, Right Reverend, Very Reverend etc.) is: Pope, Cardinals, Archbishops, Bishops, Auxiliary Bishops, Abbots, Monsignors, Canons, Parish Priests, Priests, lay preachers and other laity – about 12 levels (similar to the military) provides one example among many. The infallibility of the Pope (i.e. God ensures that he is error-free when pronouncing officially on matters of faith and doctrine and at a gathering of the Church leadership) adds the ultimate weight to his authority. But given Jesus's account of the Day of Judgement and the crucial importance of responding to simple, unambiguous, cross-cultural, human needs, I wonder at the need of infallibility other than to enforce obedience. And given that in 2013, the Vatican Palace was exposed as the home of a substantially *Mafia*-run bank and of a *paedophile* ring including clergy, one wonders at the usefulness of infallibility. A hopeful sign is that the present Pope is clearly attempting to deal with the situation and abandon the customary practice of hiding it. Another hopeful sign is that Pope Francis seems remarkably normal as a human being.

Of course, from my personal experience, the RC and other

churches and especially the individuals within them can do great good. The huge social benefits of belonging and being connected are referred to earlier. Without being a believer either in God or the RC Church, it is possible to think that most of the <u>individual</u> clergy are principled, moral people doing their best. As stated earlier, I know this to be true from my personal experience of numerous priests and nuns, many of whom are wonderful people by any standard. And the RC and other churches have contributed hugely in terms of schools and hospitals.

Jesus as an atypical, amateurish example of a leader

But as an *institution*, the RC Church, and other 'successful' (i.e. numerous adherents, rich and powerful) religions, is much preoccupied with owning the 'truth' as if it were a commodity and fighting off other religions who wrongly believe that it is they who own the truth.

Compare the RC institution/Vatican and the New Testament in terms of Jesus's attitude to power/survival. There is a huge gap. In fact, in the New Testament, it is hard to see any sign from Jesus whatsoever of legitimate, primate survival approaches such as networking with Rabbis and powerful Romans with a view to acquiring influence and power. In flat contradiction to the current education of priests, Jesus amateurishly chose a small, local, loose and inclusive group of friends – men and women, including a former sex worker ('allegedly'). Maybe he had no trust in or need for years of indoctrination. Why not?

He is characterised by advocating generous, personal and individual responses to the needy. His entry into public life is thought to have started with the statement (initially from the Old Testament prophet, Isaiah) 'I have come to give hope to the poor'. Recently, Archbishop Tutu of South Africa referred to Jesus's 'notorious' bias towards the poor. Indeed, his criteria for entry to Heaven or Hell, given in the Parable of the Sheep and the Goats (Matthew's gospel, see earlier regarding core teaching of religious prophets), are described in terms of responding to human need. Once more, they bear repetition: feed the hungry and thirsty, welcome strangers, clothe the naked and visit the sick and imprisoned. This teaching is entirely compatible with the ideas of the sages of the Axial Age referred to earlier regarding good *behaviour* being key rather than statements of 'faith'. It's not necessary to have a brilliant intellect to understand this, but it does require the ability to override some of our primate instincts to follow such teaching. Without trying grossly to simplify Jesus's message, a reading of the New Testament might lead one to conclude that being a follower of Jesus mainly involved an emphasis on responding to the needy and giving hope to the poor. This is not a behaviour characteristic of primates, expert at biological survival: in fact, it's the opposite. In terms of social status and class, Jesus had been a carpenter and he did not live in a palace, as do Bishops. One might ask, why not? Or perhaps we should ask why *do* Bishops live in palaces and the Pope in the biggest of all?

The answer is obvious in terms of primate power phenotypes. *Of course,* the Pope lives in the biggest palace (except the current Pope Francis does not); he's the alpha-male leader! But the Pope believes that Jesus is God, and Jesus (God) did not live in this way, and he wore ordinary clothes (not a uniform) and had 'ordinary' friends, including women, one of whom (Mary Magdalene) had possibly been a sex worker. Again, maybe Jesus may *not* have regarded prostitution as the worst sin and not worthy of forgiveness and maybe Mary Magdalene was likeable, kind and altruistic? Her friendship with Jesus would suggest that she was indeed kind and altruistic. Unsurprisingly, Jesus did *not* exhibit the primate, alpha-male power phenotype as typically exhibited by Generals, Emperors, Bishops, Popes, celebrities and 'top' people in general.

There are strong hints that the new Pope Francis is thinking along these lines (his new name gives a clue). And, of course, Jesus did not survive the Jewish/Roman institutions. It seems a likely possibility that religious leaders who *actually* oppose the powerful and *actually* change things to improve the lot of the poor and needy will likely meet the fate of Jesus. It doesn't take much imagination to predict what would happen if religious leaders spoke out, not regarding evil in general, but about *specific*, socially explosive issues. Among many possible reasons for silence is the potential for upsetting the powerful, especially when a state religion is hand in glove with them. There are numerous things that need specific denunciation. Slavery has existed for millennia and was accepted in the Bible. The lowly position of women and their abuse has also gone on for millennia, as seen in their social inferiority, in slavery, female genital mutilation, they are still unable to vote in many countries *today*, and they are unable to share the same space as men in some religious ceremonies. Why? The answer is surely <u>biology</u> and not the will of any God.

Need for social control

It would seem that the overriding need for control, to aid the 'survival' of the institution in primate terms, turned the priority from helping the needy towards control. Control probably stems not from evil motives, but rather from the necessity to keep the 'Church' together and <u>*hence also the overall society and culture of the state*</u>. Who controls and decides what are sacraments; which pious practices to support; which miracles and 'holy' relics to authenticate; whom to raise to sainthood? Who decides which books (numerous religions have sacred books serving the same purposes of education and also control and all written by men) are suitable for 'the faithful' to read? Who decided (for long periods) that even the Bible should not be read under pain of <u>*burning in Hell for all eternity*</u> and more briefly in this world? The answer to all – it was the 'Church'. A sleight of hand changes the meaning of church from 'the people of God' into, essentially, the papal Curia – the Pope. And who decides on the education of the clergy and arrangements in seminaries? Surely, this involves indoctrination over many years in the 'correct' <u>beliefs</u> as opposed to selecting adults *already* leading good lives, e.g. the Apostles, chosen by Jesus? The use of the words 'belief' and 'faith' is questionable. Religions *instruct* their adherents in what to believe.

As mentioned elsewhere, we Roman Catholic (Irish Christian Brothers) pupils had a book entitled 'What We Believe', from which we memorised what we believed. Numerous, if not all, religions have similar arrangements for indoctrination.

Apart from 'sins of the flesh', an important and most prominent aspect of the teaching of Catholicism during my childhood (many decades ago), was the Eucharist. The Apostles, with Jesus in imminent danger of arrest, gathered together to commemorate the flight of the Jews from Egypt with a meal involving bread and wine. It is recorded that Jesus referred to the bread as his body and the wine as his blood. Massive discussions and disputes have occurred over centuries about the meaning. It has split Christianity. Does the bread *actually physically, chemically* turn into the flesh of Christ? And does the wine *actually* turn into his blood? The idea that the bread and wine actually turn into body (muscle, nervous tissue, fat and bone) and blood (white and red cells, serum, antibodies) is obviously not true. And yet, as a boy, I have often served at Mass with priests who were neurotically and obsessively worried about dropping even a crumb of Christ's body. One possible and obvious explanation about the 'Last Supper' is that when people <u>with Christ's intentions</u> gather for a meal, then he is present (his ideas, teaching and life). Jesus was obviously well aware of the real, deep, basic significance of sharing a meal. Whatever else are the Last Supper and the Passover meal, they are basic human events that bind people together as well as to remember past participants. Personally, I wonder at the obscure theology about the reality of Christ's body and blood. Is it an unconscious attempt to 'magicify' the Mass with authenticity controlled and verified by clerical magicians?

And how about the other doctrines and creeds that resulted in wars, torture and cruel executions for deviants? And the Trinity – what is that about? Three persons in one God? The Axial Age mystics and prophets thought that these (mysterious) doctrines were harmful: <u>kind behaviour</u> is what they taught. And just before Jesus was executed he taught the same. Help people in need: *the ill, naked, thirsty, hungry, imprisoned, and strangers.* But if the clergy have a tendency to 'magicify' the Eucharist and the Mass, i.e. by controlling the symbols, then they think that they control what is signified. The ritual family meal becomes a magical ceremony. Thus, the clergy specify the nature of the bread and the wine. They also precisely specify all the other arrangements that are part of the Eucharist. For example, whilst personally helping organise a 'Family Mass', a suspicious, 'conservative' priest demanded confirmation from me that the candles used contained the appropriate, *legal* proportion of beeswax! Without the correct clerical candle specifications, the magic does not work, and the Mass is not valid. In such and other ways, a meal that contains God-like significance can be turned into a kind of magic ritual controlled by socially authenticated, clerical, uniformed magicians. And in such ways, we can have Christian people apparently indifferent to the plight of the poor, yet being regular attendees at a church, participating in its pious practices, and immune to Christ's first public statement, 'I have come to give hope to the poor'. And also indifferent to Christ's teaching that the price of entry to Heaven is responding to human need. The need for *biological* survival, aided by our primate instincts, forms a tsunami swamping all.

I have long wondered at how the key symbolism of 'the cross' arose as opposed to, say, active altruism? The reasoning seems to go as follows. Jesus died on the cross to atone for our sins. We, not Jesus, are the guilty ones and should feel guilty. As well as widespread representations of a cross, Catholics are reminded of Jesus's crucifixion by a major service called 'The Stations of the Cross' in which the priest and servers follow representations of Jesus's journey with his cross to Calvary, the place of execution. But how and why did this image of the suffering Jesus swamp all others? According to the New Testament, Jesus himself taught and emphasised love and altruism. It seems likely that the cross and associated guilt is an effective way of attaining *clerical control*. The cross is a very indirect way to imply love and altruism. But the imagery serves a biological purpose: guilt effectively facilitates obedience as does fear of burning in hell. We do good things because we are guilty of Jesus's execution and our sins can be redeemed by doing 'holy' (as defined by the official clergy) things. But Jesus did not emphasise that. Just before his execution, describing the key criteria for entry to Heaven, he said we must help the needy (ill, naked, thirsty, hungry, imprisoned, stranger). Few members of the clergy (probably because of their indoctrination) understand that by responding to one's impulse towards altruism, one is *actually* changed for the better – and not by clerical magic. It's the way humans are. I've mentioned elsewhere a huge Islamic poster near where I live that said 'Be one with the needy'. It could, and should, also be a reminder to followers of Jesus as well as followers of Muhammad. And why do many clergy (definitely RC clergy) wear uniforms? A uniform serves to separate people and reduce individuality, with those in charge being clearly visible. And, in addition, the uniform came from the Court of the emperor, Constantine and is a symbol of power rather than of the sacred. And titles? Does the title 'reverend' mean the official is to be revered? Does the title 'His Holiness' mean that all Popes are holy by virtue of their office?

If it were not from such deep, <u>biological</u> needs, could anyone see any connection whatsoever between the Jesus of the gospels and the Pope in his palace in Rome? But mindlessly, people obediently do! And bizarrely, this reality is independent of whether the Pope is unintelligent, ill-read or of evil intent. Not seeing that the Emperor has no clothes on is the consequence of *biology*, not Satan. As I revise these words (July 2013), Catholics have a new Pope Francis and one of his first acts was to move out of the papal, Vatican apartments. Another was to ring up his milkman back home in Argentina and cancel his normal, unclerical milk order. He is not your normal cleric. I can only wish him well. I really do.

Moral choice: between truth, morality and institutional survival – war

Religious institutions commonly use variations of Heaven and Hell as rewards and punishments for disobedience to the institution's own rules, and to an unwarranted extent. Physical violence or burning alive is acceptable if it's for the 'saving of souls' or if it's 'God's will'. Without suggesting any uniqueness in this respect to the RC Church, the Vatican and the Curia clearly have characteristic primate structures. Even today, many wars and acts of violent terror are justified on the grounds of God's will, believed to be uniquely conveyed to specific religious groups. Thus, some Israelis believe that God gave them personally the so-called 'Holy Land', some Muslims believe that God/Allah requires them to wage a 'Holy War' against specified non-believers, and some Protestant Christian groups believe and teach that the RC Pope is, *literally*, the Devil in the form of a man. Vicious Christian crusades against the Muslims were blessed by Popes as, indeed, virtually any army in history and across cultures is blessed by the indigenous clergy. And yet the world's leaders conduct affairs as if rational discourse alone will solve our problems. At the end of war after war after war, leaders give speeches saying that this must never happen again. We do not learn the lesson that the causes are commonly instincts, always present, and that this explains the repetition. It could be helpful if all religious groups claiming an exclusive channel to God be asked to carry a notice to that effect so that one might avoid them. If only!

This is <u>not</u> to say that all 'successful' churches are run by power-hungry men, consciously plotting to take over the world; or that they are likely to lead evil personal lives. More often, it is the consequences of our instincts, leading to powerful men instinctively acting in ways intended <u>to lead to their group surviving</u> in their world: the power phenotype. Control (and often secrecy) is needed for a concerted response to the numerous threats constantly around us. Survival and safety – such as when Constantine began to favour the Christians and became one – comes from power, money, territory, increased numbers of adherents and group obedience to authority. Indeed,

Constantine and his court gave rise, among many things, to the style of today's 'sacred' vestments referred to earlier, used in the RC Mass and, more importantly, to the 'sensible', political expedient of the official Church bowing to and nurturing relations with the powerful. Clergy bless armies, bombs and warships: this is intelligent, popular, *primate* survival behaviour.

The fifth commandment

The fifth commandment of the Bible is 'Thou shalt not kill'. However, there now exists the doctrine of a 'Just War'. An influence here was Saint Augustine (who also taught that sex is intrinsically evil and only tolerated if used directly and solely for procreation!). In a 'Just War', proclaimed as such, it is okay to kill people in a uniform, especially if the killer is also wearing one? Why is it okay? As I write, an 'enemy' has been bombed, killed and we, the 'goodies', rejoice. Except that, as it turns out, others were killed at the same time by 'drones'. As I revise this in September 2016 there is another accidental slaughter of innocents by drones. Lethal, unmanned USA 'drones' are notorious for killing a much higher proportion of innocent nearby humans than 'terrorists'. No matter, apparently the ends justify the means ('the war on terror'). Also, very importantly, American controllers of the drones are not killed with the bad political consequences in the USA. *But the ends do not justify the means.* Collective punishment is morally wrong, whatever it is called, even if it is called collateral damage. We have endless examples of state religions ignoring large-scale murder, especially during wars. Even something as crystal-clear evil as the Holocaust was not officially and publicly condemned by the official German (or Polish) or Roman Church. The systematic, factory-efficient, large-scale killing of Jews (and other hated people such as homosexuals and gypsies) occurred with a massive, regimented turning of the 'blind eye'. The obvious reason is that attacking one's government, especially a Nazi one, would damage the survival of the Church in terms of the number of adherents and the amount money and influence it has. Similar considerations apply to the Church confessing about its priest paedophiles today (see later).

During this Second World War (and likely all wars), atrocities were committed by both sides with silence by the churches reigning – but often not from courageous individuals. Biologically and from the perspective of (Church) survival, of course the churches were silent. There was indiscriminate bombing of cities with massive civilian casualties and deaths in UK cities such as Coventry, London, Liverpool and elsewhere by Germans. On Tuesday 13th February 1945, the British fire-bombed Dresden with huge civilian casualties. We used 4,500 tons of explosives, destroyed about 13 square miles of the city centre and about 25,000 people were burnt alive in the predicted *firestorm*. At the time, and even since, this was 'justified' as it would end the war sooner against the evil Germans and Nazis. Indeed, in the UK recently, a memorial has been built to *commemorate and glorify the leader of the Dresden atrocity* and the war crime! Of course, the memorial does not refer to war crimes. But human morality is not satisfied with such an animal-like 'justification' as 'shortening' the war. Again, the ends do not justify the means. It was an evil thing to do and is described in horrific detail by Frederick Taylor in his book 'Dresden'.

The biological justification is that we were at war, and in war there is only one rule for *animals* – survive at all costs. And, on an even greater scale, the USA used the nuclear bombs that *incinerated* the entire populations and physical structures of the Japanese cities of Hiroshima* and Nagasaki. And the official Church was silent. ** Nor was the Church vocal about the individuals involved in the process of bombing. The nuclear weapons that incinerated these cities were designed and constructed by numerous humans. They were transported to the war planes by individual drivers. The planes were manned by humans and a human pulled the switch that dropped them. Today, worldwide, nuclear weapons are stored and maintained by humans. Why does the Church not forbid any assistance to this process by any church member under pain of excommunication?

Similarly, why not excommunicate any church member who assisted the Holocaust in any way whatsoever. Anyone reading this knows the answer: it is biologically very dangerous for an institution (or person) to oppose such things.

Notes:

* See earlier re the book 'Hiroshima' by John Hersey about the utter devastation.
** I'm wrong to say that the Church was silent. There was much talk about whether it could *ever* be justified to use nuclear weapons. For example, the policy of 'mutually assured destruction' (MAD) was seriously discussed as preventing nuclear war, although it did not prevent Hiroshima and Nagasaki. And the unofficial Church *as the 'leaven'* protested strongly and actively, i.e. the women at the nuclear base Greenham Common, UK – not all were Christians in name but truly they were in the important sense of following Jesus's teaching. The leaven was the term used by Jesus to describe his true followers who leavened society as yeast did for bread.

Moral choice: between truth, morality and institutional survival – paedophile priests

As well as the above, what follows proves beyond doubt that it is not just a few rotten apples that are corrupting the RC Church. Roman Catholicism is sick.

In 2010 and continuing, we had the dreadful example of the Catholic Church, notably in the USA and in Ireland, with numerous hidden priest paedophiles. It gave a clear example of the choice between responsibility to the organisation's image, affecting its power and status, and the moral need to admit to the evil scandal, deal with the paedophiles *and the culture that maintained them* and help the victims in every way possible. Several successive Archbishops in Ireland knew about and chose to cover up the evil, and *some clergy viciously condemned the victims as part of the cover-up* – most likely to protect what they call 'Holy Mother Church'. The previous Pope Benedict, whilst a Cardinal, writing about a priest paedophile in a letter now widely publicised, advised that consideration be given to the effects on the 'Universal Church' when considering whether the paedophile be exposed. Cardinal Brady of Ireland was accused of a cover-up. Earlier in his career, he investigated paedophilia involving a priest, Eugene Green, known to have abused at least 26 victims.

Interviews with the abused children were held in secret, participants sworn to secrecy and parents not told!

I repeat.

Interviews with the abused children were held in secret, participants sworn to secrecy and parents not told!

This was not the work of a single mad cleric but the work of the official 'Church' that claims to stem from Jesus and in the 21st century. How did these criminals (the paedophiles <u>and</u> those covering up) get away with it? The abuse continued for <u>years</u> *after* the 'Church' knew of the crimes and Green was moved from parish to parish. Subsequently, Father Brady was promoted to be a Cardinal! It's hard not to believe that his loyalty to the unholy secrecy of the Church assisted his promotion. As I write these words, I feel physically sick. Is it at all necessary to point out that the scandal (defined as 'stumbling block before God') is actually the abuse of the child and also the existence of the priest paedophile? *The scandal is <u>not</u> people finding out about the evil, or the bad public relations for the Church.* Significantly, as yet, only one Bishop, but no Archbishop or Pope, has been charged as an accessory to the crimes by 'covering up'. Why? Answer: the <u>primate</u>, worldly power of the Church (i.e. not acting as the leaven of the gospels).

As I revise this section, the new Pope Francis has spoken about the number of paedophile priests and seems determined to do something positive. Further to this, in 2014, it emerged that an active paedophile ring existed within the Vatican! And the

Mafia was a major influence in running the Vatican bank. Why on Earth is it necessary for me to include the biology affecting religion in this book – it's all staring us in the face. All powerful organisations that are secretive tend towards corruption of all kinds. In 2016, Francis proposed that any Bishop who hides paedophilia should be dismissed and sacked. And I would add that all his details should be passed onto the police authorities and should also include medical treatment for the criminal priest. It appears possible that Pope Francis is doing his best to reform the RC Church at the same time as keeping the Church 'together'. But keeping a biologically alpha organisation and its members 'together' and obeying Jesus's clearly expressed wish to focus on the needy is perhaps impossible. Being a biologically active, male-dominated, secret, mega-alpha organisation has consequences which have now been revealed: widespread paedophilia and the Mafia running the Vatican bank. Being a secret alpha organisation has a price that is far too high to pay. Why not change the focus from clergy-controlled, 'sacred', pious practices to a focus on helping the needy as per Jesus's clear statements in Matthew's gospel?

Further evidence of a deeply sick church that has lost its way. As a shocking, sickening postscript to RC Church corruption, the UK's newspaper The Guardian published (March 7th 2017) an account by Emer O'Toole of recent evidence of the massive extent of the state-funded, Church-perpetrated abuse of women and children. It began when Catherine Corless, a local historian from Tuam, County Galway, discovered death certificates for 796 children at the Tuam home for unmarried mothers between 1925 and 1961, but burial records for only two! It turns out that the children's bodies were dumped into a septic tank adjacent to the home run by the Bon Secours Sisters. In 2009, The Ryan Report (2009) documented the systematic sexual, physical and emotional abuse of children in church-run, state-funded institutions. The report revealed that when confronted with evidence of child abuse, the 'Church' would transfer abusers to other institutions where they could *continue their abuse*. The Irish Christian Brothers *legally blocked* the report from naming and shaming its members. The same year, the Murphy Report on the sexual abuse of children in the Archdiocese of Dublin revealed that the Catholic Church's priorities in dealing with paedophilia were *not child welfare*, but rather secrecy, avoidance of 'scandal', the protection of the Church's reputation and the preservation of church assets.

In 2013, the McAleese Report documented the imprisonment of more than 10,000 women in church-run, state-funded laundries where they worked in punitive industrial conditions without pay for the crime of being unmarried mothers.

Emer O'Toole's article refers to the moral bankruptcy and hypocrisy of the Catholic Church after so many enquiries and the consistent, hypocritical expressions of 'shock' by the hierarchy at each new revelation: Ryan Report, Murphy Report, McAleese Report, Cloyne Report, Ferns Report, Raphoe Report and most recently the Tuam scandal.

Later, I make numerous suggestions for the RC Church. But at this point, I briefly suggest that the Irish State prosecutes the Nuns, Priests, Bishops, Cardinals and any Pope (via an international court) who has been covering up the brutal treatment, with a view to imprisonment. Any paedophiles should receive medical help as well as punishment such as imprisonment. Any clergy directly involved in brutality, however long ago, should be prosecuted, again with a view to imprisonment. Pope Benedict should be judged regarding his suggestion that alongside considering the disclosure of abuse should be considered the effects of such disclosure on the Church. He should be put on trial via a theological court in equating the exposure of crime and its just consequences in terms of Church PR, with the actual abuse of children. Pope Benedict has obviously failed in moral theology. Worse, he gave sustenance to the hiding of abuse, as indeed happened for decades.

As for inappropriate evolutionary forces, the RC Church,

enmeshed with the Irish state, clearly is and was an alpha force with appalling powers as perceived by its adherents in terms of 'literally' hellfire/burning alive for all eternity for sinners such as unmarried mothers. Even their children were thought to be tarnished in some way. And sadly, instinctive, biological obedience to these synthetic, manufactured alpha powers, even when reinforced by hellish threats, is totally inappropriate.

Moral choices: Church's use of Public Relations (PR)

Consider Jesus's 'Public Relations' approach. He had none. Despite being recognised by some as the Christ, the Messiah, Jesus was incompetent! Even the least gifted of people can see the merits of Jesus toning down just a little the expression of his beliefs, making friends with the more sensible Roman hierarchy and influential Rabbis, ignoring their minor faults to some extent and starting to build a power base. It is not evil, and it makes sense – *primate* sense. In this respect and in the light of expert, professional Vatican diplomatic behaviour, Jesus was obviously and hopelessly incompetent. I wonder what would have happened if Jesus had asked a suitable friend to help manage his public image? How would a PR advisor handle Jesus's unsuitable friendship with a prostitute (alleged – surely it would have to be alleged)? Horror of horrors, maybe Jesus did not think that prostitution was the greatest evil of all, even if carried out in the past, and not worthy of redemption? As mentioned earlier, maybe Mary Magdalene was a good person, kind and altruistic? Or how to manage Jesus's (the Christ) rather humble trade as a carpenter? And, possibly most tricky of all today in the West, was not Jesus a dark-skinned, Palestinian Jew?

Or maybe Jesus wasn't hopeless. Maybe he was deeply disinterested in such things. Christian theology teaches believers that Jesus (Christ, the Messiah) was fully God and fully human. Much human behaviour and social structure is primate by nature, i.e. it is territorial, experiencing fear of the foreign, suppressing women, with alpha males and obedience to them. What strikes me with great force is that Jesus was indeed fully human – not simply in the sense of separately being God (which I do not believe) and human. His behaviour and teaching, together with that of other major prophets, were *human as opposed to primate,* i.e. he stressed altruism rather than personal survival. Many Popes and church leaders have behaved in a <u>natural</u> (biological) way when confronted with the Hitlers and warlords of this world: 'now is not the right time to speak out'. During the BBC's 'Thought for the Day' on Radio 4, on this very day that I write, a cleric used <u>exactly</u> those precise words to justify silence/inactivity about oppression: '*Now is not the right time to speak out.*' Yet, in the gospels, Jesus appeared not even to consider such things. Why not? For those who believe in his divinity, this must be hugely significant.

Moral choices: Pope Benedict's state visit to the UK
An example that illustrates the modern use of public relations to divert attention from institutional embarrassment is the visit of Pope Benedict to the UK in 2010. It would be difficult to think of a worse time to come to the UK. His visit was undertaken when the UK press and TV were showing considerable hostility over the issue of the widespread paedophilia in the RC priesthood referred to above. An associated issue was the Church's complicity in the worldwide 'cover-up' over at least several decades, including a letter by Pope Benedict before he was Pope (and mentioned above), advising that consideration of the effects on the 'Universal Church' be taken into account before going public. Clearly, he was confusing the real scandal (sin) of the priestly paedophilia and the abused children with his perceived 'scandal' of the Church being found out. At least one of his considerations would have been the possible effect upon 'the faithful' (i.e. those with mindless obedience) and the loss of numbers and prestige. The corporate image of the church would be tarnished.

In the event, his visit was widely judged a success, even a triumph. The handling of the media was described as 'brilliant' and 'sensitive'. The state visit included official meetings with the UK Head of State (the Queen) who is also Head of the established Church of England, the Prime Minister (David Cameron) and meetings and church ceremonies with the Archbishop of Canterbury, together with many Cardinals and Anglican dignitaries. In other words, all the UK alphas. And clearly, in this modern world, his visit required massive security arrangements costing tens of millions of pounds. All went well, surprisingly well. Surprisingly because, unmentioned, was the fact that the RC Church formally teaches that *Anglican orders are invalid*. The Pope believes and teaches that *none* of the non-RC clergy are clergy at all. According to RC teaching, the Archbishop of Canterbury is not an Archbishop or a priest.

In worldly, business terms, an obvious reason for Pope Benedict's willingness to participate in such an 'ecumenical' series of events is that there was the possibility, not of an ecumenical merger, but of a *corporate takeover*: similarly, for the acquiescence of the Vatican. Many Anglican clergy and laity were deeply upset by issues that do not occur in the RC Church, such as accepting women clergy, especially women bishops, gay people of any kind and the widespread liberal attitudes to social issues. They see the RC Church as free of these issues. The idea of an attempted corporate takeover is supported by the relaxing of the previously rigid RC celibacy rules for Anglican 'converts', but not for existing RC clergy. This strategy was successful and resulted in many Anglican clergy converting to Catholicism. The Church of England voted in favour of women priests in 1992. Married Anglican 'priests' (who are *invalid* according to RC teaching) were allowed to remain married when they eventually became validly ordained RC priests. The ban on marriage for existing RC priests remains. Can anyone imagine Jesus being so brilliantly devious and crafty?

A postscript to this story is that Pope Benedict subsequently created a special, ring-fenced category associated with the RC Church to accommodate the immediate movement of clergy (including married clergy) from the Anglican Church. It's called the 'Ordinariate of Our Lady of Walsingham' for Anglican dissenters,

with a designated leader, Keith Newton, previously an Anglican
Bishop. In an historic ceremony on 15th January 2011, Newton and
two other Anglican bishops were ordained as RC priests. Obviously,
plans for this must have been in process well *before* the Pope's UK
visit. Part of their motive was objection to the Anglican plans to
appoint women bishops. The logic is baffling, because absent.
Hatred of the idea of women priests and bishops (and possibly gay
ordinations) is linked to a *sudden* 'belief' in the infallibility of the
Pope, the invalid nature of all Anglican orders (including their own),
possibly ideas about the Eucharist, and the sinfulness of gay sexual
activity. How can anyone suddenly believe such doctrines as a result
of opposing women and gay power? There is no link – except maybe
an instinctive male primate fear of women and gays. Fear can often
disable thought – definitely, something has.

At the end of the Pope's visit, the Prime Minister thanked the
Pope for coming and for his 'religious' influence and assured him and
the country that 'faith' would play a key role in the life of the country.
The political and PR success of his state visit cannot be denied.
But, there is a huge 'but'. The Pope claims to be the representative
of Jesus, of someone who spoke of bringing hope to the poor and
proclaiming that Heaven awaits those who respond to the needy (ill,
naked, thirsty hungry, imprisoned, stranger – acronym 'in this') and
Hell for those who do not. Whilst the Pope did have an unavoidable
meeting with some victims of priestly paedophiles, his main purpose
was a state visit. Why have state visits? Why have a papal state?
Why represent normal, worldly, alpha power? Why not make the
primary (even sole) purpose for his visit to speak about the UK's
successes and failures in gospel terms and make visits involving the
poor and homeless, immigrants, hospitals and prisons? Why not
visit all countries to do this on a regular basis: a gospel-based audit?
The effects of any Pope doing this would surely be massive. It would
indeed be good and useful for all religious leaders to speak out about
such issues: less focus on pious practices, 'holy' relics, miracles, the
censorship of books, how to increase membership and deciding on

saints to create, and more focus on wars, famine and injustice to the needy. Such a change would probably lead to the persecution of church leaders and even to their being killed. Such was the fate of many Old Testament prophets, as well as Jesus, who followed truth rather than political expediency.

Q. Why not do this?

A. The papal state is a worldly, primate structure and the associated hierarchy with their symbols of primate power, disguised as signs of fake holiness, are mainly concerned with status, the number of adherents, dangers from competitors, enforcing pious practices and institutional survival generally.

Postscript: Another shocking exposé of corruption in the 'holy' Roman Curia

The above accounts of unchristian behaviour by the RC Church are shocking, even though it's virtually inevitable that secret, powerful, alpha organisations will have corruption. But it's an especially powerful statement about the importance of primate instincts regarding alpha organisations and alpha males when it applies to a religion claiming to be the expression of God's will.

Nevertheless, recent revelations of the inner workings of the Roman Curia are truly horrifying. Two recent books disclose further corruption in the Vatican. One is 'Merchants in the temple: inside Pope Francis's secret battle against corruption in the Vatican' by Gianluigi Nuzzi. Another is 'Avarizia: Le carte chef Svelano. Ricchezza, scandali e secreti della chiesa di Francesco' by Emiliano Fittipaldi. Happily for English-only readers, 'Avarizia' written in Italian has been reviewed in the London Review of Books 18 February 2016 by Tim Parks, together with 'Merchants in the temple' (already translated). What is revealed in both books is less about paedophilia than about deep-seated, widespread financial corruption throughout the Vatican administration.

The two books were assisted by the leaking of documents from an *ad hoc* Vatican committee set up by Pope Francis. The one woman on the committee was charged by the Vatican state with leaking information to journalists, and *another member went to prison on the same charge*. This is truly sick. The author of 'Avarizia' was given numerous documents and a list of the things that should be known about greed and corruption in the Vatican. Together with Nuzzi's revelations in 'Merchants in the temple', we have the following list of disclosures that speak for themselves:

- specific cardinals' wild spending on their lavish apartments,
- *the hijacking of offerings for the poor for other ends*,
- priests and nuns stashing away money in tax havens,
- transforming the process of canonisation into a lucrative business,
- the dodgy exploitation of the Vatican's tax-free status,
- a diplomat priest using a diplomatic bag to *move Mafia money* across the Swiss border, Salerno priests granted money for an orphanage for the poor who built a *luxury hotel instead*.

There are many more appalling examples. Why are we shocked? Maybe it's because people have been conned about symbols. Clerics are all *officially* holy people, belonging to officially *holy* organisations. The 'proof' is shown by wearing *holy* clothes and other fake symbols of *holiness*. A true symbol of true holiness according to all of the humane prophets, including Jesus, is the actual behaviour of someone who is actually helping needy people.

An agnostic's view of a possible, rational God

Perhaps I should mention again my own personal position on religion. I am no longer a Roman Catholic. My best description might be as an agnostic leaning towards atheism with a strong attraction to the morality portrayed in the New Testament and by many prophets, i.e. altruism. As for the conventional God, I am certainly an atheist. It is not that I do not *believe* in the conventional God; it's that I *know* that such a being cannot exist. I also have some logical issues with my ex-Church. In the case of Christianity, the teaching is that God is all-powerful and all-loving. A frequent definition of God is that 'God is love'. But Christians already have a definition of love (or God-like activity) in St Matthew's gospel – one's response to human need. So why does God, himself, not respond to the human needs of the starving, thirsty, naked, homeless, ill, strangers and imprisoned? So, something does not follow here. It seems to me that God cannot be *both* all-powerful and all-loving. And the idea of 'allowing' us free will does not easily obscure this problem. Unborn infants with Aids or the Ebola infection have neither committed any offence nor used 'free will' sinfully, and people without food might simply be suffering from a climate catastrophe. Also, the idea of free will is being eroded by emerging evidence about the influence of genetics and child development on personality and behaviour. Also, as mentioned earlier, total free will cannot easily be squared with the fact that more 'sin' and crime is committed in unequal societies. That is, God and Satan are both influenced in their behaviour towards individual humans by *social* inequality, i.e. tempting, punishing, rewarding. The idea of God, propagated by numerous religions, is to me clearly irrational, varying and remarkably anthropomorphic.

What is God's plan?
For believers, the following question requires an answer. Did God intend to give different messages at different times to different people, and sometimes directly contradictory messages? Did God allow these myriad teachings about him to exist whilst he (in effect, secretly) gave the real truth only to one of these religions or sub-religions or sects? On the face of it, this does not seem a good way to convey the truth by anyone and certainly not by a supremely intelligent God. On the other hand, if 'official' religion's function is biological, to provide a social glue and offer meaning about the universe and thus help a particular society to survive, then diversity of religions is a reflection of this biological need for survival in different societies and changing environments.

Some features are common across religions. For example, in wars, it is common for all religions to bless the troops and the weapons, even when the war is between states with the same religion. Thus, biological necessity for survival trumps theology.

An alternative view

If one accepts the existence of God, it could be that God is not controlled by the clergy (magic by magicians), but speaks to each person individually, directly and unambiguously and speaks about the same truths as in Matthew's gospel (25, 34). That is, about what is good and bad behaviour, about what God wants. To support this view, it is universally evident and *supported by empirical sociological studies* that humans of different cultures agree closely about what is good and what is bad behaviour, and it coincides with Matthew's account of the Last Judgement in the New Testament. It also accords with the teaching of the major prophets, including those of the Axial Age mentioned earlier, namely: the supreme good is to respond to human needs and to ignore them is bad. One might ask if this makes altruism a human instinct, or at least gives rise to the common belief that it is good. In 'Zen and the Art of Motor Cycle Maintenance', Robert Pirsig has an initial page with the following quote from Plato:

> *'And what is good, Phaedrus,*
> *And what is not good –*
> *Need we ask anyone to tell us these things?'*

Yes, indeed: we need not ask. But such following of individual conscience could clash with the biological survival of one's culture and clash with the clerical control of the particular religion upholding that culture. And numerous authors have offered biological explanations for inherent tendencies towards altruism. Such altruistic behaviour can contribute to social happiness and hence it glues us together and increases the likelihood of the survival of our group and of our genes. But how about altruism towards non-group members and foreigners?

How to increase expression of altruism and control basic instincts. RC Church as exemplar

Suggestions for improvement by answering human needs, assisting the expression of human instincts, harmonising basic instincts and humanising the organs of religion

Given my familiarity with Christianity, especially Roman Catholicism, I will not make suggestions for other religions, although the same principles apply. For Christians, I make suggestions with little hope that they would be followed. But they are serious suggestions that I believe would help, so I list them. Namely, that religious leaders (e.g. Pope, Bishop, Parish Priest or equivalents of other religions) visit their constituencies (e.g. countries, dioceses, parishes, societies) and regularly check that there is a focus on the insights of their own prophet, e.g. Jesus, and perform an audit. Christian churches claim <u>not</u> to seek 'worldly' power, but to further God's (Christ's) wishes.

Suggestions for Pope Francis and the bishops

Broadly. Abandon the materialistic, corrupt, political machinations involved in the 'papal state' (happily, it seems that the new Pope Francis may have already started). Amazingly, as far as I can learn, the Pope Benedict Vatican has not denied the existence of a *paedophile* 'ring' in the Vatican, nor has he or Pope Francis denied the major influence of the *Mafia* on the Vatican bank! A combination of secrecy and power so often, maybe always, leads to extreme corruption. Abusive nuns and priests worldwide in children's homes, and a hierarchy cover-up, a Vatican paedophile ring, the Mafia and the Vatican bank! I wonder why the Western media has not been more horrified? If it were a Muslim (or Russian) Vatican, it would surely have been attacked at more length and with more self-righteous vigour. Re-reading Matthew's gospel account of the Day of Judgement and remembering my Catholic education suggests some radical and worthwhile actions.   I have <u>rarely</u> heard a sermon telling me that helping the needy or not was the key to Heaven or Hell.   And did Jesus say that the clergy had an exemption?

Clearly, the *official* Catholic Church (and numerous other official churches) has gone off the rails.   They have condoned evil, covered it up and allowed paedophiles to continue abusing children.   The Church still has a huge focus on obedience, i.e. biological, social, survival glue.   Hellfire for those who ignore the needy?   Forget it (literally)!

Hellfire (for eternity) is for those who miss Mass and otherwise <u>*disobey the institution*</u>*!*

That <u>is</u> its biological role: to glue society together to gain obedience.   Hellfire is for those who did not go to 'confession' as often as prescribed.   Hellfire is for those who use contraception and have fewer Catholic children.   Hellfire is for those who masturbate or for boys who touch girls below the waist and for the girls too.   Touching a girl above the waist (breasts were never mentioned in my schooling) is a grey area and maybe a venial sin, punished by Purgatory.   A similar grey area is kissing – maybe Purgatory.   This was my conventional Catholic upbringing.   My real, actual teachers were wonderful people, including numerous 'ordinary' priests, as well as Jesuits and Dominicans and members of a women's lay order 'The Grail' who were *all* more or less at odds with the machinery of the 'system'.   The cold, relentless, heartless system is the Devil, if I believed in one, which I do not (see below).   Or maybe it's well described as Saint John's 'the face of the beast'.   That is what Daniel Berrigan told me was his view of the 'system'.

Specific suggestions for increasing the expression of human instincts and controlling basic ones

1. All Catholics (and other religious people) should abandon their mindless focus on dogma, creeds and so-called pious practices and *individually and actively* work for change to help the needy.   And not just the obviously needy, as in Matthew's gospel.   We all need kindness, so all Christians

should aspire to be kind to everyone. For Christians, they would have the comfort of knowing that Jesus more than approves, he demands it. It would seem evident that a crowning characteristic of human biology is its capacity for altruism. Jesus agrees to the extent that his criterion for entry to Heaven consists of helping those in need. In other words, cope with our primate, basic instincts re territory, fear of the foreign and alphas, and express the human ones.

2. I seriously and respectfully (truly) suggest to Pope Francis that he first publicly <u>closes down</u> the entire Catholic Church, including the deeply corrupt Irish Church, and publicly confesses its sins, and admits that it has lost its way. And there should be no quibbling that the sins have been exaggerated and are not as bad as made out. Then the Church could restart after everyone has had time to re-read the New Testament, especially the key requirements in Jesus's 'last will and testament' regarding the Day of Judgement in Matthew's gospel. Note that Jesus, via Matthew, mentioned <u>*only*</u> attending to human need, defined in cross-cultural examples. He omitted to make any mention of adherence to clerical, 'pious' practices or the 'so-called' spiritual life. And remember that Jesus was not having a chat in a local tavern with a few friends; he was speaking shortly before his predicted execution and emphasising how he would return on the Day of Judgement as the Messiah, and he gave the criteria for that judgement – which should be massively significant for believers. Also, it's important to note that Jesus was <u>*not*</u> *mindlessly obedient to his own Church* that was behind his imminent execution.

Then, the Pope should sell all the awe-inspiring churches, cathedrals and buildings that are normally empty or give them away or use them for helping the ill, naked, thirsty, hungry, imprisoned or strangers or otherwise needy. Currently, we have refugees escaping the horrors of war and persecution coming towards Western Europe, notably from Syria, Iraq and Afghanistan. The Pope could urge that neighbouring church buildings be offered as temporary homes, with extra cooking and toilet facilities. Of course, he'd have to ignore the appalling screams from the British press about the lazy, unpleasant, scroungers whom they frequently castigate. Did Jesus miss something about the needy that the UK Daily Mail has seen? And the so-called 'fundamentalist' Christians ('Magic Circle' religion, see above) would scream too. I am reminded of a sermon at a Mass, whilst I was an 'active' Catholic, that was unique for me. It was a Dominican priest denouncing in a calm, rational way, the existence of expensive, mostly underused churches and he included the building that we were in – a university chaplaincy. It was a pleasing and exceptional happening also because the priest was a good friend of the resident priest who took no offence (and likely agreed with him – I knew them both slightly).

3. Enter the political fray solely on behalf of the starving, thirsty, naked, homeless, ill, strangers/foreigners, imprisoned or otherwise needy as emphasised by Jesus. *This* is the sacred, holy behaviour demanded by Jesus for entry to heaven. It also accords with our *human* nature.

4. Abandon the idea that any buildings are sacred. Have buildings useful to help the needy. Where unwise to sell, allow others to share existing buildings. Imagine the symbolism of turning the Vatican into homes for the homeless and the poor! And consider the current actual and real symbolism of Bishops and Popes living in palaces and dressing in special, 'sacred' garments: 'sacred' in the sense of coming from the converted Emperor Constantine's royal dress code. They were old symbols of power. Biologically it was a smart survival move. Now, they are symbols of a peculiar religiosity. In terms of the gospels, it's wrong and bad.

5. Abandon the practice of having Junior Seminaries. There

is much evidence that removing young children from their parents and their home causes problems in their development. In the case of Junior Seminaries, there is the added component of indoctrination regarding sacred dogma, sacred biblical texts, sacred practices and separation from the normal, mixed human community.

6. Turn seminaries in the UK into colleges for the dissemination of best practice for helping the needy and for the study mainly of the New Testament, Christian theology and the basic teachings of other religions. Have mostly short or, at most, one-year courses.

7. Allow ordination to the priesthood of people *already carrying out the teaching of the* gospel, i.e. those already helping the needy. This, whether married or not. The Apostles did not attend seminary.

8. Abandon the priestly emphasis on the church-directed duties of holding services, buildings maintenance and so-called pious practices. One such pious practice is kneeling down to remind an all-knowing, all-good, all-powerful, God repeatedly that he is all-knowing, all-good and all-powerful, i.e. a primate, improbable God who likes adulation and has a bad memory. Focus instead should be on the needy, including the needs of their own Christian people, as well as non-Christians – anyone. They might do well to consider the practice of Sikhs who build temples with four doors facing in different directions (north, south, east and west) to allow entry of anyone at any time who seeks food, warmth and shelter.

And specifically check:

9. The degree to which the unit (country, diocese, parish) directly responds to the human needs specifically of the starving, thirsty, naked, homeless, ill, strangers and imprisoned, etc. etc. Yes, this is repetition, needed and in line with Archbishop Tutu's comments about Christ's

notorious bias towards the poor.

The Pope and Bishops could stop the practice of piously denouncing evil in general. They should specifically denounce relentlessly and attempt actually to change such things as:

i)   the wars and atrocities that occur regularly; advise Catholic soldiers, Catholic designers and manufacturers of nuclear and other arms and Catholic drivers of such weaponry and the many who play small but necessary roles in wars however evil. Think about their involvement which might carry excommunication. Make explicit that the wearing of a uniform does not exempt anyone from their moral duty.

ii) the existence anywhere of hunger and homelessness;

iii) the lack of healthcare for the sick;

iv) the attacks on foreigners anywhere;

v)   the condition of and lack of rehabilitation arrangements for the imprisoned.

The Pope could remind all that these matters were the subject of Jesus's account of the criteria for entry to Heaven or Hell on the Day of Judgement (Matthew's gospel, 25). The Pope could praise and point out best practice wherever it exists. Similarly, for other Christian leaders such as Bishops and Priests. Again, like the little boy who points out that the Emperor is naked, I point out Jesus's basic teaching, so often and widely ignored by Christians.

10. The Pope could also check the degree to which the services have been clericalised, dehumanised and 'magicified'. Happily, this is now mostly long changed, but as an altar boy, the altar was cut off from the rest of the church by a low barrier as we (me and the priest) got on with the Mass in <u>Latin</u> – in Latin! The people 'participated' by watching what was going on; few/none would understand the Latin. But they felt that somehow they benefitted from attending

the service and watching what was going on as a spectator. It's not far, *if at all*, from benefitting from magic conducted by a magician. A small minority of wrongly described 'fundamentalists' are allowed to continue this alienating practice. Why? In what sense is it fundamental? In what sense does it repeat Jesus's last *meal* with his friends? It is no longer a real meal – it has been clericalised and magicified. Even the bread has been transformed into a clericalised, white wafer almost devoid of any nutrient whose 'baking' is closely controlled by the subservient women clergy/nuns. Often, the clergy distinguish the superior, 'spiritual side' of religion, such as pious practices of the rosary, benediction, stations of the cross and Mass from the inferior, 'social side' of helping the needy.

11. The degree to which everyone is welcomed into the community (e.g. the parish) and everyone is helped to feel that they belong should be monitored. Happily, this welcome does occur frequently, almost always. It's a hugely important asset, especially for people moving towns.

12. Give notice to abolish all the hierarchical categories of biological, alpha-male power (Pope, Cardinal, Archbishop, Bishop, Monsignor, Canon, etc.) and discuss ways and means for people to be involved in decisions about who are leaders where necessary. The Quaker systems strongly merit consideration.

A summary – magicifying 'the Church'

For the clerical alphas (the 'Church'), the laity are the 'faithful'; i.e. they are faithful to clerical control. Clergy have changed the *focus* from helping the needy ('the social side of religion' – a prime focus of Jesus and of Isiah) to a magical side, also called the 'spiritual' side, i.e. Mass (non-attendance meant hellfire for eternity), benediction, stations of the cross, and the rosary that could reduce the time in Purgatory by an amount decided by the alpha clergy. This reduction sometimes could be affected by payments to the clergy. Magic means that control of the signs indicates control of what is signified. Clerical alphas say magic words and display magic signs. God is often portrayed as the great magician: doing this, doing that, manipulating. The 'Last Supper' with Jesus and his Apostles is the basis of the Mass. 'Meet together for a meal to remember me and I'll be with you' has been replaced by a ceremony, throughout my youth and ages before, that was performed *in Latin* – mostly incomprehensible – and behind a low marble wall (for Anglicans there was a wooden Rood Screen separating off the clergy). The bread was replaced by sacred 'bread' consisting of 'pure' white wafers, devoid of nutrition made by holy nuns. A meal with friends to remember Jesus is quite different and is indeed truly spiritual. It is most certainly not magic, controlled by clergy. For biological reasons, the Vatican 'spiritual life' is about control – biological control for the biological survival of the Vatican Corporation and indirectly society. The use of the word 'corporation' is not for sarcasm, but because it is accurate.

Following *biological* inner drives, clergy replaced the God of Jesus with their own creations, called 'spiritual' practices. Jesus advised addressing God as 'Papa'. The later, clerical God requires adoration, constant praise and, as mentioned previously, is forgetful – he needs reminding of his (definitely 'his') power. The Vatican Corporation teaches that Heaven can be achieved (redemption) only by following their orders, i.e. do as they say. In Matthew's gospel, and at the end of his life, Jesus emphasises *only* the need to help people. The Vatican Corporation is largely a conventional, primate entity wanting to survive and expand its power. Jesus was fully human and fully altruistic.

Note: I suggest to any Christian cleric, Pope, Bishop or whatever hierarchical rank who may object to these suggestions as being impractical, to go into a quiet room and re-read the New Testament. The bit in St Matthew's gospel about the criteria for entry to Heaven could be a start. Jesus was not socialising with his friends in a pub. He gave this firm teaching a couple of days before his anticipated execution, so his mind was sharply focussed. It's also worth bearing in mind Jesus's statement (from Isaiah) at the start of his Ministry – 'I have come to give hope to the poor'. This was emphasised in recent decades by the unmistakable followers of Jesus, the wonderful Archbishop Tutu and the fully human, fully normal Daniel Berrigan whom I was proud to know personally.

HOW WE MIGHT TACKLE HUMANITY'S PROBLEMS

(iii) Recognising the influence of biological evolution on Commerce, Media, Habitats and Culture

Contents

COMMERCE AND BUSINESS: DRIVEN BY CAPITALISM, SOCIALISM OR COMMUNISM

Introduction
First of all, are listed definitions, quotations and pithy sayings from some of the world's most eminent thinkers and serious politicians. The latter quotations make clear that the world's major problems have long been clearly recognised. Notably, the problems of the USA in dealing with corporations and their influence on politics have clearly been recognised by presidents listed earlier and who were unable to achieve their goals. Some readers may find this list too much, but I ask them to continue.

Definitions from dictionaries
Oxford dictionaries – 'Capitalism'
> An economic and political system in which a country's trade and industry are controlled by private owners for profit, rather than by the state: *an era of free-market capitalism – private ownership is a key feature of capitalism.*

Vocabulary.com – 'Socialism'
> These days, the word socialism gets tossed around so much, it's almost lost all meaning. Originally, though, it was the bedrock of Marxism and meant that the workers and their community should control the market relating to what they made.
> Because the Soviet state eventually strayed far from Marx's idea of socialism and towards Lenin's totalitarian communism, *socialism* is now often used to mean everything from 'fascism' to 'progressivism'. But in its purest form, socialism was a political, social and economic system meant to empower the working class. In Marxist theory, socialism is a transitional social state between the overthrow of capitalism and the realisation of communism.

The Free Dictionary – 'Capitalism'
An economic system in which the means of production and distribution are privately or corporately owned and development occurs through the accumulation and reinvestment of profits gained in a free market.

> *Advocates of capitalism are apt to appeal to the sacred principles of liberty. But liberty is not the freedom to harm others. Russell satirised 'liberty' in one maxim: 'The fortunate must not be restrained in the exercise of tyranny over the unfortunate.'*
>
> **Bertrand Russell** (1872-1970), British logician and philosopher

Oxford Dictionary – 'Communism'
1. 'Community of goods' as a social system, with the necessary provisions for labour and distribution
2. Movement or political party advocating the above
3. Party affirming the need for a dictatorship of the proletariat

Oxford Dictionary – 'Socialism'
State ownership and control of the means of production, distribution and exchange

Definitions and comments from economists and philosophers

> *'The decadent international but individualistic capitalism in the hands of which we found ourselves after the war is not a success. It is not intelligent. It is not beautiful. It is not just. It is not virtuous. And it doesn't deliver the goods.'*
>
> **John Maynard Keynes, British economist, 1883-1946**

'Capitalism is the astounding belief that the most wickedest of men will do the most wickedest of things for the greatest good of everyone.'

John Maynard Keynes, British economist, 1883-1946

'Civil government, so far as it is instituted for the security of property, is in reality instituted for the defence of the rich against the poor, or of those who have some property against those who have none at all.'

Adam Smith, 'The Wealth of Nations', 1723-1790

'But what all the violence of the feudal institutions could never have effected, the silent and insensible operation of foreign commerce and manufactures brought about. These gradually furnished the great proprietors with something for which they could exchange the whole surplus produce of their lands, and which they could consume themselves without sharing it either with tenants or retainers. All for themselves, and nothing for other people, seems in every age of the world, to have been the vile maxim of the <u>masters of mankind</u>. As soon therefore, as they could find a method of consuming the whole value of their rents themselves, they had no disposition to share them with any other person.'

Adam Smith, 'The Wealth of Nations'

'To expose a 15 trillion-dollar ripoff of the American people by the stockholders of the 1000 largest corporations over the last 100 years will be a tall order of business.'

Buckminster Fuller (1895-1983)

'The history of all hitherto existing society is the history of class struggles... Our epoch, the epoch of the bourgeoisie, possesses, however, this distinct feature: it has simplified class antagonisms. Society as a whole is more and more splitting up into two great hostile camps, into two great classes directly facing each other – Bourgeoisie and Proletariat.'

Karl Marx and Friedrich Engels, 'Manifesto of the Communist Party', 1847

(**Note:** 'alphas and non-alphas')

As mentioned in the main Introduction to the book, evolution affects every aspect of life and inevitably it's not possible to be expert in every aspect of life, however many years were spent in study. May I remind the reader that the book started as jottings of ideas when I was in my early 20s and developed continuously ever since. In dealing with this section on commerce, business, socialism, communism and capitalism, this handicap applies as strongly as elsewhere. And as elsewhere, I've had to read widely and for a long period. But I still remain far short of being a professional economist. Nevertheless, my basic question immediately below remains the same as for other chapters on social structures.

Do our activities in business and commerce reflect our origins in evolution?   How can they assist community and personal belonging?

I have quoted numerous authorities, to emphasise that the potential evils of capitalism have been widely recognised for centuries, especially its influence on society via political parties being *bribed*. My searches revealed an absence of any mention of anything regarding innate impulses and biological instincts. Why do stockbrokers and many businesses repeatedly manipulate entire markets for their advantage? Why do *multi-billionaires* loot and hide billions of \$/£ in tax havens and harm their *fellow* citizens? The Queen of England (Head of the Church of England) has been using off-shore banking, probably unknowingly. There are mentions of self-interest, evil people and greed. 'Irrational movements' of markets are also often mentioned, but overwhelmingly there is either an assumption of rationality or of evil. Here is a metaphor. There is a large pile of stones at the bottom of a steep hill. More and more stones pile up. Why? People are measuring the exact shape of the stones, the surface characteristics of friction, their weight and also amassing data about the constancy of the accumulation. In this 'reasoning', no attention is given to the existence of the hill and that at the top of the hill there are large quantities of round stones. Gravity has similarities to instincts: it's there, always influencing, but not always noticed.

In the case of instincts, there's also an instinct *not* to see – as in the case of the fable, 'The Emperor's New Clothes' by Hans Christian Andersen. Thus, an explanation of the looting is the presence of inappropriately expressed instincts ('innate impulses') regarding alpha males and obedience to them.

Clear role of basic instincts
I repeat something elaborated on elsewhere. The money spent on armaments by all nations is variously estimated to be around $1,700 billion. Why are the nations of the world so divided as to spend such sums? The answer is in our basic instincts inherited from small groups of apes living in trees whose survival was aided by their instinctive behaviour. That is, fearing the foreign (including men fearing women), massive concern about their territory, obedience to their alpha males and also the instinctive behaviour of the alphas to take the best. These are all about the survival of apes in trees. But these instincts that aided the survival of small groups of apes in their arboreal existence, are often unsuitable in our modern world with massive populations and access to previously unimaginable weaponry of world-destroying power, _already_ *used twice* and with several recorded near accidents. On top of weaponry, we have capacity for our alphas to steal finance also on an unprecedented scale with modern digital, computing technology. About 20-30% of

the *world's* GDP is owned by a handful of people. This looted finance is removed from its 'natural' local economy where it could circulate and reappears elsewhere in the world as empty mega properties or mega expensive works of art kept in locked vaults. This looting is rarely mentioned in the world's media. For example, I have rarely heard any reference to it on any BBC programme or reported in any reputable newspaper. If any species of any other living organism behaved like this, they'd soon become extinct. If only all the humans in the world could cope with their basic instincts and give expression much more to human ones, especially altruism? This was advised by all the major world prophets.

Compelling evidence of the drawbacks of the 'commercial' alpha male
In the commercial world, there is current attention given to the CEO genius or 'transformational leader'. I have referred elsewhere to evidence from several workers and notably Meredith Belbin who uses management approaches that are highly compatible with human biology, including the existence of instincts. In modern, human society it would seem certain that problems are vastly more complex than in an ape society. Belbin has categorised various personality types that can play different roles in a management team and, importantly and usefully, identified combinations that are more likely to see opportunities and problems from their different perspectives. www.belbin.com/about/belbin-team-roles/; www.teambuilding.co.uk/belbin-team-role.html On the other hand, there is current evidence of the dangers of an organisation being led by a CEO genius or 'transformational leader'. In an article in the newspaper, 'The Observer' (1st December 2013), Nick Cohen wrote about industrial alpha males who contributed to or caused the recent financial crashes. He refers to the leadership of Stalin's Russia, L. Ron Hubbard's Church of Scientology, and the old UK Communist Party and makes close comparison with current bank leaders. There was also the exceptionally toxic leadership of Hitler. Moreover, in Iain Martin's biography of the alpha-male leader of the Royal Bank of Scotland, Fred Goodwin, evidence is given of his

tyrannical manner. These organisations' structures were 'top-down' in the extreme. In 'The dark side of transformational leadership', Dennis Tourish points out that while the objectives of these disparate organisations (and others) varied in terms of social paradise, divine salvation or money, the means by which they worked are very similar regarding enforcement by hierarchies. To be more precise, it involves personal enforcement by the alpha leader and obedience by the rest, i.e. a primate structure.

Before presenting the main ideas relevant to this chapter, it seemed best to start, as above, with a variety of dictionary definitions and also pithy 'sayings' by eminent thinkers conveying the essence of their thought. The driving force behind modern commerce and business in the West is often stated to be capitalism. But the biological foundation must surely include the basic primate (also present in humans) instincts, including the *alpha-male instincts of taking the best and doing so as of right, without limit and taking it for granted*. This is helpful in the primate world in that *per se* a healthy leader helps the small, 'tree-living' group in which he belongs and the 'takings' are necessarily limited by Mother Nature. Not so limited in modern, capitalist states. The early presidents of the USA (see above) were well aware of the social power of vastly wealthy corporations and of their malign and undemocratic influence on politics and laws. As mentioned elsewhere, Donald Trump now (August, 2017) has their agents in his cabinet.

The Communist Manifesto

In the mid 19th century, Karl Marx and Frederick Engels were prominent in the intellectual ferment that led to the Russian and also the Chinese Revolutions. The Communist Manifesto was published in 1847 after a large gathering in London of communists from numerous countries. It was authored by Marx and Engels. The Manifesto pointed out what was thought to be the inevitable consequences of pushing down the wages of the lowest paid workers as manufacturing, global capitalism and global markets produced ever cheaper products.

And today this description is still apt and still no revolution

I quote from the Manifesto:

1. *The need of a constantly expanding market for its products chases the bourgeoisie over the entire surface of the globe. It must nestle everywhere, settle everywhere and establish connexions everywhere.*

2. *In proportion as the bourgeoisie, i.e., capital, is developed, in the same proportion as the proletariat, the modern working class, developed – a class of labourers, who live only so long as they find work, and who find work only so long as their labour increases capital. These labourers, who must sell themselves piecemeal, are a commodity, like every other article of commerce, and are consequently exposed to all the vicissitudes of competition, to all the fluctuations of the market.* (My addition: this is similar to modern slaves and to previous slaves who were legally and officially 'converted' into commodities to enable reimbursement to the owners by the UK state).

3. *Hence, the cost of production of a workman is restricted, almost entirely, to the means of subsistence that he requires for maintenance, and for the propagation of his race. But the price of a commodity, and therefore also of labour, is equal to its cost of production.*

4. *The history of all hitherto existing society is the history of class struggles.*

In the UK in the summer of 2016 (not 1816), much light has been shone on large companies based on the above ideas. In the UK newspaper the 'i' 11th June 2016, Janet Street-Porter commented on the following. There are around 800,000 so-called zero-hours 'contracts' for part-time posts, in which the worker has no rights but must be available for work. BHS had £580 million removed in dividends and bonuses over 15 years. At this point, after being asset-stripped, it was sold with a huge pension deficit for £1. The purchaser had been bankrupted three times and had nil experience of retailing. Another large company, 'Sports Direct', had Dickensian work practices, including holding workers in a pen at the end of a shift and searching for stolen items. In this case, only 200 staff had permanent contracts and 3,000 temporary staff were *supplied by agencies*. At the same time, 'gang masters' control much of the UK fruit and vegetable picking, egg packing and food processing industries. The vast majority of the workers in these gangs are on zero-hours 'contracts'.

It seems clear that the essence of the Manifesto regarding the 'history-long' class struggle and the inevitable victory of the proletariat is incompatible with biological *instincts* (innate propensity or impulse), notably alpha males, the power phenotype and the instinct to obey. The alpha male and his instincts existed in the ape world and they continue in ours. It seems highly likely that these instincts will continue for the foreseeable future. Despite the beautiful hopes and ideals of these socialists/communists, we had disasters. Far from the proletariat triumphing, we now have a substantial proportion of the world's GDP sequestered away by elite individuals. In their own financial terms, it's their 'triumph'. Perhaps 'disgrace' would be a better word for such behaviour by humans.

It seems that the essence of the Manifesto regarding the history-long class struggle and belief in the inevitable victory of the proletariat are enshrined in the following additional extract from it.

> 'Hitherto, every form of society has been based, as we have already seen, on the antagonism of oppressing and oppressed classes. But in order to oppress a class, certain conditions must be assured to it under which it can, at least, continue its slavish existence. The serf, in the period of serfdom, raised himself to membership in the commune, just as the petty bourgeois, under the yoke of the feudal absolutism, managed to develop into a bourgeois. The modern

labourer, on the contrary, instead of rising with the process of industry, sinks deeper and deeper below the conditions of existence of his own class. He becomes a pauper, and pauperism develops more rapidly than population and wealth. And here it becomes evident, that the bourgeoisie is unfit any longer to be the ruling class in society, and to impose its conditions of existence upon society as an over-riding law. It is unfit to rule because it is incompetent to assure an existence to its slave within his slavery, because it cannot help letting him sink into such a state, that it has to feed him, instead of being fed <u>by him</u>. Society can no longer live under this bourgeoisie, in other words, its existence is no longer compatible with society. The essential conditions for the existence and for the sway of the bourgeois class are the formation and augmentation of capital; the condition for capital is wage-labour. Wage-labour rests exclusively on competition between the labourers. The advance of industry, whose involuntary promoter is the bourgeoisie, replaces the isolation of the labourers, due to competition, by the revolutionary combination, due to association. The development of Modern Industry, therefore, cuts from under its feet the very foundation on which the bourgeoisie produces and appropriates products. What the bourgeoisie therefore produces, above all, are its own grave-diggers. Its fall and the victory of the proletariat are equally inevitable.'

The Corn Laws

Another interesting historical example is the Corn Laws. They were trade laws designed to protect cereal producers in the United Kingdom of Great Britain and Ireland against competition from less expensive foreign imports between 1815 and 1846. To ensure that

British landowners reaped all the financial profits from farming, the Corn Laws imposed steep import duties, making it too expensive for anyone to import grain from other countries, *even when the people of Great Britain and Ireland needed the food (as in times of famine)*. The laws were introduced by the Importation Act 1815 and repealed by the Importation Act 1846 around the time of the publication of the Communist Manifesto. The economic issue was food prices. The price of grain was central to the price of the most important staple food, bread: the working man spent much of his wages on bread.

The political issue was a dispute between landowners (heavily represented in Parliament) and the new class of manufacturers and industrialists (who were not). The landowners wished to maximise their profits from agriculture, by keeping grain prices high. The latter wished to maximise their profits from manufacturing, by reducing the wages they paid to their factory workers. The 'problem' was that men could not work in the factories if a factory wage was not enough to feed them and their families. Thus, high grain prices kept factory wages 'high'. The Corn Laws enhanced the profits and political power associated with land ownership. Their abolition meant a significant increase in free trade. As is so often the case, including today, a key question can often be 'how little can an employer pay his employee and still keep him/her alive?' This indifference to the plight of one's employees was part of what the early communists despised.

The modern world economy
Aspects of the world economy, especially as influenced by the USA, are also considered in the section above on the USA ('The USA and the UK as special cases'). It's no exaggeration to say that our world economy is dysfunctional and is grossly biased towards benefitting the super-rich who control it. Shaxson, in his book 'Treasure Islands' (since made into a film), quotes 2010 evidence from the IMF of $18 trillion in small island financial centres alone: they thought that this was probably an underestimate. Compare this with the world's Gross Domestic Product of about $70-80 trillion. More recently, according

to Oxfam's estimates in 2013, a similar figure of about $18.5<u>tn</u> is being held for individuals in tax havens, one third of it in British Overseas Territories and Crown dependencies such as the Cayman Islands. The charity said that even on conservative assumptions, the $18.5<u>tn</u> would yield $156bn to tax authorities around the world, whilst the cost of providing every person on Earth with an income of $1.25 a day would be $66<u>bn</u>. Emma Seery, Oxfam's Head of Development, Finance and Public Services, said:

> *'These figures put the UK at the centre of a global tax system that is a colossal betrayal of people here and in the poorest countries who are struggling to get by, and they put the government on the side of the privileged few...'*

'Treasure Islands' also quotes several references to the following and disturbing statistics. Over 50% of world trade passes through tax havens, over half of all banking assets and a third of foreign direct investment by multinational corporations are routed offshore. In 2008, 83 of the USA's biggest 100 corporations had subsidiaries in tax havens. In 2009, it was shown that <u>99 of Europe's 100 largest companies used offshore subsidiaries</u>: in each case the largest user was a bank. Due to the lack of agreement regarding the definition of a tax haven, Shaxson offers a loose one. He defines a tax haven as 'a place that seeks to attract business by offering politically stable facilities to help people or entities get around the rules, laws, and regulations of jurisdictions elsewhere'. He states that the whole point is to offer escape routes from the duties that come with living in and obtaining benefits from society – tax, responsible financial regulation, criminal laws, inheritance laws and so on. He states that this is their core business. It is what they *do*. Shaxson points out that such havens can be identified by their secrecy, low or zero tax and by another interesting characteristic, as follows.

The established evidence for this 'looting' rarely appears on any of the media – newspapers or even the BBC. Similarly absent, is the established, empirical evidence about the bad social consequences of income inequality. That is, the straight-line relationship between income inequality for numerous nations and each of numerous adverse social statistics such as petty crime, burglary, murder, rape, and size of prison populations. As mentioned previously, there's a several-*fold* difference between the worst, most unequal nations (USA, Portugal, UK) at the top of the line, and Japan, Scandinavia and Iceland at the bottom (the best end). It's not being in a poor or a rich country that counts, it's being in an unequal one (see 'The Spirit Level' by Wilkinson and Pickett).

Britain as a tax haven
In 2007, the IMF highlighted Britain as an offshore jurisdiction by the criterion of having a *financial services industry that is very large compared to the size of the economy*. And this in a world where millions of people are without clean water, are hungry and inadequately housed or homeless. And many of the people benefitting from this crafty device are 'practising' Christians! On the one hand it's simply crazy, and on the other hand it's an inappropriate, pathological power phenotype, no longer benefitting the group being 'led'. Perhaps a phrase more appropriate than the word 'led' would be 'predated upon'.

These figures, bad as they are, are less striking to me than a recent personal experience. My wife and I had a package holiday on the Mediterranean coast west of Cannes. One night we were puzzled that of the numerous, huge mansions covering the surrounding hills as far as the eye could see, none had any lights showing – not one. It turned out that this was because, although furnished, they were not occupied – *none* of them: and this was also the case for the colossal yachts in the local harbour! We were told that the owners were not French – simply mega-rich people investing in property. So, a beautiful stretch of the Mediterranean coast was owned but not used (or rarely used for mega-rich parties) by the mega rich, including Russian oligarchs! It seemed to us a symptom of a serious human sickness. Recently, a similar state of affairs was revealed regarding super-expensive (£ multi-millions), empty properties in an exclusive area of London. In a capital with a bad housing problem, houses were deliberately kept empty for capital gains. 2015 data shows that more than 70% of new property purchases in London are by foreigners. AlterNet reports (July 15, 2015) that London has the largest congregation of Russian millionaires outside Moscow, and houses more ultra-rich people (owning more than $30 million in assets outside their home country) than anywhere else on Earth.

A corollary is that in a period of only three years, <u>several hundred thousand</u> relatively poor London residents have had to leave their place of birth and family area to go elsewhere. Clearly, our London alphas think that this is a price worth paying, although not by them.

A question about global capitalism

> *'The evils of capitalism are as real as the evils of militarism and the evils of racism.'*
> **Belief of Daniel Berrigan S. J. <u>and</u> of Martin Luther King.**
> **Both worked for peace and justice.**

What is so good about having an entire industry *rapidly* wiped out in one country because it's cheaper elsewhere to manufacture for the profit of the owners and directors who owe allegiance to no one? Official answer: the economy 'elsewhere' benefits. In fact, this is mostly not true. Commonly, the tendency is for money to be siphoned off from the local economy and into 'money sinks' in tax havens. *It disappears from the local economy.* In any case, why is 'the economy' seen as the highest good? For example, the USA has the current *top economy* and its adverse social statistics are *by far the worst* in the 'developed' world. The economy can be a *means* to well-being and happiness: it's not itself an end, and especially not when the money disappears from the 'successful' economy. Why not have a happy, well-fed, well-housed country with a relatively small economy?   Why not have cars and other machines and numerous other stuff, made <u>locally</u> *by* local people *for* local people that maybe are less good than the world's best?   In other words, full employment and adequate housing are higher in importance than being a 'top economy'.   One humane answer to 'why not' relates to impoverished, often 'ex' colonies that are trying to develop.   They should be helped and not predated upon as occurs now.   How to do this in a practical way, given the predatory world economy?   That is a good question.

Comments on 'Neoliberalism'

There is agreement that 'neoliberalism' describes much of the world's economic activity, notably the USA and the UK, but it is not possible to find an agreed definition.   The word has been used broadly to describe the economic principles involved in Germany under Ludwig Erhard, Chile under Augusto Pinochet, United States under Ronald Reagan, Great Britain under Margaret Thatcher and New Zealand under David Lange.   Friedrich Hayek was one notable intellectual in this area and was awarded the Nobel Prize in Economics in 1974 (in conjunction with Gunnar Myrdal).   One idea was that if restraints (e.g. by government or trade unions) on economic activity were removed, then the most productive economic models would emerge.   A useful review of neoliberalism was by David M. Kotz: Globalization and Neoliberalism in Rethinking Marxism, Volume 12, Number 2, Summer 2002, pp. 64-79.

A relativel late publication by Hayek is 'The Political Order of a Free People' (1979) and is essentially about abolishing government monopolies.   For instance, this passage summarises his views: 'any governmental agency allowed to use its taxing power to finance such services ought to be required to refund any taxes raised for these purposes to all those who prefer to get the services in some other way. This applies without exception to all those services of which today government possesses or aspires to a legal monopoly, with the only exception of maintaining and enforcing the law and maintaining for this purpose (including defense against external enemies) an armed force, i.e. all those from education to transport and communications, including post, telegraph, telephone and broadcasting services, all the so-called 'public' utilities', the various 'social' insurances and, above all, the issue of money.'

In the context of this book, what can be said about such ideas in terms of evolutionary forces of alpha leaders, fear of foreign and territory? First of all, in reading Hayek's material and especially that of his followers, it's striking how much of it is *assertions*. Also striking is that much of his ideas/assertions are highly likely to be attractive to the rich, powerful alphas. It seems obvious that rich alphas, rich bogus think tanks, bankers and the rich owners of bogus and politically oriented magazines would all approve of and support the above. Surely, the powerful alphas will have pushed and continue to push these ideas. Such Hayek-based ideas have already led to the inhuman, western 'Gig' (analogous to musicians doing a session at an event – a gig) economy and 'zero hours' contracts that offers no powers to the workers, but all powers in the hands of 'employing' companies. The workers have no rights, no holidays, no sickness benefits and minimum wages and are simply called upon for work when and if convenient to the company. This injustice is mis-represented as the workers being 'self-employed'. Given the close link between inequality and social pathology, Hayek's assertions above are a recipe for social disease.

Scientific evidence given earlier strongly supports the idea of humans being intrinsically community-oriented. Humans are constitutively social animals. The prophetic, cultural leaders at widely different times and places all intuitively advocated altruistic ideology summarised in 'love your neighbour'. Also, the activities of any living organism or of any group, especially higher organisms, all need co-ordinating. The idea of a complex, multi-million population of humans being served best without central co-ordination is absurd. Such a society is advocated by Hayek. Is he and his followers unaware of the existence of biology regarding instincts such as territory, the foreign, alphas and obedience to them and the public suppression of femininity by men? For thousands of years, prophets and philosophers have agreed that 'man is a social animal'. Today, science underlines this statement by Aristotle. I end by quoting him.

> *'At his best, man is the noblest of all animals; separated*
> *from law and justice he is the worst'.*

Finally, it must be accepted that the USA and the UK are leaders in a neoliberal approach to economics and they are at the top, *bad* end of the line describing adverse social ailments versus degree of inequality for the world's nations (for which there's reliable data). They are *world leaders* in bad statistics for social ailments described earlier. These are not merely assertions but are based on relevant, reproducible data. The idea that the definition of a good business is solely the degree of profit is *socially* not true. Money should not be the only criterion.

I finish this section with quotations from another economist, the human, rational John Maynard Keynes.

'The decadent international but individualistic capitalism in the hands of which we found ourselves after the war is not a success. It is not intelligent. It is not beautiful. It is not just. It is not virtuous. And it doesn't deliver the goods'.

'Capitalism is the astounding belief that the most wickedest of men will do the most wickedest of things for the greatest good of everyone'.

'When my information changes, I alter my conclusions. What do you do, sir?'.

Postscript

Cadbury staff told 'Change your ways or hit the road'

UK Birmingham Post, front page headline, October 16th 2014

An example of primate, alpha bosses

Workers at Cadbury's chocolate firm in south Birmingham, near where I live, were handed the above ultimatum by the company's new American bosses (Mondelez). This 'process' demonstrates the change in working practices since being established in this area of Birmingham by the Quakers, George and Richard Cadbury in 1879. They called it Bournville. Modern management practices, common in the USA, the UK and elsewhere, often do not see workers as participating people but as disposable objects, preferably with little or no input into the business, no pensions, so-called 'zero-hours contracts' and who are anti-union. They are commodities as were slaves so described. It is a stark contrast to the humane involvement of the workers in the company and the humane treatment of the work force by the company <u>135 years ago</u>. In the context of investigating whether commerce is influenced/controlled by primate instincts and to what extent it is human, there is no doubt. This is primate and 135 years ago it was much *more* human, treating and involving workers as humans and not as objects.

The detailed setting up of Bournville all those years ago is well worth noting. Perhaps today, Mondelez Inc. would care to consider following a similar path? Then, Cadbury workers were treated with respect and had relatively high wages and good working conditions. Cadbury also pioneered *pension schemes*, joint *works committees* and a full staff *medical service*. In 1893, George Cadbury bought 120 acres (0.5 km²) of land close to the works and planned and created, at his own expense, a model village which would *'alleviate the evils of modern, more cramped living conditions'*. By 1900, the estate included 313 cottages and houses set on 330 acres (1.3 km²) of land, and many more similar properties were built in the years leading up to World

War 1, with smaller developments taking place later on in the 20th century. These almost 'Arts and Crafts' houses were traditional in design but with large gardens and modern interiors, and were designed by the resident architect, William Alexander Harvey. The gardens still have lawns, fruit trees and space for vegetables. These designs became a blueprint for many other model village estates around Britain.

The (Quaker) Cadbury brothers were particularly concerned with the health and fitness of their workforce, incorporating park and recreation areas into the Bournville village plans and encouraging swimming, walking and indeed all forms of outdoor sports. In the early 1920s, extensive open lands were purchased and laid to football and hockey pitches, together with a grassed running track, acres of sports playing fields, several bowling greens, a fishing lake and an outdoor swimming lido, a natural mineral spring forming the source for the lido's healthy waters. In 1900, the Bournville Village Trust was set up formally to control the development of the estate, independently of the Cadburys or the Cadbury company. The trust focussed on providing schools, hospitals, museums, public baths and reading rooms. A campus-like feel evolved, with a triangular village green, infant and junior schools, the School of Art and the Day Continuation School (originally intended for young Cadbury employees) and a host of communal events such as fêtes and dances. The Quaker Cadburys were truly humans.

A further postscript
In 2014, Mondelez was able to *pay no UK corporation tax* as a result of a Channel Islands-based bond, despite Cadbury making £96.5m profit. An investigation by the UK Sunday Times found the company was wiping out Cadbury's bills using interest payments on an unsecured debt, which is listed as a bond on the Channel Islands' stock exchange. The interest paid on the loan can be 'legally' offset as a loss against gains made elsewhere in the company. So, that's okay then? A modern way forward to *humanise* the Cadbury workplace

would be to use a time-machine to <u>go back to 1879</u> and ask the Quakers to take over the 'new' Cadbury's.

Suggestions for improvement of the organs of commerce and of their impact on society

With a view to answering needs, harmonising primate instincts and expressing the human

Making practical suggestions is hard, given the nature of business. In terms of the listed primate characteristics (notably regarding territory, fear of and being competitive with the foreign/different, including women, alpha-male leadership and associated obedience), commerce more or less enhances all of them. Indeed, territory, competition and the elimination of opponents (but not by death or starvation!) is typically a key part of the activity of business *per se*. Nevertheless, all businesses are not equally and socially beneficial as the former Cadbury's.

Aims

1. Improve the answering of human needs by assisting the social expression of the human instincts of creativity, altruism and art – similarly for employees.
2. Humanising the organs of commerce *per se* and their impact on society.
3. Reducing the influence of inappropriately or over-expressed primate instincts: territory, the foreign, anti-feminine, blind obedience to alpha-male leaders.
4. Facilitate the convergence of commerce and 'community' as did Cadbury's so long ago. (See above)

How

Using social media, sympathetic political organisations and any peaceful means, encourage and press for:

1. National and international laws to halt the long-term ecological damage caused by the environmental

plundering of the seas, forests and land in general occurring now.

2. Increased <u>participation</u> of the 'workers'. National and international laws are needed revoking anti- <u>union legislation.</u>

3. In addition to profit, have social goals as a purpose in the <u>legal articles of all businesses</u>.

4. Common social facilities, including catering, and facilitate the mingling of 'staff', management and 'workers'.

5. Prevent the current, 'buying' of political influence by financial donations to a political   party.

Note: Alas, alas, USA presidents over two centuries failed to do this and now we effectively have representatives of corporations in President Trump's cabinet. But even so, we must continue to try to stop such corruption.

RADIO, TELEVISION, INTERNET, SOCIAL MEDIA, 'PUBLIC RELATIONS', HABITATS AND OVERALL CULTURE

With a view to answering needs, harmonising primate instincts and expressing the human

Recognising the influence of biological evolution on the 'media' and overall culture

Learning about their external environment by 'primitive' organisms

Microbes learn about and respond to numerous aspects of their environment constantly: temperature, salt concentration, acidity/ alkalinity, toxic compounds. Also, they respond to fluctuations in the availability of essential nutrients. In fact, a growing culture anticipates the disappearance of an essential nutrient several generations before the nutrient concentration is so low as to cause a cessation of growth. For anyone interested, an example is 'Effect of iron deprivation on the production of siderophores and outer membrane proteins in *Klebsiella aerogenes*. Journal of General Microbiology. Volume 130, pages 2357 – 2365. 1984. Williams, Brown and Lambert. Even dormant spores recognise environmental change and germinate when conditions become appropriate. When a suspended cell approaches a surface, it recognises this by a change in the diffusion of excreted compounds. It then makes itself sticky, adheres to the surface and thereby increases its chance of survival by being able to control its environment as part of a 'biofilm'. Over billions of years microbes have evolved to keep a close 'eye' on their environment.

The media

Given our human intelligence and access to IT, then we might expect that we humans could design a much better, super-*efficient* system for accurately learning about every significant aspect of our environment. We humans need to know about ourselves and our immediate society and also about wider social issues: opportunities and dangers, international trends and the possibility of war. But we have not. We have defective, heavily biased systems for learning. An exception is the amazing, almost limitless information gathering carried out by the world's secret services, notably exposed by Edward Snowden. In terms of the regular media, the world very largely (but not entirely) has information from the perspective of powerful, right-wing owners of the media. In 'You are still being lied to': subtitle Disinformation' (editor: Russ Kick), numerous authors include chapters (447 pages). On an inside page it is also entitled 'The REMIXED disinformation guide to media distortion, historical whitewashes and cultural myths'. This important book has much varied content, but contains many indications of a biological underpinning of the 'way things are', notably by Howard Bloom in 'Reality is a shared illusion' (page 10) and Noam Chomsky in 'What makes mainstream media mainstream' (page 19). Articles are written about social influences on perception, reality, culture, myths. But any explicit reference to evolution and inherent human tendencies is lacking. Nevertheless, it goes further than simply uncovering evildoings by controllers of the media. An issue about press quality is that over recent years, numerous journalists have been accused and convicted of 'hacking' into individuals' private communications on a massive, criminal scale ('Dial M for Murdoch' by Tom Watson and Martin Hickman; 'Hack Attack' by Nick Davies; 'The fall of the house of Murdoch' by Peter Jukes).

A major concern is the high concentration of media power placed mainly in the hands of a small number of right-wing, so-called 'barons'. They are elite, alpha males (typically ultra-rich) with the power phenotype fully functioning, including the habit of taking of the best of everything *as of right* and being above 'normal' social conventions and rules. This feature of the world press is probably more significant than individual acts of criminality, such as the hacking undertaken by their employees. Their outlets give a consistent, right-wing view of reality, i.e. a primate reality. That is, much concerned with short-term survival regarding territory, fear of the foreign, anti-feminine, accepting that 'alphas' can more or less do or take whatever they wish and hostile to any deviation from their norm. It would seem <u>un</u>likely to me, despite the accusations made against many of them, that they are personally evil. Even so, evil does follow from many of their activities. It also seems to me that such accusations miss the point that they are 'motivated' by instincts, i.e. primate, non-rational impulses such as the power phenotype. They 'know' that they are right because they recognise the authenticity of their primate, basic instincts representing the 'real world'. In fact, I cautiously have some regard for Rupert Murdoch in that he is well known for questioning 'the establishment', self-serving bureaucracies and the upper class, ruling elites. In the UK we have Rupert Murdoch's 'The Sun' and 'The Times', the pornographer Richard Desmond's 'Daily Express', Lord Dacre as editor of the 'Daily Mail' and the Barclay brothers' 'Telegraph'.

Rupert Murdoch closed the salacious 'News of the World' in 2011 (intending to replace it with the 'Sunday Sun') after the allegations and court cases over the hacking into individuals' private data. All owners are well known for their relentless, right-wing 'views' (i.e. their expression of primate instincts). Similar considerations of bias and of a narrow range of ownership apply to commercial TV channels. 'The Independent', 'The Independent on Sunday', the 'i' newspaper and 'The Evening Standard' are owned by a Russian oligarch, Alexander Lebedev. Despite early work for the KGB, his background is relatively liberal with personal support for the arts and medical charities. With the former Russian Prime Minister, Mikhail Gorbachev, he partly owns a newspaper that is prominent for its criticism of the current Russian government. And his papers have not taken a swing to the right.

Judging the UK media

If one 'judges' the UK press, then the fact that the UK is a Christian nation, with the Queen as Head of the Church, influences any judgement. Conveniently, Jesus is explicit on how, on his return as the Messiah, he will judge us all. While there is a comic element in applying Jesus's criteria to the press, it should be borne in mind that these were truly and seriously the criteria stated by Jesus and when he knew he was shortly to be crucified. He demands an absolute requirement for helping the needy. The Roman Catholic Church (*itself* lucky if it achieved Purgatory in terms of actually helping the needy as a priority as opposed to pious, clerical practices that were not mentioned in Matthew's gospel) has added to Jesus's possible judgement of Heaven or Hell by adding Purgatory as an option, i.e. temporary punishment, often described as purification by fire. The 'Morning Star' has content closely similar to a Methodist Christian publication, in advocating social justice and workers' rights. St. Matthew would approve.

So, somewhat subjectively and depending on their direct or indirect help towards the ill, naked, thirsty, hungry, imprisoned and strangers, we have the fate of the UK newspapers *and their personnel* (Jesus did not say that obeying orders is a defence for not helping the needy) as follows. Over many years, I have checked the front pages of the national press whenever in a newsagent's shop (most days) and I subscribe to various magazines and daily, read independent newspapers. I've added the BBC and ITV and the RC (my former religion) and Protestant Churches, for good measure, together with magazines. I've also added UK political parties. If the USA political parties were to be judged by Jesus's standards, then only the Democratic Socialists would go to Heaven. And much of their media are bound for hellfire.

Day of Judgement according to Jesus' criteria in Matthew's gospel
(Jesus's criteria were helping, or not, those who are ill, naked, thirsty, hungry, imprisoned and strangers. An acronym for the categories of needy is '*in this*'.)

Heaven
Daily Mirror, The European, Guardian, Morning Star, London Review of Books, New York Review of Books. Methodists, Quakers. Green Party, Plaid Cymru, Scottish National Party

Heaven/Purgatory?
The Independent, The 'i'
Co-operative Party, Liberal Democrats, the Labour Party

Purgatory
Financial Times, Evening Standard, the BBC, ITV
The Roman Catholic Church, the Church of England
Democratic Unionist Party

Hell
Daily Express, Daily Mail, Daily Star, The Sun, Daily Telegraph, The Times,
The USA Evangelical Church, the Irish branch of Roman Catholicism (the clergy),
Conservative Party, UKIP

This judgement of Hell might seem harsh to Protestant members of the Conservative and UKIP parties who have never read or understood Matthew's gospel and who lack feelings of empathy for those people listed by Jesus for help.

The British Broadcasting Corporation
The BBC has a worldwide reputation for reliably high-quality programmes, both for its home and for its overseas output. Also, it's a medium with which I'm familiar. For these reasons, I'm giving it prominence with special attention to its contribution to the overall culture of the UK and elsewhere. Similar considerations apply to other media worldwide.

It could be helpful to mention some recent developments. It has a relatively unchanged mandate from the 1920s to 'inform, educate and entertain'. In a recent UK government 'Green Paper' on the review of the BBC's charter, the government said the founding principles set out by its first Director General, Lord Reith, were 'no longer sufficient' as a yardstick by which to judge the corporation's performance. After nearly two years of consultation with the public, academics and rival broadcasters, the Tory government said the BBC needed to have a 'more closely defined set of purposes', proposing five new criteria by which the broadcaster should be judged. The BBC should sustain citizenship and civil society; promote education and learning; stimulate creativity and cultural excellence; reflect regional and cultural identities; and make British audiences aware of international news and events.

The 'Green Paper' suggests that instead of judging the BBC simply by the amount and scope of its public service programming, the corporation should be defined by the wider measure of how much it contributes to public life. 'To retain a distinctive role, the BBC needs to have a more closely defined set of purposes that can be understood by the corporation, by commercial rivals and by the public. *The case for the public funding of the BBC, and for public service broadcasting in general, is based on the benefits it can bring to society.* The BBC should be set objectives that reflect those benefits: it should be defined by its goals as a public service – not only by its programming output.'

The italicised (by me) sentence is of special interest. It seems obvious that citizens should receive information about the nation and the outside world from an accurate, impartial source. Commercial sources, however well intentioned, cannot avoid being biased by their sponsors, the attractiveness of programmes to advertisers and so on. *A commercial enterprise is not a charity and making money is not a luxury but is essential for their survival.* But, any nation needs impartial information about its internal and external environment. Consequently, there should be no question of ever abandoning either the BBC *or a replacement by a high-quality, impartial, reformed alternative.* Handing over our acquisition of knowledge/understanding of the world to commerce is manifestly wrong and predetermined towards bias.

Media bias against the new Labour leader, Jeremy Corbyn

I recommend any reader interested in the state of the media to read an article in 'The London Review of Books' (22nd October 2015, pages 8-9) by Paul Myerscough entitled 'Corbyn in the media'. The then recently elected leader of the UK Labour Party, Jeremy Corbyn, had been subjected to relentless media *ridicule* (not reasoned argument), analysed by Myerscough. Corbyn was elected by about 50% of Labour Party members and about 84 % of registered supporters. Just before the leadership election, *40,000* new Labour Party members registered to support Corbyn – a kind of mini 'Arab Spring'. Notably, Myerscough includes a focus on the influence of the media, not only on the political weather but also on the political *climate*. He refers to a study by the Cardiff University School of Journalism showing that the BBC was *more* likely than commercial channels to use sources from the right than from the left. The banking crisis was a special case in point, with a disproportionate number of BBC interviewees being directly *from* the banking sector. He also refers (with examples) to the number of BBC media appointments with right-wing, political backgrounds. Myerscough gives examples of gross BBC bias regarding major speeches by the then Prime Minister Cameron and by Jeremy Corbyn when commentators on the speeches were chosen who were favourable to Cameron and hostile to Corbyn.

In November 2015, as I wrote this section, the idea of Corbyn as a serious leader has been openly ridiculed and sneered at by BBC presenters. Shockingly, sneering and ridicule are the typical weapons of choice for the right wing – an expression of basic, animal instincts and these should be absent from serious BBC programmes other than satirical ones. Any rational disputing or refuting of Corbyn's statements is still currently (2018) almost absent. It has been exposed in an extraordinary way that these celebrity journalists and commentators think that a change from a primate world of 'winner takes all' (or most) to an altruistic, human one is ridiculous and *not worthy* of rational discussion. As is the case for other nations, the idea of political balance is subjective. In the UK, with the BBC mandated to be impartial, Myerscough states that the balance between left and right is defined by the main parties, Labour and Tory, and that the BBC norm is currently a 'balance' between the Tories and the Labour *right*. One might expect the BBC to have a focus on the human value of altruism as well as the arts. The 'right' characteristically remains preoccupied with territory, fear of the foreign and alpha-male leaders and their 'doings'. Primate instincts are genuinely *'felt'* as being real and true: hence the 'real world'. Human instincts are wishy-washy, schoolboy ideals and not the 'real world'. But they *are* real and advocated by all the world's leading sages, but typically they are overridden by the primate ones when they clash. On a day that I revise this section several months later (24th April 2017), the UK Defence Minister, Michael Fallon, (on BBC radio) derided and ridiculed Corbyn for his unwillingness to back Trident until an overall defence strategy had been reviewed. He gave no reasons, simply that it was absurd not to have Trident. A former Defence Secretary, Michael Portillo, was rational and gave reasons for his negative views on Trident. Speaking on the BBC programme 'This Week' on 30th April 2015, Portillo said, 'Our independent nuclear deterrent is not independent and doesn't constitute a deterrent against anybody that we regard as an enemy.'

Another important example of insults and derision rather than reasoning about an important issue occurred in 2018. This was mentioned earlier under 'Comments on Neoliberalism'. And bears repetition in this section. It was over a UK civil service economic analysis of several scenarios regarding UK Brexit. The gloomy analysis was derided/sneered at by right wing spokesmen. The analysis was not examined for flaws of approach or omissions or illegitimate conclusions. Simply, it was condemned, without evidence, as politically biased. Unlike the politicians who made the derisory remarks and sneers, the professional reputations of the civil servants were vulnerable to any analysis that revealed poor approaches, false assumptions and illegitimate conclusions. Their economic forecasts were open to rational criticism. A leading right wing 'Brexiteer', Jacob Rees-Mogg simply made an instant, unsubstantiated assertions about bias by the civil servants. The viewer/listener was asked to accept Mr Rees-Mogg's evidence-free *assertions* rather than the reasoned conclusions of a study by a group of government civil servants, expert professionals in economics. It's hard not to conclude that the absence of reasoned adverse criticism of the report was that it was not possible. If the report was flawed, surely the flaws would have been exposed?

Dangers of celebrity journalists – the power phenotype again
The public typically listens to celebrities and is attracted to them. Commonly, celebrities are popular alpha males. It is common worldwide to have at least some celebrity journalists, *each* regularly commenting on the news of *any* kind: foreign affairs and wars, the economy, health, education, the arts. For example, I have personally heard a BBC programme dealing with listeners' comments and a senior programme manager responding. On one occasion, criticism was made of such universal pontificating by leading journalists. The manager of the programme was interviewed and flatly denied any flaw and stated that these journalists were trusted and experienced and no change in style would occur. Mention was made earlier regarding a similar situation with politicians, e.g. the Prime Minister on radio or TV speaking with 'authority' about each and every possible subject as if he/she were Leonardo da Vinci or Aristotle. It contributes to the false idea that our alpha-male (or alpha female) leaders have God-like knowledge and is a dangerous example of the power phenotype manifesting itself. The idea that we humans trust our senior journalists or politicians to know everything about everything is obviously socially destructive.

The BBC has so-called magisterial programmes such as the 'Today' programme on weekday mornings and regularly features the same celebrity journalists, prominently male. In the same way that politicians tend to offer assertions with spurious authority on each and every topic, so too do *some* of the BBC's celebrity journalists. Too often, when interviewing an expert, it is the trusted and experienced 'expert' *interviewer* that interrogates the invited expert evidently believing that they are the intellectual equal of Leonardo or Socrates and with a knowledge base superior to the invited expert. This applies, as with politicians, to the economy, wars, finance, health, social housing – anything. This is a dangerous example of the alpha journalist behaving in an inappropriate alpha way. It helps to keep sections of the public in an infantile attitude towards some (certainly not all) of the alpha BBC 'adults/parents'. Like parents, they know and are expert in all things from the child's perspective: Daddy/Mummy knows best.

Social media
There is now a relatively uncontrolled and massive social media. Individuals across the world have the option of expressing a viewpoint on numerous outlets. The recent and continuing migration to Europe from the war-torn and atrocities of Syria, Iraq and Afghanistan has been the object of vicious, hate comments on social media. This is undoubtedly the result of basic instincts regarding the foreign and the protection of one's territory. On the other hand, the human instinct of altruism has been given practical and successful expression. In some cases, individuals have coalesced into movements for social justice, sensibly uninfluenced by political parties or commerce or 'alpha males' or celebrities. Here is a small sample: Amnesty International (sct@amnesty.org.uk) (7 million), the network Avaaz (42 million) (avaaz.org), SumOfUs.org (us@sumofus.org) the 'Occupy' Movement (occupywallstreet.org), 38 Degrees (38degrees.org.uk), Truthout (messenger@truthout.org), WeMove.EU (https://www.wemove.eu/) and Human Rights Watch https://www.hrw.org/ The broad ideals are expressed well by the wonderful, non-celebrity founder of Amnesty International, Peter Benenson: 'Only when the last prisoner of conscience has been freed, when the last torture chamber has been closed, when the United Nations Universal Declaration of Human Rights is a reality for the world's

people, will our work be done'. This is similar to the champion of the homeless, the late Abbé Pierre, who said that he'd happily support public art when the last homeless person in Paris was housed.

The media and 'Public Relations'

Public Relations (PR) is commonly defined as the management of an organisation's relationship/image with the outside world, often the general public. Apart from literature and handouts, the media of radio and TV form the main mode of PR, although social media is rapidly becoming increasingly important. Almost all organisations have specialist PR officers to present the organisation in a favourable way to the world. This is especially important in politics and in elections in particular. How the 'world' sees an organisation is now typically managed by PR specialists. This is especially true for political parties. PR specialists can and do sway public and other opinion. The last General Election in the UK is a good example. The right-wing Tory party had an extraordinarily successful 'Master of Ceremonies' in Lynton Crosby. Among several quoted tactics, Crosby is described as favouring what is called a 'wedge' strategy. Thus, the party he advises introduces a divisive or controversial social issue into a campaign, supporting the dissenting faction of its opponent party. The objective is to cause vitriolic debate in the opposing party, defection of its supporters, and make legitimate what had previously been considered inappropriate. This is also described as 'below the radar' campaigning, including the targeting of marginal constituencies with highly localised campaigning, latching onto local issues and personalities.

However, it's highly significant that an earlier General Election campaign was notable for evoking basic instincts against the Labour Party, mentioned earlier. There was a relentless attack on the Labour leader's alleged lack of ability as a *leader*. Ed Milliband was so inept that he could not cope with eating a simple sandwich, shown by a much-publicised photograph. It was reminiscent of the equally relentless campaign against the leadership qualities of a previous Labour leader, Neil Kinnock. Kinnock was apparently so clumsy that he couldn't run across a beach without falling over – again with a much-publicised picture. It's easy to imagine that wavering voters might decide not to vote for a party with a hopeless leader.

These attacks required, and had, an eager right-wing press constantly taking large numbers of photographs so that damaging ones could be selected, and the rest discarded. As well, in the last UK election, Crosby focussed on *territory*, sovereignty over our nation being diminished by the *foreign* European Union: *foreigners* having much too much control over our *territory* and *borders*. In summary, the major features of Crosby's campaign were a lack of *leadership* qualities in the opposition, *fear* of the *foreign,* and *fear* about the nation's *territorial integrity*. These are the most prominent of the basic, innate instincts that motivate us. The Labour campaign was less coherent. It did not have any focus on David Cameron's alien 'poshness', posh education, not being 'one of us', and not belonging to the 'common people'. It did not have any focus on keeping out foreign migrants. And then, in 2015 we have the newly elected leader of the Labour Party, Jeremy Corbyn, instantly subjected *not* to rational (human) refuting of his policies, but to relentless ridicule, sneering and mockery by the right-wing, <u>non-UK-resident</u>, primate, mega-rich, media barons.

It is wrong that the outcome of an election can be so influenced, even <u>determined,</u> by the tactics of a PR team, aided by a few, far-right, ultra-rich media barons controlling much of the UK media. And now we have the use of mega data (likely illegal) about individuals and their behaviour, being used to target election (and other) messages with much greater precision by such as the USA billionaire Robert Mercer and his corporation 'Cambridge Analytica'. (See earlier: Early USA presidents' warnings fulfilled: Donald Trump and triumph of corporate money'.)

In a further development, mentioned earlier and I now repeat, an undercover investigation by the UK Channel 4 News (19th March 2018), in association with the Observer, Cambridge Analytica executives claimed to offer a dark range of services. The UK Guardian (20th March 2018) reported (Graham-Harrison, Cadwalladr and Osborne) boasts of the dirty tricks used to swing elections. Undercover reporters of Channel 4 were told by bosses of how honey traps, former spies from Britain and Israel looking for political dirt and fake news can be used to help their clients. The UK Information Commissioner, Elizabeth Denham, criticised Cambridge Analytica for being un co-operative with an investigation as she confirmed that her watchdog would apply for a warrant to help her examine the firm's activities. It was also reported that 'Number 10' was 'very concerned' over Facebook data breach by Cambridge Analytica.

It hardly needs emphasising that money strongly influences or decides elections.

Similar considerations apply to the regular conduct of politics. If fear can be aroused by government through its PR specialists, then fear facilitates policies involving major social changes. Examples include 'the war on terrorism' and 'the war on drugs'. Opposition, for example, against Trident nuclear weapons arouses fear because it 'weakens our defences' and 'makes us vulnerable'. But how does Trident protect us? Which nation will attack us in its absence and will not if we keep it? It's generally accepted that the most likely danger is from accidents and individual, small, fringe groups of no fixed location and to which we cannot fire back. In any case, firing back after such an assault would itself be an act not just of extreme immorality with millions of humans incinerated, but also adding to radioactive world pollution of a massive size and lasting thousands of years. Much of this thinking is very short term.

Another consideration is to weigh up the odds of nuclear weapons being used in the next decade, or in the next century, or in the next millennium. One answer is that they have *already been used twice* with the instant incineration of tens of thousands of humans and massive radioactive pollution and we've already had several near accidents. So, the odds of further use or even accidents over, say, a millennium must be huge. It is short-term, short-sighted, frightened, primate behaviour to retain such weapons. Individual PR specialists who aid serious evildoings through their lies and deceptions cannot morally justify their actions by claiming that they are 'only doing their job' or 'only following orders'.

This is now far, far from the early classic Greece democracy of the citizens of numerous small cities meeting in spaces including and related to public theatres and discussing/voting on politics and other issues of interest.

Note: Demos is the ancient Greek word for the ordinary citizens of a city-state, "the people": demo-cracy, "rule of the people".

Suggestions for improvement of organs of the media and of their impact on society

(The UK as an example: see section on USA and UK under 'States')

Aims

1. *Improve the answering of human needs, assisting the social expression of the human instincts of creativity, altruism and art.*
2. *Humanising the organs of the media per se and their impact on society.*
3. *Reducing the influence of inappropriate primate instincts when appropriate, i.e. innate impulses regarding territory, the foreign, anti-feminine, and blind obedience to alpha-male leaders.*
4. *For the UK, ensure the independence and integrity of public broadcasting (the BBC).*
5. *Humanise the conduct of elections. Policies and not spin. Stop the influence of the ultra-rich.*
6. *Reduce/eliminate the ownership of major media outlets by individuals. Have Royal Commission on*
   i) ways and means to have a balanced media, including press and
   ii) how to improve social media.

Means

1. *Stop the expensive election campaigns and have state-managed and financed elections with statements of policies advocated by the candidates and personal appearances and debates managed by the BBC. Thus, stop/reduce the battles between PR companies.*

2. *Prevent the current, frequent meetings between media barons/ representatives and BBC executives. Use channels that are open to all.*

3. *Prevent the current, frequent meetings/communications between politicians and BBC executives. Use channels that are open to all.*

4. *Reduce the competition for 'ratings' by the BBC. Have a strong focus on quality, creative programmes.*

5. *Devise new ways of maintaining independence from government and away from short-termism, e.g. have a ten-year framework, have senior appointments made <u>independent</u> of government influence.*

6. *Encourage the campaigners for social justice, including those on social media, by producing regular documentaries with examples of their work.*

7. *Have regular documentaries with <u>foreign</u> social commentators commenting on the UK with suggestions for the improvement of any social structure.*

8. *Legislate for boards of major media outlets to have varied ownership and not majority share holding by mega-rich media barons.*

RECOGNISING THE INFLUENCE OF BIOLOGICAL EVOLUTION ON HABITATS

With a view to answering needs, harmonising primate instincts and expressing the human

> *'Restore human legs as a means of travel. Pedestrians rely on food for fuel and need no special parking facilities. Forget the damned motor car and build the cities for lovers and friends.'*

> *'A day spent without the sight or sound of beauty, the contemplation of mystery, or the search of truth or perfection is a poverty-stricken day; and a succession of such days is fatal to human life.'*
>
> **Both quotations from Lewis Mumford (1895-1990)**

A habitat appropriate for the needs of an organism contributes to survival. Even microbes tend to adopt the biofilm habitat where they grow as masses on a surface, enabling them to have a degree of control over the internal as opposed to the uncontrolled and changing external environment.

Humans must build habitats suitable for humans – alphas <u>and</u> others. The arrangements of habitation, open spaces and relatively untouched nature greatly influence human well-being and happiness. Some fortunate people live in well-designed houses in natural surroundings and importantly *<u>as part of genuine communities</u>*. Other habitations can lead to human misery, squalor and even facilitate criminality. In numerous cities across the world a fraction of the population lives in such bad, inhuman conditions, often around a third. I have personally seen humans *living* on a city street in Indonesia, i.e. eating and sleeping there. It's not the purpose of this book to argue the specifics, rather that attention and finance be devoted to healthy human habitats, the requirements of which are now well understood. Such ideas are commonly/typically ignored for financial reasons. Although obvious, it's now empirically established that human well-being is helped by homes that are of adequate space, are warm, dry, *part of a community* and have access to nature. The main problem is that the powerful, the alphas worldwide, are reluctant to pay other than the minimum or even nothing towards social housing. A current example, previously mentioned, is that London property is seen as a good investment for the mega rich. Thus, property and land have greatly increased in price with the consequence that about 70,000 Londoners have been forced to leave their homes. Numerous multi-million-pound properties (£50m+) lie empty as investments: similarly, for the French Riviera.

Public amenities
Swimming pools, libraries, parks and other sports facilities, museums and art galleries

The willingness of the taxpayer in any society to pay for public amenities varies. In the UK, there are plans for selling off public land and buildings. This is similar to the selling off of public land throughout the UK many decades ago; similarly, for the USA and its lack of widespread facilities as above. All UK universities have recreational facilities, largely paid for by the taxpayer. Why should university students in public facilities have private, privileged amenities? Surely, it would help *national solidarity* if students mingled with the non-student population in open-access facilities. Special arrangements could be made for specific clubs and activities. Currently in the UK, university facilities, as above, are largely restricted to students. And how about creating jobs similar to 'Park Keepers' as per the above heading? Surely this is preferable to simply giving out unemployment benefits?

Crime prevention through housing design
There is now a large volume of literature on crime and habitat. For example, 'Crime Prevention through Housing Design: Policy and

Practice' by Rachel Armitage. This book gives numerous examples of good practice, facts and figures. The UN 'Urban planning and design' supports governments and cities with tested approaches. It provides guidelines and tools to support urban growth and improved sustainability, efficiency and equity through planning and design at all levels and scales. Efforts are focussed on ensuring that planning and designing contribute to climate change mitigation and adaptation. Within the context of multilevel governance, a special focus is most usefully placed on promoting key principles, including optimising the population and economic density of urban settlements. And, where appropriate, promoting mixed land use, diversity and better connectivity. Throughout this approach, issues of social inclusion, including ensuring a gender balance and the inclusion of vulnerable and disadvantaged groups, are addressed and, where possible, locally and regionally defined urban planning and design traditions are respected. The UN has identified that *the main problem of humanising human living spaces is the _will_ to do it.* Worldwide, the poor live in inadequate, badly funded spaces. In the wealthy USA, numerous cities have large areas that are destitute and badly served by the organs of the city. This is not human, or primate.

Another useful source of information is the Town and Country Planning Association's (UK) (www.tcpa.org.uk) 'Biodiversity by Design: A guide for sustainable communities'. Its aim is to provide guidance on how to maximise the opportunities for biodiversity in the planning and design of sustainable communities. The guide takes the user through the design process, presenting a toolkit of best practice that can be tailored according to the scale of the development opportunity. Cultural Commentary Berlin (Germany) supports one of the strongest ecological traditions in Europe. There is a strong appreciation of the *benefits of nature in towns and cities*, particularly in making cities places in which people can more easily live. This is particularly important given the preference for higher density housing. Berlin, the capital city, is an exemplar with its pioneering green infrastructure and community forestry projects. The naturalistic or ecological approach is the norm for most contemporary green spaces, though there are differences in approach. In Munich, for example, native plant listings must be used to secure planning permission. In Berlin, minimal intervention is favoured. Native and exotic plant species are encouraged to colonise green spaces and brownfield sites and few plants are considered to be 'weeds' (Kendle, T. (1997) 'Urban nature conservation: landscape management in the urban countryside'). In order to do this, Kendle draws upon lessons from over 20 international case studies, including a set of examples from the city of Berlin.

Because of the quality and current relevance of their work, I would like to introduce the reader to one or two early giants in this area. In relatively modern times, a major contribution to ideas about the healthy human habitat was given by Lewis Mumford (1895-1990). His quotations are above at the start to this section. I was given a book of his several decades ago and was greatly impressed by its rational approach to the interactions between humans and their built environment ('Technics and Civilization'). He was exceptionally <u>un</u>qualified in terms of childhood examinations. Although he studied for several years at the City College of New York, he left before receiving his baccalaureate degree. Nevertheless, he has written numerous other hugely influential books, notably 'The City in History'. Interestingly, his education was largely self-directed. He greatly admired the ideas of the Scottish intellectual Patrick Geddes (Geddes was a biologist, educator and *town planner* and was a major figure in Edinburgh's early 20th-century cultural ferment). After World War 2, Mumford was concerned with the threat of global nuclear annihilation, and in numerous publications he warned his readers that technology, left unchecked by *human reason*, would lead to mass destruction. He had an evolutionary timescale. He was active in his opposition to the Vietnam War and also to the environmental degradation brought about by industry, the automobile and, for current purposes, ineffective planning.

Although Mumford was not himself formally an architect or planner, he became the spokesman for the Regional Planning

Association of America, an informal group of architects, planners, economists and writers who came to prominence during the 1920s and 1930s. This group lobbied business and government for the establishment of regional cities as an antidote to the metropolitan congestion that was then increasing at an alarming rate. Essentially a reworking of the British 'garden city', the regional city would be planned on a sustainable scale with requisite residential, cultural, commercial and industrial components. Furthermore, the regional city would be surrounded by an agricultural green belt that would supply its food as well as delineate its borders from neighbouring communities. Among the association's best-known achievements are the planning of the Appalachian Trail along the eastern mountain ridge of the United States, the residential neighbourhood of Sunnyside Gardens in Queens, New York, and the New Jersey town of Radburn, the forerunner of today's neo-traditional suburbs. The 'townless highway', one of the association's most ambitious proposals, would have linked America's cities via limited-access parkways. Unlike today's USA interstate highways, townless highways were intended to harmonise with the rural landscape while skirting downtown districts altogether.

Another major figure was Charles-Édouard Jeanneret-Gris, who was better known as Le Corbusier (1887-1965). He was a Swiss-French architect, designer, painter, urban planner, writer, and one of the pioneers of what is now called modern architecture. For example, a design of his was that heavy traffic would proceed at basement level, and lighter traffic at ground level. Fast traffic should flow along limited-access arterial roads that supplied rapid and unobstructed cross-city movement. Pedestrianised streets, wholly separate from vehicular traffic would be placed at a raised level. The number of existing streets would be diminished by two-thirds due to the new arrangements of housing, leisure facilities and workplaces, with same-level crossing points eliminated wherever possible.

Conclusions. It's not lack of knowledge that is holding back improvements towards the healthy, human habitat. It's lack of <u>will</u>, as well as ignorance. This is combined with instinctive, primate behaviour by our alphas and right-wing media. They propagate lies about the poor who are depicted as lazy, undeserving and with criminal tendencies. They tell lies about the 'tax-paying' rich who are typically described as 'hard-working'.

Note: For any reader interested, Mumford's 'Technics and Civilization' (1934) was the first in a series, 'Renewal of Life'. The other books were 'The Culture of Cities' (1938), 'The Condition of Man' (1944), and 'The Conduct of Life' (1951).

Culture: recognising the influence of biological evolution

With a view to answering needs, harmonising primate instincts and expressing the human

Culture as a stabilising influence

Stable biological ecosystems are always complex. This is because of the abundance of checks and balances – equilibria. A change in one part is compensated by numerous small changes elsewhere, restoring the equilibrium. Simple ecosystems are relatively unstable. Human cultures are analogous to ecosystems, with stability resulting from numerous components interacting with one another and absorbing change. The major social structures 'buffering' change and maintaining stability are the ruling and elite organisations such as monarchs or parliaments and also those to do with religion, education, the military, business and 'ART' (the official kind, approved by the elite). All of these typically interact to give a stable culture within a particular climate and geography. Turning a 'blind eye' to the behaviour of others, especially the powerful, also appears to be a common feature of human cultures.

Selection of different social behaviour patterns

It seems likely that during primate evolution, a variety of different individual and group behaviour patterns were selected for in different environments. As indicated earlier, diversity is a vital and constant part of biological evolution. Some primates are relatively violent, others are relatively non-violent. Also, the biological mechanisms whereby genetic inheritance by *individuals* can lead to consistent, instinctive *group* behaviour by humans, ants, bees, birds, wolves or wildebeest seem an unfathomable mystery. We may know little about the 'how' of instincts, but they clearly exist. If one considers current and ancient human cultures and their characteristic behaviour when confronting serious threat, then we see walled (e.g. the Great Wall of

China, the Berlin Wall, walls in Palestine today and President Trump's wall regarding Mexico) and defended habitations and evidence of constant intergroup violence right up to the modern 'Star Wars'. Today, about a third of all countries are at war or in 'unofficial' conflict. Even countries enduring the extremes of poverty, the absence of health and educational provision and even starvation, typically spend much of their resources on their military. It's doubtful if it has ever been different since we humans developed large populations after the advent of agriculture. The perceived needs of survival instinctively trump everything. Of course, we can see much more than that. But, broadly speaking, a serious threat appears to evoke a consistent response. This consistency argues strongly for the existence of *instincts* in humans that greatly predispose us to modes of behaviour similar to some (not all) of our primate relatives, especially when threatened. A dead opponent is no longer a threat and also may have provided a meal. It seems likely that merely a recognisable difference or 'otherness' has constituted a potential danger in evolution.

Consciousness has given our instincts vast new dimensions to operate within and to see 'otherness', e.g. it is not the fear/survival instinct causing wars, but the need to do the work of God and exterminate the non-believers. Thus, consciousness enables us to see a large number of 'others', even though human like 'us', but differing, for example, in beliefs or skin colour or language or dress or culture. Rational moral thought condemns the collective punishment of an entire group after crimes have been perpetrated by an individual member of that group, whereas instinctive, primate behaviour may and does tend towards punishing the 'other' group collectively and indiscriminately.

Culture is the _result_ of numerous characteristics and also it contributes to the _creation_ of numerous characteristics. Improvements will come from humanising many small characteristics, notably by facilitating the empirically verified _needs_ of people: nurturing a sense of belonging, connectedness and inclusiveness.

Summary of possible broad social improvements

With a view to answering needs, harmonising primate instincts and expressing the human

1. Education worldwide re the above-mentioned causes of our problems and re our needs. <u>Science</u> helps by casting light on:
   i) the old problems of pestilence, famine, volcanoes, earthquakes and tsunamis; and
   ii) illuminating the human brain and personality development; and
   iii) the biological and genetic basis of many problems.

   Educate re the scientifically proven need for belonging/connectedness, for inclusive social structures and for an understanding of our place in the universe. Education re the basic, *common* teaching of humanism and the *originators* of major religions regarding altruism. Educate re our common humanity. There is only one race and it's in serious danger.

2. Focus on child development, based on established empirical evidence and on the humanisation of society: <u>socialise</u> children (e.g. Scandinavia), and early on include reading stories, music, art, dance, drama, poetry, sculpture, cooking. See formal education more as a part of the important <u>human</u> development of a person. Encourage anything to increase that sense of human belonging and connectedness.

3. Positively encourage and support femininity as well as equal rights.

4. Widespread deconditioning of leaders and the led: attempt to reduce our irrational fear of the foreign, increase the use of reason re territory and our blind obedience to alpha males. Start with leaders, e.g. Prime Ministers and Presidents, Cabinet Ministers, Head Teachers, Heads of Public Hospitals and Military Commanders. Use techniques described in 'The Chimp Paradox' by Steve Peters.

5. Facilitate the expression of specifically human instincts – altruism, creativity, widespread art (by children and local people, not so much monied 'ART') everywhere: in the workplace, schools, homes, public places, galleries, libraries, on transport and in the street.

6. Pay attention to the original and common insights of the major religious prophets – especially regarding altruism. For example, aim for a genuine 'living wage' and not a 'minimum wage' or less, with 2+ low-paid jobs.

7. Facilitate the *peaceful*, mass exposure of injustice via social media including the already existing mass movements. It's proposed that progress will come mainly from mass demands from *individuals* for structural changes. Reduce the instinctive (hence mindless) obedience to elites, e.g. via these non-violent mass movements of *individuals*. Currently this is very promising.

8. Facilitate the bringing together of the alpha-male leaders and the led. Small communities, reduce inequality. Make Parliament *representative* as previously described. Needed are parliaments and senates whose actual constitution represents the *community mix,* and parliamentarians and public servants who serve the people and whose members live lifestyles *at least similar* to those served. Social focus on community, belonging, inclusiveness and creativity.

9. The connection needs to be *broken* between politicians, political parties and corporations/ 'big business' with their 'big money'.

    No donations, no buying influence, <u>no buying laws</u>. <u>All</u> election expenses to be paid by the state. Similarly, for election debates, TV and radio.

    Caution again: USA presidents have failed to do this over centuries. And now the USA has President Donald Trump who acts as if (perhaps *de facto* actually is) he is a representative of corporations. It's hard to be optimistic.

10. Increase direct, individual and personal involvement in social processes and structures, *including work*. Encourage commercial enterprises that involve their employees as participating fellow humans and not as disposable objects. Humanise the workplace. Remove anti-union legislation.

11. Encourage a 'media' that informs, educates and entertains in the absence of over-powerful, individual media 'moguls' who are personally determining a commonly 'over-primate' agenda. In the UK, help the BBC to be more independent of the government of any shade. Publicise the option of a UN media re world affairs.

12. '**Provide homes**, humanise working-class and other 'habitats' (making them communal). Does this need saying? People need homes! Design them to encourage and facilitate communities. In a list of social priorities, security comes high, but alphas get something *extra* from the latest, top weaponry: alphas gain prestige and influence among other alphas. This must be curtailed so that the poor receive housing and adequate nutrition. I have already quoted Abbé Pierre who worked with the homeless and was asked if he approved of public art. He deserves repetition.

He replied, 'Public art, yes. But after the last homeless person is housed'.